Bradt

Slow
Cotswolds

Including Bath, Stratford-upon-Avon & Oxford

Local, characterful guides to Britain's special places

Caroline Mills

Edition 1

Bradt Travel Guides Ltd, UK
The Globe Pequot Press Inc, USA

CHAPTER KEY

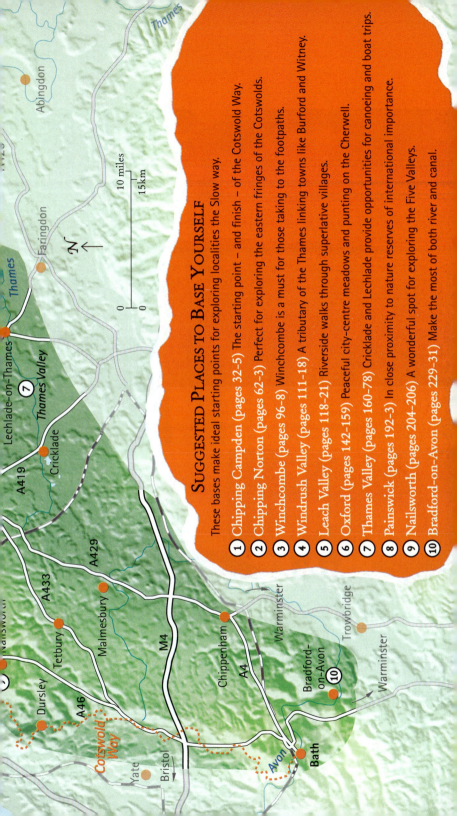

Suggested Places to Base Yourself

These bases make ideal starting points for exploring localities the Slow way.

1. **Chipping Campden** (pages 32–5) The starting point – and finish – of the Cotswold Way.
2. **Chipping Norton** (pages 62–3) Perfect for exploring the eastern fringes of the Cotswolds.
3. **Winchcombe** (pages 96–8) Winchcombe is a must for those taking to the footpaths.
4. **Windrush Valley** (pages 111–18) A tributary of the Thames linking towns like Burford and Witney.
5. **Leach Valley** (pages 118–21) Riverside walks through superlative villages.
6. **Oxford** (pages 142–159) Peaceful city-centre meadows and punting on the Cherwell.
7. **Thames Valley** (pages 160–78) Cricklade and Lechlade provide opportunities for canoeing and boat trips.
8. **Painswick** (pages 192–3) In close proximity to nature reserves of international importance.
9. **Nailsworth** (pages 204–206) A wonderful spot for exploring the Five Valleys.
10. **Bradford-on-Avon** (pages 229–31) Make the most of both river and canal.

A COTSWOLDS GALLERY

It may look like Provence but the unexpected lavender fields near Snowshill have added an alternative splash of colour to the Cotswolds and a boost to the farming economy. (CL)

The Cotswold Way provides a fantastic opportunity to get on top of the Cotswold hills and view the varied landscapes of the region. (CM)

Horseriding, here near Chipping Campden, is a popular pastime in the Cotswolds and another superb way to explore the quiet lanes and landscapes slowly. (CZ)

Views from the hillfort at Uley Bury – knobbled landscapes, the results of land slippage long ago, prevail in this part of the region. (CM)

One of the best vantage points for views over the Severn Vale is at Crickley Hill Country Park, which lies on the western edge of the Cotswold escarpment. (DM/DT)

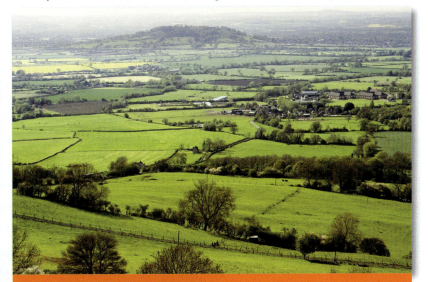

Cotswolds scenery

The Cotswolds countryside reveals some real gems to those who take the time to explore.

Six long-distance paths, including the Cotswold Way, converge in Winchcombe and the town has declared itself 'walking capital of the Cotswolds'. Here the Winchcombe Walkers savour their surroundings. (RT)

The wetland habitats of the upper Thames tributaries are considered important ecosystems within the Cotswolds. The rivers, such as the Coln, also make idyllic walking territory. (SS/P)

Unblemished Castle Combe one of the mos[t] photographed villages in the region and deserves more of your time than a single stroll along the main street. (CM)

The Arlington Row in Bibury is the epitome of Cotswold-esque architecture and a very popular attraction on the tourist trail. (SS)

Cotswolds towns and villages

Shaped by the wool trade, the picture-perfect towns and villages exemplify the iconic architecture of the Cotswolds.

Northleach is one of countless villages in the region where the wool trade really made its mark on the architecture, in particular its parish church. (SS)

Most Cotswold towns include a market hall where wool was once sold. The very yellow Market Hall in Tetbury is the focal point of the town. (MH/A)

The Shambles is one of Bradford-on-Avon's shortest streets but it is crammed with interesting shops and decorated with colourful hanging baskets. (CM)

One of the oldest market towns in the region, Burford offers fine views over the surrounding countryside, and the mismatched nature of the High Street means you'll always find something you've not seen before, no matter how many times you visit. (SS)

The steamy views of Bath Abbey and the hills beyond from the rooftop pool at Thermae Bath Spa really are this astounding. It's the ideal way to slow down the pace of city life. (BTP/CH)

Taking a boat up the River Avon through Stratford-upon-Avon is a pleasant way to escape the Shakespeare-mad crowds. (CM)

The Covered Market in Oxford is *the* place to find local delicacies and traditional foodstuffs as well as cosy cafés and interesting boutiques. (CM)

Dust off your fans and bonnets for the Jane Austen Festival in Bath – living history! (OB)

The Gloucestershire Warwickshire Railway is a superbly Slow way to visit Cheltenham. (SS)

Quite a surreal sight in the middle of this bustling city – deer in the grounds of Magdalen College, Oxford. (CM)

Slowing down urban style?

Large towns and cities can sometimes seem anything but Slow, with a frantic approach to ticking off major sights taking priority over getting to know the places you are visiting. Slow down and seek out something a bit different.

Hall's Croft in Stratford-upon-Avon is one of the quieter of the Shakespeare properties and the gardens here offer a sanctuary from the busy town. (PCL)

The Kennet and Avon Canal, just minutes away from the bustle of Bath's centre, provides a peaceful walk or an alternative, slow-paced view of the city. (TS/A)

Barnsley House (now a hotel) was the home of the celebrated garden designer Rosemary Verey. Her gardens remain open to the public. (BH)

Houses and gardens

The Cotswolds are synonymous with therapeutically cosy cottage gardens but equally there are stunning stately homes to be explored.

Batsford Arboretum is the largest private collection of trees in the UK and a real delight to explore with carpets of flowers whatever the season. (BA/MT)

The formal gardens at Nash's House and New Place in Stratford-upon-Avon create a riot of colour against the backdrop of the buildings and provide a chance for visitors to tread in the very footsteps of the Bard. (PCL)

Twinberrow Wood Sculpture Trail near Dursley aims to encourage imaginative play among children. (VLM)

The final resting place of King Henry VIII's last wife, Catherine Parr, Sudeley has much regal history and its gardens today are enchanting. (CM)

A Baroque masterpiece, Blenheim Palace is also famed for its wonderful formal gardens and extensive parkland. (OC)

When sunlight brushes against the ironstone walls of Broughton Castle, considered one of the finest fortified manor houses in Britain, the building turns a sumptuous pumpkin orange. (IM/A)

It would be impossible to overstate the significance of the Cotswold sheep (*right*, CM) and the wool trade on the region. To this day the industry is celebrated and remembered in traditional events such as Tetbury's Woolsack Races (*above*, CPL/A) and the Wool Fair at Shipston-on-Stour (*left*, PV). The Cotswold Sheep Society continues to raise the profile of this rare breed, one of the oldest breeds of sheep in the country.

The Marshfield Mummers preserve the tradition of story-telling every Boxing Day by performing a five-minute play based on the legend of St George and the Dragon. (CZ)

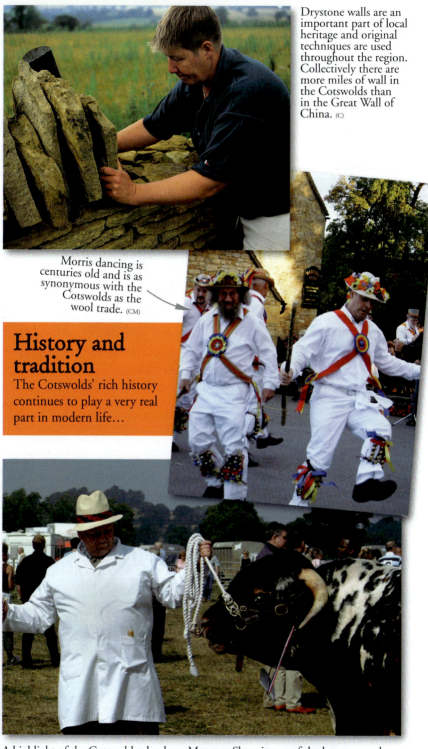

Drystone walls are an important part of local heritage and original techniques are used throughout the region. Collectively there are more miles of wall in the Cotswolds than in the Great Wall of China. (C)

Morris dancing is centuries old and is as synonymous with the Cotswolds as the wool trade. (CM)

History and tradition

The Cotswolds' rich history continues to play a very real part in modern life…

A highlight of the Cotswold calendar – Moreton Show is one of the largest one-day rural events in Britain where prize animals are judged alongside floral displays and Victoria sponges. (C)

Only in Bath can you try an original Sally Lunn Bun – still made fresh each day. (*main image* DG, *inset* BTP)

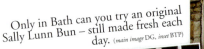

Food and drink

Celebrated across the Cotswolds, there is no shortage of first-class produce grown, reared and made locally.

Pick up local produce at one of the many farmers' markets in the Cotswolds, such as this one here in Stow-on-the-Wold. (C)

Real ales reign supreme at the Hook Norton Brewery where the original steam engine is still used in the production process. (CM)

The Cheese Festival in Cheltenham is one of many festivals held in the city. (C

Quirky it may be, but cheese-rolling at Cooper's Hill takes nerves of steel with such steep gradients! (JWL/P)

Eccentric Cotswolds

The Cotswolds have their fair share of quirky events, odd antics and unusual places....

The Chocolate Suite at the Three Ways Hotel in Mickleton – one of seven rooms in celebration of traditional British puddings! (PC)

The Olympic Games, Cotswolds style! Robert Dover's annual Olimpick Games recognises such high-profile events as shin-kicking, tug of war and sack races. (RD)

A game with a difference – the residents of Bourton-on-the-Water take to the river for this annual football match. (CM)

Set amidst glorious rolling countryside and in a designated Area of Outstanding Natural Beauty, our North Cotswolds 'home from home' at Little Compton is your great escape – the perfect location for exploring unspoilt villages and historical towns.

THE OLD SCHOOL

The Old School, Little Compton, Moreton in Marsh, Gloucester, GL56 0SL
Tel: 01608 674588
wendy@theoldschoolbedandbreakfast.com
www.theoldschoolbedandbreakfast.com

THREE WAYS HOUSE

○

A COTSWOLD VILLAGE HOTEL

Mickleton. Chipping Campden. Gloucestershire. GL55 6SB
Tel: 01386 438429
www.threewayshousehotel.com

THE
PUDDING CLUB
EST. 1985

Now in its 26th year, The Pudding Club is very much a part of Three Ways House. You can attend a Pudding Club meeting or dine in the award winning restaurant and then stay overnight in a unique pudding theme room.

Situated in the northern Cotswolds, close to Stratford upon Avon, there are plenty of things to see and places to visit. Special offers available online at www.threewayshousehotel.com

Author

Caroline Mills is a country girl. While she loves to visit the towns and cities of the world, she likes nothing better than to return to the farm where she lives on the fringes of the Cotswolds. Other than brief spells living in London and York, she has moved no more than five miles from her childhood home – also in the Cotswolds. Brought up close to Stratford-upon-Avon, she began a love affair with William Shakespeare at an early age and her dream was to become a stage manager for the Royal Shakespeare Company. Realising while studying at RADA that Saturday nights would never be the same again, she changed her mind and went to Oxford to gain an Honours degree in English and Music before diving into publishing. She now works freelance, writing travel books and contributing to various national magazines on travel, food and gardens.

Author's story

Forgive me for being frivolously biased, but I have decided that I live in the most beautiful part of the UK! I knew it all along really, but researching this book has cemented my thoughts and now I want to shout it out loud.

The Cotswolds might not be as dramatic as the Scottish glens, or as rugged as the North York Moors or even as picturesque as the Lake District on certain days. What it does have is a comforting feeling that everything is right with the world.

So when Bradt asked if I would like to write a book on the Cotswolds I jumped at the chance to explore the area some more. And then my blood ran cold. Another book on the Cotswolds – how do I make it different? How often can I write about honey-coloured stone and which villages do I include when so many of them look appealing? Am I the right person to write about the area when, I'm ashamed to say, I often take where I live for granted as I go about my day-to-day business?

My first thoughts were to re-read some 'Cotswold' literature, but I couldn't decide whether to bathe in the sublime imagery of *Cider With Rosie*, whip out a dog-eared copy of *Northanger Abbey* or brush up on some of the lesser-known sonnets of the Bard. Rebecca Tope's mix of Cotswold scenery with blood-curdling crimes I felt might leave me never stepping out to do my research so instead I thought I could return to my childhood dreams of *Alice in Wonderland*, Penelope Lively's *House at Norham Gardens* or even hide in C S Lewis's wardrobe for an hour or two.

I've had to retrain my brain to write this book – look at 'my' patch with new eyes as if removing myself from all that I know, and then put those little nuances, secret places and insider knowledge that I've gleaned over my lifetime back again but with a fresh approach.

I thought I knew a reasonable amount about the area, albeit not as much as the farmers who have toiled the land here for generations. I realise now, it will take more than my lifetime to really discover the Cotswolds. At least I've made a start.

First published April 2011
Bradt Travel Guides Ltd
IDC House, The Vale, Chalfont St Peter, Bucks SL9 9RZ
www.bradtguides.com
Published in the USA by The Globe Pequot Press Inc,
PO Box 480, Guilford, Connecticut 06437-0480

ISBN: 978 1 84162 344 3

British Library Cataloguing in Publication Data
A catalogue record for this book is available from the British Library

Photographs
Alamy: Cotswolds Photo Library (CPL/A), Michael Hawkridge (MH/A), Ian McIlgorm
(IM/A), Trevor Smithers ARPS (TS/A); Barnsley House (BH), Bath Tourism Plus (BTP):
Colin Hawkins (CH/BTP); Batsford Arboretum/Mike Tayler (BA/MT); Owen Benson
(OB); Cotswolds.com (C); Cotswold Lavender (CL); Robert Dover's Cotswold Olimpick
Games/www.olimpickgames.co.uk (RD); Dreamstime.com: Davidmartyn (DM/D);
Deborah Guber (DG); Caroline Mills (CM); Valerie L Moores/Vale Vision Development
Trust, Dursley (VLM); Oxfordshire Cotswolds (OC); Photolibrary.com: Stephen Shepherd
(SS/P), John Warburton-Lee (JWL/P); Pictures Colour Library (PCL); The Pudding Club
(PC); SuperStock (SS); Robert Talbot (RT); Philip Vial/Shipston-on-Stour Wool Fair
(PV); Crispin Zeeman (CZ)

Front cover artwork Neil Gower (*www.neilgower.com*)
Illustrations Sarah Holland
Maps Chris Lane (*www.artinfusion.co.uk*)
Colour map contains Ordnance Survey data © Crown copyright and database 2011

Typeset from the author's disc by Artinfusion Ltd
Production managed by Jellyfish Print Solutions; printed in Europe

The Slow mindset

Hilary Bradt, Founder, Bradt Travel Guides

We shall not cease from exploration
And the end of all our exploring
Will be to arrive where we started
And know the place for the first time.

T S Eliot 'Little Gidding', *Four Quartets*

This series evolved, slowly, from a Bradt editorial meeting when we started to explore ideas for guides to our favourite country – Great Britain. We wanted to get away from the usual 'top sights' formula and encourage our authors to bring out the nuances and local differences that make up a sense of place – such things as food, building styles, nature, geology, or local people and what makes them tick. Our aim was to create a series that celebrates the present, focusing on sustainable tourism, rather than taking a nostalgic wallow in the past.

So without our realising it at the time, we had defined 'Slow Travel', or at least our concept of it. For the beauty of the Slow movement is that there is no fixed definition; we adapt the philosophy to fit our individual needs and aspirations. Thus Carl Honoré, author of In Praise of Slow, writes: 'The Slow Movement is a cultural revolution against the notion that faster is always better. It's not about doing everything at a snail's pace, it's about seeking to do everything at the right speed. Savouring the hours and minutes rather than just counting them. Doing everything as well as possible, instead of as fast as possible. It's about quality over quantity in everything from work to food to parenting.' And travel.

So take time to explore. Don't rush it, get to know an area – and the people who live there – and you'll be as delighted as the authors by what you find.

Acknowledgements

This book would not be what it is without the input of those living and working in the Cotswolds who generously gave up their time to talk – thank you. On a professional level – a big thank you to the ever-patient Anna Moores at Bradt and editor Tim Locke, to Sarah Holland for the attractive illustrations and to Chris Lane for making all the copy look fantastic. And on a personal level, to my wonderful husband and to my children who barely saw Mummy for several months but, nonetheless, learnt patience, where the vacuum cleaner is kept and how to cook a roast dinner! *Slow Cotswolds* is dedicated to all the farmers of the Cotswolds who have, for generations, cared for and been the guardians of this unique and special landscape. Thank you.

CONTENTS

GOING SLOW IN THE COTSWOLDS   vi
An Area of Outstanding Natural Beauty viii, In this book x, How to use this book xi

1. STRATFORD-UPON-AVON   1
Getting there and around 1, Accommodation 3, Food and drink 4, Shakespeare's Stratford 4, Stratford without Shakespeare 14

2. NORTH COTSWOLDS   19
Getting there and around 19, Accommodation 22, South Warwickshire 23, Towards the Vale of Evesham 27, Chipping Campden and around 32, Broadway and its villages 39

3. FOUR SHIRES   47
Getting there and around 47, Accommodation 49, Southernmost Warwickshire and northernmost Oxfordshire 49, North Oxfordshire proper (and a bit of west Oxfordshire) 53, Feldon and the Stour Valley 63, Around the Four Shires Stone 69

4. HIGH COTSWOLDS   75
Getting there and around 75, Accommodation 78, Between Moreton and Stow – a triangle of villages 79, Hills and valleys – Stow and its western neighbours 84, The Guitings, Kineton and Ford – the quiet core 90, The seat of Mercia – Winchcombe and its villages 94, The Cotswolds' highest point – Cheltenham and its high commons 98, East from Cheltenham, and around the A436 102

5. THE THAMES TRIBUTARIES   107
Getting there and around 107, Accommodation 110, The Windrush Valley 111, The Leach Valley 118, The Coln Valley 121, The Churn Valley 128, The Evenlode Valley 132

6. OXFORD   143
Getting there and around 143, Accommodation 146, Food and drink 146, North of Queen Street and West of Cornmarket Street 148, North of the High Street and east of St Giles 151, South of the High Street and east of St Aldates 154, South of Queen Street and west of St Aldates 157, Oxford's outskirts 158

7. THAMES VALLEY   161
Getting there and around 162, Accommodation 163, The source – Kemble and Ewen to Cricklade 163, North of the river – the Ampneys 169, Inglesham to Kelmscott 171

8. THE SOUTHERN COTSWOLD SCARP AND FIVE VALLEYS 179

Getting there and around 181, Accommodation 182, The Frome Valley (Golden Valley) 183, The Painswick Valley and the Slad Valley 187, Stroud 194, The Cotswold Scarp – the dry valley? 195, The Nailsworth Valley 202, The commons and skinny valleys 206

9. WILTSHIRE COTSWOLDS 213

Getting there and around 213, Accommodation 215, The young Avon Valley to Malmesbury 216, Dyrham and Marshfield 220, The By Brook Valley 222, Bradford-on-Avon and the Limpley Stoke Valley 229

10. BATH 233

Getting there and around 235, Accommodation 237, Food and drink 237, Old Bath – around Bath Abbey 239, New Bath – 18th-century Bath 245, East of the river 252

INDEX 256

GOING SLOW IN THE COTSWOLDS

What is this life if, full of care,
We have no time to stand and stare.

No time to stand beneath the boughs
And stare as long as sheep or cows.

W H Davies, 'Leisure'

There are two reasons to begin this guide with a few lines from William Henry Davies other than it being a rather pleasant first few words to an effective piece of poetry. First, the poet W H Davies was a one-time traveller of sorts (more vagrant than tourist) and he was a resident of the Cotswolds. Admittedly, he wrote the poem 'Leisure' (in 1911) long before he settled in the Cotswolds but, nevertheless, he chose to spend the last years of his life in the area. Secondly, in a few short lines, the poem really sums up what going slow in the Cotswolds is all about.

In parts of the Cotswolds it is indeed impossible to do anything but go slow – narrow and contorted lanes wind their way up steep hillsides, and many villages seem decades away from the modern world. That's not to say that the Cotswolds is backward-looking, but if you happen to be gently rocking in a chair beside the embers of a log fire, just as generations of Cotswold residents have done over hundreds of years, that pressing business meeting arranged for the following morning suddenly seems ever so slightly less important.

For the rounded landscape of the Cotswolds feels cosy, snuggly and warm, even in the depths of winter. It's why everything appears to 'nestle' in the Cotswolds according to websites, tourist brochures and estate agents. There's little that's raw, jagged or sharp about the landscape and the sense of harmony between man and the land feels comfortingly organic. With 86% of the Cotswolds being farmland, the relationship between the two is where the story of the Cotswolds really begins.

You can't avoid noticing geology wherever you go. The distinctive local limestone makes the Cotswolds what they are today, both in the natural rock formations that remain and in the buildings in towns and villages. The colour of the stone varies from creamy white to a deep golden brown but its composition remains the same. Formed in the Jurassic age – 140 to 210 million years ago – when the area was awash with sea creatures, layers of sedimentary rock known as oolite were laid down. This oolitic limestone is so called because the small round particles, or ooids, look like fish eggs. Some eons later man came along and started digging up this stone for houses, animal shelters and walls to enclose livestock.

The Cotswolds stretch from Bath in the southwest towards Stratford-upon-Avon in the northeast and covers six historic counties: Somerset, Wiltshire, Gloucestershire, Worcestershire, Oxfordshire and Warwickshire. The same band of oolitic limestone continues further northeast towards Grantham and Stamford in Lincolnshire, and there are resemblances in the stone but it's here that the similarities end.

To some extent the Cotswolds divide into two. The western side is dominated by a striking line of hills that rise to 1,080 feet above sea level, running from Bath to a point east of Evesham. This escarpment overlooks the Severn Valley, the Forest of Dean and the Welsh hills beyond. Yet the escarpment, while it may look like one long ridge from a distance, is actually made up of many lumps and bumps between both wet and dry valleys that weave through the landscape. Its character is so very different from the eastern side, a plateau where the land levels out to a gentler scene with rolling hills, river valleys and agricultural plains. These are interspersed with a splattering of towns and villages that evolved with purpose – as the meeting points for the farmers and merchants who also made their mark on the landscape. For while the Cotswolds are predominantly a rural idyll now, they were by no means an industrial backwater. The quality of the stone architecture of the towns and villages that give the landscape such appeal is a potent reminder of the area's once thriving and prosperous industries.

Evidence of prehistoric man crops up here and there with Neolithic burial chambers, found mainly on the western escarpment. The Bronze Age and Iron Age residents built hill-forts, many of which can still be seen quite clearly. When the Romans arrived, they too made their mark on the Cotswolds, in the form of villas such as Chedworth. Particularly evident of their legacies today is the Fosse Way, a road that runs the length of the Cotswolds from Bath, through Cirencester to Moreton-in-Marsh and beyond to the Lincolnshire Wolds.

One of the most plausible explanations for the Cotswolds name is that 'wolds' means 'open hillsides' and 'cotes' denotes 'sheep enclosures'. Hence the 'Cotswolds' (or 'hills covered in sheep') became renowned for these woolly beasts and later the wool itself. The Cotswolds' finest hour came in the late Middle Ages when the sheep – and their prized wool – had made a name for themselves internationally. Merchants came from all over Europe to trade, 'wool towns' sprang up across the region and the wealth was pumped into magnificent houses, market halls and churches.

The woollen cloth industry began to boom during the 17th and 18th centuries, particularly along the river valleys where mills sprang up. But it was not to last; competition from large-scale mechanised mills in Yorkshire then cheap imports thwarted the industry and the area gave way to a wave of artists and craftsmen and women as the Arts and Crafts Movement began, most notably William Morris who made the Cotswolds his home and an inspiration for his work, together with numerous other associates including several of the Pre-Raphaelite Brotherhood.

The Cotswold Lion

Few breeds of animal can claim to have helped shape the economic history of England and create an entire landscape based upon their fame. The Cotswold sheep is one of them. Descended from the flocks that grazed the Cotswold hills in Roman times, it was originally a rugged animal whose characteristics evolved over time. To my mind, the Romans' greatest legacy to the area is their introduction of this breed.

Its wool was already recognised as important and of good quality by the Romans and became known as the Golden Fleece, because it generated so much wealth. It was exported during Saxon times but had its heyday in the Middle Ages, when the sheep became known as the Cotswold Lion. The sheep grew large, the coat heavy and thick owing to the herb- and grass-rich limestone pastures on which they grazed; they were big, strong and hardy. This gave the Cotswold Lion a second golden age in the 19th century when, rather than wool, rams were in huge demand. They were exported all over the world for breeding to generate the tasty meat for which the sheep had now become renowned but as Victorian-sized families disappeared, the need for large meat joints declined.

Today, numbers are increasing again. With a renewed emphasis on low-impact farming, the Cotswold Lion's traditional qualities are the focus of attention again. The breed has evolved further so it is much larger than its 15th-century forebears and creates outstandingly flavoursome meat as well as special-quality long fleece.

I spoke to Robin Leach and Derek Cross of the **Cotswold Sheep Society** (*www.cotswoldsheepsociety.co.uk*). They are both farmers in the Cotswolds and they told me what a judge is looking for to find a champion Cotswold Lion at agricultural shows.

While many of the sheep have gone from the hillsides, agriculture still plays a lively part in the local economy together with quarrying for the much sought-after stone that very much made the landscape in more senses than one. Visitors can (re)awaken their senses by sampling the sights, sounds and smells of the area, touching the landscape, tasting its fruits and encountering an altogether more organic and wholesome experience – and a slower pace of life. The Cotswolds has a character like no other.

An Area of Outstanding Natural Beauty

Much of the Cotswolds is designated an Area of Outstanding Natural Beauty (AONB), a status close to that of a National Park. Covering 787 square miles, it is the largest of all the AONBs in England and Wales. AONBs are designed to 'conserve and enhance the natural beauty of their landscapes while also taking account of agriculture, forestry, rural industries and the economic and social needs of local communities.' This sits very well with the ethos behind slow tourism.

'First, the fleece is naturally very important,' Robin explained. 'The crimp or curl should be uniform and the staple [the natural clusters of wool] should be long and wide when parted. The lustre of the fleece must be good; there should be a yellow tinge to the root.'

Derek continued, 'The sheep should have a good, wide head with a white and black nose. There should definitely be no pink noses! The 'top knot', the distinguishing feature of the Cotswold sheep, should be left on rather than sheared for judging.'

The pair explained that it is the male sheep that grows the longest wool and the first shear is always the best wool. 'Because the sheep were kept especially for their wool, the animals were that much older. Therefore the meat was actually mutton, which is why they became renowned for their flavour,' said Robin. However, today Cotswold sheep are kept more for their meat than their wool. Derek added, 'The Cotswold sheep is bigger boned so it creates a large joint. There is more fat and more marbling than the more modern breeds and this gives the meat its flavour; it is a very traditional joint of meat.'

I finished by asking how many Cotswold sheep graze the hills today. 'We have over a hundred members and we think that there are two thousand breeding ewes,' said Robin. That still makes the Cotswold sheep a rare breed, but numbers are increasing as demand for the delicious meat develops. Asked to describe the character of the breed, Robin replied, 'They are very docile and easy to handle.' Derek added, 'They are the sheep with manners.'

Butts Farm Shop at South Cerney (see page 165) is a notable place to buy Cotswold sheep meat.

The Cotswolds AONB has strikingly special attributes and the Cotswolds Conservation Board, which manages the AONB, has identified numerous landscape types and elements that are keynotes to the Cotswolds. These include more than 4,000 miles of drystone walls (longer than the Great Wall of China), ancient woodland, unimproved grassland, vernacular stone buildings, archaeological sites, settlement patterns and historic parkland.

The AONB has more than 340 Cotswold Voluntary Wardens who carry out conservation work and lead guided walks. Each warden cares for a particular area and has special knowledge of his or her patch. The Cotswolds Conservation Board website (*www.cotswoldsaonb.org.uk*) is a good starting point for finding out about activities such as guided walks (led by the voluntary wardens) and themed weeks, such as the Cotswold Wildflower Week and the Cotswolds River Week. The board also runs **Rural Skills Courses** in drystone walling (see page 90), hedging and traditional woodwork providing the perfect way in which to become involved with an aspect of the landscape that is the Cotswolds.

All the AONB events, including the courses, are listed on their website and in the free *Cotswold Lion* newspaper (available at visitor information centres) but if you prefer some face-to-face interaction, **Escape to the Cotswolds!** (see page 119) is the visitor information centre for the AONB.

Leaving the car behind really helps you get to grips with some parts of the Cotswolds. Besides, there is no other feeling like it than to climb one of the Cotswold hills under some seasonal sunshine, peek your head over the summit and find the rest of the world laid out before you. To wander the full 102 miles of the **Cotswold Way**, designated as a National Trail and waymarked with acorn motifs, in one hit requires some preparation – and in truth, you miss out on so much more that the Cotswolds have to offer. So the Cotswolds Conservation Board have come up with a series of **Cotswold Way Circular Walks** of varying lengths that take up some of the very best sections of the Cotswold Way combined with other public footpaths and bridleways. You can download maps for the circular walks from their website along with **Walks on Wheels** – short walks to explore the AONB using wheelchairs, mobility scooters or pushchairs. Also on their website is information about national **cycle routes** and paths that run through the area, and bridleways (which can also be used by cyclists). **Horseriding** is extremely popular in the Cotswolds with riding schools dotted across the area, many of them offering treks through the countryside. Some 44 miles of the long-distance riding route, the Sabrina Way, are through the Cotswolds while the Claude Duval Bridle Route, named after a notorious highwayman, is in the east of the region and covers 50 miles through north Oxfordshire and Gloucestershire.

In this book

Despite going into some detail, *Slow Cotswolds* is really a collection of choice pickings to inspire your own exciting exploration; getting out there is by far the best bit. I've lived in the Cotswolds all my life and yet, although I hope to have given a good insight into the area, I feel as if I have so much still to learn about it myself.

So I've touched upon much of the landscape within the boundaries of the AONB but I've also added in a few gems on the fringes – some of my favourite places that I feel are worth exploring too and that, in my eyes, deserve to be included as part of the Cotswolds. For many years I've watched as tourists have flown in from all over the globe, 'done' Stratford-upon-Avon, hopped on a coach to take a photograph of Lower Swell (from the coach door) *en route* to Bath before 'doing' Oxford, then climb back into an aeroplane to tell friends and family that they've been to 'the Cotswolds'. I'm not knocking this approach to travel (entirely) but I really hope that you can see a little more and get under the skin of what the Cotswolds are all about, meeting the communities that live and work here. So I've broken the area down into more manageable pieces – or 'locales'. As it is such a rural region, I've included Stratford-upon-Avon, Cheltenham, Oxford and Bath as those essential urban gateways to the Cotswolds from the four compass points.

To really appreciate the area in detail, I thoroughly recommend getting hold of a good, detailed **map**; I find the OS 1:25,000 Explorer series the most useful. Those covering the areas in this book are: OL45 *The Cotswolds*, 155 *Bristol & Bath*, 156 *Chippenham & Bradford-on-Avon*, 167 *Thornbury, Dursley & Yate*, 168 *Stroud, Tetbury & Malmesbury*, 169 *Cirencester & Swindon*, 179 *Gloucester, Cheltenham & Stroud*, 180 *Oxford*, 190 *Malvern Hills* (covers Bredon Hill in the Cotswolds), 191 *Banbury (Bicester) & Chipping Norton* and 205 *Stratford-upon-Avon*.

Perhaps better for car touring or on-road cycling is the Landranger series. Try: 172 *Bath & Bristol*, 164 *Oxford*, 163 *Cheltenham & Cirencester* and 151 *Stratford & Banbury*.

How to use this book

The **colour map** at the front of this book shows which area falls within which chapter. Each chapter begins with a more detailed **chapter map** highlighting places mentioned in the text.

To guide you round, each featured place is given a **circled number** corresponding to the same circled number on the map. Points are numbered consecutively as they occur in the text, making it easy to locate them on the chapter map.

These symbols appear on the chapter maps at the start of each chapter, as well as on the colour map at the start of the book.

To give clarity to some descriptions of locales – particularly walks – simple **sketch maps** are included. They are intended merely to set the scene rather than to provide detailed information.

Also included are suggestions of places to eat and drink, plus a very select bunch of places to stay within each area. These are all purely personal recommendations; no place has asked or paid to be in the guide.

Feedback request

There are only so many special places and aspects of Cotswold life that you can focus on when limited by word counts and book length. Much as we'd like to include them all, it simply isn't possible. We've done our best to include a good mix and to check facts but there are bound to be errors (phone numbers and websites change with alarming frequency) as well as inevitable omissions of really special places. You can post your comments and recommendations, and read the latest feedback from other readers online at http://updates.bradtguides. com. Alternatively, email us on info@bradtguides.com.

STRATFORD-UPON-AVON

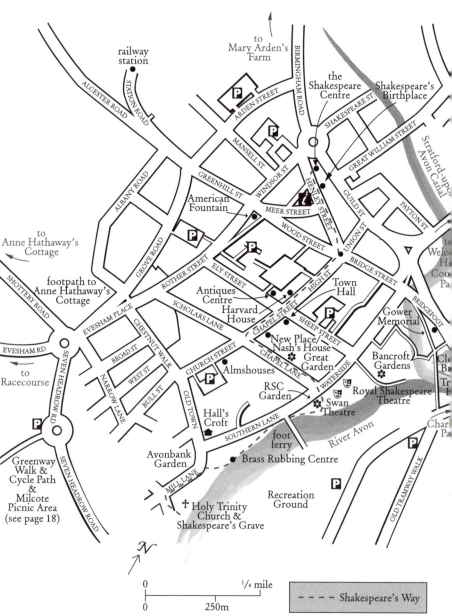

railway station

to Mary Arden's Farm

BIRMINGHAM ROAD

the Shakespeare Centre

Shakespeare's Birthplace

ALCESTER ROAD

STATION ROAD

ARDEN STREET

SHAKESPEARE ST

GREAT WILLIAM STREET

Stratford-upon-Avon Canal

MANSELL ST

WINDSOR ST

HENLEY STREET

GUILD ST

PAYTON ST

GREENHILL ST

MEER STREET

American Fountain

ALBANY ROAD

GROVE ROAD

WOOD STREET

UNION ST

to Welc H Cou Pa

to Anne Hathaway's Cottage

SHOTTERY ROAD

ROTHER STREET

ELY STREET

HIGH ST

BRIDGE STREET

footpath to Anne Hathaway's Cottage

Antiques Centre

Harvard House

Town Hall

BRIDGEFOOT

Gower Memorial

EVESHAM PLACE

CHESTNUT WALK

SCHOLARS LANE

CHAPEL STREET

New Place Nash's House

SHEEP STREET

Great Garden

EVESHAM RD

BROAD ST

WEST ST

NARROW LANE

BULL ST

CHURCH STREET

OLD TOWN

Almshouses

CHAPEL LANE

Bancroft Gardens

Cl B Tr F

to Racecourse

RSC Garden

WATERSIDE

Royal Shakespeare Theatre

Char Pa

SEVEN HEADROW RD

Hall's Croft

SOUTHERN LANE

Swan Theatre

River Avon

Greenway Walk & Cycle Path & Milcote Picnic Area (see page 18)

SEVEN HEADROW ROAD

Avonbank Garden

MILL LANE

foot ferry

Brass Rubbing Centre

Recreation Ground

OLD TRAMWAY WALK

✝ Holy Trinity Church & Shakespeare's Grave

N

0   ¼ mile

0   250m

– – – – Shakespeare's Way

1. STRATFORD-UPON-AVON

Stratford-upon-Avon. What more is there to say about this town? As the birthplace of Shakespeare, it has been written about for centuries, 'done' by coach loads of ocean-hopping sightseers on wearying whistle-stop tours of Britain, and is arguably more famous than capital cities ten times its size. And yet, despite it being so celebrated, how many visitors actually get to know Stratford?

I once overheard a Stateside tourist, clearly having been on one of those 'Britain-in-a-week' kind of holidays, respond to his wife, 'Stratford-upon-Avon? Now which one was that?' Stratford must surely leave a more lasting impression. I've also seen students from the Far East nod off in front of a play by the Bard, not because it wasn't an enthralling, gripping production that had everyone else on the edge of their seat, but because they had been told that going to the theatre was 'the thing to do' in Stratford regardless of any comprehension of language.

And yet, where would Stratford be without Shakespeare? There are apparently some who believe the town would be considerably better off if he'd been born somewhere else. Financially, I doubt that very much. I'm in the camp that's pleased as punch he was born in Stratford. Given my upbringing close to the town, he has been a massive part of my life and I consider myself extremely fortunate to live in such close proximity to his legacies.

For it is just about impossible to mention Stratford without Shakespeare; there's a gaping hole in its make-up if you don't at least acknowledge his importance to the town. So, rather than divide Stratford into geographical areas, I've split this chapter into two: Shakespeare's Stratford and – because there is more to Stratford than the literary man – everything else.

Getting there and around

Trains

Stratford struggles a little with trains. It's on a spur of the rail line from Birmingham Moor Street to Warwick so all trains must pass through one or other of these stations to get there. It means that, despite the town being so famous, trains are not as frequent as you might think. **Chiltern Railways**

The *Shakespeare Express*

Of course it couldn't be called anything else, could it? The *Shakespeare Express* (*www.shakespeareexpress.com*) steam train operates from Birmingham to Stratford every Sunday from July to mid-September. The hour-long chug through the Warwickshire countryside takes a different route each way, and you can have Sunday lunch on board.

(*www.chilternrailways.co.uk*) runs a service from **London Marylebone** and **Birmingham Moor Street** while **London Midland** (*www.londonmidland.com*) operates from **Hereford** via **Worcester** to **Leamington Spa**. There are a couple of late evening trains to cater for theatre-goers, but don't expect to squeeze in a post-theatre dinner. The station is a ten-minute walk from the town centre.

Buses

There is no specific bus station in Stratford. Bus stops line one side of Bridge Street and Wood Street; from there, buses depart for many of the outlying villages plus Warwick, Leamington Spa, Evesham and Birmingham. You can access a timetable and service numbers at www.warwickshire.gov.uk. National Express (*www.nationalexpress.com*) coaches from/to London Victoria stop at the Riverside coach park on Bridgeway (next to the leisure centre).

There are lots of buses around the town too but nearly all the sites mentioned in this chapter are within walking distance of one another. A hop-on, hop-off City Sightseeing Tour (*www.citysightseeing-stratford.com*) operates from Bridgefoot, stopping outside the Pen and Parchment public house. It's a good way of reaching the few attractions away from the town centre, including **Anne Hathaway's Cottage** and **Mary Arden's Farm**.

Cycling

The Sustrans National Cycle Network Route 5 runs through Stratford as does Route 41 to Warwick. Part of Route 5 runs along the **Greenway** (see page 18), a traffic-free cyclepath/footpath that uses an old railway line just to the west of Stratford.

The town centre is small enough to walk, but a bike is useful to reach the few outlying places of interest such as those mentioned above.

For those who like to ride in a group, **Shakespokes** (*www.shakespokes.org.uk*) meets on the first and third Sunday of each month for an organised cycle ride around the area. Rides start from the Market Place at 09.30 and everyone is welcome. The cycling is gentle and leisurely rather than race pace.

Bike hire and cycle sales/repairs

The Cycle Studio Henley St ☎01789 205057 🖱 www.thecyclestudio.co.uk. Bicycles, clothing and accessories for sale. Workshop for repairs. Open Tue–Sat.

Stratford Bike Hire The Stratford Greenway, Seven Meadows Rd ☎07711 776340 🖱 www.stratfordbikehire.com. Mountain bikes, touring bikes, children's bikes, tandems and trailer bikes plus tricycles for the very youngest. Collect from the hire centre or they will deliver to your accommodation or starting point.

Walking

American visitors brought up on the block layouts of towns and cities will find something strangely familiar about Stratford's medieval grid system, which

Shakespeare's Way

A relatively recent creation, Shakespeare's Way is described by its founder Peter Titchmarsh (who also created the Macmillan Way) as 'a journey of imagination'. Imaginary it certainly is, for it can only replicate by thought the route that William Shakespeare may have taken on his journeys between Stratford and London. The entire 146-mile route is fully waymarked and there's a complete map on www.shakespearesway.org. But for those planning on covering the full distance, a useful guide available from tourist offices and bookshops in Stratford, simply titled *Shakespeare's Way*, describes every section of the route in detail.

The route starts at the poet's birthplace in Stratford and cuts across town before wheedling its way through some of the areas covered elsewhere in this book (*see chapters 2, 3* and *5*). It continues on until reaching its destination: Shakespeare's Globe Theatre in London. Those who walk all or part of the route are invited to gain sponsorship to support the Shakespeare Hospice in Stratford, the organisation for which the long-distance path was created.

makes getting from A to B and finding one's bearings very easy.

The town has plenty of green spaces to take a quiet walk (see page 16) rather than pounding the main shopping streets. Or you can take a guided **Stratford Town Walk**, either during the day (including Christmas Day) or at night for the **Stratford Town Ghost Walk**. Both are organised by Stratford Town Walk (*www.stratfordtownwalk.co.uk*).

Tourist information centre

Stratford-upon-Avon 62 Henley St CV37 6PT ☎ 01789 264293 🖰 www.discover-stratford.com.

Accommodation

Stratford is, unsurprisingly, peppered with places to stay of every type and price bracket from a youth hostel and campsites to upmarket hotels. Two of the busiest streets for guesthouses are Evesham Place and the Shipston Road with many inevitable references to Shakespeare in their names.

Arden Hotel Waterside CV37 6BA ☎ 01789 298682 🖰 www.theardenhotel stratford.com. Short of bunking down in the wings, this is as close to the Royal Shakespeare Theatre as you can get to stay. Following a recent multi-million-pound refurbishment, it's now a boutique-style hotel with king-size beds and marble bathrooms. A brasserie, champagne bar, lounge and terrace overlooking the theatre complete the package.

Church Street Townhouse 16 Church St CV37 6HB ☎01789 262222
🖱www.churchstreettownhouse.com. In a 400-year-old Grade II listed building, this
has 12 beautifully decorated en-suite bedrooms, some overlooking the almshouses and
Shakespeare's old school. Superb bistro too, and a great location for the town centre.

Food and drink

Stratford has a wealth of dining experiences and because of the theatres you'll get food
well into the evening. Pre-theatre menus usually begin around 17.00, there's then a
second sitting for those not going to the theatre followed by dinners after the show.

Bard's Kitchen Tea room The Antiques Centre, off Ely St. Tiny (6 tables) tea room with
cosy ambience (old RSC posters decorate the ceiling). Part of the Antiques Centre, a
useful place to pick up some knick-knacks.

Countess of Evesham Stratford Marina, Bancroft Gardens ☎07836 769499
🖱www.countessofevesham.co.uk. A floating restaurant in a narrowboat. The boat
is tastefully decorated and the food, cooked on board, is accomplished. Choose from
a lunchtime cruise or an evening dinner cruise when the floodlit riverbanks create a
really atmospheric occasion.

Dirty Duck Southern Ln ☎01789 297312 🖱www.dirtyduck-pub-stratford-upon-
avon.co.uk. Also, but rarely known as, the Black Swan – look at the pub sign hanging
over the door. The Dirty Duck is a Stratford institution for being the place where all
actors from the RSC hang out after a show, it being 2 minutes' walk from the theatre.
Drink in the Actors' Bar, which is covered with signed photos of past customers, or dine
in the recently refurbished Conservatory Restaurant. Very atmospheric inside though
the best place is outside on the terrace overlooking the river and the theatres.

Edward Moon Chapel St ☎01789 267069 🖱www.edwardmoon.com. Great brasserie
serving English and colonial food. Very popular so book in advance if you can,
especially at weekends.

The Opposition Sheep St ☎01789 269980 🖱www.theoppo.co.uk. Another Stratford
institution – known as 'The Oppo' to locals – having been serving up really tasty food
for over 20 years. Great cosy ambience, superb food and owing to its proximity to the
theatre, a popular haunt for post-theatre dinners.

RSC Rooftop Restaurant and Riverside Café Royal Shakespeare Theatre ☎01789
403449 🖱www.rsc.org.uk. Open from 11.30 every day. Pre-theatre menus available. The
Riverside Café, serving snacks and drinks, has an open-air terrace over the River Avon.

Vintner Sheep St ☎01789 297259 🖱www.the-vintner.co.uk. The other renowned
institution on Sheep Street, the Vintner is classed more as a café and wine bar but still
serves excellent food in beautiful surroundings.

Shakespeare's Stratford

Stratford-upon-Avon is a relatively small town so there is no need, for the purposes
of this guide, to split it up into areas. The town is growing considerably and fast,

however, and you need to penetrate some unremarkable outskirts that give no hint of the very attractive old centre.

The Royal Shakespeare theatres

If the reason you're going to Stratford is for its connection to Shakespeare then the places, more than any other, that I would recommend visiting are the theatres, the home of the **Royal Shakespeare Company (RSC)**. Just saying or writing the words brings tingles to the spine for me. Ben Jonson, a friend and contemporary playwright of Shakespeare, once wrote about his work: '*He was not of an age, but for all time!*'

It's for this reason that I believe the theatres are *the* place to connect with the man and his work, much more so than looking at the bedroom where he was born or the school where he grew up. They are where his work really does live on for all time.

You don't have to watch a production, like the illustrative foreign students in my introduction, because it's the thing to do in Stratford – though I'd thoroughly recommend it. Just visit one of the theatres, look around the foyer or take a backstage tour and feel the energy, the vibes and the excitement that the buildings create. The chances are, the more you delve and discover about his work and how it fits a modern world, the more you will want to watch a production. The RSC is, after all, the master craftsman at Shakespeare's plays.

Three performance spaces used by the RSC in Stratford are currently open to the public: the **Royal Shakespeare Theatre** (RST), the **Swan Theatre** and the **Courtyard Theatre**.

Despite the transformation of the Royal Shakespeare Theatre, my favourite is still the beautiful Swan. Its intimacy and its warm brick and timber structure is worthy of a visit regardless of whether you enjoy a Shakespeare production in there.

However, there are other ways to enjoy the theatre spaces and make the most of the Royal Shakespeare Company's presence. Look out for their open days and special events, which may include a football match between actors in the theatre garden ('It proves that actors are human beings and not "luvvies",' said Peter Wilson, see box page 6) visits behind the scenes to the costume and scenery workshops or a hands-on demo about stage-fighting.

Theatre tours are frequently available and a free Treasure Trail lets anyone follow an easy route through the theatre to discover its history and inspirations. There are regular talks about shows in production and frequent events for families and children. No age group is left out – the RSC is adamant that Shakespeare is accessible to all.

The transformation of the Royal Shakespeare Theatre

A 3½-year transformation of the Royal Shakespeare Theatre (and the consequent closure of the Swan) saw the 'temporary' Courtyard become the only performance space. In 2010, as the Royal Shakespeare Company prepared to celebrate its 50th anniversary, the metamorphosed RST and the Swan reopened their doors to convey the Bard's words once more.

Shortly before the RST and Swan reopened, I met with Peter Wilson, the project director in charge of overseeing the whole transformation of the theatres. He had project managed the opening of the Tate Modern in London, and the RSC wanted him to do to the theatre what he'd done for the hugely successful art gallery.

Peter explained that 70% of his role had involved overseeing the physical project while 30% of his task was to explain the project to everyone and anyone, in particular the sceptics.

He described Stratford as having had 'a series of lives' in the course of its history, constantly on the fringes of being an industrial settlement. The location of the theatre today was once an industrial area of town where in the 19th century such magnates as the timber merchant James Cox (whose name lives on as Cox's Yard, now a bar and restaurant, opposite the main entrance to the RST) and the brewer Edward Flower (the Flowers logo features a portrait of Shakespeare) set up business.

Today that history has all but disappeared and Stratford's current life includes its bipolar character as, on the one hand, a place of highbrow entertainment, Shakespearean actors and academics, and on the other, as 'Stratford-on-Sea for the Midlands', as Peter described it – a place to come for recreation beside the river.

Therefore Peter's aspiration was to make the theatre building more welcoming to everyone, not just those with a ticket to see a show. A new colonnade has been designed through the theatre building that allows people to walk on a pilgrimage from the canal basin in the Bancroft Gardens to Shakespeare's grave at Holy Trinity Church in the western part of town.

I can vouch for that. My first visit to the RST was a production of *Henry V* at the age of four. I might not remember every detail, but I still have some enjoyable if vague memories of the show. And that, of course, is where the strength of Stratford lies. It all comes back to connecting with the powerful words of Shakespeare, watching a sublime performance of a play in an iconic setting and holding onto those memories forever.

The Royal Shakespeare Company Waterside ☎0844 800 1110 🖥 www.rsc.org.uk. The website has information about current and future performances of plays from Shakespeare, his contemporaries and new playwrights together with all RSC events.

A new 110-foot brick and glass tower, inspired by a tower in the Italian city of Lucca, has been designed for use as a space to house events and exhibitions. At the top is a lantern to look out over the town with views of 'Shakespeare's Church', the river and the theatre below.

Said Peter, 'Our mission is to interest everyone in Shakespeare, including those for whom he is a challenge. Our research has told us why some people don't go to the theatre and therefore the transformation is like an architectural game – to seduce people into the theatre building without realising what's going on. It's about blurring boundaries.'

He continued, 'The theatre will be a zeitgeist. We're revealing the theatre processes so, for example, while doors may be closed to allow daily work to continue safely, you can see the scenery coming in for a particular production. And on backstage tours, there will be windows into rooms so visitors can watch what's going on.'

Peter then explained the reasoning behind the change of theatre space. 'When the Swan Theatre was built with its thrust stage, everyone loved it. All the best directors and actors wanted to work in the Swan but not the RST, with its cinematic proscenium arch. It was becoming a problem. However, demolishing the main theatre would have caused outrage – the façade is a listed building. To over-simplify the process, all we needed to do was stick the plans of the Swan onto the photocopier and enlarge them.'

Peter showed me three of the 27 exquisite scale models that were made detailing the potential layouts of the Royal Shakespeare Theatre. The process of transforming the theatre he described as 'keyhole surgery, cutting out and taking away the inner areas that needed to be changed while leaving the body of the building intact. The result is a new thrust stage where actors can engage with the audience much more, whoever they may be and from whatever background they have come.'

'The Courtyard Theatre,' he explained, 'has been a prototype for the new RST. Its temporary status as a "theatre kit in a box" means that one day it will be retired but we do not "throw away" buildings and so we will find a use for it somehow.'

Shakespeare's houses and gardens

So many places in Stratford enjoy celebrating a Shakespeare connection that you half expect one day a plaque appearing on the wall of a building exclaiming excitedly that the great man 'may' have been troubled by flatulence there. Every Tudor building in the town has the possibility of some sideways association. However, five houses are genuinely linked to the man. They include his birthplace and properties owned by him and his family.

As some of the few remaining wattle-and-daub buildings left in the town, they tend to sit prominently along the street frontages.

Most of the houses have events taking place throughout the year, from readings of the sonnets to outdoor plays, Tudor living history and children's activities. The **Shakespeare Centre**, home of the **Shakespeare's Birthplace Trust** (*Henley St;*

Shakespeare's birthday

The date 23 April may be St George's Day but in Stratford-upon-Avon it is Shakespeare's birthday. There are always celebrations happening on that day in town, no more so than at his birthplace. You'll usually find a piece of birthday cake somewhere, and a pageant and procession from the birthplace to 'Shakespeare's Church', where he's buried, takes place every year on the Saturday closest to his birthday. The procession is led by boys from the King Edward VI Grammar School, where he was a pupil, and includes representatives from organisations in the town, other schoolchildren, foreign dignitaries and members of the RSC. The procession files through the church, placing flowers upon Shakespeare's grave to the ringing of the church bells and music from the organ.

01789 204016; www.shakespeare.org.uk) is the main port of call for information on Shakespeare's houses. All the properties with the exception of Mary Arden's Farm are open daily all year (Mary Arden's Farm is open daily March to October). You can buy a ticket to visit all five houses and gardens for a reduced rate.

Shakespeare's Birthplace

The beginning of the Shakespeare's Way long-distance path to London, Shakespeare's Birthplace is noticeably out of keeping with the remainder of the properties in Henley Street. Its long road frontage woos many a foreign visitor for whom this

moment might be the first time they have ever seen such a quaint-looking house. Indeed it is extremely striking for its antiquity both inside and out, and the garden in which it sits is kept beautifully.

For me though the most interesting aspect is not the room in which Shakespeare was born in 1564, but the exhibition through which you pass in order to reach the house. Located in the adjacent Shakespeare Centre, it gives a quick run-down of Shakespeare's life and, far from elevating him to dizzying heights beyond our grasp, proves him to be a human being – as if his writing doesn't prove that already. One who had to get married at the age of 18 (though this was quite usual in the period) because he'd got his girlfriend pregnant, one who was caught poaching deer in nearby Charlecote Park, fined for hoarding corn and one who was twice listed for tax evasion! There are poignant moments to pick up on too, such as the timing of writing *Twelfth Night*, a play about reuniting lost, believed dead, twins, shortly after the tragic death of one of his own children – also a twin.

With a copy of the first folio of his plays from 1623, the exhibition finishes by explaining how Shakespeare has helped to shape us into who we are, illustrating some of the many phrases from his plays that are in common usage today.

Mary Arden's Farm

Strictly speaking the Shakespeare story begins some years before at the home of William's grandparents and childhood home of his mother, Mary Arden. The 16th-century farm has been brought to life with the sights, sounds and smells of the Tudor age. Daily routines, rare breed farm animals and home-grown 'Tudor' food cooked in the farmhouse kitchen give you an insight into past lives. I asked my nine-year-old son what he thought of his visit: 'The farm is made up of lots of little fields and I got to harvest flax with my hands. I liked the pigsty; it was made of straw and wood. I dressed up as a Tudor and got to make bread in the kitchen. The bread oven [he actually described it as a pizza oven!] was made by placing a basket onto a hard base, covering it with clay then burning the basket from beneath, leaving the clay oven. I did some Tudor dancing too and a man played the violin. I remember also that the side of the house nearest the road looked very neat and tidy compared to the rear, so that it looked 'posher' than it really was.'

Mary Arden's Farm is three miles from Stratford town centre in the tiny village of Wilmcote so a bike is a useful addition to reach it. Alternatively the City Sightseeing Bus (see page 2) calls at the entrance.

Anne Hathaway's Cottage

Tucked into a quiet lane in a little offshoot village of Stratford known as **Shottery** is the childhood home of his wife, Anne Hathaway. Considered one of the most romantic of the Shakespeare houses, this is of course noted for being the place where the young and virile William wooed his future wife. One can understand how Shakespeare would have easily been seduced by the cottage alone, the timber and thatched property flirting with anyone's emotions, looking humble and meek in its idyllically rural location.

For it is the setting of the house and its gardens that is so eye-catching. Old orchards surround the house and a small patch of woodland provides the perfect opportunity for a gentle walk through the dappled shade. There's an Elizabethan-style yew maze and a living willow cabin where you can listen to the poet's sonnets being read, but of particular note is **Shakespeare's Allotment**, a garden created by

Walk to Anne Hathaway's Cottage

You can walk from the town centre along a pleasant, well-signposted, one-mile footpath to Anne Hathaway's Cottage. The footpath entrance is at Evesham Place next to the Woodstock Guest House. Follow it straight on, crossing minor residential roads, to a large open playing field (Shottery Fields) and continue to the sign on the opposite side, pointing left or right to the cottage.

The right-hand route is slightly more direct but turn left (signposted Anne Hathaway's Cottage via Shottery). Turn right on Shottery Road and follow it round, past thatched cottages and The Bell public house to a mini roundabout. Turn left into Cottage Lane and follow a short distance to the cottage on the left-hand side.

the head gardener in charge of all the gardens at the five Shakespeare properties and exhibited at the Hampton Court Palace Flower Show. The allotment is based upon Anne Hathaway's vegetable patch and features a variety of fruit and vegetables, the varieties of which date back to the 16th century.

Hall's Croft

Perhaps of all the Shakespeare houses, Hall's Croft in Old Town has the least contiguous connection to William. By contrast to the throng of visitors to Shakespeare's Birthplace, it also happens to be one of the quieter locations and is all the more pleasant for it. William's daughter Susanna and her husband Dr John Hall, the only doctor in Stratford during his lifetime, owned the property, having had it built for them in 1613. Of all the five houses this feels much more like a home than a museum. However, there is a small exhibition, up a magnificent and rickety staircase of mammoth proportions, on early 17th-century medicine and Shakespeare's references to it. Take some time to sit in the peaceful garden.

New Place and Nash's House

The Shakespeare story ends at a property on the corner of Chapel Lane and Chapel Street, right in the town centre. By 1597 Shakespeare had become really quite wealthy from his playwriting. So he bought the house with the grandest façade in town, **New Place** in Chapel Street, together with a cottage in Chapel Lane. New Place was a mansion and the second-largest house in town. It was where he kept his library of books used as reference material for his work.

New Place is also where Shakespeare died in 1616, on 23 April – his 52nd birthday. His daughter, Susanna, later moved into the house with her husband Dr John Hall from their house in Old Town and the property was then passed on to Shakespeare's granddaughter and her husband Thomas Nash.

In 1759, irritated by the number of tourists appearing at the doorstep of his house eager to see where Shakespeare lived, the then owner Reverend Francis Gastrell demolished New Place and moved into the more modest timber-framed building next door now known as **Nash's House** as it too had been owned by Thomas Nash. It's this property that you enter into, not New Place. However, you can wander the gardens and look at the foundations of the house that Shakespeare owned. The gardens, planted with formal box hedges to create an Elizabethan knot garden and rampant hedges of fig and vine, are often bursting with colour, showing off the jumbled back of the surrounding houses. Peer through the wooden gate at the far end of the garden for views across to the silvery roof of the Swan Theatre.

The Shakespeare Centre and the Shakespeare Institute

Stratford is naturally a place of pilgrimage for anyone with a passion in Shakespeare's work and, yes, you can take an MA in Shakespeare Studies at the **Shakespeare Institute** in Church Street, a part of the University of Birmingham, if you're really serious about scholastic achievement.

But if you just want to find out a little more about the man and his work, the **Shakespeare Centre** is a good start. The centre holds many events for people of all ages, regardless of academic ability, who simply have an interest in Shakespeare. Activities include literary events and evening talks, often with directors and actors from the RSC and the world's leading figures on Shakespeare such as Stanley Wells, poetry festivals, study days and short courses about Shakespeare in life, history and performance plus anything else related to Shakespeare, historical Stratford or the Renaissance world. The events are often linked to current productions being performed by the RSC.

The Shakespeare Club

The oldest Shakespeare society in existence, the Shakespeare Club (*www.stratfordshakespeareclub.org*) meets every month at the Shakespeare Institute on Church Street. The inaugurators of the annual birthday pageant, they organise talks of a slightly more academic nature, with contributions from prominent academics and leading actors. While it is a club with annual membership, visitors are invited to attend the talks. A programme list is on their website.

Holy Trinity Church

The leggy spire of what is known as 'Shakespeare's Church' dominates the skyline of the southwest side of Stratford. This is where William Shakespeare was baptised and where he is buried, though you'll find a hunt around the grounds for his gravestone fruitless. His final resting place is inside the church and you have to pay a small fee to view it and the memorial bust that sits above (although entrance to the church is free). His wife, daughter Susanna, son-in-law John Hall and grandson-in-law Thomas Nash are all buried in the chancel alongside him.

That William is granted a grave free from the ravages of weather is not owing to his status as the greatest playwright that ever lived. He paid for the privilege! Keen not to have his bones dug up and placed in a charnel house to make way for other incumbents, he placed a curse upon his grave to ensure he could lay there in peace for eternity. To date no-one has dared to test this curse.

The church sits in a peaceful part of town, its spire towering above the banks of the River Avon. A modern gateway has been knocked through the wall of the churchyard to make way for a riverside walk – and pilgrimage route – from the church to the RSC theatres.

Shakespeare memorials

You'll find references to Shakespeare everywhere throughout Stratford, not just in words but also in paint and stone. Close together is a statue of the man standing

The Shakespeare Centre Library and Archive

Archives can sound like stuffy places full of decaying books gathering dust. Not so the Shakespeare Centre Library, where the staff's enthusiasm to share their passion of Shakespeare rubs off on anyone who wanders through the door.

I met up with Sylvia Morris, Head of the Shakespeare Centre Library and Archive. She explained how the archives are open to all: 'The Shakespeare Centre needs to be accessible to anyone who wants to use it, not just students and academics. We hold the world's most important collection of material relating to Shakespeare, including early printed books, records and documents relating to Shakespeare's life and to Stratford in his lifetime as well as performance collections. We look after the entire archive of the Royal Shakespeare Company too, plus we've also got Shakespeare-related ephemera from all periods such as playbills and programmes, newspaper articles, manuscripts, original artwork, engravings, photographs and videos.'

Sylvia continued, 'It's important to us that visitors are not intimidated to come in through the doors. We really want people to be able to engage with us and the material that we have here. All we ask is that visitors arrive with some kind of preconceived interest. Rather than arriving and saying, "I want to find out about Shakespeare", it may be that they want to find out about a particular play, a certain actor's involvement with the RSC or a particular aspect in relation to Shakespeare.'

It is the RSC archives that are likely to be of interest to the casual visitor. For these include prompt books and production notes including set and costume designs for all their plays and, for example, the shooting script when filming

above the entrance to the **Town Hall** in Sheep Street and a rather fine gold mosaic above the entrance to the **Old Bank** (now HSBC) dated 1810 on the corner of Ely Street.

But the most significant memorial to Shakespeare in town is situated in the **Bancroft Gardens** near **Clopton Bridge** (see page 14). This statue, showing Shakespeare seated, is flanked by life-size statues of arguably his best representatives from his plays: Lady Macbeth, Prince Hal, Hamlet, and Falstaff, representing Philosophy, Tragedy, History and Comedy. Lady Macbeth indeed appears troubled looking out across the gardens, while Falstaff looks ready to merrily greet any passer-by.

The memorial was sculpted by Lord Ronald Sutherland-Leveson-Gower, who presented it to the town of Stratford in 1888. An MP and sculptor, he was also a trustee of the Birthplace and Shakespeare Memorial Building (now the RST).

David Tennant's *Hamlet*. Visitors can also book an audio-visual room to watch past performances from over the years.

Explained Sylvia, 'It is an absolute privilege to work here. We receive lots of material from abroad. Most recently a couple arrived from China and handed over the entire works of Shakespeare translated into Chinese by their uncle. He had been unable to leave China and yet it had been his life's ambition to visit the collection here. They came as his representatives. I find my work here really quite humbling.'

At this point, Sylvia showed me into the strongrooms where the archive material is kept. Anything from the strongrooms may be brought up to the reading area for visitors to see (they're generally not allowed 'below stairs'). Unbeknown to me, she pulled out the Ashburnham copy, a special edition of the First Folio of Shakespeare's plays published in 1623. The original is fragile, but with excitement dancing in her eyes, Sylvia showed me the pages. This edition includes a heart-warming tribute and introduction to the plays by those contemporaries who produced the book. Said Sylvia, 'Shakespeare never published his work during his lifetime. Without this book and the forethought of his friends and theatre colleagues who got it published, there would be no Shakespeare. His contemporaries knew that he was special and this book is a memorial to someone who was loved.'

Clearly, as if evidence were required, Shakespeare is still loved.

Shakespeare Centre Library and Archive Henley St ✆01789 201816 🖰 www.shakespeare.org.uk. You can follow the library's blog at www.findingshakespeare.co.uk. Access to the library is free of charge.

Shopping
Stratford is definitely *the* place to buy all your Shakespeare memorabilia.

Chaucer Head Bookshop Chapel St ✆01789 415691 🖰 www.chaucerhead.com. Secondhand bookshop next door to Nash's House. Large section on Shakespeare plus drama, literary history and historical books about Stratford.
Royal Shakespeare Company RST, Waterside. Shakespeare-related books, DVDs plus exclusive RSC merchandise including programmes, billboard posters. Also a good range of Shakespeare-related things for children.
Shakespeare Birthplace Shop Henley St. You're shoe-horned through this shop on your exit from the Birthplace (there's no other escape!), but you can enter the shop without visiting the Birthplace. Lots of souvenirs, some bordering on tat but plenty of goodies to choose from, everything with a reference to 'him' of course.
Shakespeare Bookshop Henley St ✆01789 292176. Opposite the Shakespeare Centre; you can buy all his plays either singly or in volumes, different versions together with a whole catalogue of books about him, his life, his work, that of contemporary playwrights together with Tudor and Elizabethan history.

Stratford without Shakespeare

It's an unnerving thought to mention Stratford-upon-Avon without Shakespeare, and it will be almost impossible to avoid a reference to him surreptitiously creeping into the notes about other places in town. He is omnipresent.

Without the poet, Stratford-upon-Avon would be an ordinary market town. Its name is a literal translation of 'the street at the ford on the river', the town having been an important crossing point over the Avon from the Roman town of Alcester to the Fosse Way.

The River Avon

After the Bard, it is the River Avon that is the biggest draw, for some the fun being watching inexperienced rowers steer their hire boat – and its passengers – into the overhanging trees before fighting with an unco-operative oar to get them out of strife.

Despite its 85-mile length from Naseby in Northamptonshire to Tewkesbury, where it joins the Severn, the Avon is barely navigable before it reaches Stratford and only then by a couple of locks downstream does it allow larger boats. Therefore the two-mile stretch from **Alveston**, a small village east of Stratford, to Holy Trinity Church is virtually reserved for day-tripping rowers, with members of the **Stratford-upon-Avon Boat Club** seeing sense to train at less busy times of day. If you want to witness some more proficient action on the river, they hold a regatta every June.

You can hire either traditional wooden rowing boats or engine-propelled craft – all named after a Shakespeare character of course – from the boathouse by **Clopton Bridge** and next to the **chain ferry** southwest of the theatres. This tiny chain ferry is useful for crossing the river at this side of town to avoid the walk down to the pedestrian footbridge by the Bancroft Gardens.

Clopton Bridge is the main thoroughfare over the river in Stratford; the next crossing upstream is not for several miles. Built in 1480 by Hugh Clopton, later Lord Mayor of London, the bridge spans the entire width of the river with 14 arches and houses a ten-sided tollhouse at its northern end. It is one of Stratford's most enduring images.

To my mind, with only a small stretch of waterway available to rowing boats southwest of the bridge, which is also used by narrowboats and guided tours, the nicest option for **rowing** is to travel upstream underneath Clopton Bridge towards Alveston. There you'll pass private gardens on one side of the river and open space on the other bank. Half a mile upstream is a picnic area where you can moor up and stretch your legs.

The alternative to your own muscle power is to take a sightseeing cruise. Two companies are licensed to take passengers. **Avon Boating** run half-hour cruises leaving from the Bancroft Gardens in a fleet of vintage boats while **Bancroft Cruisers** take 45-minute trips from outside the Holiday Inn on the northeast side of Clopton Bridge.

For walkers, the Monarch's Way runs through the town, along the northwest side of the river while the Avon Valley Footpath treads the southwestern bank.

The Stratford-upon-Avon Canal

You'll also find the odd narrowboat moored up along the river. They enjoy the best of both river and canal, with the two meeting at **Stratford Marina** by the Bancroft Gardens. The canal runs for just 25 miles from Stratford to the outskirts of Birmingham but there are at least two locks for every mile. You can walk along the towpath in Stratford but outside of the town centre much of it is through industrial areas.

The streets of Stratford

Medieval town planners drew up Stratford on a grid system and the centre remains very similar today. The architecture has changed though, with each street becoming a hotchpotch of styles including the few remaining half-timbered properties, Georgian town houses and glass shopping malls. Everything within the town centre sits north of the river.

Bridge Street and **Wood Street**, together with the **High Street** remain the focal points for shopping, mostly taken over by High Street clones. **Rother Street** in the north of the town holds the weekly market every Friday. **Sheep Street**, running at right angles from the river, feels as if it has more cubic feet of restaurant space than any other in town.

But the award for the most photogenic street must be shared between **Church Street** and **Chapel Street** – the two run into one another at the junction with **Chapel Lane** that runs down to the theatres. Stand outside Elizabeth House, home of the district council and look back towards the town centre. A single, monochrome view encompasses the long row of **almshouses**, the old sections of **King Edward VI Grammar School** (or 'KES' for short – Shakespeare is its most famous alumnus), the pretty tower of the **Guild Chapel** (the Guild of the Holy Cross founded 'KES' in 1269), the timber buildings that house the **Shakespeare Hotel** and **Falcon Hotel** and, at the far end, Nash's House and New Place.

Back in town, other notables include the **Garrick Inn** and **Harvard House**, side by side on the High Street. The Garrick Inn claims to be Stratford's oldest pub dating from 1594. Originally called the Greyhound, it was renamed in honour of the actor and theatre manager David Garrick following his visit to Stratford in 1769 when he arranged for the first Shakespeare Festival to be held.

Harvard House next door shows off the most delicately carved and decorative timberwork. It is a spring chicken by comparison with its neighbour, dating from 1596. It has not always been known as Harvard House, and was thus renamed for

Not just the RSC

Stratford's status as home to the Royal Shakespeare Company means that other creative organisations are attracted to the town too and there is plenty going on: from alternative drama productions, music and opera to art and craft exhibitions. A good place to start to find out what's on is the **Bear Pit** (*www.thebearpit.org.uk*), an organisation that brings together many of the visual and performing arts groups based in the town.

Or try and get along to one of the shows performed by students from the drama department at Stratford College. Many of its former students – including the likes of Ben Elton – have gone on to become well-known figures on the stage.

being the childhood home of Katherine Harvard, the daughter of Thomas Rogers who built the house, and the mother of John Harvard who emigrated to America in 1637. He helped to found Harvard College in Massachusetts and it is Harvard University who now own the house.

Finally, take a look at the area to the west of the town centre known as **Old Town**. There are no visitor attractions as such but again on a grid system, there is street after street of brick-built, back-to-back terraced houses. It provides an interesting and quiet change away from the fray of the town centre, where you'll come across the odd pub and corner shop, frequented by locals rather than tourists.

Green spaces and gardens

Stratford's abundance of green spaces is certainly one of the town's special points. The gardens around the Shakespeare properties are, surprisingly, some of the most peaceful, and colourful. They're not so much for sunbathing but they do provide a pleasant place to sit and read a book and enjoy the riot of colour from the flower borders.

Bancroft Gardens

Of the public parks, the Bancroft Gardens are the most well known and used owing

to their location next to the River Avon and between the Royal Shakespeare Theatre and marina. It reputedly attracts over a million visitors a year. There's usually a street artist performing – some more skilled than others – and boats in the marina serving as an ice-cream vendor and art gallery. On the Bridgefoot side of the marina, around the Gower Memorial (see page 12) to Shakespeare, the gardens have recently been redesigned to incorporate floral displays and a rose garden. The Bancroft Gardens are the place to watch the world go by – and often the entire world does indeed seem to be there; don't expect solitude.

Recreation Ground

On the other side of the river to the Bancroft Gardens and the theatres is the Recreation Ground (or 'The Rec'). Occupying a large area running right the way along the river from Tramway Bridge (a pedestrian-only bridge adjacent to Clopton Bridge) to beyond Holy Trinity Church, this is one of the best areas for picnics with plenty of space to play and run around. There's a large playground here too. The Tramway Bridge connects the Recreation Ground with the Bancroft Gardens while the chain ferry transports you across the river to the Avonbank and RSC gardens.

Avonbank and RSC gardens

These two connected gardens run between the northern bank of the river and Southern Lane. Nearer to the town centre, the RSC Garden looks over the Swan Theatre and is where the RSC puts on occasional events. Despite its proximity to the Bancroft Gardens – only the theatre stands between the two – it is considerably quieter and exudes a different atmosphere.

The Avonbank Garden, also owned by the RSC, is quieter still, except on days when open-air productions are performed. Sitting between the RSC Garden and the Holy Trinity Church, it is leafier than any of the other open spaces.

Within the Avonbank Garden is the **Stratford Brass Rubbing Centre** (*www.stratfordbrassrubbing.co.uk*). This is a really restful place to visit and sit quietly under the portico, with the sun warming your back while you are therapeutically concentrating on your magically emerging image of some historical figure – Shakespeare included, of course. With rubbings of all different sizes, there are small ones that take about 20 minutes to complete or larger brasses that you could spend all day working on. The centre provides all the equipment and the know-how.

The 'pilgrimage' footpath from Shakespeare's Church to the theatres also runs through these two gardens.

The Great Garden

Of all the places to sit in Stratford, the **Great Garden** is my favourite. It is a part of Shakespeare's Estate and sits behind the garden of New Place. However, it is an open public space, free to visit and accessible through a gateway in Chapel Lane. A large square garden, it is fringed with modern sculptures inspired by Shakespeare's plays, knobbly topiary and colourful borders. And just in case you seek yet another Shakespearean connection, there is a mulberry tree *said* to have grown from a cutting taken from a tree that Shakespeare planted. Regardless, it provides one of the quietest spots in the town centre.

Welcombe Hills Country Park

A mile from the town centre, the land rises from the river valley to the Welcombe Hills. Here a nature reserve open to the public provides views over Stratford and the River Avon as well as a pleasant place to find wildlife in various habitats and a hilltop picnic spot. A car park for the country park is accessed off the A439 Warwick road, on the lane to Snitterfield. Alternatively you can walk from the town centre

– beginning at the Stratford Canal next to the Pen and Parchment pub – along the Monarch's Way, which passes straight through the country park.

The Greenway

A railway until 1976, the Greenway now forms a traffic-free route for walkers, cyclists and horseriders. The route begins from a car park and picnic area off Seven Meadows Road on the southwest outskirts of the town and continues for five miles to the village of Long Marston, where there is parking for horseboxes to allow riders to use the recreational route.

Along the way are further picnic stops, one by Stannels Bridge along the banks of the Avon three-quarters of a mile from the start, the other at Milcote tucked away in a garden on the site of an old railway station.

You can take a 3½-mile circular walk starting at either the Seven Meadows Road or the Milcote picnic area entrances and using the Greenway together with the Avon Valley Footpath on the banks of the Avon. It's a pleasant out-of-town stroll that can be accessed from the centre of town when the crowds become too much and, being totally flat, is easy for young children.

Charlecote Park

The furthest green space from Stratford, Charlecote Park (*01789 470277; www.nationaltrust.org; grounds open all year, house open Mar–Dec*) is five miles east of the town centre. It is notorious for being the place, allegedly of course, where a young Master Shakespeare was caught poaching deer from the great park. Those fallows that got away – or their offspring several times removed at least – are still on show today. It is a most enticing place for a walk particularly in spring, when daffodils carpet the grounds around the house, and in autumn. The Avon winds its way through the park, which offers miles of walks and views. The brick Elizabethan house has been the seat of the Lucy family since its inception.

While the story of the young poacher provides a good anecdote and yet another Shakespeare connection, the Lucy family story is an interesting one too. There's a superb children's novel (adults will also enjoy it), autobiographical in detail, about life at Charlecote before World War I. Titled *The Children of Charlecote* it details the lives of four children who lived in the house and roamed the parkland. The well-known children's author Philippa Pearce together with Brian Fairfax-Lucy – one of the children, wrote the book.

2. NORTH COTSWOLDS

This chapter covers the northwest tip of the Cotswolds, the very fringes where the rocks and the stone peter out – or begin. Within my locale's entirely hand-drawn boundaries lie five very distinct and different areas – the northern fringe of villages running along the River Stour in south Warwickshire and the tiny part of the Cotswolds that flows into Worcestershire around the Vale of Evesham and Bredon Hill, all of which frame the start of the Cotswolds AONB near the Hidcotes and Chipping Campden. Further south, more familiar names start to crop up such as Broadway and Snowshill, by which we are well and truly immersed into the Cotswolds. This is bolt-hole territory for me, just a few miles from home and where I can spend a few hours enjoying a view or taking a walk; Ilmington Downs and Dover's Hill will always be special simply for their views, but I love the simplicity of an off-the-beaten-track walk in the Stour Valley too, described on page 24.

Getting there and around

Trains

There is a good service from London (Paddington) to Worcester and Birmingham New Street that cuts straight through the northern area of the Cotswolds. But it does just that, cutting straight through without stopping so however close you can get, there will always be the need to find an alternative mode of transport to reach your final destination.

From that route, named the **Cotswolds and Malvern Line** and operated by First Great Western, the closest stations are at Moreton-in-Marsh (see *Chapter 3*), approximately five to eight miles from Chipping Campden by road (less on foot across the fields) and Honeybourne, four miles from Broadway.

An alternative train service from Birmingham Moor Street and Snow Hill stations or Leamington Spa stops at Stratford-upon-Avon (see *Chapter 1*).

Buses

Whenever you talk to residents in this area, particularly those that live in the villages, buses are usually a big gripe. They're said to be excessively large and long, throwing out thick black smoke, and plying the narrow lanes, chewing up the verges as they go with, at best, two people on them. That's generally because the services are so infrequent, slow and inconvenient that they're barely used. It's a vicious circle. 'It would be cheaper and more environmental if the council laid on a taxi,' often comes the cry. However, there is a reasonable service from Stratford-upon-Avon to Chipping Campden and Broadway (from Bridge Street in Stratford) that runs roughly every daytime hour Monday to Saturday. It stops at several of the villages in this locale including the Quintons, Mickleton, Broad Campden, Weston-sub-Edge,

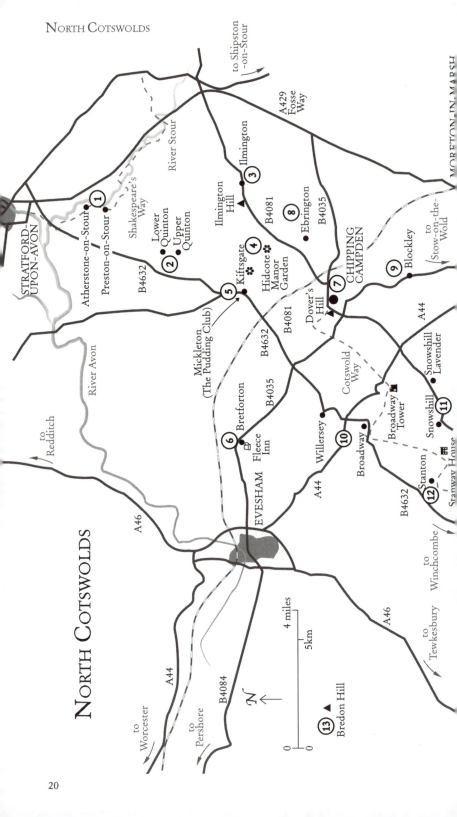

NORTH COTSWOLDS

to Shipston
-on-Stour

MORETON-IN-MARSH

A429
Fosse
Way

River Stour

Ilmington

③

STRATFORD-
UPON-AVON

①

Atherstone-on-Stour

Preston-on-Stour

Shakespeare's
Way

Lower
Quinton

Upper
Quinton

Ilmington Hill

B4081

⑧

Ebrington

B4035

②

B4632

Kiftsgate

④

Hidcote
Manor
Garden

⑤

Mickleton
(The Pudding Club)

B4081

B4632

Dover's
Hill

⑦

CHIPPING
CAMPDEN

⑨

Blockley

to
Stow-on-the-
Wold

A44

River Avon

to
Redditch

Bretforton

B4035

⑥

Fleece
Inn

Willersey

A44

⑩

Broadway

Cotswold
Way

Broadway
Tower

Snowshill
Lavender

⑪

Snowshill

Stanton

⑫

Stanway House

B4632

EVESHAM

A46

to
Winchcombe

4 miles

5km

A44

to
Worcester

to
Pershore

B4084

𝒩

Bredon Hill

⑬

NORTH COTSWOLDS

A46

to
Tewkesbury

0

0

Willersey and Blockley. You can access a current timetable at www.warwickshire.gov.uk.

Walking

The Cotswolds were made for walking, and this area is no exception. It is, after all, where the **Cotswold Way** begins (or finishes), in Chipping Campden. One of my favourite sections of the route, for a simple afternoon stroll, is at **Dover's Hill**, just outside Chipping Campden and soon after the long-distance path begins. It's fabulous in autumn when the rosehips are out to give a burst of vibrant colour against the big skies over far-reaching views. Perhaps the views with the greatest 'wow factor' as seen from the Cotswold Way should be given to those at **Broadway Tower**.

Besides the Cotswold Way, there are several other long-distance footpaths through this area. The **Shakespeare's Way** turns south out of Stratford-upon-Avon, following the River Stour while the **Monarch's Way**, the final section of **Warwickshire's Centenary Way**, **Diamond Way** and **Heart of England Way**

The Cotswold Way

Beginning or ending in Chipping Campden, the Cotswold Way is a National Trail and runs along the western escarpment of the AONB. A plaque in the town marks the official start. Along its 102 miles, walkers will see a noticeable variation in landscape between the start and the end, finishing at Bath Abbey. The views from the trail are amply rewarding for just about the whole way, mainly because you're on the high Cotswold escarpment, though you do need to be prepared for some steep climbs.

The latest information about the trail, including sections that might be temporarily closed, can be found at www.nationaltrail.co.uk while the Cotswold Conservation Board publish a booklet twice yearly titled *Walk and Explore the Cotswold Way by Public Transport*. This can also be downloaded from the National Trail website.

A useful book for walkers keen to follow the entire route is *The Cotswold Way National Trail Companion*. It's available from many of the tourist offices and, breaking down the trail into manageable chunks, provides details of accommodation within very close proximity to the footpath.

If you'd like to walk the entire length but don't fancy backpacking, there are companies that will carry your luggage ahead for you.

For the purposes of this book, I refer to the Cotswold Way as it's walked north to south, roughly in line with the chapters, which are beginning in the north Cotswolds and finishing in the south.

Both these companies will arrange accommodation, luggage transfer and route planning:

Cotswold Walking Holidays ☎01242 518888 🖥 www.cotswoldwalks.com.
Sherpa Van Project ☎020 8569 4101 🖥 www.sherpavan.com.

all play their part too in a walker's paradise. The **Wychavon Way** cuts through the Worcestershire countryside and over **Bredon Hill**, the anomalous Cotswold peninsula that juts into the **Vale of Evesham**.

You can find endless possibilities making round walks up from the OS map. The villages snuggled beneath the escarpment make rewarding objectives, such as walking through the fields from Stanton to Buckland via Laverton, climbing up onto the top and joining the Cotswold Way back to Stanton, a superb circular walk of about five miles.

Cycling

The National Cycle Network Route 5 runs through this locale starting from Stratford-upon-Avon on both roads and traffic-free cycleways, such as The Greenway recreational route (see page 18) out of Stratford. It then continues using B-roads through the villages of Lower Quinton and Ilmington and on towards Shipston-on-Stour.

For those without their own bicycles, there are two bike-hire companies close to Chipping Campden. **Cycle Cotswolds**, based in the town, provide adult and children's bikes together with helmets and safety clothing. They can also supply packed lunches, accommodation and luggage transfers. **Cotswold Country Cycles** is situated just outside the town and offers day hire of adult and children's bikes, including tandems. They will tailor-make cycling holidays for you, again with baggage transfer and accommodation provided.

Bike hire
Cotswold Country Cycles Longlands Farm Cottage GL55 6LJ ☎01386 438706
🖥 www.cotswoldcountrycycles.com.
Cycle Cotswolds The Volunteer Inn, Lower High St GL55 6DY ☎01789 720193
🖥 www.cyclecotswolds.co.uk.

Tourist information centres
Broadway 1 Cotswold Court ☎01386 852937.
Chipping Campden High St ☎01386 841206.

Accommodation
Abbots Grange Guest House Church St, Broadway WR12 7AE ☎02081 338698
🖥 www.abbotsgrange.com. An amazing medieval monastic manor house full of period features such as Gothic archways and cruck-framed ceilings. It's believed to be the oldest dwelling in Broadway and stands in 8 acres of gardens. Sit in the medieval 'Great Hall' for cream tea or take breakfast in the wood-panelled dining room. Past visitors to Abbots Grange apparently include Oscar Wilde, Claude Monet and William Morris.

Bell Inn Alderminster CV37 8NY ☎01789 450414 🖥 www.thebellald.co.uk.
Described on the website as 'Posh B&B'. Very tasteful, individually decorated
bedrooms with plenty of style and panache. Breakfast is served using local
supplies including meat from the Alscot Estate (see page 24) and jams from the
village. Dinner is available in the gastro-pub restaurant.

Three Ways House Hotel Mickleton GL55 6SB ☎01386 438429
🖥 www.threewayshousehotel.com. Elegant yet cosy Cotswold house that has
been a hotel for over 100 years. There are 48 individually furnished rooms but this
is the home of the Pudding Club (see page 28) so expect some fun – 7 pudding-
themed bedrooms eccentrically decorated according to the traditional pud that
they represent. The Sticky Toffee and Date room feels as if you're staying in a
Bedouin tent; the bed in the Chocolate Suite is the base of a box of chocolates,
with chocolate soap in the bathroom. The hotel has many green credentials,
including the Silver Award for Green Tourism.

South Warwickshire

The Cotswolds AONB peeks over the county boundary into Warwickshire in
two places: along a northwest-facing ridge (known as Edgehill) following the
border with Oxfordshire (see *Chapter 3*) and a tiny parcel south of Stratford-
upon-Avon that hooks itself onto Gloucestershire around the villages of
Ilmington and the Quintons. There's nothing significant to tell that you're
in either county; indeed these small village parishes of south Warwickshire
were actually parts of Gloucestershire until the early 20th century. But you
are right on the very fringe of the Cotswolds, the land merging with the Vale
of Evesham.

① The Stour villages

Due south of Stratford the **River Stour**, a small 'provincial' river not much
wider than a stream, pushes its way into the larger River Avon. A skinny little
thing, the Stour looks quiet and innocent enough but locals will tell you that
it has been known to make a nuisance of itself occasionally, its rising water
magnetically drawn towards residents' living rooms in times of heavy rain. It
is only 15 miles long with its source near Wigginton Heath (see page 58) in
Oxfordshire but by the time it has neared its journey's end, it passes through
seven tiny villages: Newbold-on-Stour, Crimscote, Alderminster, Wimpstone,
Preston-on-Stour, Atherstone-on-Stour and finally Clifford Chambers.

Before the M40 from Oxford to Birmingham was opened in 1990 the A3400
(then the A34) was the only main road between the two cities (and Southampton
beyond). On a Friday and Sunday night, the road would be gridlock; horrendous
for those who lived in the villages through which it passed. But overnight, as the
M40 drove its first passengers, the A34 became a ghost road – wonderful for
residents, worrying for shops and businesses. These villages are quiet once more,

particularly **Preston-** and **Atherstone-on-Stour**, who also enjoy the Stour as a barrier between them and the main road.

The land, naturally, is relatively flat though both villages enjoy the shelter from a western hummock. The road that connects the two is deserted save for farm traffic and if you arrive by car you can park close to the weir on Preston Lane (off the A3400) and walk through Preston to Atherstone along the deserted road – with magnificent views of the most northerly Cotswold hills and the Malvern hills – and back across the fields along a footpath before filling up with tea and cake at the 'traditional tea garden', adjoining the village shop (with a tiny six-seater café in winter).

As you walk over the fields along the footpath between the two villages, you'll notice a rather splendid house just across the river. It's **Alscot Park** (*01789 450451; www.alscot.co.uk*), a most perfectly proportioned Rococo Gothic house with a crenellated roof. It can also be seen from the A3400, and when passing this house daily as a teenager, I would always look longingly at it from the road, dreaming that one day I would bump into the owner (the house has been in the same family for over 300 years) who might have a son looking for a bride! As it happens the owner had a daughter, who now lives in the house with her husband. Such is life, but I did manage to visit just once when the gardens were opened to the public. The gardens filled with colourful borders, formal parterres, topiary and a traditional potager and the parkland filled with fallow deer and giant cedars, Alscot Park is truly magnificent and if you happen to be in the area when the gardens and park are occasionally open to the public, I really recommend a visit.

Alscot Park is part of a working 4,000-acre estate with many small businesses operating as tenants, particularly in connection with architecture, interior design, woodworking and furniture. Their website has links to these companies, many of which have

showrooms so you might just end up purchasing a set of chairs after embarking on your walk along the Stour.

These seven riverside villages are also linked by **Shakespeare's Way**, a 146-mile path from Stratford-upon-Avon to the Globe Theatre in London. The waymarked path uses existing footpaths and bridleways before entering the village of Alderminster where it's worth stopping to top up at **The Bell**. Now owned by Alscot Park, the pub and restaurant uses meat from the estate together with fresh fruit, vegetables and flowers grown in Alscot's kitchen garden. The rooms have been designed and furnished by the current owner of Alscot Park, Emma Holman-West.

Food and drink

Bell Inn Alderminster ☎01789 450414 🖰 www.thebellald.co.uk. Has been a popular haunt, particularly for food, over many years with 'regulars' travelling some distance to eat.

Preston-on-Stour Village Shop and Traditional Tea Garden Preston-on-Stour ☎01789 450938 🖰 www.prestononstourvillageshop.co.uk. Sells local produce including bread, milk, cakes, jams and honey. Small café and summer tea garden.

② Upper and Lower Quinton

Divided into two, much of **Lower Quinton** is modern and of little interest to a visitor travelling some distance, its unremarkable architecture virtually backing onto a decidedly ugly disused Royal Engineers depot that once housed demobilised Polish soldiers after World War II. However, the older part of

Witchcraft and the murder of Charles Walton

Charles Walton was an elderly farm labourer living in an old timber-framed cottage opposite the church in Lower Quinton. A quiet and unassuming man, he was considered to be something of a witch owing to his intense knowledge of folklore and the countryside. On Valentine's Day 1945 (thought of as the first day of February in pagan times and a good day for ritualistic sacrifice to encourage a good harvest) Charles set out to trim some hedges on Meon Hill for a local farmer. Having not returned home in the evening, his worried niece (and housekeeper) set out to look for him with two villagers, only to find him brutally murdered on the hill, pinned to the ground with his own hayfork and trouncing hook, and a cross cut deep into his chest.

The crime was so horrific that detectives from Scotland Yard were drafted in to help the nearby Stratford police with their investigations, who discovered that Charles Walton had been murdered in exactly the same way as another woman some years earlier, also thought to practise witchcraft in nearby Long Compton (see page 71). The murder was never solved.

Lower Quinton, to the east, has a small village green around the landmark spire of St Swithin's Church and an attractive pub, the College Arms. It's worth stopping for a pint if you're *en route* along the **Monarch's Way** or **Heart of England Way**, which both pass through the village.

The two long-distance paths divide at **Upper Quinton**, with houses framing a traditional village green. Upper Quinton is also the finish of the 98-mile Centenary Way, a long-distance footpath that crosses Warwickshire. The village lies at the foot of **Meon Hill**, the very last of the Cotswold ridge. By comparison with the sharp escarpments further south Meon Hill is merely a mound, said to have been put there by the devil throwing a clod of earth in irritation at the building of nearby Evesham Abbey. An Iron Age fort once sat on the top of this flat-topped hill (which puts paid to the devil's handiwork theory given that Evesham Abbey was built in the 8th century), but the villages and its southerly backdrop do hold sinister secrets from a more recent era (see page 25).

Food and drink

College Arms Lower Quinton ☎01789 720342 🖥 www.collegearms.biz. Classic village pub with pretty views of the village and Meon Hill. Cosy lounge and restaurant.

③ Ilmington

Walking along the Centenary Way, across the lower slopes of Meon Hill, you come to the village of Ilmington. The houses are built more from ironstone, still a Jurassic limestone but much darker in colour than all other Cotswold stones, having the iron deposits scattered throughout. Middle Street, right in the centre and lined by a particularly unspoilt group of cottages, is one of the prettier roads in the village, which leads to St Mary's Church – look for the carved church mice and a tapestry illustrating the old apple orchards in the village. At the core of the village is the Howard Arms, one of the best pubs in the area both for food and atmosphere and where, during the summer months, you can catch the **Ilmington Morris Men** (*www.ilmingtonmorrismen.org.uk*) dancing over a pint. You can also watch them seeing in the May Day sunrise on **Ilmington Downs**.

Ilmington Downs is not one hill but a group of hills, the highest of which, at 860 feet, is the highest point in Warwickshire. What makes it so prominent as a landmark is the sharpness of the gradient on the village side. A footpath climbs the slope from the village to the top of Knowlands Hill and Windmill Hill but for the best views, climb Stoke Hill to the southwest. On a clear day, when the visibility is limitless, you can easily see the high-rise buildings of Coventry and Birmingham; with binoculars you can even make out the Bull Ring rotunda in the centre of the latter city. There are also nearby views of neighbouring villages such as the Hidcotes, Mickleton and the Subedges, depending on what part of the downs you're on; I thoroughly recommend spending time exploring every view.

Food and drink

Howard Arms Lower Green, Ilmington ☎01608 682226
🐾 www.howardarms.com. A great gastro pub which
makes it into virtually every beer and pub guide.

Towards the Vale of Evesham

The Vale of Evesham is renowned as a market garden,
filled with mineral-rich soils growing vegetables and fruits; Evesham asparagus is
a particular speciality as are plums. As the Cotswolds drop away to this flat vale,
Cotswold stone merges with red brick, the influence of the West Midlands, but old
orchards remain evident on the hillsides too.

④ Hidcote Manor Garden and Kiftsgate Garden

Hidcote Bartrim and, half a mile to the south, **Hidcote Boyce** both lie on a
ridge that is the edge of Ilmington Downs. Residents enjoy some of the loveliest
views in the north Cotswolds over the lower slopes of Baker's Hill and the Vale
of Evesham beyond. But the name 'Hidcote' is more known as the location
of **Hidcote Manor Garden** (*01386 438333; www.nationaltrust.org.uk; open
weekends all year, plus Mon–Wed Mar–end Oct, and daily in summer; licensed
restaurant and Barn Café*) designed in an Arts and Crafts style by American-born
Major Lawrence Johnston at the start of the 20th century. What's so stimulating
about Hidcote and its garden 'rooms' is that Johnston's gardening skills were
entirely self-taught so that you can visit and wander from 'room' to 'room' with
the belief that, 'if he can do it, so can I'.

Tall hedges of beech and yew provide both the walls and the wallpaper for each
little garden room, and every individual garden has its own character, some tranquil
and calm, others raging with vibrancy. My personal favourite – I use the garden as a
bolt-hole when I'm in need of time off – is to walk to the end of the Long Walk, sit
beneath the magnificent holm oak tree and soak up the views across the cornfields;
when Johnston's mother bought the house in 1907, these fields were all that existed
before her novice gardener son set to work. Owned by the National Trust, it has
a good restaurant and tea room, but with such an idyllic location, I recommend
taking a picnic and keeping the sheep on the hillside company over lunch.

If you're going to visit one garden, you may as well visit two as **Kiftsgate Court
Gardens** (*01386 438777; www.kiftsgate.co.uk; open Sat–Wed May–
Aug, and 3 days a week Apr and Sep*) lies opposite the entrance
to Hidcote Manor Garden. They are both so very different
that it is impossible to select a favourite, though Kiftsgate
perhaps wins on its position. Absolutely on the edge of the
escarpment, the garden runs down the steep hillside (and is
not recommended for those with limited mobility). It's the home
of the rambling Kiftsgate rose (Hidcote gives its name to an electric

blue lavender) and of Anne Chambers whose mother and grandmother tended the garden before her.

Kiftsgate really is a plantswoman's garden with unusual species throughout – Anne and her husband are extremely knowledgeable on the plants growing in their little bit of escarpment – but take some time to sit and reflect in the Lower Garden, where the soaring pine trees shelter you when looking out across wooded hillsides and the Vale of Evesham. Kiftsgate has my pick of the two tea rooms in the neighbouring gardens, with fabulous homemade cakes and scones, a decent-sized pot of tea plus various daily lunch specials.

⑤ Mickleton

The village of Mickleton is where the Cotswolds and the Vale of Evesham come together. It sits at the foot of the Cotswold escarpment with Kiftsgate and Hidcote on the ridge of hills to the east, Meon Hill to the north and the Vale stretching out to the west. With the Vale renowned for its fruit and vegetable production, clusters of glasshouses and orchards begin to appear in the area.

Like Lower Quinton, it has two halves to the village, with an uninteresting collection of modern housing estates to the northeast and yet a pretty group of timeless houses spanning the roads towards Broadway and Chipping Campden. The Heart of England Way passes through the village, close to the hotel that has put Mickleton in the gastronomic headlines as home to the **Pudding Club**.

The Pudding Club

There's a time and a place for nouvelle cuisine (maybe) but it's not at the Pudding Club. For over 25 years, the club has been turning a shoulder to continental gatecrashers of the dining table, and championing tried-and-tested British fare. And tried and tested (and voted upon) these puddings are at club evenings, held at its home the Three Ways House Hotel in Mickleton, but whether *you* have room for more depends if you follow the advice of the club.

Explains Peter Henderson, proprietor of the hotel, 'The Pudding Club was founded to prevent traditional British (including the colonies) puddings such as Sussex pond pudding, jam roly poly or gooseberry fool from disappearing off menus at a time when cheap cheesecake was the only thing offered. We have a repertoire of over a hundred hot puddings and a similar number of cold puddings, from which seven are served every Pudding Club evening. We also serve these puddings, of course, within the hotel's restaurant and brasserie.'

While it's called a 'club', the Pudding Club is inclusive rather than exclusive. There is no membership required, simply a love of great British puddings. While there is a serious side to making sure that the humble British pudding remains fashionable, as

Food and drink

David Moore Family Butcher High St, Mickleton. Useful to know if you're self-catering, this is one of the best butchers in the area; all kinds of game including venison, pheasant and fresh duck.

Lower Clopton Farm Shop Lower Clopton CV37 8LQ ☎01386 438236 ✆www.lowerclopton.co.uk. Cracking farm shop selling meat and poultry direct from the farm together with fresh fruit, veg and on-site bakery. Beneath Meon Hill, mid-way between Mickleton and Upper Quinton on the road towards Stratford-upon-Avon. Beautiful Victorian brick buildings – look out for the giant clock tower.

Three Ways House Hotel Mickleton GL55 6SB ☎01386 438429 ✆www.threeways househotel.com. Besides being home to the Pudding Club, this charming hotel has a fully licensed restaurant and Randall's Bar-Brasserie serving hearty traditional fare.

The Pudding Club Three Ways House Hotel, Mickleton GL55 6SB ☎01386 438429 ✆www.puddingclub.com. Anyone can join a Pudding Club night, held every Friday and occasional Saturdays, but you must book in advance. Guests can also stay overnight at the hotel, including the unique Pudding Bedrooms. They have to be seen to be believed.

⑥ Honeybourne, Bretforton and the Subedges

Strictly speaking, you're out of the Cotswolds and into the Vale of Evesham by the time you've moved four miles west of Mickleton to Honeybourne, and

it has become since the Pudding Club was founded, the evenings are all very relaxed, jolly and informal. 'It's all very tongue in cheek and fun,' says Peter. 'Up to 70 people join us for the weekly Friday club night when a Pudding Host will start proceedings. A modest main course is followed by a parade of seven traditional puddings, full of pomp, ceremony and madness. Each pudding is cheered in and we have lots of fun eating as many as we can. Providing you follow the rules and advice of the club, most guests finish all seven – the record is twenty-three helpings!'

By late evening, once all the puddings have been gobbled up with lashings of custard, guests then vote for the 'Pudding of the Night'.

The puddings are cooked by Sheila Vincent, an unassuming local housewife and the 'Queen of Puddings', as Peter describes her. And with the hotel situated so close to the wonderful fruit farms around the Vale of Evesham, a lot of local produce is used and seasonality is key – as is a communal ambience. 'We like people to chat,' says Peter, 'so we group guests appropriately. We don't really recommend children under 12 to visit Pudding Club nights (although they're very welcome guests staying at the hotel) because they tend to get bored with the chit-chat and the time involved; most Pudding Club evenings don't end until 23.00.'

While Peter declared that his favourite pudding is passion fruit Charlotte, an 18th-century dish, I asked what the dress code is for Pudding Club nights. 'Informal and loose,' he suggested. With seven puddings that's an elasticated waist methinks.

there is little to remind you of the Cotswolds other than a look south at the hills; a shade short of two miles south and you're back in the area again. But there is something in Honeybourne worth a small detour – the **Domestic Fowl Trust** (*01386 833083; www.domesticfowltrust.co.uk*). It was set up in 1976 by Michael Roberts, a leading authority on poultry, in a bid to save many rare and pure breeds of poultry from extinction. The trust was sold on some years ago and the grounds are in need of a touch of maintenance, but I've included it because the work of the trust is vital to maintain these historical breeds of chicken and waterfowl. The owners need visitors through the gates to come and look at – and potentially buy – these beautiful creatures in order to sustain their work.

A couple of miles further west is the village of **Bretforton**, very much into the Vale of Evesham with brick architecture and nurseries everywhere. Here though, is an exception to the near-ubiquitous red brick, the famous timber-framed **Fleece Inn**, a pub of tiny, irregular proportions (with a huge orchard for a garden) and walls that defy gravity. Owned by the National Trust, it is the leading venue for the annual **British Asparagus Festival**, with the surrounding area renowned for growing this delicious vegetable.

Taking the road from Bretforton to Chipping Campden (the B4035), you'll come to the two villages of **Weston-sub-Edge** and **Aston-sub-Edge**. As their name implies, both sit below the edge of the Cotswolds escarpment, the same ridge that runs northeast on towards Mickleton and the Hidcotes. Both are tiny hamlets really, each a ribbon development of houses built from the deep golden northern Cotswold stone, with a central manor house. A public footpath connects the two villages along the foot of the escarpment.

This particular part of the ridge, sat between the two villages, is known as **Dover's Hill**. Owned by the National Trust, it is a massively famous landmark in the area, and with free access for walkers. It was one of the first places that, as toddlers, my children would go for a 'long'

The British Asparagus Festival

Forget supermarket sales of a vegetable that has travelled all the way from Peru; Evesham asparagus is simply the best. Thought of as an aphrodisiac (consider its shape) and given to 19th-century bridegrooms because of its reputed powers, asparagus is celebrated all around the Vale of Evesham through many events. The most famous is perhaps the annual Asparagus Auction, which takes place at the Fleece Inn, Bretforton, followed by a Festival Day.

The festival (*www.britishasparagusfestival.org*) takes place each year from St George's Day (23 April) to Midsummer's Day (21 June), which are the official start and end dates of the Vale asparagus season. The auction and main festival day happen over the May Bank Holiday weekend.

The Cotswold Olimpicks

Dover's Hill is named after a 17th-century lawyer, Robert Dover who, in 1612, organised a sports festival here. The festival was a huge fixture in the calendar, acknowledged by contemporary writers such as Ben Jonson and Thomas Heywood. It has continued on and off ever since and is now an annual event known as the **Robert Dover's Cotswold Olimpick Games** (*www.olimpickgames.co.uk*). While the sports festival is recognised by the British Olympic Association as being a part of the Olympic history, the participating sports are very different.

The Games (held at the beginning of June) are opened in front of Dover's Castle, a giant, temporary stage prop replicating that used in the original festival to kick-off proceedings. Events include shin-kicking, tug of war and a traditional sack race, with teams and athletes competing for the Championship/Champion of the Hill. A torchlight procession from the competition grounds to the centre of Chipping Campden is rounded off with dancing and pageantry to befit a medieval games festival.

In 2012, coinciding with London hosting the modern-day Olympics, Robert Dover's Cotswold Olimpick Games celebrates its 400th anniversary.

walk, complete with backpack hugging a picnic. What's so special about the hill is the diversity of the landscape within such a small area.

At the very top are the incredible views over the Vale of Evesham – a pictorial map pinpoints notable landmarks. Along this flat ridge run the very beginnings of the Cotswold Way, a curious dog-leg from its starting point in Chipping Campden before walking southwest. The hill then falls dramatically away yet only for a few feet before this undulating landscape creates watering holes, small pockets of woodland and warm patches in the sunlight of the open field. Further down the ridge lies the Lynches Wood, still part of the National Trust-owned landscape – a circular footpath (with steep steps back up the hillside) takes you on a journey under the canopy. My children nicknamed it 'the Gruffalo Wood' – and the name has stuck to this day. It's where we would go in search of gruffalos (the frighteningly lovable character created by Julia Donaldson in her children's book, *The Gruffalo*), establishing evidence that the beast had been there; dens were found along with gruffalo wool hooked to fences – it's really sheep wool, but please don't tell my children that!

On the opposite side of the road to Dover's Hill is Weston Park, an old estate and woodland, on the edge of which stands the **Kiftsgate Stone**. The stone is visible (blink and you'll miss it) from the Cotswold Way, and was the meeting point for the Court of the Hundred during Anglo-Saxon times, where important issues were discussed and public announcements given.

Food and drink

Fleece Inn Bretforton ☎01386 831173. Tiny bar plus restaurant all tucked into a 14th-century timber-framed longhouse. Delicious food from local produce and, keen to keep local traditions alive, there are lots of events throughout the year. Superb orchard used for the pub garden.

Seagrave Arms Friday St, Weston-sub-Edge ☎01386 840192 ⌂ www.seagravearms. co.uk. Superb pub and restaurant housed in listed Georgian Cotswold building. Food sourced from local farms and suppliers. Accommodation available too.

Chipping Campden and around

To reach the top of Dover's Hill from the Vale of Evesham in the northwest, it is a sharp incline; there is nothing gradual about it, the hill prominent and sudden. But Dover's Hill is equally as steep to reach from its southeastern side. The town of Chipping Campden, sometimes deemed the epitome of the Cotswold town, lies in a bowl at its foot along with that of Westington Hill to the south and Ebrington Hill to the north. Around the town's southeastern perimeter lie the catchment villages of Ebrington, Charingworth, Paxford, Draycott, Blockley and Broad Campden.

⑦ Chipping Campden

Chipping Campden has all the prerequisites to be the most exceptional of all the Cotswold towns, and its warm character makes it difficult not to be charmed. Yet I'm sorry to say that Chipping Campden is one of those towns I was referring to when writing the introduction to this book; I reluctantly take it for granted. I've been visiting so frequently over the years that I don't look at it as a tourist might. So, occasionally I decide to visit as a tourist.

Firstly, I recommend arriving on foot or by public transport if you can. The Heart of England Way, Monarch's Way, Diamond Way and Cotswold Way all converge in the town centre – a stone pillar close to the town hall indicates 'the beginning and the end' of the Cotswold Way, with a reminder that Bath (the other beginning and end) is 102 miles away. Unless you arrive very early in the morning, parking is notoriously difficult. However, if you do decide to arrive by car with the intention of walking the early stages of the long-distance footpaths, the recommended parking is at **Back Ends**, which runs parallel with the High Street.

And it's the **High Street** that I wish to begin with – an S-shaped ribbon that lures the visitor around each bend, curious to find out that which is hidden from view. It's this S-bend that possibly makes the town one of the cosiest of all Cotswold towns simply because there is no long and elegantly grand straight avenue. The stone is one of the darkest of the Cotswold stones, almost ginger in colour, the houses portraying a display of historic wealth and mellow grandeur.

This wealth, like that of most other Cotswold towns, was derived from wool. William Grevel, considered one of England's most successful wool merchants, built his 14th-century house in the High Street. **Grevel House** (almost opposite the entrance to Church Street) still stands and remains one of the most prominent buildings in the town. Though on the other side of the High Street, the **Woolstaplers Hall** is equally impressive, a symbol of importance for the town as a collecting point for fleece, which was later sold to Flemish and Italian clothiers.

Other wool-related locations include the Noel Arms on the southern side of the High Street, the archway of which leads to George Lane. This was once a packhorse track for transporting wool from the town to Bristol and Southampton. The Noel Arms (originally known as the George) was an important coaching inn and stopping point for the horses.

The open-sided **Market Hall**, in the centre of the High Street, close to the Noel Arms was therefore used by other traders for selling foods. It is still used occasionally though spends most of its time as photographic fodder for tourists, potentially one of the most photographed market halls in the Cotswolds.

What is refreshing about the High Street is that, while it retains several shops selling gifty items and expensive jumpers, there are still some ordinary (in the best sense) shops too – a butcher and greengrocer, delicatessen and wine shop, post office and bank. These are interspersed with tea rooms, pubs, hotels and restaurants all eager to continue the rich trading traditions that the town became accustomed to centuries ago. They, on the whole, are of the cosy variety with log fires and snugs. The High Street is indeed alluring and it can be easy to remain locked to this one thoroughfare, but if you do, you'll miss out on some treats.

Continue from the High Street up Cidermill Lane and you'll come across the parish church of St James, built upon the prosperity of the wool trade. Next to it you'll see an imposing set of lodge gates through which to have a nose at the remains of **Campden House**. It was once a fantastically grand and ornate pad that was struck by fire only 25 years after its excruciatingly expensive build in 1613. It's the banqueting house, with its spiralling chimneys, that is still intact and now let out as a holiday home by the Landmark Trust. If you fancy a clearer view of the remains, you can see much more from the Shipston road (round the corner past the church). The grounds are open once a year when you can just make out the lavish Jacobean gardens.

Close by the lodge gates of Campden House and opposite the gabled row of almshouses is the **Court Barn Museum** (*01386 841951; www.courtbarn.org.uk; closed Mon*), celebrating a hundred years or so of the Arts and Crafts Movement in and around Chipping Campden.

In 1902 the architect and designer C R Ashbee moved his Guild of Handicraft from the East End of London to Chipping Campden. With him he brought cabinetmakers, blacksmiths, silversmiths and jewellers to set up workshops in

Ernest Wilson – plant collector

Wander along the High Street away from all the shops towards Mickleton (where the High Street becomes 'Leysbourne') and you'll come across a tiny archway in the wall that leads to the **Ernest Wilson Memorial Garden**, just before Cidermill Lane. The garden, dedicated to a Chipping Campden-born botanist and explorer, is a little haven of tranquillity away from the bustle of the High Street shops. Ernest 'Chinese' Wilson (or E H Wilson) was a renowned plant collector to whom many 21st-century gardeners are indebted. Born in a house on the Lower High Street in Chipping Campden (a plaque on the wall indicates the building) in 1876, he began his employment with a local nursery as a gardener before working at the Birmingham Botanic Gardens and later the Royal Botanic Gardens at Kew.

Posted to China as a plant collector for an English nursery, he explored much of Asia over several years, returning with the seed for hundreds of species that were then unknown to Western gardeners. In all he is attributed with introducing over 1,200 species of plant into Western horticulture – more than any other botanist – including many garden favourites such as varieties of clematis, rhododendron, Japanese cherry, the handkerchief tree and the regal lily. He was awarded the Victoria Medal of Honour by the Royal Horticultural Society for his work.

an old silk mill in **Sheep Street** (at the western end of the High Street). It was a turning point in the fortunes of the otherwise declining town, with artists and designers attracted to the rural idyll, keen to follow traditional skills. The museum celebrates this history in a magnificent 18th-century stone barn.

For contemporary artistry, the attractive **Old Silk Mill** in Sheep Street is the place to visit. Many of Ashbee's guild returned to the industrial towns but some of the best craftsmen remained at the mill, including the silversmith George Hart. The Hart silversmith workshop, run by the same family, is still working today at the mill, along with other artists, craftsmen and women working with paint, textiles and pottery. The whole enterprises is known as **TheGallery@TheGuild**; you can wander around the studios, watching the artists work and purchase their wares. The renowned silversmith and designer Robert Welch also had his workshop in the Old Silk Mill. His family continue to sell his designs from the nearby Robert Welch Shop.

Food and drink

Chipping Campden caters for every kind of eating and drinking from tiny tea rooms to fine dining.

Bantam Tearooms High St ☎ 01386 840386 🖰 www.bantamtea-rooms.co.uk. The large bay window stuffed full of homemade cakes, giant meringues and treats tempts you down the steps to sit by a roaring log fire.

Campden Coffee Company Old Silk Mill, Sheep St ☎01386 849251 🖰 www:campdencoffeecompany.co.uk. My pick of the tea rooms – while many tourists stick to the High Street, this is where the locals go. Great coffees and hot chocolates and fabulous homemade cakes served in the same building that houses TheGallery@TheGuild. Comfy sofas and welcoming, chatty owners. It's also where members of **Creative Campden** (🖰 *www.creativecampden.co.uk*) meet, an organisation of artists, designers, craftsmen and musicians, which runs various creative events throughout the year.

Eight Bells Inn Church St ☎01386 840371 🖰 www.eightbellsinn.co.uk. Beautiful pub just off the High Street with good food and beer. Accommodation too.

Maylams High St ☎ 01386 840903. Long-standing deli.

Meg Rivers Cakes & Café Lapstones, Westington Hill GL55 6EG ☎01608 682858 🖰 www.megrivers.com. This world-renowned mail-order cake company now has a café in a beautiful converted Cotswold stone barn, three miles from Chipping Campden on the B4081. Peaceful surroundings (in the middle of open fields) and upmarket shopping in same building.

Noel Arms Hotel High St ☎01386 840317 🖰 www.noelarmshotel.com. Historic building serving British fare in Dover's Bar and Austrian cakes and pastries in the Coffee Shop.

Shopping

Campden Bookshop High St ☎01386 840944. Specialises in books on the Arts and Crafts movement, art, painting and antiques.

TheGallery@TheGuild Old Silk Mill, Sheep St ☎ 07870 417144 🖰 www.thegalleryattheguild.co.uk. Contemporary arts and crafts including Hart Gold and Silversmiths.

Robert Welch Lower High St ☎01386 840522 🖰 www.robertwelch.com. Selling goods from the designs of the late Robert Welch, including a vast collection of cutlery.

⑧ Ebrington

As with so much of the Cotswolds, agriculture and horticulture are still major sources of income for the area and the north Cotswolds are no different. Taking the road out of Chipping Campden towards Ebrington, you'll pass Campden BRI, a research institute for food and drink and the largest employer in the community. The large complex includes laboratories and food processing halls to test and research a vast range of issues connected with the science and technology of the food and drink industry. Continue on up the hill into Ebrington and you'll come across the other end of the food spectrum – a lookout point over the fields growing vegetables and crops, fruit farms and cattle.

Food and drink

Ebrington Arms GL55 6NH ☎01386 593223 🖰 www.theebringtonarms.co.uk. Fine old village pub serving great food from locally sourced produce. Superb views.

Morris dancing in the Cotswolds

It was at the Baker's Arms, Broad Campden, where I went to watch morris dancing one balmy summer's evening. Far from being stereotypically daft, it was the most fabulous rural entertainment that you could have over a pint of local brew and a bag of crisps, while that great big ball of fire on the horizon made its way beneath the chimney tops and slid down the gables of the inn. It's one of many hostelries throughout the shires that welcome these merry-making men during the summer, where you can catch a glimpse of centuries-old dancing and summer frolics.

If there is one area in the country most associated with morris dancing, the Cotswolds stakes its claim. This traditional form of dancing is far from antiquated, with a thriving community of morris dancers in several towns and villages keeping the heritage alive – and keeping fit at the same time, for the dances are both lively and invigorating.

I went to watch the **Gloucestershire Morris Men** perform alongside the **Ilmington Morris Men** (see page 26), their colourful costumes brightening up the already colour-filled gardens of the Baker's Arms. Mike Thomas, Gloucestershire's 'Bagman' (the melodeon player) and Bob Pierce, the 'Squire' or head of the team, helped me out with some of the history.

With his baldric (a crossbelt that would have held a sword or powder for cannon in days of old) laced with gold to lift him up to the lofty position of Squire, and his long beard flowing as much as the beer was (most morris dancers seem to down at least one pint, drunk from a pewter tankard, before the dancing begins), Bob explained, 'Every village has its own dances and its own movements of hands, feet, handkerchiefs and sticks. The Gloucestershire Morris Men perform dances from lots of different villages, mainly from Gloucestershire, but also from Worcestershire, Oxfordshire and Warwickshire.

'Most dances are performed by six or eight men together with musicians (melodeon, pipe, tabour and fiddle) and a "fool" who helps to entertain the crowd. Sometimes a beast, usually a horse, will also become involved. These characters evolved from the old mummer's plays, the beast being an animal that villagers would have been accustomed to seeing in the fields.' I looked on as the 'Deputy Fool', dressed in black with multi-coloured socks and a silly hat, tickled the dancers under the arms with a feather duster as they danced to heighten the audience's enjoyment. It sounds ludicrous – and it is – but it's entertainment.

Continued Bob, 'You'll also see morris men using sticks within their dancing to tap on the ground or against another. These can be short or long sticks depending

⑨ Broad Campden, Paxford and Blockley

Southeast of Chipping Campden lie a cluster of villages, the closest to the town being **Broad Campden**. It's a useful focus for walks, with the Diamond Way, Monarch's Way and Heart of England Way all converging, conveniently near to the Baker's Arms, the central hub of the village. These long-distance routes give on which village the dance originates from. And while the dance might be the same from village to village, the tune might be slightly different, handed down through the generations.'

Bob then went off to join his fellow men as they leapt and turned around the pub garden, accompanied by a twinkling of bells wrapped around their legs and hankies fluttering in the late summer evening breeze. The banter as they danced was amusing in itself, for while these morris men take their dancing very seriously, their evident enjoyment at larking about is a crowd-pleaser. What is it about men dressed in smocks with one yellow and one blue football sock to complete the look (the Fool's costume of the Ilmington Morris Men) that we find so entertaining?

These athletes from the seven ages of man – many morris-dancing troupes will have father and son dancing alongside each other – have just as nifty footwork as any expensively paid footballer, the steps intricate and complex to coincide with the hand movements and shake of a bell. One wrong move and a hurdle over a long stick could be excruciatingly painful to all concerned.

What I found so appealing, in a world of ever-widening boundaries, was the localised rivalry. The chattering dance troupes, while united in their entertainment, were from differing counties. It mattered. As the Squire announced each dance, with Arcadian names like, 'How do you do?', 'The Postman's Knock' and 'Ring O'Bells', he would describe them as being a 'foreign dance' originating from a village in neighbouring Oxfordshire (the county border being all of four miles away).

All were invited to join in with the final dance, 'Bonny Green Garters', the steps by now lacking in finesse and a thirst acquired by all. 'A pint of your strongest ale please,' came the morris men's cry.

Morris dancing can be seen throughout the Cotswolds, usually in pub gardens but also at various festivals.

Chipping Campden Morris Men ✆ www.chippingcampdenmorrismen.org.uk.
Gloucestershire Morris Men ✆ www.glosmorrismen.org.
Ilmington Morris Men ✆ www.ilmingtonmorrismen.org.uk.

plenty of opportunities for circular walks using other footpaths and quiet lanes, in particular around the Sedgecombe Plantation and Wood to the southeast.

Sedgecombe Wood is a part of the **Northwick Park Estate**, which lies between the villages of Broad Campden and **Blockley**. Once belonging to the Spencer-Churchill family (relations of Sir Winston Churchill), the estate was taken over as an American field hospital during World War II. However, from 1947 until the end of the 1960s it became one of several camps in Gloucestershire used to house displaced Polish people. Here several thousand Poles lived with their families in small Nissen huts, which they decorated with climbing flowers and planted gardens. Children were born on the site and went to school. In 1952 General Wladyslaw Anders, the leader of Free Poland, visited the camp, a major event during their lives.

Northwick Park is the only one of the Polish camps to survive intact; with the manor house turned into flats, the remainder is now a rather scruffy-looking business park. These businesses run from the very same Nissen huts that were used as residences and in 2007 a monument was erected on the site to commemorate all those who lived at Northwick Park and the importance of this and other camps for displaced persons. At the back of the business park, the plaque is at a grotto built by the Polish people during their residency.

I went to this business park several times over the years, unaware of its former life until I was researching this book. A fascinating website (*www.northwickparkpolishcamp.co.uk*) created by Zosia Biegus Hartman describes her life growing up at Northwick Park, and what it felt like having arrived with her parents at the age of five. Before going, do have a look at the website, which is full of remarkable photographs of the era, and which for me made the visit particularly poignant.

I then went on to visit the cemetery in Blockley where, I discovered, there are over a hundred graves of Polish residents from Northwick Park who once dreamt of returning to their homeland but were never able to do so. Up on a hillside in the centre of the village, they have a beautiful landscape to look upon but I couldn't help feeling that, however picturesque their final resting place is, it's not exactly where they wanted to be.

Even though the camp at Northwick Park had closed long before I was even born, I felt ashamed that I did not know the story of these people that had unfolded within a few miles of where I live, and within yards of places that I have trodden, and came away with a tear in my eye at their plight. Their history is such an important part of the area and yet I wonder how many other residents or visitors of the Cotswolds know about it.

The village of **Blockley** is, to my mind, one of the most compelling destinations within the north Cotswolds. Lying on the side of a steep hill and running into a small valley carrying Blockley Brook, it has all the classic Cotswold village elements – a charming collection of houses to look at, a few places to stay, plenty of good, scenic walks (providing you don't mind beginning and/or ending with a hill), a reasonable pub, a cracking village shop and café and a pretty garden open to the public.

Take time if you can to visit **Mill Dene Garden** (*01386 700457; www. milldenegarden.co.uk; open Apr to Sep, Tue to Fri; see website for certain open weekends too*) while in the village. It is privately owned and you'll inevitably come across one of the owners weeding the 2½-acre garden, which is filled with seasonal colour and which sits comfortably around one of 12 mills mentioned in the Domesday Book; this mill, as well as grinding flour, has also had a life as a piano factory. Head up to the top of the garden for views over the mill stream (Blockley Brook) towards Blockley where the church tower mingles with the Cotswold rooftops or pad across the stepping stones and spend a moment chatting to the ducks on the millpond. The family's passion for cricket is also evident with a cricket lawn and pavilion.

Take the road northeast out of Blockley, past Northwick Park, towards **Paxford** and you'll pass what appears to be an anomaly in an area where Cotswold stone predominates. The Northcot Brickworks, the tall brick-kiln chimney an iconic landmark along the road, still makes wire-cut bricks by hand. Its material comes from the neighbouring quarry, though in this instance of a Jurassic lower lias clay rather than limestone. Still, the village of Paxford remains in the Cotswold tradition of stone houses, the material also used to build the Churchill Arms, its name a nod to the Spencer-Churchill family who once owned the brickworks (and Northwick Park).

Food and drink
Blockley Village Shop & Café Old Coach House, Post Office Sq; ☎01386 701411 ⌂ www.blockleyshop.com. A community-owned shop with superb café all run by volunteers. Lots of local produce and a popular meeting place. Free broadband access.
Baker's Arms Broad Campden ☎01386 840515. Small and rustic village pub with a good atmosphere and reasonable garden.
Churchill Arms Paxford ☎01386 594000 ⌂ www.thechurchillarms.com. Fresh local produce served. Popular Sunday lunches. Very limited parking so come on foot or by bike if you can.

Broadway and its villages

Broadway is one of the best-known of Cotswold villages, though I've never quite understood why visitors flock there in preference to other, equally pretty destinations. It's a centre for smaller satellite villages too – **Willersey** to the north, **Snowshill** and its famous manor to the south together with lesser-known settlements like **Stanway** and **Stanton**. It's around here that you could say the Cotswolds 'proper' begin, with some of the more dramatic views of the north Cotswolds obtained from **Broadway Tower**.

⑩ Willersey and Broadway
The village of **Willersey** is worth a mention because of its boulevard-like main street. The outskirts include some undistinguished modern houses but the centre is truly lovely. For, unusually, the stone houses along the High Street do not butt up to the road but sit well back with wide, grassy verges that give the village an appearance of space. A central village pond finishes off the picture. The village shop, Willersey Stores, has been a regional finalist in the Countryside Alliance Awards

while drinkers at the Bell Inn can make the most of the views along the High Street by sitting outside overlooking the duck pond.

One of the few Cotswold settlements that fall into Worcestershire, **Broadway** is another of those gateway villages, providing the link between the Cotswolds and the Vale of Evesham. Situated in the district of Wychavon – a not very ancient (1974) local government renaming of the area – Broadway nods towards the west and the towns of Evesham and Pershore, and yet has all the hallmarks of a Cotswold destination, its broad way (the High Street) attracting coach loads of visitors a year. There are few 'everyday' shops; those that are there play to the tourist's wallet.

I find it more interesting to visit Broadway as part of the Vale of Evesham's **Blossom Trail**, a 45-mile signed circular route through the fruit orchards, of which Broadway is a part; plum trees – and their delicate springtime blossom – are particularly prevalent just west of Broadway. On the trail, and approximately half a mile out of the village, is the **Barnfield Winery and Cider Mill**, which uses an old 1920s press to make cider, perry and wines from the fruits in the district. September to January is the best time to visit when the fruits are being pressed but you can visit for a cider-tasting at any time of year.

Within Broadway's centre is the **Gordon Russell Museum**, housed in the restored workshops of his furniture company. Much like the Arts and Crafts Movement within Chipping Campden at the turn of the 20th century, Sir Gordon Russell enthused a new crowd of craftsmen in Broadway to design and make furniture, having been asked to restore antiques to furnish a hotel run by his father. The hotel became one of the most famous in the country, the Lygon Arms; Russell went on to be appointed head of the Design Council and was knighted for his services. His workshop and museum lie just behind the hotel away from the main street.

Broadway sits in a hollow, tucked up against the foot of the Cotswolds. The escarpment on its eastern side is known as Fish Hill. Why it was named so is something of a mystery (though it could be something to do with monks storing fish), with Snake Hill being a more appropriate name as the main A44 slithers its way down. Along the ridge from Fish Hill, and south of the main road, stands the landmark **Broadway Tower** (*open daily*), a crenellated folly built in 1798 for the Earl of Coventry based upon an idea from landscape designer Capability Brown.

There are few superlatives to match the view from the top on a gin-clear day, along the bumpy ridge and out across the Vale of Evesham to Bredon Hill. If heights are not your thing (allegedly it's 'the highest "castle" in the Cotswolds' – though there are not actually that many castles in the area), the views are equally spectacular from the ground. You can get to the tower and the views along public footpaths – the Cotswold Way saunters straight past the front door – and an entry fee gets you inside where there's an exhibition on the history of the folly, including its holiday-home status to the likes of the artist William Morris and his Pre-Raphaelite chums (see page 177). Next to the tower is Broadway Tower

Country Park, a fee-paying deer park with basic café, though I give the whole place a thumbs up as one of the best picnic spots in the Cotswolds on a sunny, wind-free day. An alternative is to walk the Cotswold Way from the tower, down the hill in the direction of Broadway. You'll then wander through the beautiful Clump Farm, which is National Trust-owned land and an important site for rare flowers and yellow ant hills.

Directly opposite the narrow road that leads to Broadway Tower and on the other side of the main A44 is a picnic site. With the noise of traffic changing gear to make it up Fish Hill, it's not the quietest place for a picnic but it is a pleasant place to stop if you're passing by. There's a half-mile circular walk for those who need to stretch legs after a cramped car journey with northeasterly views across open farmland towards Ilmington Down before tramping through beech woods. In part of a former quarry, it is speckled with limestone-loving flowers like the ox-eye daisy.

A little further along Fish Hill, between Broadway and Willersey sits the **Farncombe Estate**. During the week it's used as a hideaway retreat for business conferences but at weekends it hosts music, poetry, literature and history courses. Attendees to the courses have access to accommodation on the estate too, with views that stretch across the Vale of Evesham, to the Malvern Hills and beyond.

Food and drink

As to be expected, Broadway has a large range of places to eat and drink given its size. I've selected my favourites.

Broadway Deli 16 High St ✆01386 853040 🖰 www.broadwaydeli.co.uk. If we all had a shop like this on our doorsteps, we would not go to the supermarket at all. The best delicatessen I've come across, the range of local produce includes a comprehensive selection of cheese. A member of the Slow Food Movement, the shop may be small in size but it's massive in content. Visit here and you will not want to eat out, although there is a small café at the rear.

Lygon Arms High St ✆01386 852255 🖰 www.barcelo-hotels.co.uk. Now part of a hotel chain but still retains the character for which it is famous. You don't have to stay here to experience dinner in the Great Hall, complete with its 17th-century minstrels' gallery. The hotel also serves up a reasonably priced set-meal Sunday lunch.

Tisanes Tea room 21 The Green ✆01386 853296 🖰 www.tisanes-tea rooms.co.uk. Lovely tea room that is regularly awarded the Tea Guild's Award of Excellence. A selection of over 30 teas, served 'properly' with luscious cakes and tasty lunches.

Activities and attractions

Farncombe Estate Broadway WR12 7LJ ✆01386 854100 🖰 www.farncombeestate. co.uk. Talks and activities include art history, textiles, painting, music, photography and literature.

Gordon Russell Museum 15 Russell Sq ✆01386 854695 🖰 www.gordonrussellmuseum.org. Closed Mon.

⑪ Snowshill

So much has already been written about Snowshill being the epitome of an English village, its narrow, hillside lanes and 'quaint' gable-windowed houses – and its use in the popular film *Bridget Jones's Diary*. The village does attract lots of tourists for all the reasons above and, not least, to visit the National Trust property, **Snowshill Manor** (*01386 852410; www.nationaltrust.org.uk; open Mar to Oct, Wed to Sun*), which houses a bizarre collection of toys and knick-knacks. Charles Wade's appetite for 'stuff' was clearly insatiable, near-on bonkers, choosing to use the house as an exhibition space to display his bits and pieces from around the world rather than live in it. Indeed Wade, an architect and craftsman living at the turn of the 20th century, bought the semi-derelict old farmhouse specifically for his adored collection. He would spend hours there tinkering with the objects (all 22,000 of them) while he lived in a much smaller property in the farmyard.

The house is filled to the rafters with anything and everything – historic children's toys, costumes, primitive bicycles and even Samurai armour – none of it is behind glass or in showcases but on the floor, on tables, stacked on shelves, hanging from ceilings and leaning against walls. The Wade family motto was 'Let nothing perish', a mantra Charles took to heart, but what's astonishing is that you

would perhaps expect his objects to have been collected on expeditions to the colonies and trips around the world. Not a bit of it; most items were acquired from antique shops and dealers in the UK.

Wander around the village midweek and you can find life returned to something akin to near normality, with residents tending to the roses that climb the cottage walls helping to give Snowshill its undeniable beauty – also helped by the characteristics of the houses, the roofs made from one type of Cotswold slate. Look on an Ordnance Survey map and you'll find the area around Snowshill littered with centuries-old slate pits and quarries. They have long since seen the workers' tools and are now a natural part of the up-and-down landscape. Names like Upper Slatepits, Scarborough Pits and Hornsleasow Quarry give the game away.

⑫ Stanway, Stanton, Laverton and Buckland

From Broadway the Cotswold ridge runs north to south dividing Snowshill from a quartet of villages linked by the Cotswold Way. Each one tucks itself close to the base of the hill for shelter, using the natural folds of the land for added protection. **Buckland** and **Laverton** are furthest north, each one only accessible by road along a no-through route, though a bridleway and several footpaths bring the two together. Their tucked-away character makes them particularly restful.

The furthest south of the four, just as the sharper inclines of the ridge slow down

Snowshill Lavender

The brashy, shaly limestone ground hereabouts has helped to generate a new landscape, bringing a touch of Provence to the area – and a boost to the farming economy. A couple of miles east of the village, Hill Barn Farm is the home of **Snowshill Lavender**, where on summer days, a hazy purple hue smothers the stony soil.

With 420 acres of farmland covered with poor, stony soil and a micro-climate that sees average temperatures 3ºC lower than nearby Broadway, Charlie Byrd decided he needed to look for alternative crops to cover the diminishing returns he and his family were receiving from growing the usual British fare. He noticed that lavender in his garden was growing well, so at the turn of the millennium, he bought 500 lavender plants, dotted them into the ground and waited to see what would happen.

The resident population of rabbits didn't munch through all the plants, which also seemed to survive the climatic conditions of a Cotswold hillside, so he bought 30,000 more, planting up 55 acres with 40 different varieties of lavender. The diversification of a small part of the farm had begun, intended merely as a helpful addition to the farm income.

Now Snowshill Lavender (*Hill Barn Farm, Snowshill WR12 7JY; 01386 854821; www.snowshill-lavender.co.uk; visitors welcome Wed to Sun, Easter to Christmas and daily Jun to Aug*) is producing scent on a commercial scale for the perfume industry, keeping 10% for its own use. The lavender is harvested over a fortnight in July and August, using a specially adapted machine that just snips the heads off the plants. The flowers must be distilled within three to four hours from cutting, so the process is completed on site to create a lavender oil.

The farm grows two species of lavender for commercial purposes: the higher-quality *Lavandula augustifolia* (well-known varieties such as 'Hidcote' and 'Munstead') and *L. intermedia*, a higher-yielding but lower-quality variety that is used in products such as room fragrances. Many other types are also grown, providing a collage of colour over the fields, which are purely there for display so that visitors can see, smell and choose lavender for their own garden. The peak season, when the lavender is at its best for viewing, is from early June until mid to late August. Growing sunflowers has extended the viewing season and the sight of a brilliant yellow against the puffed indigo rows and the green of the surrounding hills is magnificent, especially with the wafts of fragrance that lift the air as you brush past a lavender bush. What was once a small sideline has become the main focus of the farm.

As well as wandering the colourful fields, you can buy Cotswold lavender toiletries and fragrances, lavender plants (not grown on site) and eat in the tea rooms, a converted stone barn, where they serve lavender scones; for me, the lavender shortbread is to die for.

a touch, the hamlet of Stanway is little more than a house and a church, but this is some house. At **Stanway House** (*01386 584528; www.stanwayfountain.co.uk; house and garden open Jun to Aug, Tue and Thu*) sumptuous Jacobean architecture, full of knobs and furbelows, fill the grounds and Britain's tallest fountain (and the highest gravity-fed fountain in the world at 300 feet) erupts from a Cotswold water garden like an Icelandic geyser. J M Barrie, author of *Peter Pan*, was a regular visitor here in the 1920s. He donated the village cricket pavilion, an unusual structure in that it rests on staddlestones.

My favourite of the quartet, **Stanton**, sits just north of Stanway and pushes its way up the ridge. As with the others, the Cotswold Way passes through (Laverton has a spur), straight along the main street past many pretty cottages and slightly grander manor houses. At the far end of the village, high on the hill (just like the other four villages, Stanton has no through route) is the **Stanton Guildhouse** (*www. stantonguildhouse.org.uk*) a manor house serving as a venue for summer schools and workshops in arts and crafts, including woodwork and textiles. At other times of the year, there are retreat-like 'quiet days' where you can simply sit, relax and reflect in a conducive environment away from everything but the countryside.

Food and drink

Buckland Manor Hotel and Restaurant Buckland ✆01386 852626 www.bucklandmanor.co.uk. Smart restaurant in a beautiful hotel within large private grounds.

Mount Inn Stanton ✆01386 584316 www.themountinn.co.uk. Locally sourced wines, food and Donnington ales (see page 84). A steep walk up, at the top of the village, within 100 yards of the Cotswold Way and just below the Guildhouse. The views over the Vale of Evesham reward the effort. The small patio is the place to savour them, or you can look out through the pub windows over the rooftops of Stanton and beyond.

The delectably varied escarpment here makes for some of the choicest short circular walks in the Cotswolds. For a three-mile taster from Stanton, follow the well-marked Cotswold Way up to Shenberrow Hill, and look down over the Vale of Evesham towards the jagged mountain-like outline of the Malverns. Carry on northwards, and return to Stanton by the track that once served local quarries. As you drop back into the village you pass the Mount Inn, very handily sited as a final reward.

You could extend this route to five miles by turning right at Shenberrow Hill, then dropping past Parks Farm, through Lidcombe Wood and down to the B4077, then branching off past the grand gates to Stanway House. If it's open, I recommend you visit. The road and the Cotswold Way bear round to the left and, just past the church, to the right. Out of the village, the route is wonderful. With parkland and the escarpment on your right and passing

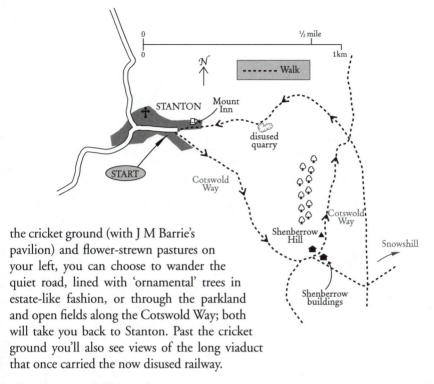

the cricket ground (with J M Barrie's pavilion) and flower-strewn pastures on your left, you can choose to wander the quiet road, lined with 'ornamental' trees in estate-like fashion, or through the parkland and open fields along the Cotswold Way; both will take you back to Stanton. Past the cricket ground you'll also see views of the long viaduct that once carried the now disused railway.

⑬ Bredon Hill

Bredon Hill is a Cotswold anomaly, an island of Cotswold stone sticking out sore thumb-like from the flatness of the Vale of Evesham and the river plains of the Avon.

Most of the architecture in the nine villages that circle the base of the hill bears little resemblance to the typical Cotswold village, with modern brick and the odd black-and-white half-timbered structure featuring more than stone. **Overbury** is by far the prettiest. However, **Bredon Hill** itself is a landmark, owing to its anomalous mass in otherwise flat territory. A long and wide hill, it is circumnavigated by endless footpaths and bridleways accessed from the base-camp villages, including one that runs around the rim of the steepest part of the escarpment – on the northern side. It's here that you'll come across the outline of an Iron Age fort, **Parson's Folly** and the Banbury Stone, just below, also known as the Elephant Stone because of its shape. Parson's Folly is the highest point, bringing the total hill height to just over 1,000 feet. The hill is a National Nature Reserve for its great importance to wildlife, which includes rare beetles.

Depending on which side of the hill you walk along, there are views to Broadway Tower, Ilmington Down, Tewkesbury and the Severn Valley, the Malverns and Cleeve Hill.

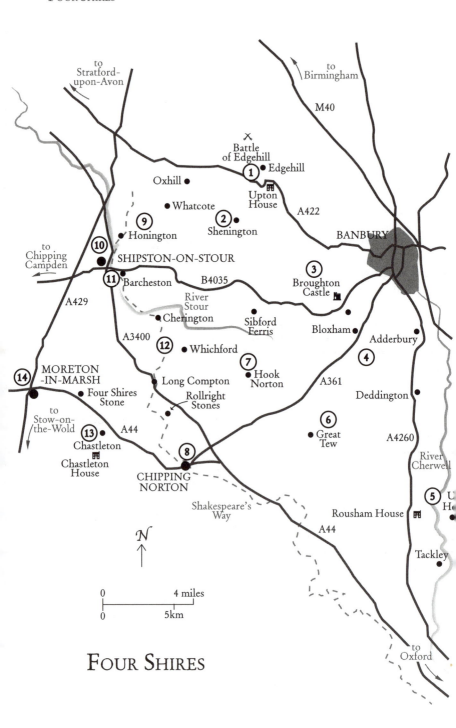

Four Shires

3. FOUR SHIRES

This is the hidden part of the Cotswolds, the forgotten part, the part that the coach tours leave out – and it is all the better for it. Not as dramatic as the western escarpment, it's cosier and has just three small towns in the west – **Shipston-on-Stour**, **Moreton-in-Marsh** and, one of the most rural, **Chipping Norton**.

Strictly speaking, there are only three shires within this chapter – Warwickshire and Oxfordshire, plus a tiny scrap of Gloucestershire. The 'four shires' refers to the **Four Shires Stone**, not far from Moreton-in-Marsh (on the southwestern point of the map for this chapter). It marks the point where four counties once met – Warwickshire, Oxfordshire, Gloucestershire and Worcestershire. The borders have changed and now Worcestershire begins several miles away.

Within these boundaries, the areas become even more localised. We're at the very southern tip of Warwickshire, and the most northern part of Oxfordshire. Residents in these borderlands will feel much more akin to one another than they will to the remaining parts of their respective counties. Even the term '**Banburyshire**' (referring to the market town of Banbury just east of this locale) is still used today, demonstrating the closeness of the two counties at this point.

The bond between south Warwickshire and north Oxfordshire is perhaps because of their shared heritage and style of architecture. This is still the Cotswolds – just. We are on the very fringe here and, though there are still plenty of rolling hills, it is the flattest part of the Cotswolds overall, leaving the sharp western escarpment behind.

I've quartered the chapter further, the B4035 from Shipston-on-Stour to Banbury cuts the area in two (it's almost the county boundary) and then a line from Oxhill in the north to Chipping Norton in the south divides it further still, utilising another county boundary. This is a very localised area, and if you've lived here for many years, you'll understand.

Getting there and around

Trains

Two lines serve the area. **Banbury**, to the east, is a mainline station, with trains from London Marylebone, Paddington and Oxford. Trains from the southwest stop at Oxford, where a change needs to be made. Trains come from the north via Birmingham. **Chiltern Railways** (*www.chilternrailways.co.uk*) operate services from the southeast, **Cross Country Trains** (*www.crosscountrytrains.co.uk*) operate from the north via Birmingham and **First Great Western** (*www.firstgreatwestern.co.uk*) operates from the southwest via Oxford.

To the west of this chapter, **Moreton-in-Marsh** is the main station on the **Cotswolds and Malverns** line, with stations at Charlbury and Kingham, a few miles to the south.

Buses

Buses are extremely sporadic throughout the district. Some routes to the villages operate only once a week to reach market days in the nearby towns of **Moreton-in-Marsh** (Tuesdays) and **Banbury** (Thursdays). A daily (Monday to Friday) service operates between Banbury, Stratford-upon-Avon and Shipston-on-Stour calling at some of the villages in the very north of Oxfordshire. Similarly there is a daily service between Chipping Norton and Stratford. The only bus route in the area that operates every hour is from **Chipping Norton** to Banbury. This is operated by **Stagecoach** (*www.stagecoachbus.com/Oxfordshire*).

The **Cotswold Line Railbus** (*www.railbus.co.uk*) can get you to **Chipping Norton** from railway stations at Charlbury and Kingham but no further.

Sadly, unless you are prepared to do lots of walking and waiting (or cycling), a car is pretty much essential in this part of the Cotswolds.

Walking

The area is too far east of the main Cotswold escarpment to pick up the Cotswold Way. However, the **Shakespeare's Way** (see page 3) continues its journey from Stratford-upon-Avon to London through this area from **Shipston-upon-Stour** to **Chipping Norton**.

This being predominantly rural territory, the local footpaths accrue a handsome mileage and because the terrain is hilly but not dramatically so, the walking is attractive without being harsh on the legs. So it is easy here to create any length of walk that you like to suit the abilities of the walkers concerned, from a short and gentle stroll through the woods picking up acorns with children or a grand-scale pub-to-pub walk.

Cycling

The **National Cycle Network Route 5** from Stratford-upon-Avon to Oxford via Banbury continues through the area. Two sections of this are traffic-free but they are minimal. There are few other designated traffic-free cycle routes, but plenty of tiny lanes. See page 22 for **cycle hire**.

Horseriding

This activity is extremely fashionable hereabouts, and livery yards, stables, riding schools and training are big business. You will inevitably see some horses wherever you go, particularly on the quiet lanes. There are also bridleways aplenty and much of the 50-mile **Claude Duval Bridle Route** crosses this area, from Upper Heyford in the east to Chipping Norton in the west.

Tourist information centres
Banbury Castle Quay Shopping Centre ☎ 01295 753752.
Moreton-in-Marsh High St ☎ 01608 650881.

Accommodation

George Hotel High St, Shipston-on-Stour, Warwickshire CV36 4AJ 01608 661453 www.georgehotelshipston.com. Hotel with elegant Georgian façade in the centre of Shipston. Completely renovated and refurbished recently to create 16 boutique-style rooms, each individually furnished and named. King-size beds in all rooms and period bathrooms, including roll-top baths. Good restaurant or for private dining – book the cosy Library.

Gower's Close Sibford Gower, Main St, Banbury, Oxfordshire OX15 5RW 01295 780348 www.gowersclose.co.uk. Lovely rambling thatched and beamed house with absolutely beautiful gardens (Judith, the owner, is a garden writer). Pretty kitchen with Aga breakfasts and a sunny terrace, wonderful living room with log fires. Only 2 bedrooms so you'll feel looked after exclusively. Conveniently located for much of the north and lesser-known Cotswolds.

Holycombe Whichford, Warwickshire CV36 5PH 01608 684239 www.holycombe.com. Run by Sally and Andy Birtwell, who organise retreat weekends and holistic therapies in their home; they also provide tipis, a yurt and bell tents for some luxurious camping in their extensive garden. Stunning location in the grounds of the old Norman castle, next to the moat, it's about as far removed from a campsite as you can get.

Old School Little Compton, Moreton-in-Marsh, Gloucestershire GL56 0SL 01608 674588 www.theoldschoolbedandbreakfast.com. Atmospheric B&B beautifully decorated with rich, warm colours. The Victorian schoolhouse has many quirky features and inviting places to rest and relax, including a cosy rooftop drawing room with a Gothic arched window. Delectable breakfasts, supper trays, dinners and picnic hampers are offered using local (sometimes from the garden) produce.

Southernmost Warwickshire and northernmost Oxfordshire

Other than a county sign on the roadside there is little to distinguish Warwickshire from Oxfordshire, at least not at first glance. But talk to an elderly someone who has lived in one county all their life – and whose ancestors have preceded them in the same manner for generations – and they will fiercely proclaim to be in one camp or the other. And yet the boundaries become more blurred: Edgehill has an Oxfordshire postal address but is physically in Warwickshire. Other boundaries exist in this area; the traditional hedges that were installed during the Enclosure Act of the 18th and 19th centuries are very evident in these parts. The traditional 'Saxon Mix' includes hawthorn and blackthorn interspersed with field maple, ash, hazel and elm; the elm of course all but gone. You'll occasionally come across a hedge-laying competition to see who can make the neatest hedge. They are works of art when done properly compared with their machine-trimmed counterparts.

① Edgehill

As the Cotswold Hills formed, two ridges appeared to the west, the more dramatic Cotswold escarpment that ends with Meon Hill (see page 26) just south of Stratford-upon-Avon and, slightly further east, a thinner spine that now forms the Warwickshire/Oxfordshire county boundary. It is this more easterly line of Jurassic limestone that stop–starts its way further northeast towards Lincolnshire.

However, the Cotswold ridge dramatically stops at a place inevitably known as Edgehill. Known to locals for its castle-shaped pub, the **Castle Inn**, and for the beautifully named Sunrising Hill that drops down the ridge to the plains below, Edgehill is known by most for the raging battle that took place 350 years or so ago. This whole locale is big English Civil War territory and almost every village, major house or stately home and even field has something to say about its connection with the Civil War; many local families became involved, their ancestors still living in the area today. The 1642 Battle of Edgehill was the first pitched battle of that war, and one that ended inconclusively. The October battle involved approximately 28,000 men (3,000 of whom perished), with the Royalist camp set up on the top of the escarpment, where the Castle Inn now stands, and the Parliamentarians on the plain below. It was the Royalists who made the first move, charging down the escarpment.

The battlefield is now inaccessible, covered, ironically, by one of the UK's main ammunition depots and much of the escarpment is covered with trees. But there are good vantage points of the battlefield (especially from the Royalist viewpoint) from the Castle Inn. The Macmillan Way and Centenary Way run along the top of the ridge, generally through the trees, but a stone obelisk just below the pub and alongside the footpath gives good views.

The unusual Castle Inn has an octagonal tower, the building of which was begun in 1742 to commemorate the 100th anniversary of the battle. It opened in 1750, on the anniversary of the death of Oliver Cromwell. Every October the historical society, the Sealed Knot (*www.thesealedknot. org.uk*), re-enacts the battle in neighbouring fields (though I'm not sure whether the outcome ever changes!).

Not surprisingly, there are other pubs in the area connected to the Civil War. In **Whatcote**, one of those villages that take a bit of seeking out, just like neighbouring **Oxhill** (which really is worth finding), the pub sign of the **Royal Oak** depicts two pikemen, a crown and an oak tree. The pub was reputedly used by Parliamentarian officers following the battle at Edgehill. However, its name is derived from the hollow oak tree that Charles II hid in during his escape from the 1651 Battle of Worcester in part two of the English Civil War. The pub has good views of the Edgehill escarpment.

Just south of the village of Edgehill, and close to Sunrising Hill, is **Upton House** (*OX15 6HT; 01295 670266; www.nationaltrust.org.uk; closed Thu and part of winter*). Its history is a little more modern, the grand ironstone house being the one-time home of Lord Bearsted, the first chairman of Shell, a company that his father had founded. There is an exhibition about the company, in particular old advertisement posters from a bygone era, but it is the 1930s décor that is the real eye-opener – including the sumptuous Art-Deco bathroom. Owned by the National Trust, the house puts on events where visitors can experience the house parties of a 1930s millionaire as well as view Lord Bearsted's remarkable art collection, which includes works by Canaletto, Hogarth, El Greco, Stubbs and Bosch, and some notable porcelain.

Food and drink

Castle Inn Edgehill ☎01295 670255 🖰 www.hooky-pubs.co.uk. Plenty of Civil War history on show with muskets, breastplates, halberds, maps and relevant paintings adorning the walls in this historic pub and setting. Unique architecture and good pub garden. Owned by Hook Norton Brewery, so Hooky beers on tap are the norm.

② Shenington, Hornton and Wroxton

All around these villages are the past and current quarries lifting out great lumps of rock. It's known locally as Hornton ironstone, getting the name from the village of **Hornton**, though the quarries reach out towards Radway, Alkerton and Wroxton. It's a ferruginous limestone with colours ranging from deep brown to golden brown and even tinges of grey and blue, the harder, veined blue stone used mostly for stonemasonry. Many of the houses in the area are built from this material, though the colour and size of the stone varies depending upon where it was quarried.

Run along the top of the escarpment from Upton House towards **Shenington** and you'll come across views over south Warwickshire including Stratford-upon-Avon and Warwick. From this height (almost 700 feet) the land below appears incredibly flat stretching to the horizon – you can see all the way to Birmingham on a very clear day.

In Shenington is **Brook Cottage Garden** (*01295 670303; www.brookcottage garden.co.uk; open Mon to Fri Mar to end Oct*), a four-acre hillside speckled with bulbs in spring, roses and peonies in summer, and hips and berries in autumn. Natural slopes, filled with several decades of a plantswoman's thoughts and ideas, are linked with terraces and lawned areas to create a magical theme.

In the not too distant past (in my lifetime at least) the village of **Wroxton** was known as Wroxton-St-Mary which was a reference to the 13th-century Augustinian priory that was built in honour of St Mary. The abbey was razed to the ground to be replaced by the captivating Jacobean house called Wroxton Abbey, now known as **Wroxton College** (*grounds open all year from dawn until dusk, except all Aug and during Christmas holidays; house open 14.00 to 17.00 on spring and summer bank holiday Mon*). This was built at the start of the 17th century. Ownership has rarely changed hands, though at one time it was the home of the North family, a prominent local bunch of earls and lords, one of whom became prime minister at a time when England lost claim to the American colonies. In an ironic twist, an American university now owns the house, which is closed to the public most of the time but you can walk through the landscaped park full of woods, lakes and cascades where you can catch a glimpse of the house. A public footpath, close to the entrance to the college, leads you through the park and on towards the villages of Drayton and North Newington.

③ Broughton Castle

While the fan-shaped village of Broughton is mostly modern, Broughton Castle (*OX15 5EB; 01295 276070; www.broughtoncastle.com; opening times vary but generally Wed, Sun and bank holiday Mon afternoons Easter–mid-Sep*) is anything but. Of all the castles (it's actually a fortified manor house) in Britain, this is the one I love most for its sheer visual impact, and the one I would recommend others to visit more than any other. I'm not the first to say it sums up England, but it certainly does. Broughton Castle has received plenty of accolades over its 400-year history, one of the more recent coming from the author and historian Sir Simon Jenkins who gave it five stars in his tome *England's Thousand Best Houses;* only 19 others were awarded the same rating.

As it is just about on my doorstep, I've visited the house on many occasions and driven by hundreds of times and yet I never tire of its sight, especially towards dusk when the fading sunshine lights up the soft brown walls until they glow a pumpkin orange. These colours are reflected in the square moat, the sweet little gatehouse and bridge allowing owners and visitors to approach without getting their feet wet.

The owners are Lord and Lady Saye and Sele, one of the loveliest couples you could wish to meet, and meet you they probably will as it is often they who are collecting the entrance takings or showing you around. The couple are part of the Fiennes family – the very same one as the explorer Sir Ranulph Fiennes and the actors Ralph and Joseph.

If upon arriving you feel that the house, and in particular the Great Hall, looks strangely familiar, you may well be right. For Broughton Castle has been used on several occasions as a location for films, advertisements and television programmes, including Hollywood blockbusters like *Three Men and a Little Lady* and more notably *Shakespeare in Love*, which featured Joseph Fiennes as the young Shakespeare.

Cannonballs dredged from the moat, now on display, show its direct link (or hit) with the English Civil War, along with hiding holes, secret doors and tiny passageways making it the stuff of children's storybooks. But it's the Great Hall that is indeed great, as is the garden.

You can also wander through Broughton Park, north of the house, at any time of year (several footpaths cross it); the views of the house from here are magnificent.

North Oxfordshire proper (and a bit of West Oxfordshire)

Oh, what it is to pigeonhole places. If I work to district council boundaries then much of this area is considered the Cherwell Valley. I've narrowed it down a little and put the Cherwell Valley, for the purposes of visitors, as comprising those villages that are within very close proximity to the River Cherwell. And yet, move a few paces west to the Tews and you are officially in West Oxfordshire. I hope you can tell the difference; the clue is in the colour of the rubbish bins – green for Cherwell, grey for West Oxfordshire!

④ Bloxham, Adderbury and Deddington

Bloxham is sadly spoilt by the busy A361 running through its centre but both the church here and the one at **Adderbury** are renowned for their spires and their music, with many jazz and classical music concerts (*www.coffeeconcerts.co.uk/music-in-adderbury* and *www.bloxfest.org.uk*) that attract both local and international musicians.

You can walk between the two villages along the disused railway line, accessed south of the church in Bloxham and from Manor Road in Adderbury.

Three miles south of Adderbury lies **Deddington**, with the old part of the village clustered around a wide market square. It's the furthest south that the deep brown Hornton ironstone reaches; from here on most of the villages are in the paler forms of oolitic limestone. Deddington is well known in the area for its popular farmers' market held each month. On the eastern edge of the village are the embankments to **Deddington Castle** (administered by English Heritage) of motte and bailey design, built in the 11th century by William the Conqueror's half-brother, Odo of Bayeux.

Shopping

Bread and Milk High St, Bloxham. Tiny deli selling delicious local produce plus a couple of tables in the window and a courtyard garden for coffee and cake.

Deddington Farmers' Market Market Pl. Held every 4th Sat of the month. Considered to be one of the best in the region with over 50 stalls.

Eagles Market Pl, Deddington ☎01869 338500 🖥 www.eaglesinfood.co.uk. Butchers (renowned for the quality of their meat), deli and greengrocer selling mostly local produce. Also well known for homemade ready meals and picnics.

Fired Earth Twyford Mill, Adderbury ☎01295 814399 🖥 www.firedearth. co.uk. Factory shop selling discontinued lines and seconds in floor and wall tiles, bathrooms and furniture. Cooking demonstrations using Aga cookers too. Sale days are extremely popular.

Wykham Park Farm Shop Wykham Park Farm, Banbury OX16 9UP ☎01295 262235
🖥www.wykhampark.co.uk. Beef, lamb, pork, seasonal fruit and vegetables (asparagus a speciality) from the farm and a fully stocked farm shop. Also at Deddington Farmers' Market.

⑤ The Cherwell Valley

We really are on the far eastern fringes of the region here, but there are still traces of the Cotswolds. The **River Cherwell** (pronounced 'Charwell' officially but not by all locals!) begins life well away from the Cotswolds in Northamptonshire and flows virtually due north to south, but for its meandering nature, until it joins the Thames in Oxford (see page 155). For most of the time it runs parallel with the **Oxford Canal**, a waterway that is popular with holidaymakers owing to its easy access via the Thames and because of the pleasant river meadow scenery that runs alongside.

The villages that do run alongside – North Aston (with a fantastic upmarket garden centre at Nicholson Nurseries specialising in trees), Middle Aston, Steeple Aston, Somerton, Lower Heyford, Rousham and Tackley – begin to revert to a much creamier limestone and are well worth a mini tour if you are in the area. Of particular note is **Rousham House and Garden** (*01869 347110;*

Banbury cakes

Secret recipes always intrigue – mystery ingredients held under lock and key. It's a sure sign that you're on to something good, something that others would like to have. The ingredients of the Banbury cake can no longer remain a mystery; regulations on packaging have seen to that. But Philip Brown, owner of the recipe for Brown's Original Banbury Cakes, still holds the quantities and combinations firmly to his chest. For it's those quantities that make a true Banbury cake as delicious as it is: the right proportion of meltingly light puff pastry to fruit, and just enough spice to give the cake bite without being overpowering.

Philip is the latest in a succession of Browns who have held the secret of the Banbury cake; from father to son and, before that, aunts and great grandparents, a direct association beginning in 1868 when Wilks Brown (Philip's great-grandfather) bought the bakery business for his wife, Elizabeth, from other relations. Banbury cakes were just one of the products made within their thriving enterprise, run from a bakery in Parson's Street, Banbury, for a long time known as the Original Cake Shop. As Philip explained, 'My family were all Quakers and, as such, women and men were not allowed to work together in the bakehouse. Hence there were two bakeries within one – the men and women given separate tasks.'

But the Original Cake Shop dates back much further than Victorian times, built around 1550, *www.rousham.org; open daily*), an architectural gem that has been left almost unmodified since it was built in 1635. Ownership has also remained in the same family – the Dormers – ever since. It's an uncommercial site – without tea rooms or gift shops, and with no entrance for children under 15. The 18th-century landscaped park and walled garden, including a delightful parterre, make a good place for a quiet walk and picnics are allowed. Rousham House is open only for groups and by arrangement, but the garden is open every day of the year and makes for an excellent winter outing. If you simply wish to catch a great view of the house, stand on **Heyford Bridge** (on the B4030 from Hopcroft's Holt to Lower Heyford) that crosses the River Cherwell.

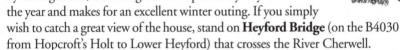

A mile west from Rousham, the crossroads of the main Banbury to Oxford road with a smaller B road is known as **Hopcroft's Holt**. An ancient crossing and meeting point, there is little there now except a garage and a small hotel but it is synonymous with a notorious 17th-century highwayman, Claude Duval. French-born, he was considered to be very gentlemanly in his conduct while he robbed his victims! He would frequent the Holt Hotel, then a small coaching inn, to spend his

the Banbury cake already famous and depicted by the playwright Ben Jonson in his play *Bartholomew Fair*. It's believed that the cake was introduced at the time of the Crusades when, in the early 13th-century crusaders would bring back dried fruit and spices from the Middle East.

The recipe remains very similar today although before the introduction of raising agents, a yeast-leavened pastry was used. The elliptical shape has been maintained – believed to represent Christ's cradle when, in days gone by, the cakes were used for religious festivals and celebrations. And over the years, royalty, presidents of the United States and mere humble citizens have enjoyed Banbury cakes for the medieval mix of pastry, fruits and spices.

Sadly, the Original Cake Shop was demolished in 1968 but Philip has continued to bake the traditional cakes by hand. Many try to replicate, though few succeed, often adding non-traditional ingredients such as sponge or stale cake (an idea to use leftover food). None quite hit the mark of the original. I think that the Banbury cake is best served slightly warmed, which brings out the flavour of the spices, the light pastry contrasting with the crunch of the sugar cane crust. It's one of those simple masterpieces that make British food so delicious.

You can buy Brown's Original Banbury Cakes online at www.banburycakes. co.uk. The cakes are also sold at various locations in Banbury and the surrounding area including Banbury Museum Visitor Centre, Castle Quay, Banbury (where an exhibition on the Banbury cake also exists), Eagles in Deddington, Taste Buds in Adderbury and Wykham Park Farm Shop, Bloxham.

earnings. However, his conduct did not spare him and he was executed in London; rumour has it that he still frequents the hotel.

Food and drink

There are no venues of outstanding merit in this area but Steeple Aston is home to two pubs at either end of the village – the **Red Lion** and the **White Lion**. Both serve food.

> **Holt Hotel** Hopcroft's Holt OX25 5QQ ☎01869 340259 ✆www.holthotel.co.uk. Old coaching inn that has been extended into a small hotel. Nothing extraordinary but a useful place to stop in the area. Highwayman's Bar and Duvall Restaurant.

⑥ The Bartons, the Wortons and the Tews

As you move west, back towards the true Cotswolds (at least the AONB), a strange landscape unfolds, or rather folds. One of the least-populated parts of Oxfordshire, it encompasses a beautiful valley and series of hummocky hills that makes you feel in the middle of nowhere; a strange sensation given the increasing population in the area. The National Cycle Network Route 5 runs right through it, and it's on a bike that I'd recommend exploring if you can cope with the ups and downs, for while there are numerous footpaths, they are somewhat random and don't necessarily take you from A to B.

A string of tiny villages and even smaller hamlets are scattered in among the hills and valleys. There is nothing particularly distinguishing about any of them in terms of visitor attractions or even a local pub. But it's this seclusion from society that provides the charm, simply a few clusters of comely looking houses in restful countryside. Furthest south are Steeple and Westcote Barton (ignoring Middle Barton, which is unremarkable) and **Sandford St Martin**, unusually for the area not paired with another village of a similar name. Next come Ledwell and the Wortons, **Over Worton** first and then **Nether Worton**, barely a hamlet with one beautiful manor house and an additional dwelling.

To either side of you now, the hummocks intensify as a ridge creases the landscape, the folds flowing in and out of each other. One has been named Steepness Hill, its title justifiable. Spinneys, copses and traditional hedges break up the pastures and leys, and there are numerous bubbling springs with many tiny streamlets.

Furthest west are the Tews – Little Tew and Great Tew. Slightly larger than all the other villages, **Great Tew** has already made a name for itself, regularly described as chocolate boxy owing to its numerous thatched cottages. Visitors have been arriving for decades to sit on the grass and sup a pint from the minute bar at the Falkland Arms, which also very quaintly sells snuff. Despite its seemingly fossilised qualities – properties were not connected to mains facilities until the latter part of the 20th century – Great Tew is a thriving village with most of the houses and land, as well as the atmospheric house at Great Tew Park, still owned by the Great Tew Estate. A bridleway leads through the park, itself clutching to the twists and folds of the land. Great Tew Park is also the new home for the annual summer **Cornbury Festival**

Upper Heyford Airbase

Not all of this region has the air of cosiness and warmth. On top of a hill near Upper Heyford are the remains of one of the most important sites of Cold War history worldwide. I knew there was something remarkable about the place as I was growing up nearby – American cars wider than the roads, the sale of Mountain Dew, and *Top Gun*-style aeroplanes that would hum quite quietly overhead as they came in to land. I didn't appreciate how momentously important the place was though, the Soviet Union (as it was then) and the Eastern Bloc just words on a newscaster's script.

While protesting women latched themselves to the fences of Greenham Common under the gaze of the media, **USAF Upper Heyford** continued relatively unscathed from the watchful eye of the world and the protestors' wire cutters; only a handful of hippies would hang about in the nearby woods.

Having already been in service since 1915, the airbase was leased to the Americans after World War II as a part of NATO, when it was used first by B47 bombers, then by U2 reconnaissance and later fighter aircraft, the F111 a familiar sight in the sky over northern Oxfordshire. What I didn't realise at the time was that these sleek machines were armed with nuclear weapons and ready to strike at the press of a button, kept in domed hangars made from yard-thick concrete behind infallible fences and walls that couldn't whisper.

After 43 years of operations, including involvement in Desert Storm over Kuwait during 1990, the base closed in 1994. I drove through a part of the 1,250-acre site quite recently and found an eerie reminder of the past. Once home to thousands of personnel and their families, it is now ghostly, left as it was the day the Americans went home. Brown street signs remain standing, the Bowling Center, the Community Bank, the USAF signs leading to the Officers' Mess, the old tennis courts and lead-in lights to the runway, the grass-laced bomb-proof hangers – and the old petrol station that sold gasoline for those big American cars.

English Heritage have put in numerous bids for the base to be preserved, such is its importance to world history – but without success so far. I recommend a look – drive down Camp Road and you'll find the experience really quite surreal. There is also a small **museum** on site (*01869 238200; www.raf-upper-heyford. org; visits to the museum must be booked in advance and take place on Tue, Wed and Thu afternoons*). You get to see a video on the history of the airbase, take a look at the Command Centre as it was and then take a tour around the base.

(*www.cornburyfestival.com*). Originally based at nearby Cornbury Park, the music and camping fest is making the most of its new surroundings at Great Tew, with improved 'glamping' facilities, and all camping areas closer to the stage. Festivalgoers should take the opportunity of being able to stay here; Great Tew Park really is an idyllic venue.

Food and drink

Falkland Arms Great Tew OX7 4DB ☎01608 683653 🖰 www.falklandarms.co.uk. The charms at this widely admired pub have something of a cult following. Cosy bar and restaurant with log fire. Good food. Accommodation too.

⑦ Wigginton, Swalcliffe, Sibford and Hook Norton

Wigginton might well be considered sleepy. It has no distinct village centre – the church is at one edge of the village, the pub is on the other. However, Wigginton grabbed the headlines worldwide a few years ago when rumours sprang up that actually quite a lot had been going on back in 1940 with the apparent temporary residency of Unity Mitford at a hush-hush maternity home for the gentry. Unity, one of the renowned Mitford sisters, who lived a few miles away at both Swinbrook and Batsford (see page 80), was allegedly in residence to give birth to Adolf Hitler's love-child.

With argument and counter-argument, the story remains as the kind of tittle-tattle that makes it into the script of a village soap opera, but it did drag Wigginton into the limelight for its 15 minutes of fame, however truthful or false the story is.

Climb the hill northwards from Wigginton towards **Swalcliffe** and **Sibford**, and you'll come to an area known as Wigginton Heath and Tadmarton Heath. It houses not one but two golf courses teeing off against one another. **Rye Hill Golf Course** is open every day for visitors to play the championship golf course and test their skills on the practice ground. The restaurant, Nineteen, is open every day too for both golfers and passers-by; and, being on top of an undulating hill, the views are pretty good. **Tadmarton Heath Golf Club** has a reputation for having a rather special course and being quite exclusive. Visiting golfers must make arrangements in advance to play.

Continue along the single-track road towards Swalcliffe and Sibford and you'll cut across what is known to locals as the Prairie. It's a most inviting strolling ground, as being so open there are some fabulous views west right along the valley of the **River Stour**, which rises at Wigginton Heath. In the distance is **Brailes Hill** with its clump of trees on the top, a notable landmark for miles around (see page 68), and **Oatley Hill**.

Swalcliffe is unfortunately affected by a busy road that cuts straight through but there is an impressive 15th-century half-cruck **tithe barn** (*01295 788278; open Easter to end of Oct; Sun and bank holiday Mon 14.00 to 17.00*) that is considered to be one of the finest in the country. Built by New College, Oxford, who owned considerable land and property in the area for centuries, the barn houses agricultural vehicles from the County Museum Collection along with a display of Romano-British artefacts from nearby Roman encampments like Madmarston Hill, a landmark hump just east of the village.

Sibford is made up of three villages: **Sibford Ferris** and **Sibford Gower** combined with **Burdrop**. The two enclaves are divided by a steep river valley and some worthwhile village walks will take you past beautiful houses made both of Hornton ironstone and the paler Cotswold stone.

A couple of miles to the west of Sibford is **Traitor's Ford**. This beautiful ford hidden in the trees is a well-known spot for local children keen to dip their feet in the cool waters of the River Stour (though the base is very slippery) and play Pooh-sticks from the bridge. Apparently the name has nothing to do with traitors but the tale that I was told is that a headless horseman – the traitor – rides through the ford every night at midnight. It's worth following the

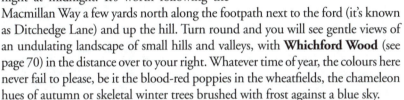

Macmillan Way a few yards north along the footpath next to the ford (it's known as Ditchedge Lane) and up the hill. Turn round and you will see gentle views of an undulating landscape of small hills and valleys, with **Whichford Wood** (see page 70) in the distance over to your right. Whatever time of year, the colours here never fail to please, be it the blood-red poppies in the wheatfields, the chameleon hues of autumn or skeletal winter trees brushed with frost against a blue sky.

By far the largest of the four villages is **Hook Norton**, of a sufficient size to warrant named parts: Scotland End (in the west), Down End, East End and Southrop. Allocated as the village to develop, it has had extensive housing built since World War II. However, it remains a very attractive village. Once upon a time, Hook Norton (or 'Hooky' as it is known) could boast seven pubs – two of them next door to one another – not a bad ratio for a village. You'd think that all the residents would have been permanently pickled but the high proportion (there are now only three pubs) is owing to the celebrated **Hook Norton Brewery.**

At the opposite end of the village from the brewery is **Hook Norton Pottery** (*www.hooknortonpottery.co.uk*). Russell Collins's hand-thrown domestic kitchenware is very distinctive and highly collectable; it displays characteristics of the earthy, rural location from which it is born. Most of his work is sent direct to clients around the UK and abroad, including Harrods and Liberty of London, but he does operate a basic showroom above the pottery studio where you can purchase some of his work – much cheaper than in London.

Hook Norton was once on the railway, running from Chipping Norton to Banbury, and, other than the brewery, one of Hooky's most distinguishing landmarks is the **Hook Norton Viaduct.** At the time of building, in 1887, the 85-feet-high viaduct was the tallest in Britain. Closed to passengers in 1951 and freight after a landslide in 1958, much of the railway route is still evident in the area through broken bridges that cross roads

and parallel lines of trees. Originally there were two iron viaducts and a lengthy tunnel; only the piers of the more southerly viaduct survive and the area is now a nature reserve that provides a pleasant walk.

Food and drink

Nineteen Rye Hill Golf Course, Milcombe, Banbury OX15 4RU ☎01295 721818
🖰 www.ryehill.co.uk. Open to all (not just golfers) including children. Full

The Hook Norton Brewery

It's the kind of morning that puts a spring in your step. As I approach my local brewery along the narrow, twisting lane, it's suddenly there, appearing like a giant friend, the sun lightening the dark brown ironstone, the familiar black-and-white timber latticework decorating the skyline. It has been a long time since I visited last and I had forgotten how beautiful this listed industrial construction is at close quarters. I say a 'giant friend' because the building, though tucked away in the west end of this thriving north Oxfordshire village, is a landmark for locals approaching Hook Norton.

Inside and out, there is a buzz of activity, the attention-to-detail repainting of the original timbers is matched to that of brewing their award-winning ales. As I step inside, the smell of brewing hops pervades the air on the first floor, the sweetness of malted barley on the second, with a maze of staircases, huge timber barrels, giant copper cauldrons and steel tanks, old wooden floors that would be the envy of any house renovation and the sunlight throwing shafts of warmth across the cool brick floor of the racking room. And at the very top of this traditional six-storey tower brewery is the architectural gem – the building providing some of the most spectacular views in the county over north Oxfordshire, south Warwickshire and Northamptonshire.

To say that Hook Norton Brewery is old-fashioned would totally misrepresent its 150-plus year history. Forward thinking, it celebrates and embraces its traditions, while keeping ahead of the competition. Its director, James Clarke, is an old primary school acquaintance of mine. In the playground the 'What do you want to be when you grow up?' line was never really discussed but I guess 'brewer' would have been an automatic answer. James followed his father into the family business, one that was set up by his great-great-grandfather John Harris in 1849, each generation handing down the secrets to the masterful art of brewing.

James is of the firm belief that, while developing regulations and consumer demands require the brewery to keep up with change, not all aspects need to.

menu available throughout the day with popular Sunday lunch, snacks, cream teas, drinks. Local, seasonal produce used.

Pear Tree Inn Scotland End, Hook Norton 📞01608 737482 🖥 www.hooknortonbrewery.co.uk. The closest Hook Norton Brewery-owned pub to the brewery itself, about 150 yards away.

Wykham Arms Sibford Gower 📞01295 788808 🖥 www.wykhamarms.co.uk. Gastro pub with comfortable bar (including a covered well) and restaurant areas. Log fires in winter. Expect to rub shoulders with the local farmers.

The steam engine, installed over a hundred years ago to run the brewery, is still in daily use, driving several pieces of essential equipment such as the grist mill, used for crushing the malt, and the Steeles masher, where the malt and water are mixed. Hook Norton is the only brewery in the UK still brewing under steam.

It is also only one of two breweries left in the country transporting its beer by the traditional shire horse-drawn dray wherever possible, delivering to local pubs and a magnificent sight on the roads around the village.

These energy-saving beliefs run through the heart of the brewing process too. The water (obtained direct from the brewery's own well) used in the brewing process is reused as much as possible and the surplus spent grains and yeast are sent to local farmers for cattle feed.

The range of beers has grown significantly in the past decade with a series of seasonal beers added to the four staples. 'Our four core beers account for 80% of our production', says James. 'Old Hooky is the beer we are most well known for but Hooky Bitter has the greatest output and is very drinkable.' Of course I knew that already, it being one of the most available drinks in the area. 'Then Hooky Dark, a chestnut-coloured ale and Hooky Gold, its name describing its pale, golden nature, are the other two beers that make up the core. We then have a seasonal programme with a different beer released every two months.'

The list of Hooky pubs is ever growing. The brewery has been presented with many awards over the years; Double Stout was winner of the World's Best Stout (Standard) category in the World Beer Awards while the brewery scooped three awards in the International Beer Challenge to find the World's 50 Best Beers. Twelve Days, Hooky Gold and Old Hooky were all listed. Hook Norton was the only UK brewery to have three winning beers within that Top 50.

Brewery Visitors' Centre 📞01608 730384 🖥 www.hooknortonbrewery.co.uk; brewery tours available by appointment Mon–Fri. Housed in the original maltings, open Monday to Saturday with a shop selling all the bottled beers and a brewery museum. Alternatively there are over 40 tenanted pubs owned by the brewery in and around Oxfordshire, Warwickshire and Gloucestershire (and Northamptonshire). Serious aficionados may like to try the **Hooky Ale Trail**, visiting as many pubs as you can and collecting prizes (which includes a brewery tour) along the way.

⑧ Chipping Norton

Chipping Norton is one of those places that I ashamedly take for granted, visiting so frequently but usually with too much to do. Every so often, I have a few moments to sit and look up. Then comes the comment at how pretty the town is. Often known as 'Chippy', this is the highest town in Oxfordshire, and has particularly good views. As you enter the town from the east along the Banbury road, there are glimpses across the rooftops to the Cotswold hills beyond; catch the light at just the right moment, especially with a grey-blue thundering sky, and the whole place glows. The town, along with its environs, also has the envied status of being one of the best places in the UK to live, regularly receiving the thumbs up from property pundits. Judging by the number of celebs who have chosen to make it their home in recent years, there must be something in it.

The Georgian façade belies the town's age, having been granted a charter by King John to hold a market (hence its name Chipping, from Old English *cēping*) in 1205. The town is even older than that, with evidence of Saxon history and the earthworks of a Norman castle behind the hospital.

The 'new' market town was built on the hillside above the village and evidence of the thin burgage plots east of the High Street are still there, in the form of thin strips and narrow alleyways, quite apparent if you walk along Albion Street behind the High Street. The market flourished and, naturally, wool was traded bringing prosperity to the town, hence the 'new' Georgian façades that were added to buildings. A new town hall was built to show off the town's wealth too.

The most striking building in the town – or rather just on the edge surrounded by Chipping Norton Common – is the **Bliss Tweed Mill**, its slender chimney reaching for the clouds. What began as a small cottage industry, Chipping Norton tweed gained a reputation for its quality. The mill closed in 1980 and has now been converted into flats.

More recent history includes the location where many a pop star was to be found, the **Chipping Norton Recording Studios** in New Street responsible for lots of '70s, '80s and '90s hits from bands like the Bay City Rollers, Duran Duran, Status Quo, Level 42 and Dexy's Midnight Runners. The studios closed in 1999.

The **museum** (opposite the town hall) on the High Street gives a community-eyed view of the town's history from its earliest roots, the industries that have come and gone, the railway that came and went and the town's brush with fame as the inventor of baseball, long before the Pilgrim Fathers sailed to America.

The **High Street** and large **Market Square** sit on a hillside that has slipped up many a shopper on an icy morning. And it's really here that everything happens in this compact town. A few High Street names in small-branch sizes mingle with plenty of independent shops, all clustered around the central town hall. As a lively town, there are good butchers and a traditional bakery. Just around the corner from the bookshop, along Spring Street, is the **Chipping Norton Theatre** (*01608 642350; www.chippingnortontheatre.co.uk*). The building alone is worth a look, for the theatre is one of the smallest that you will find (just over 200 seats) and yet it's also one of the loveliest with its iconic cream and bottle-green façade (the building was once a Salvation Army citadel) and the sweetest of interiors, too. But it also has a superb reputation; many well-known faces come to the theatre, often at the start of a run to try out a show, with live theatre, music, films and workshops adding to the attraction. A gallery also holds art and photography exhibitions.

Southeast of the High Street (*with access off Albion St*) is the **lido** (*Fox Close; 01608 643188; www.chippylido.co.uk; open Apr to Sep*), an outdoor pool that is perhaps showing its age but which is a well-loved friend to the town, with regular fundraising events held to help keep the pool open. Generations of families have enjoyed basking in the sunshine for an afternoon on the lido's grassy picnic area and taking a dip to cool off. Since 2010 the pool has been heated by solar energy.

Food and drink

Chequers Goddards Lane, Chipping Norton ☎01608 644717. Right next door to the theatre, this is a terrific town-centre pub full of character, and with appetising bar and restaurant food. Open all day.

Crown Inn Church Enstone OX7 4NN ☎01608 629305. Actually 3 miles southeast of the town, in a tiny but very pretty hamlet. Great location with a good restaurant.

Jaffé and Neale Bookshop & Café Middle Row (in the Market Pl) ☎01608 641033 🖰 www.chippingnortonbooks.tbpcontrol.co.uk. A superb little independent bookshop with some of the best coffee I've ever come across, and Ceci's homemade cakes are sublime. Run by Patrick and Polly, it's often rated as one of the best bookshops in the UK. However, it's simply a very pleasant place to sit – indoors or out – and view the world. Events are held there regularly too.

Wild Thyme Restaurant with Rooms New St (just off the Market Sq towards the Worcester Rd) ☎01608 645060 🖰 www.wildthymerestaurant.co.uk. Modern, regional British food using local, seasonal produce. Everything is homemade including the bread and chocolates. Three 'boutique'-style bedrooms too.

Feldon and the Stour Valley

We've moved northwest now to the top-left quarter of our locale. This is very definitely south Warwickshire – no blurring of the sacred county boundaries here courtesy of Royal Mail. Except that once upon a time this quarter was in Worcestershire – an enclave surrounded by Warwickshire.

On the very edge of the Cotswolds, the **Stour Valley** falls between the two northern Cotswold escarpments, with Chipping Campden, Dover's Hill and Meon Hill in the west and the Edgehill escarpment in the east. The **River Stour** (one of five in the country) rises at Wigginton Heath (see page 58) and flows west until it reaches **Shipston-on-Stour** and then north before joining the Avon at Stratford. And yet it is really the central part, around Shipston, that is considered the Stour Valley.

Warwickshire was also, centuries ago, split into locales. Most famous is Arden, or more specifically the Forest of Arden, north of Stratford and the Avon. This particular part of south Warwickshire around Shipston, **Honington** and Idlicote is also known as Feldon, a 'feld' being an old English term for 'open, cleared land'. Parkland and agriculture are clearly evident in the area.

⑨ Idlicote and Honington

Ordinarily there is no reason to go to **Idlicote**. It is a couple of miles from the main road along twisting narrow lanes and the few houses that are there do not offer grand visitor attractions. But it's worth coming this way to look out towards the Edgehill escarpment, the ridge so prominent all the way around to the village of Shenington. It's also much more evident from here just how tree-smothered the hill is now, though not so in the days when Cavalier soldiers marched (or slid?) down to battle.

Take the quiet road to **Honington** and you'll appreciate how agricultural this area is – and has been, with noticeable ridge and furrow fields demonstrating the ancient art of ploughing. You'll cross through open parkland meadows with views west over Ilmington Hill and the slender spire of Todenham's church, a well-known landmark when travelling in these parts. Climb Idlicote Hill on foot – there's a footpath from Idlicote and the **Centenary Way** passes straight over the top – and you'll be able to see even further across several counties.

The village of Honington is particularly attractive. A blend of Cotswold stone, ironstone, brick and rendered houses, where the obligatory climbing rose and cottage garden sit alongside village greens and open spaces; no wonder that it has won numerous 'Best Kept Village' awards. On the banks of the River Stour, behind lofty metal gates – you can't help but notice them – sits **Honington Hall**. A symmetrically precise mellow brick manor house from the 1680s, it has been described as the perfect model for a doll's house. Unfortunately it's not open to individual visitors, but make up a group of ten people and you're allowed in if you book in advance (*01608 661434*).

Shakespeare's Way having come from the north and following much of the River Stour, passes through Honington. It uses the footpaths and quieter back roads to reach **Shipston-on-Stour** rather than the busy A3400 as most travellers do. While in Honington, take a look at **Honington Bridge**, which crosses the Stour close to the main road. It's a pretty little thing with Grade II listed status and the river is at its loveliest around here running along towards Tredington.

⑩ Shipston-on-Stour

By its very name, Shipston – or 'Sheep Wash Town' as it was called, translated from the Old English Scepwaeisctune – lies on the west side of the River Stour, with only one bridge crossing on the road to Brailes, close to the Old Mill Hotel.

A part of the Kingdom of Mercia during Saxon times, Shipston became an enclave of Worcestershire, surrounded by Warwickshire, until a change of county boundaries in 1931 when Warwickshire swallowed it up. Granted a charter for a weekly market and an annual fair, Shipston prospered as a centre of trade, mainly in sheep given the lie of the land around it, and later in spinning and weaving, and became an important stopping point on a drovers' route, along which cattle were transported from Wales to the markets in London. The town became well known for a woollen velvet known as 'shag' during the 17th century. The annual **Shipston Wool Fair** (*www.shipstonwoolfair.org*) is held on the late May bank holiday to commemorate this heritage.

Shipston is a thoroughly appealing town for **shopping**. The town has been developed over the decades so its borders are sprawling out, but its shopping heart remains focused around the High Street and Market Place and a few other roads that extend from these – Sheep Street, New Street and The Bury. The town has some nicely traditional clothes shops, and yet they must have kept up with the times by the very fact that they are still in business – some have been there for decades. It's perhaps their old-fashioned approach to customer service that keeps them going, but shops such as **Spencer's**, **Sandra's** and **Chris's** (formerly 'Marguerite's') have many loyal followers.

Then there are the housekeeping shops – the cook shop, the electrical appliance shop, the gift shops, the much-loved toy shop Walrus (which has also been in town for decades), the haberdashery, the needlecraft shop, the art gallery, the hardware store, the antiques shop, the home furnishing shop, the jewellers and the clock shop. In fact, most of these purveyors of goods have survived for years and years.

But the absolute gem of Shipston is the quality of its food stores, with two cracking butchers, **Rightons** and **Taylors** (whose plain sausages are outstandingly good), a fresh fish shop, greengrocers mainly selling produce from the nearby Vale of Evesham, **Taste of the Country**, a terrific local produce store, and **Edward Sheldon**, one of the most respected independent wine merchants in the country. Gourmets are truly spoilt.

On the corner of **New Street** and **West Street**, Edward Sheldon has been supplying wine in Shipston since 1842 and is a Warwickshire institution. It gained a reputation for the quality of its wine, vintage port, sherry and Madeira, supplying affluent country gents and university colleges in its early days. The brick building is interesting enough at ground level, with a wine cellar kind of smell inside that will never leave you. But it is below ground that the building becomes really interesting, having over 12,000 square feet of labyrinth cellars to store wines at just the right temperatures.

Edward Sheldon (or just 'Sheldons') was purchased in 2009 by another well-known local wine merchant, Bennetts of Chipping Campden, and the cellars have now been opened up again to visitors for tours and tutored wine tastings.

I remember visiting the cellars many years ago and it really is an interesting old place, full of ambience, echoes and dark passageways. You can imagine the dusty, old wooden boxes of port and sherry being stacked up following a lengthy sea voyage.

Food and drink

George Hotel and Restaurant High St ☎01608 661453 🖥www.georgehotelshipston. com. The grandest façade on the High Street, a recently refurbished hotel with smart restaurant open to non-residents.

Mrs Browns Tea Rooms Sheep St ☎01608 662217. Traditional tea rooms selling sandwiches, cakes and a good cuppa.

Old Mill Hotel Mill St ☎01608 661421 🖥www.theoldmillshipston.com. 'British food with a classical influence' prepared by head chef Ashley James. It's a tricky one, this; the building and location are enviable, tucked up against the River Stour, with a gorgeous riverside garden in which to sit. But no restaurant owner ever seems to stay that long; perhaps it's because every time the river floods, so do the ground-floor rooms. Maybe Ashley James will have better luck.

White Bear High St ☎ 01608 661558. Cosy town pub with window seats overlooking the High Street.

Shopping

Edward Sheldon New St ☎01608 661409 🖥www.bennettsfinewines.com. Wine merchants in a superb and historic building and a great range of wine from inexpensive plonk to Château Pétrus.

Rightons of Shipston Sheep St ☎01608 661445 🖥www.rightonsofshipston.co.uk. Traditional butchers (and farmers) with superb meat – selling their own beef – and award-winning pies.

Taste of the Country Market Pl ☎01608 665064 🖥www.tasteofthecountry.co.uk. Fabulous deli selling local everything plus homemade bread and cakes.

Taylors Butchers Market Pl ☎01608 661429 🖥www.taylorsofshipston.co.uk. The tastiest plain sausage in the kingdom and a loyal following. At Christmas, customers queue out of the door.

Taylors Deli & Bakery High St ☎01608 661429 🖥www.taylorsofshipston.co.uk. The other part of the Taylors 'empire', selling great cheese, cold meats and bread.

⑪ Barcheston and Brailes

Just east of Shipston, a matter of a few hundred yards away over the River Stour is **Barcheston**. It is a tiny, tiny rural hamlet among the fields and yet for its size, its importance has been mammoth.

William Sheldon established England's first tapestry-weaving enterprise in the manor house at Barcheston in the second half of the 16th century. Living in Weston Park (see page 70) a few miles south, he acquired the village and, keen to utilise the wool trade in Shipston, he set up workshops and installed looms in the manor house.

A local man, Richard Hyckes was employed to oversee things and he and his team of weavers were responsible for creating the finest Tudor tapestries – indeed some of the finest ever made. Their initial output was mostly of commonplace items (though still spectacular in quality) – bed valances, cushion covers and cuffs for gloves. But pictorial wall hangings were soon created, commissioned for country houses as the workshop's fame grew for the quality of work. When William Sheldon died his son Ralph Sheldon acquired Weston Park and he commissioned Hyckes to create a series of pictorial maps to hang in his house. These are known as the **Sheldon Tapestries**, though other work tapestries from the same workshop are also known under this guise. It's believed that he went on to receive commissions from Queen Elizabeth I.

Richard Hyckes died in 1621 aged 97 and is buried at Barcheston. The tapestry industry at Barcheston survived for only 90 years, with work coming to an abrupt end at the outbreak of the Civil War in 1642.

Being such a tiny hamlet – barely more than two houses – there is little to look at in Barcheston except to appreciate its location. However, little **St Martin's Church** is a gem in peril. The tiny 12th-century church, sunbathing in a grassy garden accompanied by yew trees and past residents, is known as the Pisa of Warwickshire. Its castellated tower leans precariously from the remainder of the building. This is merely a quirky feature that is, surprisingly, relatively stable, but the church needs a new roof urgently before the existing one, made with Cotswold stone slates, slides off. An appeal, St Martin's in Peril (*www.stmartinsinperil.org*) has been set up. Barcheston is also on Shakespeare's Way long-distance footpath.

There are three Brailes villages, **Upper Brailes**, **Lower Brailes** and **Sutton-**

The Sheldon Tapestry Maps

All the tapestry work that survived from the looms at Barcheston is impressive – there are examples that hang in the Victoria and Albert Museum in London – but none more so than the Sheldon Tapestry Maps. Created in the 1580s and 1590s by Richard Hyckes for his employer and landlord Ralph Sheldon, the tapestries form a set of four maps that illustrate the four counties of Warwickshire, Oxfordshire, Gloucestershire and Worcestershire.

Woven in wool and silk, the tapestries are absolutely exquisite, technically unrivalled, with the landscape, rivers and towns depicted in vibrant colours and immaculate weft. Some are decorated with flowers and mythological motifs too. However, these are more than just decorative masterpieces. The four tapestries are of major cartographic importance.

Three of the impressive-sized tapestries – Oxfordshire, Gloucestershire and Worcestershire – are held at the Bodleian Library in Oxford. The fourth, Warwickshire, measuring 13 feet by eight feet, is held at the County Museum in Warwick.

under-Brailes. Of the three, my favourite is Sutton, a quiet village set on its own with some really pretty houses around a large village green and the odd ancient oak tree to picnic under. Lower and Upper Brailes are barely indistinguishable from one another (though residents may correct me on that), the ribbon development along the Banbury to Shipston road linking the two. Upper Brailes lays claim to a motte and bailey castle, though its only evidence is a mound on the top of Castle Hill. It's easily seen from the perimeter roads and there are numerous footpaths to it from the village. Lower Brailes is home to **Birdy the Blacksmith** (*www.birdyblacksmiths. co.uk*), one of the few remaining blacksmiths in the area, creating beautiful ironwork in the traditional way.

In terms of renown, all three villages are overshadowed by their neighbour, **Brailes Hill**. A Cotswold outcrop, at 760 feet high it is a landmark for miles around. Its distinguishing feature is Highwall Spinney that, from a distance, appears like a line of trees on the top of the hill. Unfortunately there are no public footpaths to the top, but you can climb the first slopes from Gillett's Hill Lane in Upper Brailes.

A cycle ride around Feldon

The Cotswold and Feldon Cycle Route has been created from Shipston-on-Stour around the Feldon area. With Feldon being open lowland, this is an easy, signposted cycle ride around quiet country lanes without too much strenuous effort. A 14-mile-long circular route (although there is an additional, more challenging seven-mile section), it provides the perfect excuse to pass through villages and countryside that you otherwise would not think to visit but are nonetheless very attractive and worth seeing. Details of the route can be downloaded from www.warwickshire. gov.uk.

From Shipston-on-Stour, follow the road towards Banbury, over the River Stour. Take the first right (opposite the recycling centre) towards Barcheston and follow the road on to Willington then Cherington. Continue past the Cherington Arms pub to Stourton, and at a T-junction turn left for Sutton-under-Brailes.

In Sutton follow the road round towards Lower and Upper Brailes. At the T-junction with the main B4035 turn left (take care as this is a busier road) and within a few yards turn right off the main road towards Whatcote (down Castle Hill Lane), next to the village hall and playing field. Prior to this, you could take a quick detour by turning right at the T-junction in Brailes to visit St George's Church, known as the Cathedral of the Feldon.

Continue along Castle Hill Lane towards Whatcote. Pass a turning for Winderton on your right and Aylesmore Farm on your left. At the next crossroads turn left signposted for St Dennis, past fields of ridge and furrow, illustrating ancient ploughing techniques when the shire horse was used to pull a plough, and return to Shipston.

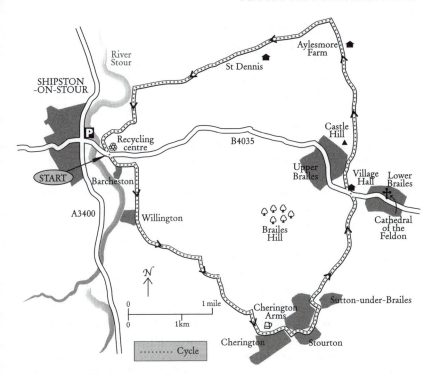

Food and drink

George Hotel Upper Brailes ☎01608 685223 🖰 www.hooky-pubs.co.uk. Owned by Hook Norton Brewery this is an old coaching inn with flagstone floors and a snug. Large restaurant and pretty pub garden. Accommodation too.

Around the Four Shires Stone

The final quarter, in the far southwest of this locale, is, I think, the prettiest of the four that make up this chapter. Around the Four Shires Stone, charming villages create a fan shape converging on Moreton-in-Marsh, the Gloucestershire town. Naturally, with Worcestershire gone, the stone pinpoints the coming together of the other three counties, Oxon, Warks and Glos – using their abbreviated names.

⑫ Cherington, Whichford and Long Compton

Swinging round to the southwest from Brailes, **Cherington** and its conjoined partner **Stourton** lie at the southern foot of Brailes Hill and, below that, Cherington Hill. They are beautiful villages, with very little modern infill to detract from the many Cotswold stone cottages and elegant Georgian façades. It's a pastoral community, with Home Farm still at its centre where I remember going, as a child,

69

each Christmas for preposterously ancient spinster sisters (as they seemed to me) to despatch, pluck and dress our goose. I always returned home with a plate of meltingly light shortbread biscuits, the likes of which I have never tasted since.

There are no visitor attractions to speak of, other than the beauty of the place in its own right, being an ideal afternoon strolling ground after a lunchtime drink at the Cherington Arms, either along the River Stour, or across the fields from Stourton to Sutton-under-Brailes.

Southwest of Cherington is the **Weston Park Estate**. A narrow gated road runs straight through the centre where you'll usually see some sheep or cattle grazing beneath the many oak and ash trees. Weston Park was the seat of the Sheldon family in Tudor and Elizabethan times, the name synonymous with the Sheldon Tapestries from Barcheston. What an amazing house this must have been, in such magnificent grounds. But it was pulled down long ago, the site now covered in trees close to the Cherington road. Legend has it that the Sheldon family could drive a coach from Weston Park to Coventry (some 35 miles away) while staying on their own land. A new Weston House was built in 1830, designed by the architect Edward Blore who also drew up Buckingham Palace. Weston House too has now gone but old photographs show it to be an overtly ornate neo-Gothic palace.

If you happen to be wandering down Hack Lane and past Little Wolford Heath – on the western edge of Weston Park – during May, glance into the trees for a stunning sea of bluebells, one of the best woodland floral displays in the area.

South of Cherington is the Cotswold-fringe village of **Whichford**, with its little tag-on, Ascott. Spread around a large village green, it has significant Norman roots, evident in the names of some of the roads, in the naming of the pub as the Norman Knight, and in the fact that some of the villagers still have the French names inherited from their French forebears. Hummocky remains exist of a moated Norman castle (the moat is still there too, though privately owned). The tiny church of St Michael's, also of Norman origins, is of mellow moss-strewn stone, with its castellated tower, and is one of the prettiest in England. But then I am biased – I got married there! Its calm interior houses the De Mohun Chapel, a reference to the Norman knight who was given the village by William the Conqueror, and includes a 15th-century tomb with a pair of spectacles carved on the side – one of the earliest references to glasses.

Yet it is the exterior that is so joyful to look at. One of my favourite views in the country is from the road that comes into the village from Weston Park. Turn a corner, and the church is there sitting so comfortably in its landscape. Take some time to listen to the church bells if you can; it's one of the few churches in the district to have a full octave.

Whichford lies in a bowl, the surrounding hillsides once lined with sheep. Less so now but the old farm buildings have evocative country names like Gottenham, Doctor's Barn and North Leasow. To the west of the village is **Whichford Wood**, a sizeable landmark woodland on a hillside of mixed evergreen and native trees that put on a vibrantly colourful display in autumn. It's a well-known spot for walkers and the Macmillan Way runs along the southern perimeter of the wood with some fine views of the neighbouring valley, though for the best views, you need to climb the tree-lined avenue to the top of Whichford Hill. At 775-feet high, it's second only to Ilmington Downs in the area, with a notable panorama from the top.

The Normans may have got things started here but Whichford is now more synonymous with clay. **Whichford Pottery** (*01608 684416; www.whichfordpottery.com*) is run by Jim and Dominque Keeling; their pots are renowned – and sold – worldwide and there are numerous trophies in the cabinet awarded for their displays at Chelsea Flower Show. It is truly a local business, though with an evident community atmosphere – most of the staff commute a few paces from their doorsteps in the village. The pottery's buildings are beautiful, the gardens inspirational and the craftsmanship the quintessence of quality. Most well known are the terracotta garden pots – all of which are available to purchase from the outdoor showroom, but Jim and Dominique also make their unique sgraffito earthenware pottery for the home. Visit the Octagon Gallery to see more and look out for their extremely popular pottery sales, events, often including well-known garden designers, and open days when you can visit the workshops.

In the most southerly tip of Warwickshire, the village of **Long Compton** stretches nearly three-quarters of a mile along the main A3400 Oxford to Stratford road, beneath a ridge of Cotswold limestone. The village was allegedly home to no fewer than 17 witches in the late 19th century – with one of them murdered in 1875 for bewitching a man.

There's no evidence of covens now though their earlier presence is thought likely owing to the proximity of the Neolithic **Rollright Stones** that stand on the Cotswold ridge south of the village. These might not have the grandeur of Stonehenge but they have some fun stories worth mulling over. There are three sets of stones: on one side of the road that divides them is a circle of stones known as the *King's Men* and, some yards from these, another group of stones huddled together and known as the *Whispering Knights*. Then, opposite the *King's Men* is the slender, yet crooked figure of the lonely King Stone.

Some five-thousand years old, the *Whispering Knights* is a burial chamber of a long barrow, and some claim the stone circle and King Stone are astrologically aligned standing on a prehistoric path. Whatever the reality and the reasoning behind the presence of these Neolithic stones, the myths particularly stir the imagination. The legend goes that a would-be king of England reached this particular spot on his travels when a witch challenged the king with the words, 'Seven long strides thou shalt take and if Long Compton thou canst see, King of England thou shalt be.'

Whether the ground rose up in front of him upon his seventh stride or he simply misjudged the lie of the land, he didn't make it. The witch responded, 'As Long Compton thou canst not see, King of England thou shalt not be. Rise up stick and stand still stone, For King of England thou shalt be none. Thou and thy men hoar stones shall be, and I myself an eldern tree.'

Hence the would-be king, his men and the conspirators across the field were all turned to stone. The witch, in the hedge along the road, is meant to bleed if cut when in blossom. Every child likes to have a go at taking the seven strides and they can also attempt to count the number of king's men in the stone circle. Two myths exist, one somewhat more pleasant than the other: one is that if you count the stones in the circle three times and reach the same number every time, you won't live; the other is that the person that you love will be yours.

Despite the ambitious king's fruitless efforts, there are actually some sweeping views from the top of the ridge over Long Compton and south Warwickshire. But head to the Whispering Knights and you look out far over Oxfordshire, Chipping Norton and yet more Cotswold hills.

Food and drink

Cherington Arms Cherington ☎01608 686233. A 'Hooky' pub with a basic bar. Great restaurant and lovely garden that runs down to the River Stour. One for the summer. **Red Lion** Main St, Long Compton ☎01608 684221 🖰 www.redlion-longcompton. co.uk. Cotswold stone pub with cosy flagstones-and-rugs bar. Excellent food, using local produce. Regularly included in beer and pub guides. Good accommodation too.

⑬ Todenham, Great Wolford and Chastleton

It would take appreciable effort to cover every village in this small pocket of south Warwickshire but virtually every one is worth taking the time to explore. **Todenham** has a fine church, its spire is a landmark for miles around. **Great Wolford** has one of the cosiest pubs in the area and **Barton-on-the-Heath** has Barton House, a fine Elizabethan manor house (redesigned by Inigo Jones in 1636) that stands opposite the village green and is now used for luxurious bed-and-breakfast accommodation. The house also has some attractive gardens. **Little Compton** has all the requisites to be a pretty Cotswold village and then **Chastleton** is the secret gem, tucked across the border in an oddly jutting corner of Oxfordshire, with Warwickshire and Gloucestershire extremely close by. The Diamond Way and Macmillan Way converge at Chastleton, with a bridleway taking you on a spur to Chastleton Barrow, an Iron Age hillfort.

However, the architectural masterpiece is **Chastleton House** (*01608 674981; www.nationaltrust.org.uk; open Mar to Oct, Wed to Fri*), one of the finest examples of Jacobean architecture. It is simply a cosy home and one that remained in the same family from 1612 (when Walter Jones built the house having bought the estate from Gunpowder plotter Robert Catesby) until 1991. The family lost their money in the English Civil War by staying loyal to the wrong side (that is, the Royalists) – there was much plotting that took place in the secret rooms – and the house gradually decayed because of the cost of the upkeep. Without the trappings of modern life it has remained virtually unchanged for 400 years with the bits and pieces collected over time lying as they did when the family left. The Long Gallery at the very top of the house, with its creaky floorboards and cracking plasterwork on the barrelled ceiling, is a delight; one wonders how many mischievous children have, over the centuries, made the most of the room length and slippery floorboards as a socked skating venue. In the rooms below, in a seamless drift of time, pewter plates sit side by side with equally historic tins of beans, golden syrup and some kind of linament, ageing tennis rackets are juxtaposed with Civil War 'memorabilia'. The National Trust, which have conserved rather than restored the house, now owns Chastleton. I remember visiting the house as a young child, when it was still lived in by the Jones family, long before the National Trust took over or it was widely known. Even at a tender age I was mesmerised by the beauty of the architecture, sitting on the lawn to paint a picture of the house. If you're an artist of any kind, take your watercolours or your pencils with you when you visit; the house and its surroundings have a bewitching effect. You can spend an afternoon playing croquet in the garden too; and this is very much the place for it, being the very spot where the rules of lawn croquet were first laid down in 1865.

Food and drink
Fox and Hounds Great Wolford ☎01608 674220 🌐 www.thefoxandhoundinn.com. Very pretty Cotswold stone pub with courtyard. Authentic, cosy interior brimming with character. Great food. Accommodation too.

Simple Suppers Ditchford Mill, Todenham, Moreton-in-Marsh GL56 9NU ☎01608 650399 🌐 www.simplesuppers.co.uk. Superb quality foods from own farm kitchen and shop including cracking sausages, bacon and pork (own pigs), savoury pies, ready meals, cakes and puddings. Good food to take home and perfect for self-catering holidaymakers.

⑭ Moreton-in-Marsh
Receiving its charter in 1227 to hold a market, Moreton-in-Marsh is still one of the Cotswolds' main market towns today, with the district's largest market held every Tuesday. It's a busy day, with shoppers bussed in from the surrounding area. It's not a high-quality or classy market, and not the place for a quiet browse among the dozens of stalls, but there is a certain buzz in the town centre on market day.

With an extraordinarily broad High Street, Moreton does give off a sense of space and offers the visitor a good selection of shops, from cheeses to chocolates, candles to carpets, all sold behind the elegant pale stone façades and beneath the mixture of rooflines of the 18th-century town houses.

The town has long been important to travellers, with the Roman **Fosse Way** passing through the town and crossing the main A44 Oxford to Worcester road; a list of tolls charged in 1905 is still marked up on the side of the town hall today. In fact no fewer than seven roads converge on the town. Moreton also received one of the country's first ever railway stations in 1826 when the Moreton to Stratford tramway was built. The railway line is still considered one of the most important

Moreton Show

One of the highlights of the Cotswold calendar, the Moreton Show is the largest one-day rural show in the country, with up to 20,000 visitors enjoying the sights each year. And with the demise of the Royal Show, Moreton's has become even more important to those who live off the land. It has turned into an all-family attraction now but agriculture and rural life are still at its heart. Cattle, sheep, poultry and goats are still judged to determine 'Best in Show' and everything from vintage tractors to giant onions and gladioli is displayed. A food marquee brings together many of the region's finest food producers and horseriders compete in the showjumping ring. It's also the main showcase for the Cotswold Sheep Society.

Moreton Show Moreton Showground 📞01608 651908 🖥 www.moretonshow.co.uk. First Sat in Sep.

today cutting across the north Cotswolds (though heading for Worcester these days, not Stratford).

Unusually for a Cotswold town, Moreton is neither built on top of a hill or in a river valley, but sits in the centre of a relatively flat and large bowl. On the outskirts is the old airfield that was once RAF Moreton-in-Marsh. During World War II, bomber crews were trained here to fly Wellington aircraft, a number of which crashed in the district. There's a quirky museum in the town centre dedicated to those who trained at the base. With its tiny façade and propeller blades guiding you in, the **Wellington Aviation Museum** (*01608 650323; www.wellingtonaviation.org; open daily all year, except Mon*) reveals itself Tardislike inside, stuffed full of artefacts – thousands of them.

The old aerodrome (inaccessible to the general public) is still in use for training purposes, though for a different personnel. Laid out on the old runways are full-size models of every construction you can imagine required for firefighters to train – it is now now home to the world's leading fire service training college. It includes the M96, the only motorway in Britain that you're not allowed to drive on!

Food and drink

Moreton is noted for its food shops. Even the local supermarket, Budgens, is dedicated to selling food from local farms and producers.

Manor House Hotel High St 📞01608 650501 🖥 www.cotswold-inns-hotels.co.uk. High-class food in the Mulberry Restaurant; four-star hotel accommodation too.
White Hart Royal Hotel High St 📞01608 650731 🖥 www.whitehartroyal.co.uk. A refurbished 17th-century coaching inn where King Charles I reputedly stayed; the entrance hall has a copy of his unpaid bill. Choice of three eating venues – the Courtyard Restaurant, al fresco in the courtyard or by the fire in the Snug Bar.

4. High Cotswolds

There's a little bit of everything in this locale. In the east, the curvy hills remain with interlocking valleys and vistas that make you feel a part of the landscape. Some of the most-visited villages and towns are here: the Swells, the terrifying-sounding Slaughters and the hyphenated beauties of Stow-on-the-Wold and Bourton-on-the-Water. I've also slipped in some lesser-known jewels that rarely make it onto the tourist trail itinerary, such as Salperton and Longborough, Kineton and Hampnett.

In the north, the town of Winchcombe is keen to establish itself as a base for walkers and proud of its image as a working tourist town without the trappings of being 'too pretty'.

Further west, you begin to see the more aggressive side to the Cotswold Hills, rugged escarpments that on a windy day make walking on the edge feel somewhat threatening. Places such as Cleeve Common, the highest point in the Cotswolds, and Leckhampton Hill – alternately sublimely calm or alarmingly volatile when a storm approaches and the air is thick with deep mauve thunderclouds.

These hills envelop the spa town of Cheltenham, struggling to cling onto the glory days of its former life as a fashionable health resort yet still retaining that charisma in places.

For me, my heart lies somewhere between them all – the high points in the west and the simple beauty that comes with clusters of wild flowers painting a rugged canvas, or those mellower pastures in the east, striped with flourishing hedgerows and guarded by stone walls, standing defiant whatever the weather throws at them.

Getting there and around

Trains

Cheltenham is served well by rail with three mainline routes. **First Great Western** (*www.firstgreatwestern.co.uk*) runs direct from London Paddington and from the West Country. The town sits midway on the **Cross Country** (*www. crosscountrytrains.co.uk*) route from the southwest and the northeast plus East Anglia via Birmingham. Services also run from Cardiff and Gloucester using **Arriva Trains** (*www.arrivatrainswales.co.uk*).

The **Cotswolds and Malverns Line** (*www.firstgreatwestern.co.uk*) from London to Worcester serves the east of the locale, the closest stations being at Kingham and Moreton-in-Marsh (five and four miles respectively from Stow-on-the-Wold).

A special steam train (see page 95) also runs from Toddington in the north of the locale to Cheltenham Racecourse via Winchcombe, operated by the **Gloucestershire Warwickshire Railway** (*www.gwsr.com*). The timetable is irregular and the train does not run every day, so check the website before travelling.

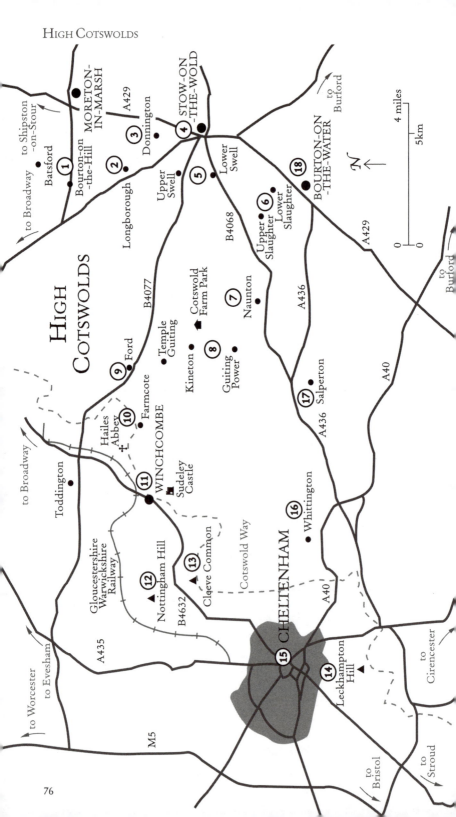

Buses

National Express travels countrywide to Cheltenham, stopping in the Royal Crescent, right in the centre of town. **Local buses** run daily between Moreton-in-Marsh and Cheltenham via Stow and Bourton-on-the-Water. A further route runs between Cheltenham and Winchcombe. Elsewhere in the region, buses are extremely sporadic and cannot be totally relied upon.

Cycling

Cycling is one of the best ways of seeing this particular part of the Cotswolds, with idyllic country lanes and small villages providing numerous rewarding stopping-off points. The roads may undulate gently but apart from the main A40 and A416 in the south of the area the large tract of rural land in the middle is excellent cycling territory.

In the east, a good straight north to south-ish route (an old Roman road known as Buckle Street) with fine rural views and few undulations begins at Cutsdean Hill, just east of the village of Cutsdean, ending at Bourton-on-the-Water. It gives ample opportunity for taking short detours to small villages to the right and left such as the Guitings and the Slaughters.

The Cotswolds AONB has devised a circular cycle route within the eastern area of this locale. Titled Bourton, Bulls and Beer, the 26-mile ride encircles Stow-on-the-Wold and takes in sites such as the Cotswold Farm Park, Bourton-on-the-Water, Donnington Brewery and several pubs along the way. A map and details of the route can be downloaded from www.cotswoldsaonb.org.uk.

Cotswold District Council has also devised a series of circular on-road routes, the details of which can be downloaded from www.cotswold.gov.uk. Of particular note Cycle Route 2 takes an interesting, if hilly, ride through Winchcombe, Belas Knap, Guiting Power and several other villages in the centre of this locale. Route 3 provides a circuit from Bourton-on-the-Water around Lower Slaughter and Lower Swell plus the lesser-known villages of Aylworth and Notgrove.

Cycle hire and cycling holidays

Bourton Cycles Bourton Industrial Park, Bourton-on-the-Water GL54 2HQ
☎01451 8223232 🖰 www.bourtoncycles.co.uk. Cycle hire, sales and repairs. Five minutes from the centre of Bourton. Free delivery within 3 miles of Bourton and a minimal charge for delivery within 15 miles, which includes most of this locale.
Cheltenham Cycles 61 Winchcombe St, Cheltenham ☎01242 255414
🖰 www.cheltenhamcycles.co.uk. Bike sales and repairs.
Compass Holidays Cheltenham Spa Railway Station ☎01242 250642
🖰 www.compass-holidays.com. Packaged cycling holidays including accommodation, bike hire and luggage transfers around the Cotswolds.
Hartwells Cotswold Cycle Hire High St, Bourton-on-the-Water ☎01451 820405
🖰 www.hartwells.supanet.com. Choice of mountain bikes, hybrid and touring bikes plus tandems. Free car parking for the day is included with bike hire.

Walking

Long-distance walkers are spoilt here with so many longer routes criss-crossing the area in addition to local footpaths. These include the Heart of England Way, Monarch's Way, Macmillan Way, Gloucestershire Way, Diamond Way and Kenelm's Way in addition to the Cotswold Way.

Of particular note, two footpaths that cross the locale are the **Warden's Way** and the **Windrush Way**. Both take separate journeys beginning and ending in the same two places – Winchcombe and Bourton-on-the-Water. The Warden's Way, travelling slightly further north than the Windrush Way, is the one to pick for good stopping-off points, including Guiting Power, Naunton and Upper and Lower Slaughter. The 13-mile route sticks mainly to the valleys. The 14-mile Windrush Way travels much more through open countryside over the hills and, but for the tiny hamlet of Aylworth, doesn't pass through a settlement at all. Remember to pack a picnic.

Winchcombe has declared itself the 'walking capital of the Cotswolds', with the town awarded 'Walkers are Welcome' status. This honour is given to towns and villages that have something special to offer walkers. Further information on walking around Winchcombe, including their annual walking festival, is available at www.winchcombewelcomeswalkers.com.

Tourist information centres

Bourton-on-the-Water Victoria St ☎01451 820211.
Cheltenham 77 Promenade ☎01242 522878 🖥 www.visitcheltenham.gov.uk.
Stow-on-the-Wold 12 Talbot Court ☎01451 870150.
Winchcombe High St ☎01242 602925.

Accommodation

Aylworth Manor Aylworth, Naunton GL54 3AH ☎01451 850850
🖥 www.aylworthmanor.co.uk. Impressive yet comfortable 3-storey manor house in its own 165-acre grounds, in a tiny hamlet close to the village of Naunton (itself on the Diamond Way footpath). The 2 guest rooms have wonderful views. Breakfast features homemade produce. The Granary, a 2-bedroom self-catering cottage housed in a listed building is in the grounds.

North Farmcote B&B North Farmcote, Winchcombe GL54 5AU ☎01242 602304
🖥 www.northfarmcote.co.uk. Spectacular location. One of only 6 handsome properties along a lengthy no-through road. Perched on a steep escarpment with wide-ranging views over the Cotswolds and as far as Bredon Hill, the Malverns and the Welsh hills. The mellow Cotswold stone farmhouse has been lived in by David Eayrs for 55 years; it is cosy and the gardens, with superb mature walnut trees, are inspirational. There's a magnificent terrace for sunny breakfasts and afternoon tea, or you can relax in front of the log fire. The Cotswold Way passes within a few yards of the front door.

Whittington Lodge Farm Whittington GL54 4HB ☎01242 820603
🖰 www.whittingtonlodgefarm.com. A 4-star, gold award B&B on a working farm,
which has been in the same family for over 80 years, this has 3 bedrooms and a lounge
warmed by a log fire. Visit Britain award-winning breakfast with home-grown fruits,
homemade bread and produce from the farm. The farm has also won national wildlife
and conservation awards; Ian and his wife are happy to give guests a tour. In a village
close to Cheltenham.

Between Moreton and Stow – a triangle of villages

Between Moreton-in-Marsh and Stow-on-the-Wold, the Roman Fosse Way, now
followed by the A429, stretches south. The main A44, meanwhile, heads due west
from Moreton before peeling off towards Broadway. And the stubby A424, known
as Five Mile Drive for obvious reasons, forms a triangle that also connects up with
Stow. This creates a triangular frame in which sit three villages: **Bourton-on-the-
Hill**, **Longborough** and **Donnington**. Together the villages form a pretext to
explore this small pocket of countryside.

① Bourton-on-the-Hill

On the northern edge of the triangle is
Bourton-on-the-Hill, its suffix added in the
15th century to distinguish it from nearby
Bourton-on-the-Water. As its name implies,
it sits on an (east-facing) escarpment with
some spectacular views over the bowl in
which Moreton-in-Marsh lies and beyond to the
eastern edge of the Cotswolds.

Bourton-on-the-Hill's 17th- and 18th-century roadside cottages are very good
looking with mullioned windows and Cotswold dormers, but unfortunately the
busy A44 splits the village in two, with the cabs of articulated lorries at roof height
to the houses. Hence most people simply see this particular Bourton from the
comfort of their car, *en route* between Moreton and Broadway.

Since the 18th century, Bourton has been well known for training racehorses
– there are still several stud farms on Bourton Down west of the village – and, up
until the middle of the 19th century, for being the location of a gibbet on which the
bodies of highwaymen were hung. But the village has happier associations today,
with a fine gastro pub and three great sights on its doorstep in the form of Bourton
House Garden, Batsford Arboretum and Sezincote.

Bourton House Garden

Surrounding a fine neo-classical manor-like house made from large slabs of smooth
cream-cheese stone and perfectly proportioned sash windows, are the accompanying

Cotswold farm walks

Enjoy the countryside around Bourton-on-the-Hill by going on a walking tour – free of charge. Robin Dale, farmer at Manor Farm, takes visitors around the area for a minimum of two hours during which time you'll learn about the farm, local history, wildlife, birds and wild flowers. Visits must be booked in advance by telephoning Robin on 01386 700312 or 07774 693720.

gardens (*01386 700754; www.bourtonhouse.com; open Wed to Fri, Jun to early Sep; drinks and homemade cakes available in the tithe barn or outside in a sheltered corner of the garden*) that show off a brilliance of light and colour. Ten interlinked areas of the garden provide different aspects towards the house and exhilarating changes of mood. Of the ten, my favourites are the long borders full of riotous colours, the raised walk facing the house, where a gentle brush against the shrubs erupts amazing scents into the air and, by contrast, the White Garden, where monochrome shades mingle with green foliage, against immaculately clipped box hedges and lichen-covered stone pillars. At the far end of the White Garden are scrolled-iron gates through which you can look over the hillside.

You enter the garden through a most impressive tithe barn. One of the largest in Gloucestershire, it retains its 16th-century timbers under which you can sit to sip tea and devour homemade cakes.

Batsford Arboretum

A hundred yards east of Bourton-on-the-Hill, towards Moreton-in-Marsh, is the entrance to Batsford Arboretum (*01386 701441; www.batsarb.co.uk; Garden Terrace Restaurant with panoramic hillside views open throughout the day and for evening meals and sunsets; renowned garden centre*), the largest private collection of trees in the UK with over 63 acres and 3,300 labelled specimens. The arboretum holds the National Collection of Japanese flowering village cherries and an extensive collection of acers, making spring and autumn obvious seasons to visit. Except that in winter aconites and snowdrops carpet the floor of this south-facing hillside, followed by drifts of daffodils and later summer bulbs. Great American redwoods tower above swathes of flowers in winter, the largest handkerchief tree in Britain displays its tissue-like bracts in May and the 'cathedral' lime offers respite from the sun in summer – stand beneath it and gaze skywards; you will feel as if you're in an enormous church. Autumn, of course, is the time to experience bursts of glistening gold, firework reds and shiny copper.

In among the glades are features such as a Hermit's Cave, bog garden and Japanese Resthouse, installed by Algernon Freeman Mitford, grandfather to the famous Mitford sisters, in the late 19th century. He designed the arboretum with a restful, informal layout around the grand neo-Tudor house (not open to the public) that stands within the grounds of Batsford Park. From the top of the arboretum you look across to the house and the Evenlode Valley (see page 132) beyond.

The Mitford sisters continued to live in the park until 1916, when the house and estate were sold. The eldest sister, Nancy, based the early part of her novel *Love in a Cold Climate* on the family's time at Batsford. Algernon and other Mitford family members are buried in the tiny church of St Mary's on the far northeast edge of the arboretum. This church, with its unusual apsidal-ended chancel reminiscent more of the French countryside than the Cotswolds, is accessible from the arboretum – although you cannot enter the arboretum from this side.

Today the arboretum is owned by the Batsford Foundation, a charitable trust that ploughs any profits back into maintaining the park and awarding gifts to other charities such as the Gardeners Royal Benevolent Society as well as local schools and churches.

Sezincote

Opposite the entrance to Batsford Arboretum, on the other side of the A44, is an unassuming gate. Continue along the lengthy driveway and you'd be forgiven for forgetting that you're in the Cotswolds at all.

Sezincote (*01386 700444; www.sezincote.co.uk; garden open Jan to Nov, Thu, Fri and bank holiday Mon afternoons; house open May to Sep, same days as gardens; no children under 15 allowed in the house; drinks and homemade cakes served in the orangery*) is a somewhat poetic word in itself. The 'cote' or shelter is obvious enough but Sezin- is derived from *la chêne*, the French for oak tree, hence 'home of the oaks', the odd few of these oaks you'll see in the parkland once you've entered through the entrance gate. Such an unusual name should prepare you for something extraordinary, for instead of a grand traditional manor house with classic Cotswold architectural styles, Sezincote is Indian-inspired.

Built in 1810 by Charles Cockerell to a design by his brother, Samuel Pepys Cockerell (the pair were related to the diarist Samuel Pepys), Sezincote is in the Mogul style of Rajasthan, with a central dome, minarets, peacock-tail windows, jali-work railings and pavilions. A long, sleek orangery curves around the Persian Garden of Paradise with its fountain and canals. In 1812 the Prince Regent visited Sezincote and, inspired so much by the architecture, adapted a farmhouse into the Royal Pavilion in Brighton. Sir John Betjeman described 'exotic Sezincote' in his autobiographical poem, *Summoned by Bells*.

Sezincote is a startling incongruity in the cosy uniformity of the Cotswolds. Its deep golden Cotswold stone – quarried from Bourton-on-the-Hill but allegedly dyed – contrasts with the copper-blue onion domes and metalwork railings. Bizarrely, the Indian theme disappears inside, where a much more conventional classical style takes over. The gardens, however, continue the exotic theme with water gardens, an Indian bridge and a temple to the Hindu sun god – all within a very English parkland setting.

Food and drink

Horse and Groom Bourton-on-the-Hill &01386 700413 www.horseandgroom. info. Gastro pub run by the Greenstocks family, renowned locally for great food and attention to service in several pubs in the area. Superb food and drink; local suppliers include beef and pork from the neighbouring Sezincote Estate. Accommodation available.

② Longborough

From Bourton-on-the-Hill, the Heart of England Way runs due south along the east-facing escarpment, past Sezincote and on to the village of Longborough. This footpath meets up with the Monarch's Way from Moreton-in-Marsh, conveniently a few yards from the Coach and Horses public house. There are fine views from the hillside but it's very much a local pub with darts and cribbage teams still keeping the leather seats warm. To confuse matters there's another cosy Coach and Horses a mile away at Ganborough on the main A424 road to Stow, where the Longborough-based artist Caroline Green (*www.carolinehgreen.com*) exhibits much of her work.

Longborough Festival Opera

As with so many of the settlements around here, Longborough could easily be the film set for a period drama, but it is opera for which the village has truly made a name.

The Cotswolds unleash quite a few surprises, and arriving at the home of Longborough Festival Opera on selected dates from mid-June to the end of July (*GL56 0QF; 01451 830292; www.lfo.org.uk*) is one of them, not least that there is a permanent opera house, with glistening chandeliers and all the glamour of a London-based production, deep in the Cotswolds countryside.

Far from being buried, Longborough Festival Opera sits on a hillside – the same east-facing escarpment as Bourton-on-the-Hill and Sezincote. The views from the 'picnic field' – more on that later – and the opera house terrace are part of its very special character and certainly something that the Royal Opera House couldn't possibly compete with. They scan a full 180 degrees of the surrounding countryside including the Evenlode Valley and a variety of landmarks such as Brailes Hill and Ilmington Downs even though, from this position, they appear to be ironed out to a uniform plain.

The opera house has been set up in the grounds of an extremely handsome house owned by Martin Graham. Martin grew up in Longborough and from an early age was inspired by listening to music, in particular Wagner. He began to organise charity performances using a travelling opera company and eventually his idea to create a permanent opera house came to fruition when an old cattle barn next door to his house was transformed. Today you'd never guess the building's former use, with a striking pink-tinged classical façade topped with the figures of Wagner, Puccini and Mozart – sculpted by the local potter, Jim Keeling of Whichford Pottery

Food and drink

Coach and Horses Ganborough ☎01451 830208 🖥 www.thetoppub.co.uk. Child-friendly pub with a garden and roaming chickens. Food served. Pub is just outside Longborough on the A424.

Coach and Horses Longborough ☎01451 830325. Traditional village pub serving food and local Donnington ales (see page 84). Pub garden with good views.

Cotswold Food Store & Café Near Longborough GL56 0QN ☎01451 830469 🖥 www.cotswoldfoodstore.co.uk. Admirable food shop selling top-class produce, much of it sourced from local farms (meat, cheese, milk, ice cream, fruit and vegetables) and suppliers (breweries, cake makers, etc). The deli counter offers many Cotswold-made cheeses, and the café uses seasonal produce from the shop. Terrace offers views over open farmland around Condicote and the Swells. The shop and café are off the A424 2½ miles north of Stow-on-the-Wold.

Longborough Village Shop & Café Moreton Rd ☎01451 833534. A community-owned shop, following the threat of closure, and run by a team of 30 volunteers. Lots of locally produced food and drinks on sale in the shop and a café menu including hot

(see page 71) – and elegant reception rooms awaiting the arrival of guests.

An artistic director is appointed each season to create an imaginative programme; Martin's ambition is to stage Wagner's full Ring Cycle. Far from amateur, the live orchestra is made up of instrumentalists from the top orchestras in London and Birmingham, who enjoy performing for a season in the Cotswolds, with professional singers, backstage and production crews. And, to keep costs down, local residents put up the performers.

Community spirit is evident elsewhere too, the opera house providing education programmes in local schools and giving young singers stage experience, despite the opera house being completely unsubsidised by Arts Council grants.

Perhaps the most appealing aspect of visiting Longborough Festival Opera is complementing a sublime performance with a truly memorable meal. Guests are invited to picnic anywhere in the grounds of the opera house, or dine in the purpose-built festival restaurant, a convivial, typically Cotswold atmosphere. A lengthy mid-performance interval allows guests to dine and after the curtain down, visitors may sit around for as long as they wish by candlelight to soak in the sunset, eat and drink while chatting about the performance. It's all part of a highly civilised and magical experience.

For those who want to enjoy a private party before or after the show, guests may book the use of two follies that Martin has built in the grounds of his home.

sausage rolls, wraps and pasties cooked on the premises, sandwiches and homemade cakes. The café will put together a traditional picnic lunch (advance booking only) for visitors planning a day out in the area.

③ Donnington

That east-facing slope upon which Bourton-on-the-Hill, Sezincote and Longborough sit suddenly turns a corner and creates a short, stumpy ridge of hills sandwiched between the A424 and the Fosse Way as they begin to meet at Stow-on-the-Wold. The ridge drops off and then dramatically climbs higher again approaching Stow, but on this particular ledge is the village of Donnington.

Donnington is known around Gloucestershire for its eponymous brewery, though this is some way from the village in about as picturesque a location as you could possibly find. You can walk to the brewery from the village, west across the ridge using a local footpath before joining up with the Heart of England Way – it's approximately 1½ miles on foot.

Donnington Brewery

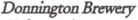

Unfortunately, visitors are not allowed in the brewery any more, but do spend a few moments enjoying its position. It's housed in a striking 16th-century Cotswold stone watermill – the millwheel is still used to drive some of the machinery – that bridges the barely known River Dikler. To one side is the millpond through which the river flows. This river ultimately flows by Upper and Lower Swell towards Bourton-on-the-Water in a steep-sided valley.

Donnington Brewery (*www.donnington-brewery.com*) was set up by Richard Arkell in 1865 and it's still run by the Arkell family (also known for Arkell's Brewery in Swindon) today. Its beers are produced in much the same way as they were back then, using spring water from the spring beside the millpond.

Fifteen pubs are tied to the brewery, all of them within a few miles of the watermill. For the ultimate of pub crawls, drinkers can walk the **Donnington Way**, a 62-mile circular route that links all 15 pubs and wanders through some of the most iconic and gentle Cotswold scenery. All the pubs are listed on the brewery's website, though ironically the village of Donnington doesn't have a pub of its own.

Hills and valleys – Stow and its western neighbours

Stow's full name – **Stow-on-the-Wold** – offers some clue to its location. It sits on a high hill, the slender tower of the parish church providing a beacon for miles around – every approach road must climb to reach the town. That there are eight approach roads illustrates the town's prominence as an important meeting point.

To the west is the Dikler Valley, where **Lower Swell** and **Upper Swell** lie on two arteries into Stow, the villages themselves linked by the river, a quiet country lane and the Heart of England Way.

Further west again, in the next parallel valley are **Upper** and **Lower Slaughter**, this time lying on the tiny River Eye. Finally as the landscape shifts and pivots, the village of **Naunton** lies on a river valley running west to east, at least for a few moments. In this area the valleys, escarpments and interconnecting roads twist and turn, accommodating the changing folds in the rock beds. Many quarries, disused and working, are in evidence.

④ Stow-on-the-Wold

On a hill 800 feet above sea level, Stow has the enviable status of being the highest town in the Cotswolds. That in theory should make it one of the chilliest or windiest too. However, somehow it feels far from bleak, particularly thanks to the **Market Square**, at the heart of the town, being sheltered by the tall buildings that surround it providing something of a microclimate.

Stow as a settlement dates from the Iron Age, and witnessed one of the last skirmishes of the English Civil War in 1646, the Battle of Stow, in which Royalist troops were driven back from the outskirts of the town to fight in the Market Square. It has been a trading place since Norman times; sheep that were so instrumental to the town's prosperity were grazed on The Green, once considerably larger than now, at the northern end of the Market Square.

Today the trade is in antiques and horses, the two standing uncomfortably cheek by jowl twice a year in May and October when the Stow Horse Fair takes place on the edge of town and thousands of Romany Gypsies from across Europe descend. During the remainder of the year, the antiques shops, secondhand bookshops and increasing collections of sellers offering products for the home, encouraged by the renowned mail-order company **Scotts of Stow**, attract thousands of visitors to browse and enjoy the charm of the town.

The notoriously abrasive restaurant critic A A Gill once remarked of Stow that it was 'catastrophically ghastly'. The hordes of tourists who flock to the town each year would clearly disagree. And every one of the numerous restaurants, pubs and hotels that string along Sheep Street in between the antiques dealers and bookshops look inviting, particularly as lights begin to twinkle at dusk. However, I must confess to finding the numerous tea rooms that frame the Market Square have not kept up with the times and, even if the old-world premises look appealing enough, the food is considerably superior in cafés and tea rooms elsewhere in the area.

That said, Digbeth Street is the place to visit to put a picnic together, with a great butcher's selling local Gloucester Old Spot pork, several competing delis offering superb goodies and a chocolate shop where the chocolates really are made on the premises. Add in the farmers' market, held on the second Thursday of every month, and you will have a feast.

If it's the history of Stow rather than the window-shopping that interests you, you can use your mobile phone to grab information on the move. The audio guide from **Walking Past** (*www.walkingpast.co.uk*) allows you to either take a complete historical tour of the town by hiring an audio player from **Go-Stow**, the tourist information centre in **Church Street**, or by calling a designated telephone number to pick up on a particular thread such as stagecoach travel in Stow, legendary figures or gruesome stories.

Food and drink

Conservatory Restaurant at the **Grapevine Hotel** Sheep St ☎01451 830344 www.thegrapevinehotel.com. Candlelit restaurant where a huge vine scrambles across the ceiling. Top-quality contemporary food. La Vigna Brasserie offers a more relaxed setting for pizza and tapas.

Royalist Hotel Digbeth St ☎01451 830670 www.theroyalisthotel.com. A relaxing ambience in an ancient building. Excellent and imaginative food in the AD947 restaurant. Located right on the end of Digbeth Street where it joins with Sheep Street. Connected to the hotel is the **Eagle and Child**, a character pub with low-beamed ceilings, flagstone floors and classic pub food such as steak and ale pie.

Shopping

Hamptons Fine Foods Digbeth St ☎01451 831975 www.hamptons-hampers. co.uk. All the sorts of treats that you expect from a deli including homemade cakes and pastries made in their own kitchens. Renowned for their hampers – make up your own or try a Gloucestershire hamper – created using foods produced in the county.

Lambourne's Butchers Digbeth St ☎01451 830630 www.lambournesbutchers. co.uk. Fine traditional butchers with much of the produce reared on farms within the Cotswolds. Includes game in season. Closed Mon.

Maby's Digbeth St ☎01451 870071 www.mabys.co.uk. Homemade breads and patisserie products, foods from around the world.

Miette Digbeth St ☎01451 833543 www.miette.co.uk. Delicious chocolates handmade in Stow.

⑤ Upper and Lower Swell

There's nothing to suggest a height difference between these two villages, the pair sitting comfortably in the narrow Dikler Valley with sharpish inclines either side. If anything, Lower Swell is slightly higher up the hillside than its neighbour – it doesn't actually sit over the river, but it's simply that Upper Swell lies north of Lower Swell.

Sadly both villages are strung along their own twisting road with cars that venture far too fast and this does hamper their likeability even if the buildings are aesthetically perfect. So my recommendation is to explore the village's neighbourhood off the main road by walking the mile-long footpath between the two, along the valley floor; it's part of the Heart of England Way.

Arts and crafts around the Stow area

Aside from the art galleries selling both antique and contemporary art in Stow, the area attracts a large number of artists, craftsmen and women who offer opportunities for visitors to make the most of their rural surroundings for inspiration through workshops and courses.

In the picturesque village of **Condicote**, three miles from Stow, the **Cotswold Art Studio** (*www.cotswold-artstudio.com*) offers a programme of art and craft courses in watercolour painting, calligraphy, jewellery design, batik making, glasswork and tile-mosaic work.

Meanwhile, Stow itself is the venue for 'Start to Art Workshops' at the **Walton House Gallery and Studio** (*www.lindyallfrey.co.uk*) in Sheep Street. Half-, whole- and three-day courses are designed for those just beginning or getting back into painting. Courses are taught in small groups with a maximum of four people.

For those living relatively close to Stow or taking an extended break in the Cotswolds, **Jill Jarvis** runs weekly lessons over a ten-week term in drawing and painting at all levels including beginners. Holiday workshops for children are also offered. She can be contacted on 01451 831862.

Jill is the inspiration behind the **Stow Art Group** too, which presents an annual exhibition in Lower Slaughter (see page 88) every July. The standard of work is high and most of the paintings and artwork on show are for sale, giving visitors the opportunity to take away a piece of artwork as a souvenir. To check the dates of the annual exhibition, contact the head of the art group, Priscilla Peace, on 01451 830459.

⑥ Upper and Lower Slaughter

Few villages in the Cotswolds are better known or attract more visitors than the Slaughters. Their name sounds as if they hide some grisly past and yet 'slaughter' comes from the Old English 'slohtre', which simply means 'muddy'. Where this mud comes from, I've not been able to establish but can only presume that it must have some link to their location on the tiny River Eye.

The pair of villages are approximately a mile apart by narrow lanes but less so if you take the Warden's Way (see page 78) that runs through and between them. The Eye of course connects them too, and it's the water that seems to make them all the more idyllic – and all the more attractive to visitors. North of Upper Slaughter the river runs through a series of lakes. The most northerly of these is inaccessible, on private land, but the one nearest to the village is in line with the Warden's Way. This and the lake are sandwiched by a line of trees and it makes a pleasant short walk out of the village.

Upper Slaughter proves less popular with visitors than Lower Slaughter, but take the trouble to wander around the village, attractively tucked as it is between steep-sided hills and with a quintessential Cotswolds quaintness, and a small ford. If you're not partaking in afternoon tea at the celebrated Lords of the Manor Hotel

Thankful villages

A prominent feature of most Cotswold villages – indeed most British villages – is the war memorial but there is one missing in Upper Slaughter. For it is considered a 'thankful' village, a name given to the very few settlements in Britain that did not receive any fatalities among its volunteer servicemen during World War I. It can be even more thankful that this feat was repeated again in World War II. However, a roll of honour in the village hall commemorates the lives of all those villagers who did their duty.

(*www.lordsofthemanor.com*) – it's reputedly one of the best places to do so, even if it does lighten your wallet substantially – you can catch a glimpse of the building at least by taking a wander up the hill towards Lower Swell and turning right into the field just past the last house.

Or visit Simon Weaver's **Cotswold Organic Dairy** (*www.simonweaver.net*), which makes a very tasty organic Cotswold Brie at Kirkham Farm, on the road to Lower Swell. You can buy the cheese direct from the creamery.

The River Eye is much more noticeable in Lower Slaughter, running past cottages and miniature gardens. Tucked against the river is the **Old Mill** (*www.oldmill-lowerslaughter.com*), its square brick chimney rising above the Cotswold slate roofs. A small shop in the mill attracts plenty of tourists, but the greatest lure for me is the handmade organic ice cream manufactured on the premises. Sitting by the river, licking sumptuous creamy ices while your toes play in the shallow waters is one of the ultimate pleasures of summertime visits here.

The village hall, on the other side of the narrow river, is also well known for putting on art exhibitions throughout the year, usually with work for sale.

One of my favourite local views is from the little road that runs just to the right of the villages, turning off the B4068 Stow to Naunton road. Turn down this road and you'll see both villages tucked among the trees, with the church spire of St Mary's in Lower Slaughter peeking above.

⑦ Naunton

Naunton is to one side of the road that passes high above from Stow to Cheltenham. It's very easy simply to pass by, but amply repays the small diversion, lying at the bottom of a steep-sided valley, with the River Windrush gushing through on its way to Bourton-on-the-Water and beyond. From the Stow road that passes up above the village there are three prominent buildings: St Andrew's Church on the west side of the village, the Baptist chapel in the form of a long, low building perched on the hillside and a dovecote below it.

In front of St Andrew's Church is a wooden bench with an apt inscription from *Alice in Wonderland*. The Reverend Edward Litton, a friend of Lewis Carroll (real name Charles Dodgson) lived in the fine old vicarage during the latter part of the 19th century, where the author would come and stay.

The Baptist chapel, I think, makes Naunton. It is certainly the building, with its long, arched windows, which draws one's eye from a distance, along with the dovecote below and to one side. That this 15th-century dovecote was built in a valley right next to a river is unusual itself, for these shelters are usually built on higher, more prominent ground. But, owing to its unusual position, it was converted to a mill for grinding corn. The village community bought the four-gabled building in 1997 to save it being turned into a bed and breakfast. Take a look inside: the odd dove and pigeon still enjoys their own bed and breakfast accommodation but beware of the deposits that these visitors leave behind on the floor. The Naunton Village Trust is keen to raise funds to maintain this listed Grade II Ancient Monument, so buying a postcard or a tea towel helps the coffers.

An alternative way to enjoy Naunton and the Slaughters is by taking a **Treasure Trail** (*www.treasuretrails.co.uk*). I took my children on the 'murder mystery' trail, solving clues by looking at the village environment as we walked to discover a 'culprit'. The children enjoyed the game very much and it encouraged us to look more closely at the villages. A little booklet with all the directions and clues is available to download from the website or you'll find it available to purchase at several of the tourist information centres in the area.

Take a look at an Ordnance Survey map and you'll see that the area around Naunton is full of disused quarries. Much of the stone used for the historic buildings in the area came from these but many of the quarries also dug out the kind of stone used to make the traditional Cotswold roofing slates, many of which made their way onto some of the finest buildings in Oxford.

There are several quarries still operating in the vicinity today chopping out stone for building, roofing and paving. For safety reasons it's obviously not possible to wander around these work sites but you can gain an idea of how they operate by taking a virtual tour on the website of **Huntsmans** (*www.huntsmansquarries.co.uk*), one of the main quarries in the area.

×◦×◦×

Food and drink

Black Horse Inn Naunton ☎01451 850565. On the main street, a thriving village pub connected to Donnington Brewery. It's a good stop-off for walkers on the Warden's Way, or a small detour for those on the Windrush Way.

Dry as a stone – Cotswold walls

One of the most important features of the Cotswolds, and for which it is so renowned, are the miles and miles of drystone walls that break up the landscape into contained parcels. The sedimentary formation of the limestone means it is easy to split making it the perfect material for wall building. With the lichens and mosses that subtly weather the stone into those famous mottled colours, these aesthetically pleasing walls are an integral part of the landscape, either cascaded with vibrant aubrietia in a cottage garden or extending into the horizon enclosing a great estate, capped with coping stones.

The Cotswolds Conservation Board run weekend-long drystone walling courses throughout the AONB. Far from being a closed shop to builders and farmers, these courses are open to anyone. They make a memorable way to be out in the open, at one with the environment and your surroundings, as well as putting something back to the area. For the walls that are built during the time on the course are 'proper' drystone walls that will be around for centuries, not a quick makeshift partition ready to be pulled down again at the end of the weekend.

I knew that drystone walls are built without a mortar to hold the stones together, but that was about the extent of my knowledge. So I went along to one of the courses run by the board, close to Naunton, and learnt so much about this iconic Cotswold feature.

Our tutor was Jonathan Bendle, a professional landscaper and instructor of rural skills. He demonstrated the different kinds of stones used – walling stone is different from building stone – and how they differ according to the area of the Cotswolds from which they're quarried. My dozen or so companions on the course and I learnt how some perish over time once the frost and heat travel into the sedimentary layers,

The Guitings, Kineton and Ford – the quiet core

By comparison with other places in Britain the area around the Guiting villages is far from remote. And yet, when you're there you get a delicious sense of isolation, finding secluded pockets of countryside, yet with the odd tiny village to remind you that civilisation is never very far away. And you're still only within a few miles of Stow, Bourton-on-the-Water, Broadway or Winchcombe.

The valleys are unpredictable as the folds of the earth dart this way and that with tiny streams that bubble along. It's what makes the landscape here so interesting. I prefer this area to that around the Slaughters, for it does not attract the visitors in anything like the same numbers.

⑧ The Guitings and Kineton

As the crow flies, or indeed if you're travelling along the Warden's Way, the village delaminating the stone, when to mix old stone with new and when it's time simply to start again with fresh stone. We found out about the different qualities – what to listen for when you tap a stone and how long it takes to weather.

By now it was time to get cracking on the physical work. 'An experienced waller', said Jonathan, 'will think one step ahead all the time to conserve energy and get to the end result quicker.' That was what he wanted us to do as we went about sorting the stone, getting an eye for the right-sized piece, making sure that it has a good long 'tail' to tie the two sides of the wall together like a jigsaw puzzle before chipping and shaping, then laying the stone down and filling the middle with 'hearting', the smaller rubble that helps to hold the wall together.

I looked along the length of the wall that we had completed. The aesthetic beauty lay in its rhythm – the layers and the irregular uniformity of the stone. I'd spent a weekend among poppies, field scabious and ripening blackberries, a gentle breeze had quashed any notion of the physical hard work and the tap, tap, tap of the walling hammer striking stone sounded therapeutic as it echoed across the cornfields. And I can leave with the knowledge that a hundred years from now, the wall will still be there, long, long after I've gone.

For information on future dry-stone walling courses, as well as the other rural skills workshops on hedge laying, woodland coppicing and green woodworking in the Cotswolds, visit www.cotswoldsaonb.org.uk.

of **Guiting Power** lies approximately 1½ miles northwest of Naunton. By a narrow and twisting country lane, it's somewhat further. Preposterously photogenic, the heart of the village lies around a small green and its war memorial, overlooked by a village stores that fits right into the 1950s. Large stone barns, a mix of houses that anyone would be eager to live in and the Norman church of St Michael, which has one of the most pleasing exteriors of any church in the area, complete the picture. The **Guiting Festival** (*www.guitingfestival.org*), with its series of classical music concerts, runs every summer.

Temple Guiting lies two to three miles north. Unlike the clustered Guiting Power, Temple Guiting is stretched out, crossing the River Windrush. The two villages are linked by the Diamond Way. Considered a hideaway, Temple Guiting is the place to visit if you wish to be treated like a celebrity (or indeed if you are a celebrity), the estate around the manor house having been taken over by Sophie Conran to run bespoke country house parties. Under the guise **Sophie Conran for Temple Guiting** (*www.sophieconrantg.com*), it offers packages involving personal tutelage from top chefs and restaurateurs – many of them celebrities themselves

The Cotswold Farm Park

A mile or so east of Guiting Power is the **Cotswold Farm Park** (*01451 850307; www.cotswoldfarmpark.co.uk; open daily mid-Mar to Sep then weekends only to end of Oct; special events take place throughout the year including lambing, milking and sheep shearing*), the home of *Countryfile* presenter Adam Henson. I caught up with Andy Cole, Assistant farm manager, who explained how the farm came into being.

'It was Adam's father, Joe Henson, who set the farm park up, together with his business partner, John Neave. Joe had a passion for rare breed animals and having taken over the tenancy of Bemborough Farm [where the farm park is based] in the 1960s, he wanted to put some animals on it, and bought his daughter some Cotswold sheep. Then came other breeds – Gloucester Old Spot pigs and Gloucester cattle – and he and John decided to show their increasing collection to the public.' Continued Andy, 'The pair had tremendous opposition from the planners and local people. It was at a time when intensive farming was the in-thing and people had decided that the Cotswolds were not for tourists!'

But Joe was becoming increasingly concerned about the number of native breeds of livestock that the country was losing, so in the early 1970s he helped to found the Rare Breed Survival Trust in what was the world's first farm park.

The park is now run by Joe's son, Adam and his business partner and friend from agricultural college, Duncan Andrews. Said Andy, 'We've had to change over the years but we want to keep things simple; there are over 1,500 farm parks now and the Cotswold Farm Park is one of the few to still keep rare breeds.'

Those rare breeds number over 300 – of sheep, cattle, pigs, poultry, horses and even oxen, though Adam's affections ultimately lie with his sheep. These are positioned around the farm in an informative history trail. Said Andy, 'Each paddock refers to a different period in history. We begin with native breeds from the Neolithic period, then Roman and Viking right up to modern, commercial breeds.' People can see how farmers have changed and adapted to meet demand. And aside from these animals Adam and Duncan continue to run the 1,600-acre Bemborough Farm, which also includes a commercial flock of sheep and mixed arable crops.

In addition to visiting the farm park, visitors are free to wander a two-mile waymarked Wildlife Walk around the farm and view a farming landscape that has been shaped over 6,000 years. There are butterflies and birds, and over a hundred species of wild flowers and grasses on the walk, including typical limestone-loving flowers and some unusual species as well as the very rare Cotswold pennycress.

– renowned interior designers, beauty specialists as well as the option to top it off with a range of country pursuits. On the same estate, self-catering accommodation is available at **Temple Guiting Manor** (*www.templeguitingmanor.co.uk*), one of the most graceful Tudor manor houses you're likely to see.

In between the two villages is the tiny hamlet of **Kineton**, which slopes down a steep hillside to rest at two fords and the even tinier **Barton**, merely a couple of large houses and a tiny river crossing.

If you can stomach the constantly undulating landscape, cycling the quiet lanes is a good way to appreciate the beauty of the area. One of my favourite lanes to cycle or wander along, **Critchford Lane**, runs west of Kineton. Approaching from the west, the gated road begins by cutting through a very steep-sided valley. The landscape then opens out and sheep nibble the pastures down to the next, perpendicular-running valley. The Diamond and Warden's ways both run through this valley, just to one side of a tiny riverlet and the site of a medieval village. There is a ford that is simply perfect for paddling and also a tiny car park for walkers. From here, look west for views of a superb manor house, behind which is the vast expanse of **Guiting Wood**. Both aforementioned footpaths lead you into the woodland.

Food and drink

Halfway House Kineton ☎01451 850344. A 17th-century pub tied to the Donnington Brewery. Traditional pub food.

Hollow Bottom Guiting Power ☎01451 850392 🖑 www.hollowbottom.com. A 17th-century pub once owned by Peter Scudamore and Nigel Twiston-Davies, the Hollow Bottom continues to be a horseracing-themed pub owing to the number of top racehorse stables in the vicinity (Nigel's race stables are a few hundred yards up the road). You'll almost certainly find a racehorse trainer or jockey in the pub and possibly a winning racehorse tethered up outside. One of the current owners is also the chef and has impressive credentials.

Old Post Office Guiting Power ☎01451 850701 🖑 www.theoldpostoffice.biz. Very pretty house right in the centre of the village opposite the green, with a couple of tables inside and out serving exemplary coffee, homemade cakes and a few savouries. Also sells country interiors.

⑨ Ford

North of the Guitings and cut through by the Stow to Tewkesbury road is the tiny village of Ford, sitting across the River Windrush with no more than a few houses and a pub. But the **Plough Inn** is another celebrated horseracing pub, sitting opposite Jonjo O'Neil's famous Jackdaws Castle racing stables, considered one of Britain's premier National Hunt training facilities; the accommodation overlooks the gallops. Craig, the landlord, can provide you with all sorts of tips about visiting Cheltenham Racecourse (see page 102).

Food and drink

The Plough Inn Ford ☎01386 584215 🖑 www.theploughinnatford.co.uk. Fresh, seasonal food. Specialises in game and dishes using asparagus from the Vale of Evesham when in season.

The seat of Mercia – Winchcombe and its villages

As we head further west towards **Winchcombe**, the ridges of the Cotswold hills become greater, higher, steeper and then suddenly plunge into the flat lands of Tewkesbury and the Severn Vale, where the M5 motorway thunders through. Then there's just the odd isolated hill or hummock, such as Alderton Hill and Oxenton Hill close by and Dumbleton Hill followed by Bredon Hill in the distance.

Mercian kings made it this far and declared the town of Winchcombe as a capital. Nearby **Sudeley Castle** has royal connections too, though of a different era, while the remains of **Beckbury Camp**, northeast of Winchcombe, and **Belas Knap**, due south, show signs of an age long before any kings stamped their mark on the area.

⑩ Farmcote, Hailes Abbey and Toddington

I find that if you drive towards this part of the Cotswolds from the east – from Stow and through Ford – you don't really appreciate the lie of the land and how it has been getting steeper, because the car's engine has ironed out all the ups and downs. But walk or cycle around these parts and you appreciate that you are now on the western Cotswold escarpment. By the time you've reached the hills just west of Ford you're standing roughly 930 feet above sea level and with some captivating views of the Severn Vale and the Malverns.

We're now sufficiently far west to pick up the Cotswold Way again; having come from Stanton and Stanway (see page 42) north of this locale, the route runs along an old sheep-drove road known as Campden Lane and then to one side of Beckbury Camp, an Iron Age hillfort that teeters on the edge of the escarpment. There's evidence too, on the hillside, of the 'strip lynchets' or long parallel terraces that were created by centuries of ploughing with oxen.

A few yards south of the camp is the minutest of hamlets, **Farmcote**. It comprises little more than a farm, a tiny Saxon church, bed and breakfast (see page 78) and a half-dozen other dwellings but these fortunate residents have, arguably, one of the best locations in the Cotswolds, with a sharply rising hill behind for shelter from the cold northeasterly winds and views out to the west beyond compare as the land drops away below. To add to the idyllic setting, the settlement is only accessible via a tiny little lane that runs along the top of the escarpment from the south, or a footpath that links up with the Cotswold Way to the north.

Within this cluster of dwellings, in what would seem the most unlikeliest of settings for passing trade, is **Farmcote Herbs and Chilli Peppers** (*www.farmcoteherbs.co.uk*), a little nursery specialising, as the name gives away, in growing and selling dozens of different kinds of herbs and numerous varieties of chilli peppers. The setting is under the shade of giant walnut trees on the edge of the escarpment; plant selection takes some considerable time as you gaze at the views. In addition the owners Tim and Jane sell chilli chutneys, chilli chocolate and chilli sausages and burgers, the last cooked up during the couple's annual chilli festival, held every August Bank Holiday Monday. Opening times are variable throughout the year so check on the website.

To the west of Farmcote, the land falls away sharply into a short steep-sided valley, the open ends of the V-folding out at right angles to itself to create further escarpments. Running parallel with the road to Farmcote, on the other side of the valley, is the **Salt Way**, an ancient route that crosses **Salter's Hill**, used for transporting salt from the Midlands to London. From its foot, Salter's Hill is frighteningly prominent. It looms large and anyone making an ascent on foot via the Salt Way will really feel the calf muscles working hard. But the views from the top are amply rewarding.

At the point where the aforementioned valley opens out, tucked at the foot of Salter's Hill, **Hayles Fruit Farm** has made the most of the mineral-rich soils (there are no fewer than six springs bursting out from the surrounding hillsides, all heading for the farm) and planted acres of fruit trees and soft fruit bushes. Accessible along a quiet no-through road – which becomes the Cotswold Way up the hill towards Farmcote – it's a most bucolic fruit-picking location with a scenically placed campsite getting views of Salter's Hill and Hailes Wood.

Just below the fruit farm are the remains of **Hailes Abbey**. It's run by English Heritage and the National Trust now, but until its dissolution in 1539 housed a small group of Cistercian monks. The abbey became a place of worldwide pilgrimage after it was alleged that a phial of Christ's blood was held there. Benefiting from perhaps one of the greatest scams of the Middle Ages, the abbey grew rich off the proceeds from the religious tourists, and the phial turned out to be nothing but some coloured water! A group of beech trees on the hill above, close to Beckbury Camp, is known as **Cromwell's Clump**, believed to be the place where Thomas Cromwell, Henry VIII's commissioner, watched the dismantling. One wonders what was going through his mind as he looked upon the destruction of such a majestic building in such a glorious location. Atmospheric ruins, draped with ivy and fighting against large horse chestnut trees, are all that remain today in this peaceful spot.

Approaching Hailes Abbey from the northwest, you'll cross over a railway line, which carries the **Gloucestershire Warwickshire Steam Railway** (*01242 621405; www.gwsr.com*). The railway uses a part of the old Great Western Railway's main line from Birmingham to Cheltenham via Stratford-upon-Avon. Steam trains now run for ten miles between the village of **Toddington** and Cheltenham Racecourse, no mean feat given that the track and the stations have been restored entirely by volunteers and enthusiasts. The next part of the project is to open the line from Toddington through to Broadway. The current route from Toddington to Cheltenham passes through some pleasant Cotswold countryside with views of the surrounding hills and further afield to Tewkesbury Abbey and the Malverns on a clear day. Trains run from March to December with occasional special events and a meticulously restored Pullman carriage offers

Saturday evening dinners and Sunday lunches. There's also the opportunity to step on the footplate and learn how to drive the locomotive.

Food and drink

Elegant Excursions ☎07866 556719 🖥 www.elegantexcursions.net. Four-course Saturday evening dinner or 3-course Sunday lunch on board the Gloucestershire Warwickshire Railway, with 1st-class rail travel.

Hayles Fruit Farm Hailes GL54 5PB ☎01242 602123. Pick-your-own fruit sales plus good farm shop. Sales of their own apple juice – lots of varieties from which to select. Small campsite too.

⑪ Winchcombe

When I spoke to Carole Price, the visitor assistant in the tourist information centre at Winchcombe, she described the town as 'rustic'. She commented, 'Winchcombe is not pretty like Broadway but it has its own kind of prettiness as a self-contained, working town. You can buy everything and anything from the shops here.'

I agree with Carole. With over 60 shops crammed into the three main roads in the town centre, every one independent from those giant national retailers, Winchcombe is a pleasure to visit. Combine this with its architectural diversity and a good choice of places to eat – it abounds in special qualities .

Sat in the middle of a horseshoe of steep escarpments, the town has been a crossroads, a meeting place and a focal point for travellers, traders and religious pilgrims over hundreds of years. Its origins go back approximately 3,000 years although it wasn't until the 8th and 9th centuries that the town became really important when Offa, the Anglo-Saxon king of Mercia made it his capital. His successor, Kenulf, had a son, Kenelm who, as a young boy, was murdered at the request of his envious sister. Many miracles were then attributed to Kenelm as a result and the town became a place of pilgrimage; St Kenelm's Well on the escarpment to the east of Winchcombe, is believed to be one of the miracle locations and the water is reputed to have healing properties. Coupled with the pilgrims who began descending on nearby Hailes Abbey in later years, Winchcombe became a busy and prosperous place.

Now walkers with alternative motives descend on the town, with six long-distance paths converging on the High Street: the Cotswold, Warden's, Windrush, Salt, Wychavon, Gloucestershire and St Kenelm's Way. Winchcombe has promoted itself in recent years as a town for walkers and has been awarded 'Walkers are Welcome' status as having something special to offer those travelling on two feet. The town plays host to an annual walking festival.

But don't assume the beauty or the grandness of Chipping Campden or Broadway – Winchcombe doesn't sell designer sweaters. Take time to explore its streets and alleyways (not forgetting the renowned collection of gargoyles hanging from St Peter's Church); Vineyard Street, which descends down to a little bridge across the River Isbourne particularly deserves seeking out, as does Dents Terrace, a row of almhouses built by Emma Dent, the owner of Sudeley Castle in Victorian times and a relative of the present owners.

Vineyard Street also takes you to the entrance for Sudeley Castle and the start of the Windrush Way. From this you can take a quick detour to Spoonley Wood to see the stark remains of **Spoonley Villa** together with its small mosaic. It was one of three Roman villas situated around Winchcombe indicating the importance the Romans placed on the area prior to King Offa.

Sudeley Castle

When Henry VIII died in 1547 his widow, Catherine Parr, married Sir Thomas Seymour, the brother of Henry's earlier wife, Jane Seymour. They moved to Sudeley Castle (*01242 602308; www.sudeleycastle.co.uk; open Apr to Oct*), where Catherine gave birth to a daughter and died shortly after. She was buried in the chapel of St Mary within the castle grounds. Her husband was later executed for treason and, among other things, lascivious acts towards the young Queen Elizabeth.

Sudeley has had many other royal connections throughout its thousand-year history, including an attack by Parliamentary forces when Charles I used it as his headquarters during 1643. The battle scars are still evident on the castle walls today.

I love visiting Sudeley. The atmospheric ruins of the old banqueting hall with rampant plants escaping through the rooftop and the cannonball-shot window frames are inspirational. The knot garden with its design based upon a dress worn by Elizabeth I and the dilapidated ruins of the vast tithe barn, now filled with ornamental colour, the unusual octagonal tower and the Secret Garden, commissioned by the present owners to celebrate their marriage are all masterpieces. I love them all. But don't expect to see four-poster beds slept in by past royals or cosy kitchens from a bygone age. The interior of the castle is reserved for an exhibition about its history and relevant themes.

Both the Warden's Way and Windrush Way pass through the estate so you still catch a glimpse of the castle even if you're not visiting.

Food and drink

Winchcombe is a Fairtrade town with many of the shops and restaurants selling or serving Fairtrade goods.

Food Fanatics Delicatessen 11 North St ☎01242 604466. Notable deli selling tasty picnic goodies including homemade breads, pies and pastries, cheese, salads, etc plus plenty of regional foods.

Juri's, The Old Bakery Tea Shop High St ✆01242 602469 🖰 www.juris-tea room. co.uk. Cakes and dishes handmade on the premises using organic produce. Summer garden and winter fires.

Vegetable Garden 2 High St ✆01242 609500. Wide selection of locally sourced – within a 20-mile radius – seasonal produce and fruit juices.

Wine and Sausage at the **White Hart Inn** High St ✆01242 602359 🖰 www.wine andsausage.co.uk. Specialising in good-quality simple, unpretentious classic British food plus local ales, regional ciders and wines personally selected by the owner. Plenty of atmosphere in the 16th-century coaching inn. Wine shop in the pub too.

The Cotswolds' highest point – Cheltenham and its high commons

Leaving Winchcombe via the Cotswold Way heading south, the land becomes dramatically steeper quite quickly. For walkers it's a punishing climb although the legs have to appreciate that the higher you go, the better the views become. Within a few short yards, the hill ascends to almost 1,000 feet above sea level. Close to the top is **Belas Knap,** a very fine Neolithic long barrow, which, when excavated in the mid-19th century, was found to hold the remains of 31 people.

To the west of Winchcombe are first Langley Hill then **Nottingham Hill,** home to the Bugatti Owners' Club and the celebrated Prescott Hill Climb. And cutting a diagonal line across a map, splitting Winchcombe from **Cheltenham,** are Cleeve Hill and **Cleeve Common,** the highest point in the Cotswolds. These are serious hills now, the escarpment really making itself noticeable as it continues around the eastern and southern sides of Cheltenham to **Leckhampton Hill.**

⑫ Nottingham Hill

Nottingham Hill is less well known than its neighbour Cleeve Hill. Like a spur or growth, it juts out of the main line of the escarpment, its southern edge wrapping itself around **Woodmancote** a village split from **Bishop's Cleeve** by the Gloucestershire Warwickshire Railway. Both villages have attractive historical centres but the latter grew dramatically in the last century and is due to grow larger still over the next few years with several hundred new homes.

The southwest-facing side of Nottingham Hill holds the steepest slopes while the north side periodically hums to the tune of burning rubber on the hillside racetrack. The Bugatti Owners' Club owns the 60-acre Prescott Estate as their headquarters and built the **Prescott Hill Climb** (*www.prescott-hillclimb.com*). It's considered one of the world's greatest motor racing venues where visitors can watch as vintage, classic and modern racing cars and bikes make their way up the 1,127-yard course.

While the Hill Climb may be considered the prerogative solely of those who love the smell of engine oil, the countryside is scenic in the extreme and the events are invariably exciting. Anyone who enjoys a picnic in the fresh air and a wander through the woods will like it here. Perhaps one of the most exhilarating events is the Cotswold Trial, where truly ancient motor cars slide through the mud and the trees. Alternatively, you can take your own car up the hill-climb track under the tutelage of an instructor.

More ancient still is the fort on the top of the hill. It is the largest of all the Cotswold hillforts but not a lot is known about its origins, although there are some magnificent Bronze Age swords dug up while ploughing that are exhibited in the Cheltenham Museum and Art Gallery. The whole of the hilltop is fortified and you can walk – or ride a horse – straight across the middle of it on the Sabrina Way, the long-distance bridle route. From the top you get 360-degree views that reach as far as the north Cotswolds in one direction and across Cheltenham to Leckhampton Hill and the continuing Cotswold escarpment in the south.

If you don't fancy walking the full distance to the top, a very steep road leads to a car park close to the top near Longwood Farm.

⑬ Cleeve Common

Three masts close to the highest point on Cleeve Common make this hill an obvious beacon for miles. To the west are huge views over Cheltenham, with Prestbury Park, the home of the Cheltenham Gold Cup looking to be just a few furlongs away from the foot of the hill. Take a set of binoculars and you may have the best seat in the house on Gold Cup day. The Severn Vale and the Black Mountains in Wales are clearly evident too – at least on a day when the wind is not blowing the rain sideways. To the east are views over Winchcombe and Sudeley Castle; you realise from here just how undulating that particular area of the Cotswolds is.

With little shelter, the vast expanse of limestone grassland blows cold on a winter day, but summers here are divine. In geology terms this has some of the thickest sections of oolitic limestone in the country – there's evidence of numerous quarry workings on the slopes – and that creates an amazing display of wild flowers and grasses throughout the spring and summer months, with harebells, field scabious and perennial cornflowers making a regular appearance.

The Cotswold Way passes along the very western edge of the escarpment, precariously so in places. Yet, if you can stomach the sheer drops below that appear just west of the three masts, this is where some of the finest displays of wild flowers are. This area is known as the **Prestbury Hill Reserve**, owned by Butterfly Conservation. It has some of the best unimproved grassland on Cleeve Common, with steep, stony slopes rich with butterflies such as the chalkhill blue and Duke of Burgundy feeding off the flowers.

Plenty of other footpaths in addition to the Cotswold Way cross Cleeve Common to create any number of circular walks. And with the land undulating so much, the parts of the common change abruptly in character, from gorse bushes one minute, immaculate lawns of the Cleeve Hill Golf Club the next and then sheep-grazed pastures, making it a spectacular place to spend a few hours.

Numerous paths climb the common from the surrounding area but there are two car parks close to the top, one by the golf club off the Winchcombe to Cheltenham road and one by the masts, accessed along a narrow country lane from the village of Whittington. A weather forecast for the common is accessible from www.cleeve-weather.grg.org.uk, monitored by the weather station set up on top of the hill.

⑭ Leckhampton Hill

With the escarpment swinging round the eastern side of Cheltenham, Leckhampton Hill, far from facing west, faces north to enclose the town. The Leckhampton Hill Local Nature Reserve close to its summit incorporates Charlton Kings Common and creates an upturned horseshoe shape pushing towards the town. The area is designated as a Site of Special Scientific Interest (SSSI) for its diverse flora and fauna. Roe deer, badgers and woodmice coexist with adders, lizards and slow worms as well as Roman snails, rare butterflies and glow worms. Wild thyme, vetch and everlasting peas colour these rich grasslands too.

The Cotswold Way runs along this escarpment, through a strangely shattered landscape, variously quarried and thrust up by natural forces within the earth, and a good place for fossil browsing. Park at the southern tip of the reserve in the disused quarries and you can see the thick bands of limestone strata. Look out for the **Devil's Chimney** too, a limestone pinnacle that, legend says, is the chimney to the devil's underground home.

⑮ Cheltenham

According to tourist literature, Cheltenham is named a 'Centre for the Cotswolds'. Personally I find this title a little far-fetched, the town being neither central nor in the Cotswolds. But it is a useful gateway town for those travelling from the west and important for making travel connections.

To give it its official title, Cheltenham Spa, its heyday was in Regency times when bold, classical architecture and wide tree-lined avenues were the fashion. Parts of Cheltenham have lost their sparkle in a big way and are in serious need of an overhaul. The High Street and the Strand, for example, and the Regent Arcade, *the* place to shop in the 1980s, are now little more than locations for pound shops. My recent visits to Cheltenham town centre have been really quite disappointing.

To find the best of Cheltenham, you need to move away from the High Street to areas such as the **Montpellier Quarter** and the **Suffolks**, where small independent shops, boutiques and restaurants look more in keeping with the architecture. The Montpellier Gardens with their towering lime trees provide a pleasant place to sit when the sun is shining as do **Sandford Park**, full of ornamental water features and a large summer lido, and the **Imperial Gardens**. Full of colour, even if it is from bedding plants out of tune with the town's Regency heritage, the Imperial Gardens provide a home to a recently introduced statue of Gustav Holst, the classical composer who was born in the town.

For me the **Holst Birthplace Museum** (*www.holstmuseum.org.uk; open Tue to Sat, mid-Feb to mid-Oct*) is one of the most interesting places to visit in Cheltenham. Although the name of the street has changed from Pittville Terrace to Clarence Road, the museum is located in Holst's actual birthplace and childhood home. While his personal possessions will be of interest to those who enjoy his music, the house and period rooms also provide a good glimpse into the Victorian age, a time when Holst was growing up here. His working years were spent elsewhere but Holst composed considerably more than his most famous work, *The Planets*, and the museum provides plenty of opportunities to discover his other music.

Elsewhere in the town, particularly if you're looking for somewhere with free admission, **Cheltenham Museum and Art Gallery** (*www.cheltenham.artgallery.museum*) is a good find. It provides exhibitions and displays on local history and archaeology, international paintings plus an internationally significant collection from the Arts and Crafts Movement, especially of that originated in the Cotswolds. However, do check which galleries and collections are open before arriving as a massive building extension and refurbishment means that some areas of the museum will be closed for the foreseeable future.

One other leading attraction in the town is the **Pittville Park** and **Pump Room**. The town's largest ornamental park, full of specimen trees, lakes and walkways to 'promenade', is home to the town's most flamboyant Regency building, the Pittville Pump Room, full of pomp in its columns and domes. As a spa town and health resort, this was the focal point for social engagements, and the source of Cheltenham's spa water.

Food and drink

Brosh 8 Suffolk Parade 📞01242 227277 🖥 www.broshrestaurant.co.uk. Modern Middle Eastern restaurant in the Montpellier quarter. All the food served is made on the premises, from sourdough bread to ice creams and preserved lemons.

Maison Chaplais 52 Andover Rd 📞01242 570222 🖥 www.maisonchaplais.co.uk. Deli, bakery and café owned and run by the renowned Maurice Chaplais, artisanal master baker. Products are carefully selected to be of the finest quality and from companies with an ethical ethos.

Royal Oak Prestbury GL52 3DL 📞01242 522344 🖥 www.royal-oak-prestbury.co.uk. On the outskirts of town, close to the racecourse, Cotswold stone 'village' pub with cosy snug bar and dining room. Well-kept ales and imaginative menu.

Cheltenham festivals

Cheltenham was once *the* place to take the waters. Now it's the place to celebrate, wherever your interests lie. Folk, jazz, science, food, cricket, even ballroom dancing – they all have a festival dedicated to them in the town. But the two for which Cheltenham has truly made a name are literature and horseracing.

The **Cheltenham Literature Festival** (*www.cheltenhamfestivals.com*) has become one of the most important occasions in the literary calendar worldwide. It's when big-name authors sign copies of their latest tome, make speeches, read poetry and draw illustrations (or the illustrators do). Held every October, over 400 events usually take place, with plenty to interest children too.

Meanwhile, spring sees the area around Cheltenham explode with bookies and punters as millions of pounds are won or lost on the National Hunt Festival. The four days of utter madness culminate in the **Cheltenham Gold Cup**, one of the most prestigious horseraces in the world. With the backdrop of Cleeve Common and Nottingham Hill, Cheltenham Racecourse (*www.cheltenham.co.uk*) at Prestbury Park is considered one of the most scenic courses. Though be prepared for a serious drought in accommodation during the festival week. Rooms around this whole locale get booked up months if not years in advance.

East from Cheltenham, and around the A436

Heading east out of Cheltenham, cutting through the sharpest escarpments, you can deviate from the A436 and follow the little villages either side of the main road towards Bourton-on-the-Water. This itself is known beyond compare but some of the little villages *en route* are gems that barely make it onto a road map let alone the tourist brochures. There's no reasoning behind it. Villages like **Whittington** and **Salperton** are quite enchanting and the scenery in which they sit is quiet, out of the tourist's spotlight.

⑯ Whittington, Dowdeswell, Sevenhampton and Brockhampton

Leaving Cheltenham through the suburb of Charlton Kings, the A40 runs parallel with the River Chelt, which runs in the opposite direction towards the Severn. The river flows through the Dowdeswell Reservoir, a flood-defence mechanism to prevent Cheltenham from becoming awash. The reservoir and the massive dark green swathe of evergreen woodland on the steep slopes behind make up the **Dowdeswell Wood and Reservoir Nature Reserve**.

The reservoir sees many migrant birds overwinter on its waters and lays permanent home to other waterfowl including little grebes and great crested grebes. Though, perhaps of most significance to the reservoir is its population of common toads, for which the site is a major spawning ground. With many toads migrating to the reservoir and its surrounding watery grasslands from the south, special toad tunnels have been created underneath the A40. But many prefer to take the overland route; it's quite a sight to see dozens of toads crossing the road at any one time. Some clearly won't make it but there are 'warning of toads' signs that are put up each year for the migration season. The grasslands around meanwhile support orchids and cowslips and the pine woods behind allow roe and muntjac deer to roam freely. The areas of mixed deciduous woodlands give bluebells the chance to bloom in spring. Waymarked paths thread Dowdeswell Wood, but these are only accessible from the Cotswold Way, which skirts the western edge of the trees.

As the Cotswold Way crosses over the A40, it travels through another area of woodland owned by the Woodland Trust. **Lineover Wood** is totally different in character from Dowdeswell Wood. Sandwiched between the main A40 and A436 roads, the wood spreads up another steep escarpment and features some rare large-leaved limes. One of the limes dates back over a thousand years, making the reputedly second-oldest beech tree, also in the wood, a mere baby at 400 years old.

With wide tracks between the trees, the wood feels much more open than Dowdeswell. In addition to the Cotswold Way it has two waymarked circular walks of different lengths. If you fancy getting your hands dirty, the Woodland Trust is always looking for volunteers to help maintain this wood.

There is no parking at Dowdeswell Reservoir/Woods and only space for a couple of cars at Lineover Wood. My recommendation is to have a drink or a meal at the Reservoir Inn, within a few yards of the Cotswold Way, and park your car in their car park. The landlord is perfectly happy for customers to do this. Or you may be fortunate to catch a bus from Cheltenham and have a bus driver set you down outside the pub, but don't count on it.

The tiny stone villages of Lower and **Upper Dowdeswell** just east of Lineover Wood are worth a quick look if you're passing by; the parish of Upper Dowdeswell is one of the highest villages in the Cotswolds, while in the Chelt Valley the village of **Whittington** is a must-see location. There are only a few houses strung out along a country road just off the A40 but with the hills looming large behind, its location is pretty. The Elizabethan **Whittington Court** (*01242 820556; open 14.00 to 17.00, during Easter and late Aug*) is just about visible from the main road but take a visit if you get the chance. Very much a family home, it's open only for a couple of weeks a year in April and August, but the Elizabethan interiors (panelled rooms, ornamental mantels, large fireplaces and ranges) and the exterior architecture (including the remains of an old moat) have seen few alterations in 300 years.

You can take a footpath up and over the hill northeast from Whittington to the villages of, first, **Sevenhampton** then **Brockhampton**. These two really do nestle, tucked into a very tight and tiny river valley, the cottages clinging to the hills either side and, between them they have over 40 listed buildings.

Food and drink

Craven Arms Brockhampton ☎01242 820410. Cosy pub with a sofa-filled snug and restaurant serving classic pub food. Great views from pub garden.

Reservoir Inn London Rd, Charlton Kings GL54 4HG ☎01242 529671 ♻ www.reservoir-inn.co.uk. Roadside pub opposite Dowdeswell Reservoir and next to the Cotswold Way. Breakfasts and coffee served from 11.00. Lunches and evening meals.

⑰ Shipton, Salperton and nearby villages

Where the A40 from Cheltenham meets the A436 to Bourton-on-the-Water, two tiny villages appear, once again on a valley floor with wavy lines of hills either side. This time the valley is the River Coln (see page 121), at this point no more than a trickle emanating from numerous springs around the two Shipton villages. Based upon two separate manor houses, **Shipton Solers** (also known as Solars and Sollars) lies to the west of the larger **Shipton Oliffe**. The Gloucestershire Way runs through both.

Shipton Solers has an atmospheric 13th-century church, with little more than fields for company. Unbelievably, the tiny St Mary's was used as a cowshed in the 19th century. One wonders if the beasts learned anything from the fragments of medieval text that are painted on the walls. Now a Grade I listed building, the church is cared for by the Churches Conservation Trust.

Continue along towards Bourton-on-the-Water and you cross over the ancient Salt Way, which heading north takes you over Salter's Hill near Winchcombe and south towards Bibury and Lechlade. I enjoy approaching **Salperton** off the Salt Way through the Salperton Park Estate.

The park is surrounded by a very long and high Cotswold stone wall; having taken a course on drystone walling I could very much appreciate the effort that must have gone into its making. As you venture through the gates to the park and crossing the open parkland, the grand Georgian façade of Salperton Park is directly ahead of you with the tiny All Saints' Church to its side. The village, some distance away, is barely visible until you turn a corner and drop into a tiny valley. The village name is clearly derived from its association with the Salt Way but Salperton is also on an old wool trade route from Chipping Campden to the southern Cotswolds, and much of the agriculture around here was once sheep farming. The deeply rural landscape is free from hordes of visitors and the tree-studded parkland a joy to wander through. With desolate roads and farm tracks, it's perfect for a circular walk or longer trek across the fields.

The villages around here in these more open wolds – Salperton, **Notgrove**, **Hampnett**, **Turkdean** and **Cold Aston** are all inconspicuously stunning. Each one of these unassuming farming communities deserves a visit and between them they make a very worthwhile walk, with footpaths and bridleways connecting them. Take a picnic though – eateries to stop off at are scarce.

Food and drink

Plough Inn Cold Aston ✆01451 821459. Tiny 17th-century pub serving food and local brews. Plenty of character and period features – beams, flagstones and inglenook fireplace.

⑱ Bourton-on-the-Water

Yes, it's very picturesque; yes, the shallow River Windrush flowing through straddled by miniature bridges adds greatly to the character of this most visited of Cotswold honeypots; yes, the architecture, from humble rose-clad cottages to elegant Georgian 'town' houses-cum-hotels is certainly special. But, Bourton is not so idyllic when the coach parks fill up and the streets throng with tourists – and the grassy banks that border the river become a pleasure beach so cramped that the resident mallards' only respite is to stand on one leg on a protruding pebble in the river.

Unfortunately Bourton is a victim of its own quaintness and in becoming so has acquired something of a tacky reputation. The shops are firmly aimed at the souvenir-seeking day tripper. At least, that's the picture on a summer day. To appreciate Bourton at its best, visit midweek during the winter – especially if you can get there when it snows – or early spring before the masses from the towns have awoken once more to the village's charms. You may need to wrap up warm, but at least you'll find a seat on which to sit to admire the trees that dangle their shadows into the river and the smell of stale chips won't hang in the air.

Of all the attractions to visit in the village, the one I most recommend is the **Living Green Centre** in the High Street, a traditional Cotswold home (with shop attached), with a peaceful secret garden providing inspiration for modern eco-living. Alternatively, take one of the many footpaths leading from the centre of the village and get out of Bourton altogether – from the High Street, the Oxfordshire and the Diamond ways reach the **Greystones Farm Nature Reserve** on the edge of the village. Summer evenings reveal potential sightings of barn owls gliding over the flower-rich water meadows and farmland while spring heralds the arrival of traditional Cotswold wild flowers such as lady's smock and cowslips. Or several footpaths will take you through a series of both large and small lakes. Once gravel pits, these are now embedded in their surroundings, filled with fish and make a very pleasant focus for a short walk, with the wolds rising behind.

A game of two halves – football in the river

The Cotswolds are known for odd antics and Bourton adds to the reputation with an annual football match. Nothing strange about that, except that members of Bourton Rovers Football Club divide every August Bank Holiday Monday to play against one another in a far-from friendly civil-war clash in the River Windrush.

Events begin when the real-live ducks take a swift exit to make way for the plastic variety swimming their way to the winning line in the annual duck race. Then makeshift goals are erected between two bridges and everything turns slightly serious.

How serious the pre-match training is taken is anyone's guess – team tactics discussed around the bar. The crowd size is far greater than at an average Bourton Rovers weekend game; most spectators are wet before a ball is even kicked with the prelim warm-up moving on from passing round cans of beer to jogging on the spot, sidesteps and press-ups, each stamp of the foot placed with gusto to create the biggest splash.

When I went along to watch, the referee arrived with the ball and declared the rules, with the Greens at one end and Reds at the other. 'No getting wet and no splashing.' It was a bit late for that. With the first blow of the whistle, 30 minutes of combat ensued with a comical gravity and some dubious tackles. A drench-inducing throw-in from the 'sidelines' was clearly designed to create maximum distress for the spectators – much to their delight given the evident screams and squeals. Those who escaped the pre-match soaking were certainly wet-through now.

And then the ref produced a yellow card from his sock, sternly presenting it to a player for a harsh tackle. It mattered not. As the Greens hit the back of the net, goal celebrations involved diving into the watery depths and the crowd received a soaking once more.

The final score? Who really knows or cares? Everyone had a great time and as for anyone who went home dry, well, they didn't see the half of it.

Food and drink

Cotswold Brewing Company College Farm, Stow Rd GL54 2HN ☎01451 824488 www.cotswoldbrewingcompany.com. Recently developed microbrewery specifically creating British lager. The 3.8 Lager and the Premium Cotswold Lager are among the best I've tasted, rivalling the top European varieties. The Willis Arms sampling pub on the site of the rural brewery gives you the chance to try them all.
Dial House Hotel and Restaurant High Street ☎01451 822244 www.dialhousehotel.com. First-class dining plus afternoon teas served in a comfy sitting room or out in the garden. Excellent accommodation too.

5. THE THAMES TRIBUTARIES

It might seem bizarre to be referring to both the Cotswolds and the River Thames within the same sentence, as the Thames Valley, London and Thames Estuary seem a different world. But the source of the Thames bubbles out of the Cotswold hills and a large swathe of the Cotswolds lies north of the Thames, within which are five small river valleys – the Churn, Coln, Leach, Windrush and Evenlode – each a tributary of Britain's most famous river.

Not one of the rivers here is particularly well known, but the villages and towns that they flow through are more acclaimed, such as **Cirencester** on the Churn, or **Burford** on the Windrush or the village of **Bibury** on the Coln. Yet each river valley has very much its individual character.

Two counties fall into this chapter – Gloucestershire and a large chunk of Oxfordshire. Often referred to as the **Oxfordshire Cotswolds**, it is an area of the Cotswolds that is occasionally forgotten about when so much emphasis is placed upon the western escarpment.

Getting there and around

Trains

The **Cotswolds and Malverns Line** (*www.firstgreatwestern.co.uk*) runs direct from London Paddington via Oxford to Worcester. There are small stations at Hanborough, Combe, Finstock, Charlbury, Ascott-under-Wychwood, Shipton and Kingham, *en route* to Moreton-in-Marsh. Be aware that most of these stations are away from the villages so there may be a walk of some distance involved unless you take the Railbus (see *Buses*, below).

The Gloucestershire part of the locale is less well served by train. **First Great Western** travels from London Paddington to Gloucester with the most convenient stations for this locale at Swindon (though still some distance away) and Kemble, only four miles from Cirencester. Travelling from the north or southwest requires a change at Gloucester.

Buses

The **Cotswold Line Railbus** (*www.railbus.co.uk*) is a frequent and reliable service that connects the train stations of Charlbury and Kingham with the surrounding villages. There are four main routes: two from Charlbury to the Wychwoods and an off-peak, on-demand service to/from Leafield and Finstock; and two from Kingham station to Chipping Norton, Churchill and the Wychwoods midweek plus a very useful Sunday service from Chipping Norton and Kingham to the Wychwoods, Burford and Witney. Both stop off at other smaller villages on the way. All the buses have good access, with low-floor entrances and wheelchair space. **Stagecoach** operate regular buses from Oxford to Witney, Burford and Milton-

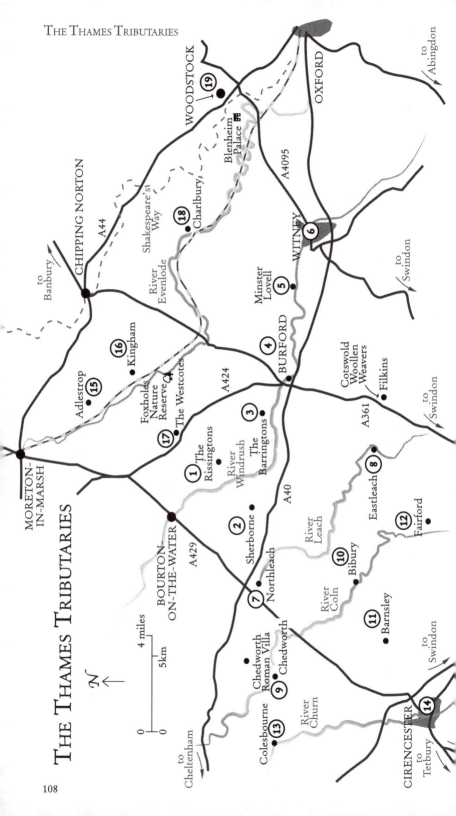

THE THAMES TRIBUTARIES

N

4 miles

5km

0

0

to Cheltenham

MORETON-IN-MARSH

CHIPPING NORTON

to Banbury

A44

Shakespeare's Way

WOODSTOCK

⑲

Blenheim Palace

Charlbury

⑱

River Evenlode

OXFORD

to Abingdon

Kingham

⑯

Adlestrop

⑮

Foxholes Nature Reserve

⑰

The Westcotes

A424

A4095

Minster Lovell

⑤

WITNEY

⑥

to Swindon

BURFORD

④

Cotswold Woollen Weavers

Filkins

A361

to Swindon

The Rissingtons

①

River Windrush

The Barringtons

③

②

Sherborne

A40

Eastleach

⑧

River Leach

Fairford

⑫

BOURTON-ON-THE-WATER

A429

⑩

Bibury

River Coln

Northleach

⑦

Barnsley

⑪

Chedworth Roman Villa

⑨

Chedworth

River Churn

Colesbourne

⑬

CIRENCESTER

⑭

to Tetbury

to Swindon

under-Wychwood plus Woodstock and Charlbury. A service by **Swanbrook** from Oxford to Northleach also serves villages and towns alongside the A40 including Burford and Witney.

Covering the west of the locale, **Pulham's Coaches** operate a reasonably frequent Monday to Friday service from Moreton-in-Marsh to Cirencester and Kemble station, stopping at Northleach and Bourton-on-the-Water (useful for the Rissingtons). Unfortunately buses in the Coln and Leach valleys are woefully inadequate and cannot be relied upon; in fact you'll be lucky to find one at all.

Cycling

As much of this area contains gentle, rolling hills, cycling is pleasurable without the strains of excessively steep slopes. Main roads such as the A40, A429 and A361 are fast and busy all day and generally to be avoided.

The Sustrans National Cycle Network **Route 48** travels from Northleach to Cirencester; however, none of it is traffic-free. **Route 57** runs from Oxford to Witney and then turns south towards Cricklade.

The **Windrush Valley Cycle Route** uses the quiet lanes of the National Cycle Network Route 47 to create a 17-mile wiggly cycle ride from Witney to Northleach through Burford and some pretty villages such as Minster Lovell and Great Barrington. The detailed waymarked route can be downloaded from www. oxfordshirecotswolds.org.

The Cotswolds Conservation Board has devised seven well-conceived circular cycle routes that all begin at **Kingham station**. The grade of each ride varies from easy to medium according to the route and the number of miles, but tours take in much of the countryside around the Oxfordshire Cotswolds. Each map can be downloaded from www.cotswoldsaonb.org.uk.

Bike hire/repair

Bourton Cycles Bourton Industrial Park, Bourton-on-the-Water GL54 2HQ
☎01451 8223232 www.bourtoncycles.co.uk. Cycle hire, sales and repairs. Five minutes from the centre of Bourton. Free delivery within 3 miles of Bourton and a minimal charge for delivery within 15 miles, useful for cycle trips along the Evenlode, Windrush and Leach valleys.

Ride 247 6 The Woolmarket, Cirencester GL7 2PA ☎01285 642247 www.ride-247.co.uk. On-site bicycle repair workshop. Bike sales too. Closed Sun and Mon.

Walking

Gentle hills make for gentle walking. The views may not be quite so dramatic as those obtained from the 'extreme' heights of the Cotswold escarpment, but there are views nevertheless obtained from the tops of hills such as **Habber Gallows Hill** near the Rissingtons. Woodland walks abound too here, in particular the great **Wychwood Forest**, one of the last-remaining centuries-old royal hunting forests, or **Foxholes**, an important nature reserve. But the main focus for walking in this chapter is a gentle stroll alongside small, bubbly and vivacious rivers.

Tourist information centres

Burford The Brewery, Sheep St ☎01993 823558.
Cotswolds AONB Visitor Centre The Old Prison, Northleach ☎01451 862000
🖰 www.cotswoldsaonb.org.uk.
Cirencester Corinium Museum, Park St ☎01285 654180.
Witney 3 Welch Way ☎01993 775802.
Woodstock Oxfordshire Museum, Park St ☎01993 813276.
🖰 www.oxfordshirecotswolds.com.

Accommodation

Abbey Home Farm Burford Rd, Cirencester GL7 5HF ☎01285 640441
🖰 www.theorganicfarmshop.co.uk. Several choices: a hideaway self-catering cottage; the romantic Hut by the Pond, secluded among trees and by the water's edge; the Shepherd's Hut, on the edge of the ancient Wiggold Wood, complete with log burner and outdoor fireplace; the summer Eco-Camp comprising 4 yurts accommodating 18 people as a group, with compost loos and a 'bucket shower'; a single 5-person yurt in a secret woodland glade; and 'Greenfield Campsite', a traffic-free campsite for tents.
Asthall Manor Burford OX18 4HW ☎01993 824319 🖰 www.onformsculpture.co.uk. The house where the famous Mitford children grew up (see page 115). A self-catering flat above the ballroom using the rooms where the Mitford children stayed; the names that they gave their bedrooms are still pinned above the doors. Murals by Nancy Mitford are in the main bedroom. Large kitchen. Sleeps 5.
Barnsley House Hotel Barnsley GL7 5EE ☎01285 740000 🖰 www.barnsleyhouse. com. The former home (and gardens) of celebrated garden designer Rosemary Verey. A gardening theme runs throughout the hotel, including the Potting Shed – a suite with private garden and terrace. The whole house has a special feel, as if you are stepping into a comforting country house rather than a hotel. Excellent food, with many of the fruit and vegetables grown in the hotel gardens.
Bruern Holiday Cottages Bruern OX7 6QA ☎01993 830415 🖰 www.bruern-holiday-cottages.co.uk. A collection of 12 luxurious self-catering cottages hidden on the estate of Bruern Abbey, an imposing country house built upon the foundations of a 12th-century Cistercian monastery. Admirable attention to detail in the décor, furnishings, facilities, gardens and management. Facilities and equipment excellent. Spa facilities listed as one of the top spas in the world.
The Mill and Old Swan Minster Lovell OX29 0RN ☎01993 774441 🖰 www.oldswan andminstermill.com. Two recently restored buildings in 60 acres of countryside next to the River Windrush and in an attractive village. Both traditional Cotswold-stone buildings are full of character, the Old Swan particularly so. Gastro-pub food at the Old Swan in relaxing surroundings. Fishing available on the Windrush for guests.

The Windrush Valley

The previous chapter on the High Cotswolds has several mentions of the River Windrush, the source of which is actually some way north of this locale, in the tiny village of Taddington. From there it flows southeast through the villages of Cutsdean, Temple Guiting, Kineton, Barton and Naunton as a racy little stream before being tamed by the formal stone-clad banks of Bourton-on-the-Water.

However, once past Bourton, the landscape seems to change as the river broadens. The Oxfordshire countryside through which the Windrush flows has different characteristics from those more northern parts – shallower slopes and a more open look to the water meadows and pastures.

After leaving Bourton, the Windrush doesn't flow through any settlement until it reaches the town of **Witney** some 16 miles or so downstream. Villages such as **Little** and **Great Rissington** wisely sit upon the hillsides of the valley some distance away from potential flooding. Others allow the river to skirt their boundary, such as **Little Barrington**, **Minster Lovell** and even the town of **Burford**, where the river crosses the bottom of the High Street.

From Witney the Windrush flows past Ducklington and Standlake before entering the River Thames at Newbridge, some way out of the Cotswolds AONB and 40 miles from its source.

① The Rissingtons and Clapton-on-the-Hill

A mile south of Bourton-on-the-Water, the Windrush joins the Dikler. The Dikler flows east of the Windrush first through the Slaughters and the Swells, before drifting through open meadows between Bourton and **Wyck Rissington**, a tiny scattered village that has escaped the ravages of modernisation and thoroughly deserves a detour. Approach it if you can from the east, down the hill from Wyck Beacon.

From the confluence of the two rivers, the Windrush wriggles for miles in a series of tight loops and squiggles. The valley floor is broad here, with your best sight of the river from New Bridge, on the road that links **Clapton-on-the-Hill** in the west with **Great Rissington** opposite. From the Bourton to Great Rissington road, as you climb the hill towards the village, look back for some vintage sunsets melting over the village of Clapton.

Little Rissington and **Great Rissington** are sat part way up the valley hillside. A bridleway links the two, with views over the river valley. **Upper Rissington** originated as a featureless collection of married quarters for officers attached to RAF Little Rissington. It once housed the famous Red Arrows flying display team. The connection with the Red Arrows is not forgotten in the tiny church of St Peters, which stands alone in open fields. A window in the church remembers the lives of those servicemen who served at the base.

Food and drink
Lamb Inn Great Rissington 📞 01451 820388 🖥 www.thelambinn.com. Rambling Cotswold stone country pub with large open-plan restaurant. Accommodation too. Great views from the pub garden over the valley.

② Farmington and Sherborne

The villages of Farmington and Sherborne might not seem to have much to do with the Windrush Valley, set as they are at right angles to the river. Farmington, furthest west, sits on top of a hill with valleys and escarpments all around unsure which way to turn.

Farmington frames a triangular village green and an octagonal-shaped pump house with stone columns to support its gabled roof. Built in 1874, the roof was 'presented' to the village in 1935 by the residents of Farmington in Connecticut, USA. A huge sycamore tree provides the shade for summer picnics. Close by, the village church has a clock that's very hard to tell the time by – it has no hands.

The village has been known for many years for the quality of the stone in the area, with Farmington stone a much sought-after product for making features such as fireplaces. More recently, the village has gained renown for the **Cotswold Ice Cream Company** (*01451 861425; www.cotswoldicecream.com*). The small on-farm ice-cream parlour, in its infancy, is basic but pleasant, especially given its location at Hill House Farm in an old Cotswold stone barn. Using organic milk from their own herd and other Fairtrade ingredients, the farm enterprise aims to get 'from cow to carton' in just one day. The farm also provides two short walks with notes explaining the basics of organic farming.

As the Sherborne Brook drops down the valley, it widens quite rapidly. As with so many villages around here, **Sherborne** is no exception to the Cotswold prettiness, though this time it is in linear fashion, stretching for a mile alongside Sherborne Brook. Roughly in line with the middle of the village is a weir on the brook that was used as a sheepwash in bygone days, a sign once again of the significance of the wool industry in these parts.

The focal point of the village is the very grand **Sherborne House** and the steeple of the village church next door. Sherborne House has now been turned into a series of private apartments but the surrounding 4,000-acre **Sherborne Estate**, which is owned by the National Trust, is accessible to the public. Cars may park by Ewepen Barn, just off the A40, from where the National Trust has drawn out a series of walks. My favourite waymarked route here (follow the purple arrows) is through the Pleasure Grounds, a traditional parkland setting with fine views of the house and church, before darting off into Ragged Copse. The path exits this wood in the village centre, where you look out onto the Windrush for a time, passing old stone cottages with long gardens brimming with vegetables, before returning to the parkland at the rear of Sherborne House and walking across fields to return to Ewepen Barn. At just over a couple of miles in length, it's a lovely walk to take with children.

③ Windrush and the Barringtons

Shortly after Sherborne Brook enters the Windrush, the river turns at right angles to flow east. On a hillside above, the village of **Windrush** clusters around a tiny green. The village was known for centuries as providing some of the best Cotswold stone, renowned for its longevity and used variously for St George's Chapel in Windsor in 1478 and for the Houses of Parliament in 1839. By 1911 though the quarries were defunct, and are now marked by grassy knolls.

The **Barringtons** have a similar history, created as estate villages built upon the wealth of quarrying and stonemasonry in the area. Their location by the river aided their fortunes – barges full of the prized stone were floated down the Windrush to the Thames and on to London. Barrington stone was used in prominent London landmarks such as St Paul's Cathedral and the Royal Hospital in Greenwich.

Little Barrington has a slightly warmer character than its more commanding northerly relation, the houses clustered together more on the southern slopes of the river valley while **Great Barrington** stretches out north of the river. Remains of the great estate are still evident: the mansion, Barrington Park, tucked into a vast deer park, seen just north of the village through iron gates.

⤫⤫⤫⤫⤫

Food and drink

Fox Inn Great Barrington ☎01451 844385 🖰 www.foxinnbarrington.com. A fine location on the banks of the River Windrush, with views across the river from the dining room and garden. Annual Foxstock folk and blues music festival held every August bank holiday weekend.

④ Burford

Doorways, windows, roofs, chimneys – every aspect of every building is unique in Burford. I love wandering up and down the High Street gazing at all the little nuances that make up the architecture and always manage to find something that I've not seen before. It may be the arch over an alleyway, a tiny gabled window in a rooftop or something as simple as an ornamental doorknocker.

There's rarely a moment when the High Street is not lined with cars, visitors attracted to the mix of shops, from cookware to wine-making equipment, garden ornaments to wood-burning stoves as well as old-fashioned sweet shops and gourmet delicatessens. The town takes on an extra quality in winter at dusk when the twinkling lights shine through the shop windows.

One of the oldest market towns in the Cotswolds, it focuses on the High Street that climbs from an ancient stone bridge over the river, on which stood Queen Elizabeth I when she first saw the town. The view over the water meadows is alluring enough, though the bridge isn't the most pedestrian-friendly, being something of a traffic bottleneck. To appreciate the river a little better, head to St John the Baptist

Church, with its churchyard by the water. It has historical importance as the place where three ringleaders from the political movement known as the Levellers were executed by Oliver Cromwell. Others faced their end in Oxford.

Like other Cotswold towns, Burford became known for its wool trade during the Middle Ages. While the northern slopes of the Windrush Valley across the river were perfect for sheep grazing, on Upton Down, southwest of the town, horses were the animal of choice, albeit a little later in history, when Burford Races were second only to Newmarket. Charles II came here with Nell Gwyn to watch the racing – the pair are thought to have had their trysts in the old Burford Priory, next to the river, and their son was named the Earl of Burford. The finest views are from the top of the High Street, south of the town where you can look over the rooftops towards the northern slopes.

Food and drink

As it grew, Burford became an important coaching centre during the 18th-century, with over 40 coaches a day trundling through the town. Its legacy is a vast number of places to eat and drink.

Foxbury Farm Shop Burford Rd, Brize Norton OX18 3NX ☎01993 867385 www.foxburyfarm.co.uk. Large farmshop with on-site butcher's selling meat from the farm alongside fresh fish, a deli counter and fruit and veg. You can eat in the **Good Food Barn** too. Children (and adults) are encouraged to ask questions about the farm and farming. There are seasonal events such as lambing and sunflower planting too.
Huffkins 98 High St. Large tea rooms and good bakery with plenty of savoury and sweet take-outs to create a picnic.
Lamb Inn Sheep St ☎01993 823155 www.cotswold-inns-hotels.co.uk. Comfy yet smart restaurant well known for the quality of its food. More informal dining in the bar, with all the distinguishing features expected of a Cotswold 'pub'. Accommodation too. Neighbouring **Bay Tree Hotel** is the more upmarket sister run by the same group. The Lamb Inn is my pick in the town.
Maison Blanc High St. It may be one of a chain, but it offers tasty patisserie and lunchtime snacks. Its location and huge plate-glass windows make it a great place from which to view the passing world.
Mrs Bumbles Delicatessen 31 Lower High St. At the bottom of the High Street; look out for the bright blue timberwork. Superb selection of produce.

⑤ Widford, Asthall, Swinbrook and Minster Lovell

Following the Windrush east, it passes between four villages, Widford and Swinbrook on the north bank, Asthall on the south side and old Minster Lovell back on the north bank once again. Each has its own crossing point.

Widford, a medieval village, barely exists any more. You can just make out the lumps and bumps of the old buildings in the ground but the church of St Oswald's still stands forlorn. A footpath crosses the old site; you're literally passing through what was once someone's kitchen or hallway. But medieval is not old enough for Widford, for the tiny church is built on the site of a Roman villa; a mosaic was uncovered during restoration work in 1904. Take a look too at the large pond between the river and the church – it provides an atmospheric photo opportunity.

Further east is **Swinbrook**. It was dominated by the Fettiplaces for 500 years until the family line died out in 1805; nothing remains of their manor house but you can just make out the remains of the Italian terraced garden on the hillside close to St Mary's Church. Here you'll find grandiose statements of their self-importance – their gigantic tombs. More recently, Swinbrook was the home of the six aristocratic Mitford sisters, famed for much of the 20th century for their social lives, scandals and political persuasions, as well as their skills as novelists and prolific letter writers. Their father had Swinbrook House built for the family in 1926, 1½ miles north of the village. Four of the sisters – Nancy, Unity, Pamela and Diana – are buried in the churchyard. Deborah, the youngest sister, became the Duchess of Devonshire, restoring Chatsworth House in Derbyshire. However, while the Mitford sisters' story may end in Swinbrook, it certainly doesn't begin there. Having lived at their grandfather's house at Batsford (see page 80) in Gloucestershire, they moved to Swinbrook's neighbouring village **Asthall** when their father inherited the Jacobean manor house there.

Asthall Manor now plays host to a biennial summer sculpture exhibition, On Form (*www.onformsculpture.co.uk*). Situated in the fully restored gardens, the exhibition focuses solely on contemporary stone sculpture, with the world's most distinguished sculptors exhibiting and providing talks.

But it's the village furthest east that I enjoy most. **Minster Lovell**, or strictly **Old Minster**, for modern Minster Lovell is on the south side of the river, does more than offer character. The old village is an inspirational place where the gentle river provides a backdrop to cricket on Wash Meadow, overlooked by a quintessentially English timber-framed pub  adorned with cascading flowers, a narrow street lined with the most appealing cottages and the spectacularly eerie ruins of a once grand manor house. **Minster Lovell Hall** tries to stand up next to St Kenelm's Church, on the banks of the Windrush, with ancient fishponds evident and an immaculately layered-stone dovecote close by. The hall was built by Lord William Lovell in the 1440s but dismantled, in part, by 1750. Now the remaining blackened walls whisper tales of yesteryear, arched doorways hang in mid-air, empty windows whistle with the wind and moss grips the foundations trodden down with 300 years of footsteps.

There's a fine walk across the water meadows too, where you can brush with the weeping willows and wild mint that mount the banks of the river and where if you're lucky you'll catch sight of a swooping barn owl. Either come back the way you came along the river or take the circular walk via Crawley, with a great pub to stop for a breather, and return across the northern meadows and Ladywell Pond.

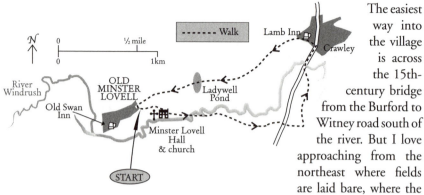

The easiest way into the village is across the 15th-century bridge from the Burford to Witney road south of the river. But I love approaching from the northeast where fields are laid bare, where the Romans once trod along the course of **Akeman Street** and the views across the water meadows to the ruined hall and church make it all the more mysterious, especially when a mist hangs through the trees.

Food and drink

Lamb Inn Crawley OX29 9TW ☎01993 703753 🖱www.thelambcrawley.com. Rustic chic pub with superb food.

Maytime Asthall OX18 4HW ☎01993 822068 🖱www.themaytime.com. Extensively refurbished following flooding in 2007 (which tells you how close to the river it is). Large bright and airy restaurant that very definitely looks like a restaurant rather than a dimly lit pub, though cosy bar area as well. Accommodation too.

Old Swan Inn Minster Lovell OX29 0RN ☎01993 774441 🖱www. oldswanandminstermill.com. In Old Minster on the north side of the river, overlooking Wash Meadow and the medieval bridge. Serves gastro-pub style food.

Swan Inn Swinbrook OX18 4DY ☎01993 823339 🖱www.theswanswinbrook.co.uk. A perfect location on the banks of the Windrush. The pub is owned by the last surviving Mitford sister, the Duchess of Devonshire; there are lots of photographs on the walls recollecting Mitford family life in a bygone age. Run by the same couple as the Kings Head Inn at Bledington, both pubs are renowned for their success as a result. A very good all-rounder.

⑥ Witney

While the Cotswolds were renowned for the 'wool trade', each town and village specialised in a specific aspect; in Barcheston it was tapestry, in the Stroud valleys, baize and broadcloth. In Witney, it was blankets. It doesn't sound like the most exciting of histories, but actually it was one that dominated Witney from the Iron Age until recently. Blanket-making mills dot the Windrush all the way from Barrington and as far west as Worsham. The town made a name for itself by about the 17th century when there were a significant number of weavers and, latterly, blankets made elsewhere could not be named as a 'Witney blanket', the title synonymous with quality.

Most of the mills around town have disappeared now, the land more valuable for housing development as Witney continues to grow and prosper. It's better known today for being the parliamentary seat of David Cameron for the last blanket-making company, Early's of Witney, closed down in 2002. We can blame the rise of the continental duvet and centrally heated houses for the demise of the humble blanket, which fell out of fashion.

While the familiar mill chimneys in Witney have gone (Worsham, Crawley Mill and New Mill west of the town still stand though used for other purposes), other buildings connected with the wool trade are apparent. Of most significance is the Blanket Hall at the north end of the long High Street, where the Witney Company (or Guild) of Blanket Weavers hung out. You can pick up a leaflet detailing the **Witney Wool and Blanket Trail,** a circular 2¾-mile walk, from the tourist information centre in Welch Way, or download one from www.oxfordshirecotswolds.org, under 'Witney'.

Witney thrives, and the population has grown significantly despite the closure of the old mills. The High Street is a pleasure to walk along, bustling and vibrant. Seek out in particular **Church Green**, at the top of the High Street and the Market Place, beyond the curious **Buttercross**, a traditional market cross that was given a roof under which traders could sell perishable goods. Sheep were once herded into pens here ready for sale and not all that long ago either – the middle of last century rather than the Middle Ages.

Sandwiched between two quiet roads lined with elegant merchant's houses all made of creamy stone, and punctuated with regularly spaced trees, Church Green is the perfect spot for a picnic, with the church of St Mary the Virgin standing at one end.

Just to the east of the church is the **Bishop's Palace**. It's a strange entrance, through two stone pillars and down a drive to the district council offices, but this is where Witney's prosperity began. Excavations, now sheltered under a large canopy, have revealed the once moated 12th-century manor house of the bishops of Winchester who ruled the town and farmed much of the surrounding area with sheep for the wool trade. Both King Henry II and King John stayed at the palace on their travels.

However, it's the river that really brought prosperity to Witney and you can get close to it at **Langel Common**, an island to the east of the town centre, about 200 yards from the High Street. Cross right over the two stretches of river and you'll come to **Cogges Manor Farm Museum** (*01993 772602*; *www.cogges.org.uk*) where historic life is played out. The first owner of Cogges Manor was clearly an important chap, for he's featured on the Bayeux Tapestry riding into battle at Hastings. The museum is a great one for children, with dozens of activities from bread-making to gardening.

Food and drink

Fleece Inn 11 Church Green ☎01993 892270 🖰 www.fleecewitney.co.uk. Sit outside this Georgian building overlooking Church Green and relax in one of the best locations in town. Great food and good beers (though not necessarily a local brew).

Real Eating Company Café 8–10 Market Sq. 'Real', freshly prepared food using local producers whenever possible. Sandwiches, smoothies, good-quality coffees and cakes. Eat in or take-out. Closed Sun.

The Leach Valley

The next valley west of the Windrush is that of the River Leach. Far shorter than the Windrush, its 18-mile stretch rises in the tiny hamlet of Hampnett (where the church has astonishingly rich Victorian stencilling, evoking the look medieval church interiors must have often had when freshly painted) and only passes through a handful of settlements, most of them taking their name from the river, before reaching the Thames just east of Lechlade close to Buscot Weir.

⑦ Northleach

Logically enough, the village of Northleach is in the north of the Leach Valley. Northleach is also the first settlement that the river flows through having sprung up from nearby Hampnett. You can follow the river between the two villages along a dog-leg of the Monarch's Way, which passes through Northleach.

The village grew up close to the Roman Fosse Way and when you're travelling along the Fosse, approaching the turning for Northleach, you soon get to appreciate the lie of the land and how steep and sudden the valley sides are for such a tiny river. At right angles to the Fosse, the village sprawls out along its High Street. A mix of tall 'town' houses with ruler-straight frontages mingle with dumpier cottages, squat to the ground, each one telling a tale of merchant or master versus minion.

Evoking its wool-rich days, in the Market Square stands a colourful sign marking the charter granted in 1227 allowing the village to hold an annual market. From then on its prosperity grew. Its wealth is obvious in the complexity and size of the **church of St Peter and St Paul**, a short stroll southwest of the Market Square. On approaching, the stained glass of the great east window, created only in 1963, reflects in such a way that it appears, like an optical illusion, to be falling out. From inside the building greens and blues change to reveal symbolism relevant to Northleach – woolsacks and shears, and the motif of a wool merchant. Memorials to dynastic wool merchant families fill the aisles and chapels. Many are remembered in memorial brasses buried into the floor and, in particular, a pair of tiny brasses pressed into the wall of a chapel.

The centre of Northleach is small and it doesn't take long to wander around. If you've arrived at the vast churchyard from the Market Place, exit via Church Walk and take a walk around School Hill, Town Row and College Row, which will deposit you back at the green, where you'll see one of Northleach's half-timbered buildings creeping into the fray of Cotswold stone.

Perhaps Northleach's most famous landmark is Keith Harding's **World of Mechanical Music** (*01451 860181; www.mechanicalmusic.co.uk; open daily*) Illustrating 40 years of dedication to restoring self-playing musical instruments, musical boxes and clocks, this is a living museum where the exhibits are likely to change every time you visit; many of them are for sale having been intricately restored by Keith Harding and his team of craftsmen. Once family entertainment, before radio and television, these self-playing exhibits 'perform' for visitors as you're guided round. And even if you're not visiting, you'll be able to hear the unique 'canned' sounds bursting through the windows.

My preference is **Escape to the Cotswolds!**, the visitor centre for the **AONB and Cotswolds Conservation Board** (*01451 862000; www.cotswoldsaonb. org.uk; open Apr to Oct, Wed to Sun 10.00 to 16.00*), alongside the Fosse Way. Housed in the Old Prison, you can find out more about the geology of the Cotswolds and what makes the area so unique.

Food and drink

Savage Selection & The Ox House Wine Bar The Ox House, Market Pl ☎01451 860896 🖰 www.savageselection.co.uk. A real find. All the wines sold are from vineyards too small for the multi-nationals and each one is hand-picked by the owners who visit the vineyards before choosing to sell the wine. Some great house red and white, and a wide price range from a fiver up. You can sip a glass of wine in the shop, or over a barrel or propped up at a bar made from wooden wine crates. There are tables and chairs too if you wish to be totally civilised, or venture out to the vine-covered courtyard at the back. Tapas-style nibbles plus teas, coffees and hot chocolate available too. If you don't fancy the wine on offer by the glass, select one of your own off the shelf, drink what you want there, and take the rest home with you.

Sherborne Arms Market Pl ☎01451 860241 🖰 www.sherbornearms.co.uk. Chips-and-peas menu but a useful pub if you're in Northleach at mealtimes. Otherwise it's a pleasant place to sit out in the Market Place for a drink, especially on a summer's evening.

⑧ The Eastleach villages and Filkins

After Northleach, the river flows steadily south, the valley sides remaining steep, through the village of Eastington then Lodge Park. Now owned by the National Trust, **Lodge Park** was a giant 17th-century playground. The lodge was never a residence but a grandstand built by John Dutton in 1634 to play out his passion for gambling and entertaining. He and his chums would stand on the balcony to watch the deer coursing, something that he'd never be allowed to get away with today.

The parkland is impressive, if windswept, and it's the only place that you can get close to the Leach before it reaches the Eastleach villages some miles further downstream. That is with one exception, at Sheep Bridge, where Akeman

Street, the old Roman road from St Albans in Hertfordshire to Cirencester, crosses the river.

A few meanders further downstream and the little river passes between two heavenly idyllic villages in the Cotswolds, **Eastleach Turville** on the west bank, and **Eastleach Martin** east of the river. Perhaps to distinguish the two, Eastleach Martin is also known locally as Bouthrop although you'll be hard-pressed to find it named so on any map. The pair are noble oases of peace, and the river running through makes them all the more uplifting. As two separate parishes, the villages have two churches, no more than a stone's throw apart; it's just the river that separates them. Of the two, the tiny church of St Michael and St Martin, with its churchyard bordering the river, is the more quietly striking. The priest and poet John Keble – the famous Keble College in Oxford was built in his memory – was a curate here in the early 19th century. The church is only used twice a year now, including Keble evensong in mid-May when the Keble choristers visit.

A footpath runs through the churchyard and along the riverbank, crossing over an old clapper bridge, known as Keble's Bridge, between the two villages. There's a wooden bench tucked by the riverside here and it is the most peaceful spot to sit among the wild flowers, listening to the dulcet tones of the river.

For an appealingly tranquil village-to-village walk along country lanes and riverside footpaths, take a circular amble from the Eastleaches via Fyfield to the equally idyllic village of **Southrop** where you can stop for something to eat at the Swan Inn. The valley here is at its quietest, and arguably most scenic; by spending even a rewarding hour or two, you can get to grips with the rural aspect of the Leach.

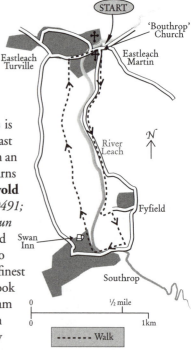

On the tiny Broadwell Brook, **Filkins** is also well known for having one of the last links to the region's wool trade. Housed in an old mill and a series of striking stone barns around a sunny courtyard, the **Cotswold Woollen Weavers** (*GL7 3JJ; 01367 860491; www.naturalbest.co.uk; open daily, Sun afternoons only*) are run by Richard and Jane Martin. Here wool is still woven into cloth – tweeds, flannels and saxonies (the finest merino wool); watch the processes and look at the design room upstairs where the team are working with some of the best-known fashion houses in the world. You can buy

Thyme at Southrop Food School

Rejuvenating the Southrop Manor Estate from its crumbling existence has included developing **Thyme at Southrop** (*Southrop Manor, Southrop GL7 3NX; 01367 850174; www.thymeatsouthrop.co.uk*). It's called a food school rather than a cookery school because it goes further than simply cooking, instead embracing the Cotswold countryside and looking at the whole story of food from source to production in addition to the enjoyment of serving, eating and drinking.

One part of the school's culinary philosophy is to encourage course leaders, chefs and class participants to work with fresh, seasonal and often locally distinct and traditional produce from small farms and artisans. An abundance of wild food can be found growing on and surrounding the estate, including wild garlic, elderflower, watercress and mushrooms and these are used too when appropriate. A love of the land and growing your own food is also instilled and some courses include forgotten skills such as butter making. Most classes last for one day with the option of demonstrations, tastings and hands-on, skills-based cooking classes.

the pre-spun wool on spools if you like, but the temptation is in the shop downstairs – one room selling stylish clothes at pounds less than designer prices and the other with items for the home – fabulous rugs and blankets, cushion covers and throws, their tactile texture calling out from the shelves to be felt. A Cotswold tweed has been developed too, using colours that evoke memories of the landscape. There is also a café serving light lunches and homemade cakes and a small museum (free to enter) dedicated to textiles in the Cotswolds.

Food and drink

Swan Inn Southrop GL7 3NU ☎ 01367 850205 🌐 www.theswanatsouthrop.co.uk. Attractive-looking pub with plenty of atmosphere but also a winner of plenty of awards for their food. Using local produce from neighbouring villages and estates, including lamb from Southrop. Accommodation too on the Southrop Manor Estate, of which the Swan is a part.

The Coln Valley

The River Coln rises at Brockhampton, east of Cheltenham. Like the Windrush, its character changes once it leaves the steep escarpments behind and begins to run through a gentler territory. It too sweeps in a south to southeasterly direction, discharging its waters into the Thames west of Lechlade.

The countryside through which it flows is the most rural of the five northern tributaries, and some of the least visited; the river never gets much wider than a few feet, the shallow banks and adjacent hay meadows teeming with wildlife.

⑨ Withington, Chedworth and Yanworth

Well, those Romans really knew a beautiful spot when they saw one, building one of their most important villas at Chedworth. They spent decades exploring this valley; this small part of the Coln Valley deserves at least 24 hours of your time.

Once crossed by the main Oxford to Cheltenham road, the first village of any size that the Coln passes through is **Withington**. The land here once again twists and turns, each fold in the earth's surface never wishing to conform to uniformity. Hence the village is squeezed between two steep ridges, the north wind funnelling down the valley; this is one of the highest parts of the Cotswolds and even on the valley floor, you're over 500 feet above sea level. The village is dissected by an old disused railway line, the remnants of which are evident but a large lake through which the Coln flows has a few short yards of a footpath to wander along, just to the west of the dismantled line.

While the village of **Chedworth** is wedged even tighter into a mile-long bottleneck of a valley, on a tributary of the Coln, Chedworth Roman Villa sits a mile north of the village. You can walk between the two using either the Macmillan or the Monarch's Way, and in doing so you'll pass through **Chedworth Woods**. This vast expanse of ancient woodland, joined in the west by Withington Woods, grows on a steep slope of the Coln Valley with masses of wildlife under the mostly beech canopy, including bluebells, primroses, wild strawberries, wild garlic, tawny owls, mammals, rare butterflies, adders and Roman snails. The Chedworth Nature Reserve falls within the woods, particularly in the area around the disused railway where you can see geological masterpieces and a tufa spring.

Chedworth Roman villa (*01242 890256; www.nationaltrust.org.uk; open Mar to Nov, closed Mon except bank holidays*) is tucked on the edge of the woods, on a bank above the river. I absolutely love this place, not just for its location but also for the chance of understanding how the Romans – or at least some of them – lived. The layout of the villa is all there, with two bathhouses, hypocausts and some fabulous mosaics too, worthy of a visit simply to see the artwork and intricate patterns. Owned by the National Trust, it's a great place to take children with lots of Roman-themed activities.

Chedworth is by no means a conventional Roman villa. It's unexpectedly large and has its own water shrine, or nymphaeum, which was much-revered during the Romans' residency. Uncovered in the 19th century, the whole place is an archaeological time-warp – it's not how they perform archaeological digs nowadays. Quaint little pitched roofs protect the shin-high remains of the villa walls, old barn-like structures sheltering the mosaics and an over-conspicuous Victorian villa sits in the middle of it all housing a museum of once buried 'treasure', very much in the spirit of a Victorian archaeologist's collection. Perhaps the most interesting aspects are the hypocausts with the mosaic floors peeled back in places to reveal this underfloor heating system, appearing like stone statues or a giant draughts board.

I would urge anyone not simply to drive straight to the villa, spend an hour there, then leave without exploring this beautiful section of the Coln. Take the time to picnic in the woods (or among the Roman ruins), and wander the quiet country lanes and the valley's footpaths through open, yet sheltered meadows. If you are driving to the villa, the National Trust signposted route takes you through the village of Yanworth. On your return from the villa, turn right just before the village and head down the valley's northern embankment, crossing the river at Yanworth Mill and exiting the valley at Fossebridge to see an alternative view of the valley that shouldn't be missed.

⑩ Fossebridge to Bibury

Running beneath the Fosse Way at **Fossebridge**, the next section of the Coln Valley gives a good opportunity to get out on foot or to explore the lanes by bike, making the most of the two roads that run either side of the Coln to create a circular route between Fossebridge and Bibury. Off the Fosse Way, the first village you arrive at is **Coln St Dennis**, with its riverside church, where the strangely shaped tower has the look of a set of children's building blocks, the blocks getting gradually smaller as they rise. The road then divides, running either side of the river, one heading to **Calcot**, on a tiny ridge above, the other to **Coln Rogers** and its Saxon church. Two footpaths join these two villages, one crossing the river to meet up with the Coln St Dennis to Coln Rogers road, the other running along the eastern riverbank.

At the village of **Ablington**, the river is wide enough to need two double-arched bridges side by side, one carrying road traffic, the other for feet. There's access to the river here, its crystal waters reflecting a village that seems to have avoided the inescapable pace of modern life. This is your last chance to savour quiet solitude by the Coln before the onslaught of coaches and day trippers at Bibury.

The 19th-century craftsman William Morris once said that **Bibury** was the most beautiful village in England. I wonder if he would feel the same way now, as coach loads of tourists spill out across the village before 09.00. Generally speaking, they've come to snap a quick shot of the much-photographed **Arlington Row** before climbing back on board. The row originated as a 14th-century wool store and was later converted into a group of weavers' cottages. The American businessman Henry Ford (founder of the Ford Motor Company) tried to buy the entire row with the idea of shipping all the buildings to America where he would rebuild them in his history theme park; fortunately he was unable to, but he did get his hands on an old house in Chedworth which now stands, stone for stone, in Michigan.

You can reach Arlington Row, the epitome of Cotswold-esque architecture, by crossing the Rack Isle – a low-lying meadow in between the dried-up Arlington Mill Stream and the River Coln. This tranquil, verdant meadow, now used to encourage rare water voles, frogs and kingfishers to habituate the area, was once used to stretch out the drying cloth, hence its name.

On the opposite side of Rack Isle you can't help but notice the vast buttresses holding up the walls of the tall Arlington Mill, once home to the famous garden designer Rosemary Verey and her family before they moved to nearby Barnsley. Built in the 17th century the mill was originally used for fulling (or degreasing) cloth that had been produced in Arlington Row.

There is more to Bibury than Arlington Row though. If you've approached Bibury and Arlington from Ablington, following the River Coln, you'll have noticed a series of lakes as you enter the villages, with the famous, ivy-clad Swan Hotel opposite. These are the lakes of **Bibury Trout Farm** (*www.bibury troutfarm.co.uk*). The gift shop and children's play area make it rather commercial but you can still fish to catch your own supper or learn about the hatchery where up to six million brown and rainbow trout ova are spawned each year.

On days when the coach fumes have long risen into the air, it's extremely pleasant to pass the time of day by the banks of the Coln in Bibury. The river is generally completely clear and it doesn't take long to discover a couple of brown trout sunning themselves in the shiny waters before shoals appear. Hunt too for the stone head of a Cotswold sheep hanging off the Saxon church; its give-away curly forelock is clear to see.

⟩⟩⟩⟩⟨⟨⟨⟨

Food and drink

Inn at Fossebridge Fossebridge GL54 3JS ☎01285 720721
www.fossebridgeinn.co.uk. Highly recommended bar, restaurant and hotel adjacent to the Fosse Way with a riverside garden on the banks of the Coln. The bar and restaurant have all the rustic features expected of a Cotswolds pub and the food is superb. Breakfasts for non-residents are served as well as cream teas. Accommodation too.

Swan Hotel Bibury GL7 5NW ☎01285 740695 www.cotswold-inns-hotels.co.uk. Renowned hotel overlooking the River Coln. Café Swan is the place for lunches and afternoon tea, though at around £8 for a sandwich you may prefer to nibble on a picnic by the river. The Gallery Restaurant is for fine dining with a dress code in place.

⑪ Barnsley

The village of Barnsley sits midway between Arlington and Cirencester on a wold four miles from both the River Coln and the next river along, the River Churn. Here lived Rosemary Verey OBE, the internationally acclaimed garden designer and writer who drew up, among others, gardens for the Prince of Wales and Sir Elton John. Her own garden at the family home, **Barnsley House**, was her most famous design, attracting up to 30,000 visitors a year up until her death in 2001. Today, the gardens remain open to the public, but Barnsley House itself is now a luxurious hotel (see page 126). The head gardener who worked under Rosemary Verey, Richard Gatenby, remains in the same position today.

Barnsley House is approached, like much of the village, from the Cirencester to Bibury road that runs through. But Richard Gatenby had asked me if I thought the back of the house looked more like the front of a house. Far from some puzzling riddle, he pointed out that the main Cirencester to Oxford road in the 16th century had actually been the little track, known as Clacton's Lane, at the rear of the hotel. It was one of the most important trade routes for transporting wool and a drover's road, taking cattle from Wales to market in London.

Wander down this lane and you'll come across another garden, the antithesis of the country glamour of the Barnsley House Hotel. This is **Barnsley Herb Garden** (*01285 851457; www.herbsforhealing.net; garden and nursery open Apr to mid-Sep on Wed and Fri plus other occasional days, including the Barnsley Garden Festival; camping and yurts available in the field*), run by Rosemary Verey's daughter, Davina Wynne-Jones. However different it may be, this secluded spot is equally special. With no particular intention of opening a nursery, Davina created her garden in 2005, using only plants that have a healing or therapeutic purpose. Herbs feature prolifically, her knowledge of the plants gained from growing up at Barnsley House and discussions with her mother. Naturally, owing to the kinds of plants in the garden, wildlife is abundant too, with bees and butterflies darting from one border to another. Davina's latest addition is a giant scrying bowl, made from thin layers of Cotswold stone, housed in a bony framework of contorted branches.

'From the garden, the rest of the business grew,' Davina said. 'I was planting herbs in rows so I began to develop the nursery, selling plants that are found in my garden. Now I concentrate on generating knowledge about these plants through workshops and courses run from my workshop, an old recycled barn.'

Courses include practical workshops on making herbal oils, ointments and creams, making tinctures, cordials and teas, flower essences or soap all using herbs.

⑫ River's end – Coln St Aldwyns and Fairford

From Bibury both the River Coln and the ancient Salt Way head towards a trio of villages, Coln St Aldwyns, Hatherop and Quenington. Of the three, **Coln St Aldwyns** is my favourite, tucked as it is into a loop in the river with the old lichen-covered cottages gathered together around a tiny village green.

There's a footpath from Quenington to walk south by the river and across water meadows for approximately one mile; thereafter the river flows through Fairford Park, a 4,200-acre estate. Though private, the estate is owned by the Ernest Cook Trust (Ernest Cook being the grandson of Thomas Cook, the very first tour operator), whose aims lie in the conservation and management of the countryside and providing educational opportunities for people to learn about the outdoors. A permissive footpath across the estate joins up with the aforementioned public footpath from Quenington allowing you to walk along further stretches of the river and the little Pitcham Brook; a route map can be downloaded from the website: www.ernestcooktrust.org.uk. The trust also has access to two miles of river frontage, including the area known as Broad Water, where the river widens before reaching the town of Fairford. Permits are available to fish for the brown trout that lurk in the shadows.

The permissive footpath onto the Fairford Park Estate is also accessible from the little town of **Fairford**, at the top of the High Street, close to where the river ducks under two very pretty bridges. Though a typically 'Cotswold town', Fairford has different connotations for me.

I recently came across an old diary of mine and in its pages discovered the entry for 27 March 2003. It read, 'Early this morning I looked to a quiet noise in the sky and saw the ominous shape of a B52 bomber returning to Fairford. Minutes later

The making of a hotel garden

I'm a little bit starstruck just at the mention of Rosemary Verey's name. While paparazzi photographers are aiming their long lenses at Liz Hurley's farm over the fields, I'm more inclined to sit back in the comfortable Gardener's Library of the Barnsley House Hotel and browse through a selection of Rosemary Verey's books as the framed garden plans on the wall peer down at me. With row upon row of inspirational garden design books filling the shelves of what was once her husband's study, I believe that here, of all places, is the place to be inspired.

That is until I stepped out into the garden to meet the head gardener of the hotel, Richard Gatenby. Far from the brusque, ruddy-cheeked estate manager that I had imagined, Richard, who has been gardening at the property for 11 years, is a gentle plantsman as enthusiastic about gardening as his previous boss. As we stood on the back lawn gazing at the oh-so-perfectly proportioned house, I envisaged him discussing, with his broad Yorkshire accent, plans for the garden with his former employer, Rosemary Verey, or Mrs Verey as he politely still refers to her.

Without appearing in the slightest bit derogatory, Richard reminded me that Mrs Verey was not, at least to begin with, a professional gardener but an amateur when she came to Barnsley House in 1952 with her husband David, an architectural historian who wrote many books on the subject. Richard said, 'At first there was no great design for the garden. Mrs Verey simply loved and collected plants, which got squashed and crammed into borders wherever they would fit. The garden today is much as she left it, a collection of mixed borders. It's certainly not a botanic garden, rather an elderly lady's rectory-style garden that appeals to many.'

As we drift past the borders of fire-red Crocosmia, everlasting sweet peas and the shiny pennies of the honesty seedheads, Richard continues, 'It's an aspirational garden because anyone who visits feels that they can aspire to something that they've seen here. No-one ever walks away thinking, 'we can't do that'. They can plant up a little piece of Barnsley in their own garden, whether they take away ideas for a tiny corner or a design for a topiary bush.'

There are glimmers of symmetry around the small follies and architectural features acquired by her husband on his travels, such as the Temple brought from nearby Fairford Park. Said Richard, 'Mrs Verey loved the clash of formality with informality.

we listened to the 7am news of further "shock and awe" in Baghdad overnight and yes, the timing would be spot on. It was especially eerie on such a gentle, sunny and quiet early spring morning to hear the sound of the aeroplane – it had a beautiful earthy sound – and yet to know exactly where it had been and what it had been doing the previous night. Did it sound so beautiful to those living in Baghdad?'

For many Fairford means the RAF airbase where USAF troops have been stationed on occasions, in particular during the Iraq War, and also as the location for one of the world's largest annual air displays, the Royal International Air Tattoo. And yet this quiet town is the antithesis of all this show of strength

So herbs would be planted within box bushes. And if something trailed over a path, she wouldn't say that it needed trimming back, rather that visitors would simply have to walk around it.'

According to Richard it is her Laburnum Walk that most visitors want to see, with unruly borders either side, filled up with anything self-seeding. 'We rely on any mechanism to keep the borders full', said Richard. 'Musk mallows, penstemons, night scented stocks, nicotiana, perennial shrubs. Anything that will reproduce in abandon.' But for me, it was Mrs Verey's potager that I was eager to see, as she had brought the whole potager way of thinking back into English gardening. A rush of silvery lavender drew the eye to a Mr McGregor kind of gate and inside, runner beans spun their way around arches while wasps devoured fallen fruit. From every point in the garden, there was a view – a tiny statue, an apple tree, a glimpse of a chimney.

I asked Richard if the idea is to keep the garden exactly as it was when Mrs Verey lived at Barnsley House. 'The garden has Grade II listed status so there are certain aspects that we cannot touch', Richard replied. 'But there are areas that we intend to renovate and restore without being rigid to the past. Mrs Verey's book about Barnsley, *The Making of a Garden*, included ideas and I still refer to it. So, for example, in the Broad Border, facing the house, I want to try something new from ideas that she had for the garden but didn't have time to implement. I don't want the garden to become too user-friendly. We need to maintain the feel and charm that Mrs Verey created. And we will continue to plant as she did, where timing is more important than horticultural excellence to maintain all-year-round interest in the garden.'

Richard ended, 'The biggest change in this garden is that it has gone from a house to a hotel. That's all.'

Keen to maintain the gardening link and utilise the assets, the Barnsley House Hotel offers many gardening events, from tours of the grounds with Richard Gatenby, gardening workshops and courses on garden photography and painting, as well as lunches in the Potager Restaurant eating produce grown in the garden. The gardens are also open to the public daily. Admission includes tea and biscuits.

and force, the only strength shown in the town from the wool trade wealth invested in the 15th-century church of St Mary the Virgin. It dominates the very attractive High Street, with its giant walnut tree at the entrance. Its near-complete set of medieval stained-glass windows are world famous, depicting scenes from the life of Christ, culminating in the Last Judgement. I also like the fact that the bell ropes hang right in the centre of the church where the bellringing is clear for all to see. Don't forget to pay your respects at the memorial for Tiddles, the church cat, in the churchyard. For the best view of the church, wander along the footpath to the west of the river.

Northwest of the High Street, close to the river, are the oxpens, ancient stalls where cattle once fed after a hard day's ploughing. They've been fully restored and the sunny courtyard is the perfect place for a picnic. You can also begin a riverside walk from here – via Back Lane. Following the river until it reaches the Cotswold Water Park (see page 164) it returns alongside a lake and back into the East End of town towards the Walnut Tree Field where the annual Fairford Festival takes place every June.

Food and drink

A standard outdoor market together with a country market selling homemade cakes and jams is held every Wednesday. A Christmas market is then held in December.

Bull Hotel Market Pl ☎01285 712535 🖥 www.thebullhotelfairford.co.uk. Informal lunches and dinners served in the bar. Full selection of ales from Arkells Brewery in nearby Swindon. Packed lunches made to order. Trout-fishing breaks available – the hotel owns 1½ miles of Coln riverbank.

Deli Allium Market Place ☎01285 711111 🖥 www.alliumfood.co.uk. Head chef from the Restaurant Allium has created a comprehensive range of Allium own products including artisan breads, soups, chutneys, cured meats and desserts.

Restaurant Allium London St ☎01285 712200 🖥 www.alliumfood.co.uk. Imaginative contemporary menu; not the cheapest (3-course lunch £25; dinner £42).

The Churn Valley

The River Churn rises close to the tiny village of Seven Springs near Cheltenham and, despite it being a tributary of the Thames, is actually longer from its source to confluence than the Thames. It is therefore argued that this theoretically should be the head of the Thames.

Overall the Churn, which is the Thames's most western tributary, is just 16 miles long before its confluence near Cricklade where, bizarrely, it gets smaller as it approaches. It passes through a series of lakes at the impressive Cowley Manor Hotel before being channelled between hills and wooded slopes taken up by, first **Colesbourne Park** and then Rendcomb Park.

North Cerney is its last village stop-off before reaching the historic town of **Cirencester**. From there, it's just a few more twists and turns until it passes through the Cotswold Water Park (see page 164) before entering the Thames.

⑬ Colesbourne and North Cerney

The tiny village of **Colesbourne** appears on a bend in the river as the Churn turns south. The village is entirely consumed by **Colesbourne Park** (*01242 870264; www.colesbournegardens.org.uk; open selected weekends Feb/Mar*), a 2,500-acre estate with significant acreages of woodland and home of the Lord Lieutenant for Gloucestershire. The park is renowned for its snowdrop collection, with over 200 varieties of the Galunthus bulbs planted throughout. Visitors come from far and wide to wander through the gardens during the **Snowdrop Weekends** in February, when they can see the church, waterfall, the woodland paths and huge banks of snowdrops fluttering in the breeze. There are lakeside walks too, the bluest of blue waters reflecting further banks of little white stars.

Elsewhere on the estate is the purpose-built **Foodworks Cookery School** (*01242 870538; www.foodworkscookeryschool.co.uk*), where some of the country's finest chefs take the classes and students can learn how to make the likes of fresh pasta or desserts.

From Colesbourne the Churn slides on through the valley and Rendcomb Park, before entering the village of **North Cerney**. Much of the village stretches up the eastern hillside while, unfortunately separated by the A435, the western riverbank includes the village's Norman church with its unusual saddleback tower and **Cerney House Gardens** (*01285 831205; www.cerneygardens.com; open Jan to July, closed Mon, Thu, Sat*), a classic Victorian Cotswold garden, secret, romantic and full of old-fashioned everything. It houses the National Collection of tradescantia in addition to an annual Tulip Festival.

Food and drink

Bathurst Arms North Cerney ☎01285 831281 🖥 www.bathurstarms.com. Warm and friendly pub with riverside garden. Regularly featured in the *Good Pub Guide*. Fabulous food, sourced from the local area including Cerney goat's cheese and meat from nearby farms. Accommodation.

Colesbourne Inn Colesbourne ☎01242 870376 🖥 www.thecolesbourneinn.co.uk. Old coaching inn with 2-acre gardens and rural views. Plenty of cosy corners, snugs and fireside seats. Accommodation.

⑭ Cirencester

Here thousands of schoolchildren 'doing the Romans' are brought every year to gain a better understanding of past lives. Understandably so, given that Corinium, to use its Roman name, was Roman Britain's second-largest city. Virtually nothing of the Roman town is now apparent, the central street plan dating from medieval

A Roman time walk

While in Cirencester I immersed myself in the history of the town through a living history walking tour. Cherry Hubbard, who was taught her living history role by the historian Ruth Goodman (known for her TV work such as *Edwardian Farm*), dresses in Roman clothes to guide you on a personalised tour of the town. Said Cherry, 'I don't like to call it a costume. These are my clothes. They are handmade using fully authentic materials and exactly the kinds of tunic and tube dress with pennanular brooches that Roman ladies of a certain standing would have worn.' While the walk lasts for 1½ hours, there's plenty of sitting down too as Cherry tells you some story of the town, drawing you into a Roman world, as you smell the potions and spices and feel the textiles of the clothes they would have worn. Every few minutes some other Roman artefact is pulled from her basket as the stories unfold and you interact with the town. She'll tell you where the old pavement of Ermin Way sits, where the oyster beds were, their jewels exported to Rome, and how the amphitheatre was used for weapons training and inter-town competitions. 'However, as social history experiences, these walks are more about the people of Cirencester rather than the places,' commented Cherry, 'how, for example, many 'Romans' that lived in Britain had no connection with Rome at all.'

Other periods of history creep in too, such as the Jacobean mansion house that once stood in the **Abbey Grounds**, a fine place for a picnic and one of the few places where you can see both the River Churn and the last remaining section of Roman wall. Cherry also takes Tudor Walks bringing the Market Place and the ancient streets to life. Her **Cirencester History Walks** (*07547 403057*) are fantastic value at just a few pounds, and suitable for both adults and children, but they must be booked in advance. Thoroughly recommended.

times, although the **Roman Amphitheatre**, known locally as the Bull Ring, still exists, a grassy arena ten minutes-walk from the Market Place (just on the south side of the bypass): there's free access to the site. Externally, perhaps the best evidence is in the form of the roads on the outskirts that show why Cirencester was so important to the Romans, as a crossing point of several major roads – the White Way, bringing salt from Droitwich, the Fosse Way from Exeter to Lincoln, Akeman Street from St Albans and the Ermin Way from Gloucester to Silchester. Most of the remains of Roman Cirencester have been brought indoors forming one of the best Roman museums in Britain. The **Corinium Museum** (*01285 655611; coriniummuseum.cotswold.gov.uk; open daily*) is full of life as well as thousands of artefacts and some vividly recreated Roman interiors, but for me, the highlight is the set of mosaics that were uncovered and carefully pieced back together. If you're in town when the museum is closed, you can still catch a glimpse of one of the mosaics through the glass-plated front doors; it will certainly whet your appetite to return. Numerous events and activities take place throughout the year for both adults and children.

Today Cirencester centres around the vast parish church with its unique entrance through the medieval town hall, in the Market Place. This town was also a major player in the medieval wool trade, as evidenced by the rich array of buildings framing the Market Place and the roads leading from it; unusually many of the buildings are pastel-painted – a rainbow of pale blues, pinks, greens and yellows sitting harmoniously together.

From time to time you see little blue plaques pinned to the walls of certain buildings. These snippets of history give clues to what went on behind closed walls and are placed by the Cirencester Civic Society, whose waymarked town walk (follow the marks in the pavements) leads you to the smart town houses of Cecily Hill, on the west side of town, near the tallest yew hedge in the world, standing at 40 feet high, and the bizarre neo-medieval Cecily Hill Castle, built in Victorian times and now home to Cirencester College. Beyond it are the fancy iron gates leading into **Cirencester Park**. This enormous expanse is five miles long and three miles wide. It is owned by the Bathurst Estate (over 13,500 acres) but permission is granted to walk or ride horses (no bicycles allowed) throughout the grounds between 08.00 and 17.00 each day. With its Broad Ride that extends into the horizon, woodland paths and wide avenues interspersed with huge specimen trees and vast grass 'meadows', it's the perfect retreat into the country while, initially at least, remaining in the town. Every July the park hosts the **Cotswold Show** (*www.cotswoldshow.co.uk*), one of the largest rural jamborees in the region's calendar, highlighting the very best of the countryside and the Cotswolds. Through entertainment and attractions, the ethos of the show is to foster links between town and country and to encourage a love, respect and understanding for the countryside and rural issues.

Finally, it's perhaps not surprising to learn that with the Cotswolds remaining one of the most important agricultural areas in Britain, Cirencester is home to Britain's most prestigious agricultural college. Located in impressive Cotswold buildings on the outskirts of the town, the **Royal Agricultural College**

The sport of Cirencester

It may be the sport of kings, but you may be surprised to learn that you don't need a king's ransom to watch a game. Matches at the **Cirencester Park Polo Club** (*01285 653225; www.cirencesterpolo.co.uk*) take place virtually every day during the season from April to September, utilising any one of the six prestigious grounds in Cirencester Park. And while their website provides grid references for visitors arriving by helicopter, arrivals by road command an entrance fee of just £10 to £15 (depending on the month) per car regardless of the number of occupants. It's recommended that you take a picnic and make a day of it but for a few pounds extra per person you can collect day membership and have lunch in the members' restaurant and tea room.

(*www.rac.ac.uk*) provides more than just a formal education for young students going into agribusiness and land management. Their food centre is open to all, providing numerous courses in the training kitchen. The working allotment brings home the 'field to fork' message.

Food and drink

Cirencester has a lively farmers' market, held twice a month on the second and fourth Saturday morning where, among the producers, you may find Liz Hurley selling meat from her 400-acre organic farm at Ampney Knowle and the Duchy Home Farm selling organic vegetables. Cirencester also has lots of very good places of all types to eat. Here's my pick.

Jesse's Bistro The Stableyard, off Blackjack St ☏ 01285 641497
⊕ www.jessesbistro.co.uk. A light and airy bistro tucked down a tiny alleyway with plenty of character. Meat comes from their own butcher's shop in Blackjack Street, specialising in Cotswold sheep and other local farmed produce. Lots of fish and seafood dishes too.

Lick the Spoon 3 Blackjack St ⊕ www.lickthespoon.co.uk. Fresh handmade chocolates (they're divine!), chocolate cakes and chocolate courses.

Organic Farm Shop & Café Abbey Home Farm, Burford Rd GL7 5HF
☏ 01285 640441 ⊕ www.theorganicfarmshop.co.uk. Very impressive farmshop genuinely selling produce from their own farm. National award-winning café serving organic food, inspired by the 10-acre vegetable garden surrounding it. Eco venue for weddings. Workshops on willow weaving, cheesemaking et al. Accommodation too.

Swan Yard Café 9–13 West Market Pl. Right in the heart of town, homemade café food – their thick lentil and bacon soup is the best I've ever tasted. Superb homemade cakes too. Breakfasts, lunches and afternoon teas.

The Evenlode Valley

The **River Evenlode** is the most easterly of the five Thames tributaries in this locale. Rising close to the town of Moreton-in-Marsh, it flows through a little corner of Gloucestershire before hopping over the county border into Oxfordshire. The river begins to gather pace at **Bledington**, cutting through wolds, dividing the Wychwood villages, skirting the vast – though not as large as it once was – **Wychwood Forest** before meeting up with its own tributary, the **River Glyme** close to **Woodstock**. It discharges into the Thames three miles northwest of Oxford near the village of **Cassington**.

The Evenlode is a relatively modern name for the river, its original title being the River Blade, hence the tiny village of **Bladon** through which the river flows. Powered boats are not allowed on any stretch of the river, so it is constantly peaceful as it drifts between villages save for the odd rumble of a train on the Cotswold Line, which uses the river valley. The beauty of the Evenlode is also immortalised by the Anglo-French poet Hilaire Belloc who once wrote:

The tender Evenlode that makes
Her meadows hush to hear the sound
Of waters mingling in the brakes,
And binds my heart to English ground.
A lovely river, all alone,
She lingers in the hills and holds
A hundred little towns of stone,
Forgotten in the western wolds.

The villages are not forgotten now. This is commuter territory for Oxford and London, and houses here are some of the most expensive in the Cotswolds.

⑮ The Gloucestershire Evenlode

From its gentle beginnings in the 'marshes' around Moreton, the Evenlode flows past several villages but not through any one of them. The first, and one of the most peaceful, takes its name from the river. **Evenlode** is a square village with its heart centred around a small triangular village green overlooking the Norman church. Both Evenlode and the next village downstream, **Adlestrop**, lie on the east bank of the river valley, and like the 'tender' river, the land is gentle too, nothing dramatic, just perfect for being simple.

While Hilaire Belloc was writing about the river, Edward Thomas penned one of my favourite poems, his famous ode to the tiny village of Adlestrop. It describes an unremarkable train journey during which the train made an unscheduled stop at Adlestrop Station. *Adlestrop* simply describes the sights and peaceful sounds of a summer's day in June 1914, witnessed from the railway carriage while waiting for the traveller's journey to resume. The station, where the A436 crosses the railway line, fell with Beeching's axe in the 1960s, but the classic chocolate and cream railway sign has been hung in the bus shelter at the entrance to the village approached from Evenlode. A bench originally on the platform is also there, with a plaque quoting the poem.

Adlestrop is one of those villages that you have to find. Off the beaten track, tucked against the bottom edge of a ridge of hills, it's sheltered from the elements and from stacks of tourists. It's a village definitely worth taking a wander around, with a tiny tea room at the post office. Footpaths southwest of the village give views of the string of lakes in Adlestrop Park.

Just south of Adlestrop, right on the county border, is **Daylesford**, the house and park once the home of Warren Hastings, the first Governor General of India and a large figure in the making of the British Empire. Daylesford is now better known for organic food, with the estate providing much of the produce for the **Daylesford Organic Farmshop**. The food is sublime, all the better for being bought in the parkland setting.

West of the river lie the villages of first Broadwell and then the Oddingtons. Of all the villages in this area, **Broadwell** has to be a favourite. The village straddles a ford, the shallow waters making their way into the Evenlode, and many of the classic Cotswold cottages, farmhouses and stone barns are focused around a large green. As a reminder of the heady days when it was a 'wool village' owned by prosperous sheep farmers, its churchyard has a series of unusual 'wool-bale' tombs (there are others at Burford), where the tops look like strands of the very textile that created prosperity for the area. A pub completes the picture.

Broadwell needs time to be properly explored, especially if you're going to while away a few hours on the village green or dabble in the stream, but once satisfied that you've discovered every nook, take a stroll across the fields to the Oddingtons. **Upper Oddington** sits on two banks facing one another and while attractive doesn't quite match its counterpart, **Lower Oddington**. From the village take a quick detour to the 'Church in the Woods'. The 11th-century **St Nicholas Church** is atmospheric enough simply for its lonesome location, buried in the surrounding woodland and along a no-through road. But inside the limestone walls are frescoed with a medieval Day of Judgement wall painting. It's so faint that the beige stencil-like artwork seems like an apparition seeping through the wall.

Two miles southeast is **Bledington**, the most easterly village in Gloucestershire. It's a village of two halves with the more recent 20th-century housing developments closest to the river – the county boundary – and the old part of the village housed around a green frequented by ducks that occasionally waddle to the little stream running through on its way to the Evenlode. The renowned Kings Head Inn provides the perfect backdrop and summer days will find locals and visitors strewn across the green enjoying the sunshine and the pastoral idyll.

Food and drink

Several pubs in the area are known either as the Fox Inn or the Fox and Hounds, showing variously the countryside's reverence for this creature or its association with fox hunting.

Daylesford Organic Farm Shop and Café Daylesford GL56 0YG ☎01608 731700 🐾 www.daylesfordorganic.com. The farmshop is renowned countrywide for its excellent produce, most of which comes from the estate, including fruit and veg from their market garden, cheese made in their creamery, breads, pastries and cakes from their bakery, and meat and poultry from the farm. Café serving first-class breakfasts, lunches and occasional evening meals – all using produce from the estate. Cookery school too.

Fox Inn Broadwell ☎01451 870909 🐾 www.donnington-brewery.com. Traditional village pub, owned by Donnington Brewery.

Fox Inn Lower Oddington ☎01451 870555 🐾 www.foxinn.net. Flagstone floors, low ceilings and beams, log fire, comfy chairs, sunny courtyard garden and plenty of good food. Accommodation too.

Kings Head Inn Bledington ☎01608 658365 🖥 www.kingsheadinn.net. An old cider house overlooking the village green and stream, a pub that is almost too perfect to be true. Superb atmosphere and a nice mix of regulars and locals, fine old furnishings and thoughtfully prepared food. Accommodation.

⑯ Kingham and Churchill

When a few years ago **Kingham** was judged by *Country Life* magazine as 'England's Favourite Village', it started attracting those looking for the right town and country balance – a quiet retreat in the countryside with a railway station nearby to make a quick exit to London. But, with its blend of thatched and slate-roofed houses and village green, it has been something of a rural idyll for decades, from long before celebrity musicians moved in or fever-pitch journalism made it known to the outside world.

Its near neighbour **Churchill** is further east, on an incline that makes its pinnacled church tower stand out for miles. However, this is 'modern' – since 1700 – Churchill, the old village ravaged by fire on the lower slopes of the hill. Only the old church remains, where a heritage museum is now explaining the history of the village and its two best-known sons William Smith, who created the first-ever geological maps of England and Wales, and the colonial administrator Warren Hastings. Close to the 'new' church in the village is an unusual-looking fountain with obelisks and flying buttresses, presented to the village in memory of the landowner who once owned the surrounding estates.

Food and drink

Kingham Plough Kingham ☎01608 658327 🖥 www.thekinghamplough.co.uk. Overlooking the village green with shady trees. Generously served bar food and a daily changing restaurant menu with seasonal ingredients from local farms and smallholdings. Accommodation.

Tollgate Inn Kingham ☎01608 658389 🖥 www.thetollgate.com. Large Georgian farmhouse with comfortable dining and drinking areas around the bar and woodburners. Cascading lilac wisteria and giant canopies on the front terrace.

⑰ The Westcotes and Fifield

Just west of the villages of **Church Westcote** and **Nether Westcote** (whose hillside positions give commanding views over the Evenlode Valley) is Brookfield Ostrich Farm, home to the painter Irene Tyack and her **Yellow Hat Tribe Gallery** (*OX7 6SJ; 01993 832042; www.theyellowhat-tribe.com*). Her bold and vibrant paintings, depicting her little brigade of yellow-brimmed figures – you never see their faces – in all manner of environments bring vitality to any wall and have attracted a cult following. Irene is often in the gallery painting, so you can watch as she works while you browse the paintings and associated gift items. Says Irene, 'I love my little characters dearly. They have become a part of my life and I'm always thinking up new situations for them to be in. I bring out two new collections every year in May and November, the next two themes being 'gardens' and 'campervans'. During the summer, you'll often find bunches of giant sunflowers for sale too, grown on their ostrich farm. You can't miss the entrance either – a bright yellow car marks the way.

There are so many tiny villages in this area that rarely get a mention because of the few facilities (such as a pub) that they can offer tourists, and yet really shouldn't be missed – hamlets such as **Foscot**, **Idbury Icomb** and **Sarsden**. These are the real Cotswold settlements, untouched by coach tours and gift shops. One such place is **Fifield**. It only takes 15 minutes to wander round the block – a 'rectangular'-shaped village on a hillside with stone houses lining the four roads and, in the middle, a church with a slender octagonal turret. The D'Arcy Dalton Way runs through, which you can use to reach the **Foxholes Nature Reserve** close to the River Evenlode to the east. The 158 acres of woodland, known for its spring bluebells, grassland and wetlands, were once a part of the ancient Wychwood Forest. It takes a bit of finding, but persevere. Here you can listen to the numerous birds or look out for bats on the waymarked wildlife walks and permissive footpaths. Oaks, beech, silver birch and sallow tower above as does the sea of woodland ferns. The reserve can also be reached by car, down a very bumpy track, off the Fifield to Bruern Abbey road.

Food and drink

Feathered Nest Country Inn Nether Westcote ☎ 01993 833030
🌐 www.thefeatherednestinn.co.uk. This pub, completely rebuilt from an old malthouse, opened in 2010. Gastro-pub food; open for morning coffee, afternoon teas and dinner too.

⑱ The Wychwoods and Charlbury

In the 11th century the Wychwood Royal Hunting Forest covered much of west Oxfordshire. It was steadily felled to make way for sheep pastures for the wool trade but several villages were already established, their names reflecting their woodland location: **Milton-under-**, **Shipton-under-** and **Ascott-under-Wychwood**. Between Milton and Shipton is the **Wild Garden** (*www.wychwoodwild garden.org.uk*), 12 acres of woodland owned by the villages with a network of paths following a line of ponds and plenty of wildlife. It was originally a pleasure garden belonging to the Elizabethan Shipton Court, the impressive building that you cannot miss through the decorative gates alongside the A361.

Having flowed south since its source, the river turns east at Shipton and makes a wide, sweeping curve in which sits most of the remaining chunk of the Wychwood Forest. Some 1,700 acres of the forest come under **Cornbury Park**, where the former royal hunting lodge is, now a private house on folded, hilly ground. Deer roam free through the woodland and more open parkland, and provide many of the pubs and restaurants in the area with fresh venison. A public footpath runs through the estate, crossing a chain of six lakes which feed into the Evenlode. Park in the village of Finstock and take the footpath into the estate opposite the old chapel, on the Charlbury Road. Cornbury Park is also the venue for an annual summer music festival (*www.cornburypark.co.uk*) with scenic camping by the lakes. An annual **Wychwood Forest Fair**, celebrating the history and the diversity of this area of countryside, is held in a different location every year. It is organised by the **Wychwood Project** (*www.wychwoodproject.org*), a community organisation that helps to conserve, restore and plant new sections of the Wychwood Forest. They are always looking for volunteers.

As the river curves back round to continue its more easterly path, it skirts the very edge of pale-stone **Charlbury**, a small market town, home to the free Riverside Festival (*www.riversidefestival.charlbury.com*), held in summer on the Mill Field island, just to the west of town. You can download details of ten cycle rides from the Charlbury Community Website (*www.charlbury.info*). Click on 'Info' followed by 'Cycle routes around Charlbury'.

Food and drink

Bull Inn Sheep St, Charlbury ☎01608 810689 🖥 www.bullinn-charlbury.com. 16th-century freehouse with plenty of charm in the centre of town.

Café de la Post Chadlington ☎01608 676461. Welcoming café serving homemade food in the old post office. Open daily.

Lamb Inn Shipton-under-Wychwood ☎01993 830465 🖥 www.shiptonlamb.co.uk. Fine wines and well-kept beers. Hearty fare at lunchtimes, separate menu for the log-fire restaurant. Pie night on Wed.

Tite Inn Chadlington ☎01608 676475 🖥 www.titeinn.com. Hillside pub with a pretty garden.

⑲ Stonesfield and Woodstock

Stonesfield was once one of the most important villages in the Cotswolds, providing some of the highest-quality roofing materials for many buildings in the area, including many Oxford colleges. Stonesfield slate is not like a grey Welsh slate but slabs of Jurassic limestone known as pendle. As a sedimentary rock the limestone splits into slate-like pieces in frosty conditions, providing the stone is kept damp. Traditionally it was quarried or mined from Michaelmas through until the end of January and once dug out, would be covered with earth to keep it moist until a frost was imminent; the church bells would toll when a frost was expected. Many years ago, I had the chance to go into one of the Stonesfield slate mines where I had to crawl on hands and feet to travel along the mine's cramped passages. Given that the workers toiled throughout the winter months, the work must have been tough in the extreme.

Evidence of Roman occupation in this area is apparent in many places but in particular, on the opposite side of the river from Stonesfield, there are the remains of **North Leigh Roman Villa** close to the riverbank. The ankle-high foundations of this aristocratic courtyard villa are pretty much all that remain (the location and the walk to it, with views over the Evenlode Valley and wooded cliffs behind, are phenomenal) except for its most special feature, a near-complete mosaic tiled floor. A grand statement, much of the house was once patterned with mosaic pavements and tessellated floors. This particular mosaic floor was in a formal reception room, and its geometric designs reveal intricate craftsmanship. The mosaic is protected from the elements by an unprepossessing but rather endearing corrugated-roofed building, which is opened occasionally (pure luck whether it's open when you're there). However, giant picture windows allow you to see the mosaic clearly at all times. Entrance is free, with access only from a knobbly footpath (not suitable for wheelchairs) 550 yards from the road, just west of the village of East End. There's a lay-by for cars to park opposite the footpath.

Nearby **Combe** has a large central green upon which centuries-old seasonal festivities take place such as maypole dancing in spring and a summer fete. The charming village, filled with houses of slender mottled stone, is considered one of the most attractive in Oxfordshire. Take your pint from the Cock Inn overlooking the village green and enjoy the tranquil atmosphere for a while. Look out for the majestic cedar of Lebanon, just to the east of the village green, close to the church.

Just south of the village is **Combe Mill Museum** (*01993 358694; www.combemill.org; open Wed and Sun, mid-Mar to mid-Oct*) at Blenheim Estate Sawmills. A working industrial heritage museum, Combe Mill is the original powerhouse of the timber mills and workshops connected to the Blenheim Estate. Traditional skills are demonstrated here such as forging, wheelwrighting and woodturning, using the original power sources – waterwheels, boilers and steam engines – put in place during the 19th century.

My husband once worked on the Blenheim Estate (helping to build the timber bridges in the maze at the Pleasure Gardens) and he recently took me to see Notoaks Wood, a woodland that he planted over 20 years ago just to the west of Combe. Unsurprisingly, he commented that 'you'd hardly recognise it now', except for the excessive number of pheasants that appreciate the cover. 'They were there even when we planted.' He commented on planting up Combe Cliff with trees too, a mini Cotswold escarpment that lines the Evenlode Valley south of the village, and prominent from the river. 'It's so steep that we could barely stand up; we needed ropes to climb down and hold on as we planted.'

To the east of Combe is the small market town of **Woodstock**. When the M40 from London only stretched as far as Oxford, Woodstock was the first small town that anyone travelling northwest would come through. It gave the town a bolt-hole appeal, somewhere to escape for the weekend. However, visitors have been coming for far longer than that: things have been distinctly prosperous since the 18th century, with the building of adjacent Blenheim Palace and the subsequent arrival of wealthy guests attending engagements there. The town became a market for finery and a glovemaking industry took off. The history of Woodstock and the county is recollected at the admirable **Oxfordshire Museum** on the High Street, which charts everything that makes Oxfordshire what it is, from the geology of the area to Oxfordshire-based inventions. Free to enter, it has regular activities, many specifically aimed at children, and changing exhibitions. A pleasant garden at the rear provides a quiet place to sit for a cup of tea. The museum is also the location of the town's visitor information centre where you can pick up a leaflet outlining the Woodstock Town Walk.

Food and drink

The Bear and **The Feathers** hotels are two of Woodstock's institutions, fine hotels with impressive reputations for both food and accommodation in age-old coaching inns, still retaining a gastro-pub feel. But, with a long-term history of pulling in tourists, there are many other places to choose from too.

Hampers Food and Wine 31–33 Oxford St ✆01993 811535. Deli selling local produce in addition to high-quality food and wine from around Britain and the world. Picnic hampers made up or eat in the café where food from the deli is served.

Kings Arms 19 Market St ✆01993 813636 🖥 www.kings-hotel-woodstock.co.uk. Upmarket restaurant and bar in fully restored Georgian building with stripped wooden floors, log-burning stove and marble-top bars. Accommodation.

Blenheim Palace

Brushing up against Woodstock is the huge **Blenheim Estate** in the middle of which is Blenheim Palace (*0800 8496500; www.blenheimpalace.com; palace and gardens open daily Feb to Dec, park open all year – see website for exact dates and times*), the seat of the Duke of Marlborough aka the Spencer-Churchill family. We're currently on duke number 11, but it was the first duke who was granted the building of the house as a gift from Queen Anne following his heroic victory over the French at the Battle of Blenheim in 1704. The hour of triumph is commemorated in one of the palace's finest treasures, the Blenheim Tapestry, just one of ten 'Victory' woven masterpieces.

The house is itself a masterpiece of Baroque, grand in scale and with all the pomp and stature inside and out that you'd expect from a status symbol used as a declaration of victory. In 1874 Sir Winston Churchill was born here, an unexpectedly early arrival while his mother was visiting relations. It's also where he later proposed to his wife. There is a large, permanent exhibition on his life and work focused around the room in which he was born. Churchill, together with his wife and parents, is buried in the churchyard in the neighbouring village of **Bladon** (see page 134), all their gravestones facing towards the Blenheim Estate.

While the house and grounds – including the Grand Bridge – were originally designed by the now celebrated, but at the time unqualified, John Vanbrugh, under the watchful eye of Nicholas Hawksmoor, the 2,000-acre grounds were later landscaped by Capability Brown. He created the two large lakes through which the River Glyme, a tributary of the Evenlode, flows; the two rivers meet on the estate.

A walk around Blenheim's Great Park

A visit to Blenheim Palace easily takes up more than a day to do it justice if you're visiting the house and formal gardens alone but the estate also includes 2,000 acres of parkland to explore. You can purchase a ticket for the park, allowing you to wander anywhere, or use a little-known entrance from the town and explore using the numerous public footpaths that criss-cross the estate.

The footpaths across the Great Park give outstanding views of the palace and vistas of the lake that Capability Brown was appointed to create. It gives the opportunity to get away from the crowds and the coaches that hang around the house and formal gardens – the majority of visitors don't step out into the park at all – and you'll find many delightfully peaceful spots to sit. Do bear in mind that the estate is private property and without an entrance ticket you must stick to the public footpaths. This circular walk through the Great Park begins at the visitor information centre on the High Street in the centre of Woodstock.

With your back to the visitor information centre, walk right and turn right down Chancery Lane (opposite Blenheim Tea rooms) to Hoggrove Hill, a footpath. On reaching the main road, turn left along the Causeway where you see a green gate that looks like a private drive. Pass through this and the next green gate and you're in the grounds of Blenheim Palace.

Follow the track round to the right, which is a part of the Wychwood Way. There will be initial views across to the palace over Queen's Pool on your left. Continue along the track between the steep banks and make a 90-degree turn between the two rows of lime trees. This is one of the main symmetrical vistas with the palace behind you and the Ditchley Gate entrance far in the distance in front of you.

Pass over two cattle crossings and turn left at the second field boundary (marked with a fence). This is Akeman Street, the old Roman road that passes from St Albans to Cirencester and forms a part of the Wychwood and Oxfordshire Way.

As you enter the first woodland, turn left and walk along the wooded track for approximately 500 yards – look out for a small yellow footpath sign on the left (it's not that well signposted), which will take you out of the wood. Walk along the field perimeter towards another small woodland. With this next wood directly in front of you, turn left for approximately 100 yards until you meet up with a metalled track. Turn right and pass through a strip of woodland before crossing the field through two kissing gates. Do not follow the metalled track around that leads to Park Farm on your right.

Through the second kissing gate, turn right and skirt round a small clump of trees. Continue until you come to the entrance of Park Farm. Follow the metalled track round to the left and where the track forks, turn back on yourself, following one track downhill. Continue until you have an open valley on your left and trees straight ahead. Turn left along the side of the valley. This is now one of the most secluded parts of the park.

At the end of the valley, with a steep bank on your left, turn left through a kissing gate and follow the path alongside the lake. From here as the ground rises slightly you will get views across the lake of the palace and the Grand Bridge.

Continue along the lakeside, past Fair Rosamund's Well and, with the Grand Bridge on your right, turn left when you reach the metalled track.

Continue for approximately half a mile along the track and at the cattle crossing turn right, over a stile. Follow along the fence until you reach the Column of Victory, erected shortly after the first duke's death. Pass by the column on your left and cross the rest of the field through the trees. Cross the stile and turn left for a short distance until you reach the small house on your right.

Follow the road around to your right (the first one that you came along when you entered the grounds) until you reach the green gate. You are now back where you entered the grounds to the Great Park. Retrace your steps back to the town centre. The walk is approximately 4½ miles.

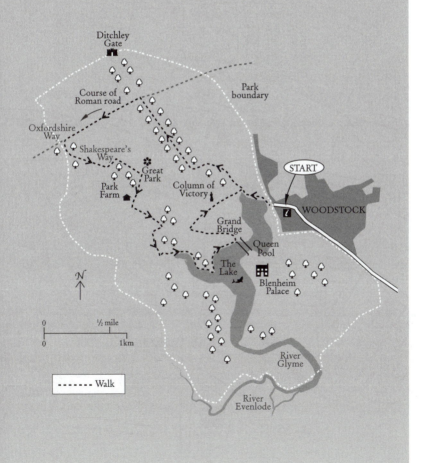

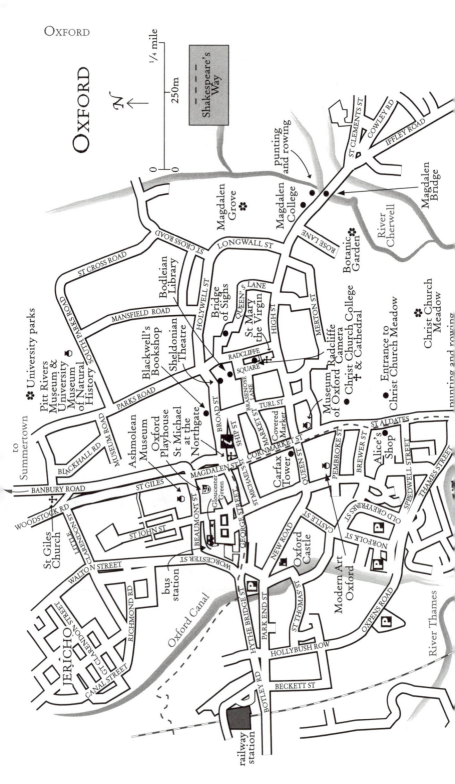

OXFORD

N

250m
¼ mile

Shakespeare's Way

to Summertown

University parks

Pitt Rivers Museum & University Museum of Natural History

St Giles Church

WOODSTOCK RD
BANBURY ROAD

BLACKHALL RD

ST GILES

ST CROSS ROAD

ST CROSS ROAD

MANSFIELD ROAD

PARKS ROAD

SOUTH PARKS ROAD

MUSEUM ROAD

KEBLE ROAD

Magdalen Grove

Magdalen College

punting and rowing

Magdalen Bridge

ST CLEMENTS ST
COWLEY RD
IFFLEY ROAD

River Cherwell

Botanic Garden

ROSE LANE

LONGWALL ST

Bodleian Library

Bridge of Sighs

Sheldonian Theatre

Blackwell's Bookshop

HOLYWELL ST

QUEEN'S LANE

St Mary the Virgin

HIGH ST

MERTON ST

RADCLIFFE SQUARE

RADCLIFFE

Christ Church College & Cathedral

Museum of Oxford

Christ Church Meadow

Christ Church Camera
Entrance to Christ Church Meadow

Ashmolean Museum

Oxford Playhouse

St Michael at the Northgate

BROAD ST

SHIP ST

CORNMARKET ST

TURL ST

Covered Market

BRASENOSE

BEAUMONT ST

ST JOHN ST

LITTLE CLARENDON ST

WALTON STREET

JERICHO

CLARENDON ST
CANAL STREET
RICHMOND RD

Oxford Canal

bus station

WORCESTER ST
GEORGE STREET

Gloucester Green

MAGDALEN ST

St GILES

Carfax Tower

QUEEN ST

ST MICHAEL'S ST

ST ALDATES

PEMBROKE ST

BREWER ST

Alice's Shop

Oxford Castle

Modern Art Oxford

New Road

CASTLE ST

NORFOLK ST

OLD GREYFRIARS ST

ST EBBE'S STREET

THAMES STREET

OXPENS ROAD

ST THOMAS ST

PARK END ST

HYTHE BRIDGE ST

HOLLYBUSH ROW

BECKETT ST

BOTLEY RD

railway station

River Thames

punting and rowing

6. OXFORD

It was the poet Matthew Arnold who first depicted Oxford with its 'dreaming spires' in 1865 and the idiom alluding to this 'sweet city' has remained ever since. He was a professor of poetry at the university when he penned it, describing the panorama of spires, turrets and pinnacles seen from Boars Hill, southwest of the city.

Seen from here or any one of the other viewpoints around the outskirts of the city, or by climbing a tower in the centre, the skyline has a magical quality that draws breath and makes even the most hurried tourist stand still for a moment. It's like seeing the Duomo in Florence for the first time or the plan of Paris from the Arc de Triomphe.

But I like the notion that in this university town, Arnold's 'dreaming spires' are all about the hopes and aspirations of the thousands of students that pass through the halls, passageways and courtyards every year. For there is no doubt that the architecture and the traditions embedded within the walls of the Oxford colleges make the city an inspirational place to study. Watching the scholars chatting in the

cafés takes me back to my own student days, poring over reams of literary notes, a novel several inches thick open on the table, while trying to make one coffee last several hours.

Oxford is certainly a vibrant place to visit. The city may be rooted in tradition, but it's not stuck in the past, the romantic scholarly buildings merely the backdrop upon which to create an exciting stay. Although, if Inspector Morse is to be believed, no-one would dare set foot in the city for the number of deadly deeds and ghastly goings-on that occur behind whispering walls and the creeping crevices of college gardens. Oxford is indeed the stuff of fiction too.

Oxford can easily be cut into four segments, with the **Carfax Tower** right in the city centre being the midpoint. Four roads, running almost due north to south and east to west, conveniently converge here – **St Aldates** to **Cornmarket Street** (running north towards **St Giles**) and the **High Street** to **Queen Street**. These I use as borderlines.

Getting there and around

As a major educational centre in a central location, Oxford is remarkably easy to get to with its excellent connections. Traffic in Oxford is, however, a problem and the cost of car parking is extortionate. I strongly recommend using one of the five park and ride sites on the outskirts if you are driving to the city.

University of Oxford

Oxford University is an umbrella institution for 39 self-governing colleges and students are affiliated to one of these for the duration of their studies. Consequently there is no campus as such but endless college halls and, in amongst them, the buildings of the various faculties – Music, History, Engineering, and so on. Many colleges, such as Balliol and Christ Church, are centuries old, begun as religious institutions and their ornamented cloistered buildings reflect this; quadrangles, chapels, formal gardens, gatehouses and porters' lodges are frequent features. The newest include Kellogg College, established in 1990, and Green Templeton College, in 2008.

Tourists may visit the grounds of some university colleges and inside some halls. The best known – Christ Church, Magdalen and New College, for example – charge nominal fees but there are several colleges that you may enter free of charge. Of these, take a look at Pembroke, All Souls and Queen's College in particular for architectural interest and a view of college traditions. Dates and times of entry for visitors vary between colleges and seasons; most display a board outside the gatehouse indicating whether they accept visitors and when.

Trains

Frequent direct services operate between Oxford and London Paddington and Birmingham New Street. Services from the north are via Birmingham, from the south via Reading and from the west via Didcot.

Buses

Two very frequent coach services operate every few minutes between central London and Oxford 24 hours a day. The journey takes approximately 100 minutes, terminating at the coach station at **Gloucester Green**. Choose between the **Oxford Tube** (*www.oxfordtube.com*) and the **Oxford Express** (*www.oxfordbus.co.uk*). Both are relatively efficient (traffic permitting) and comfortable. Services from elsewhere in the country are available by **National Express** (*www.nationalexpress.com*) and **Megabus** (*www.megabus.com*). The Oxford Bus Company also runs a frequent service between the city and both Heathrow and Gatwick airports.

There are frequent bus services between Oxford and the outlying villages too, mostly operated by Stagecoach, as are the services around the city centre.

Cycling

Oxford's streets rival Beijing's for the concentration of bicycles, the preferred mode of transport for the city student. Racks of bikes are a familiar sight – including the odd neglected sample with buckled wheels and rusty handlebars – so you won't look out of place parking up against a lamp post. Just make sure you have a sturdy lock and chain though – bikes are desirable items in Oxford.

There's traffic-free cycling alongside the **Oxford Canal**, which travels right into the centre of Oxford from the north, though you should observe the 'No Cycling' signs in places. You need to obtain a free cycle permit to be able to use the towpath, available to download from www.waterscape.com. Sustrans National Cycle Network Route 5 provides an alternative from Birmingham.

A short section of the **Thames Path** also offers traffic-free cycling from Folly Bridge to Kennington.

Bike hire/repair

Bainton Bikes 6 Bainton Rd ☎01865 365658 🖱www.baintonbikes.com. Bicycle hire, including children's bikes (though, frankly, I wouldn't recommend either children cycling around the busier streets or the use of children's trailers on the back of adult bikes). Free puncture repair and breakdown support. Repair service too with courtesy bikes offered during the repair.

Bike Zone Market St (off Cornmarket) and 202 Banbury Rd (Summertown) ☎01865 728877 🖱www.bikezoneoxford.co.uk. Bike hire, repairs and sales.

The Cycle Centre 85 Walton St ☎01865 554646 🖱www.thecyclecentre.com. Bicycle hire per day, week or weekend, repairs and sales. All hires include a lock and lights. Delivery to accommodation available.

Oxford Cycle Hire ☎07907 952 832 🖱www.oxford-cycles.co.uk. Quality bike hire with free delivery and collection within the Oxford area. Lights and locks included in hire.

Walking

The best way to see Oxford is on foot. Several of the streets in the city centre are pedestrianised and it would be a shame to miss out on the many narrow alleyways, nooks and crannies.

Walking tours are big business in Oxford, departing daily from the city's tourist information centre on Broad Street, where you can also book a tour. Pick your theme; there are twenty or so, from simple tours of the colleges or family walking tours to specific themes such as Women in Oxford, Inspector Morse, Tudor Oxford, Stained Glass, Gargoyles and Grotesques, Film Sites or Children's Stories.

If you prefer to head out on your own, the centre has several leaflets and booklets to guide you around, such as the Oxford Science Walk, taking a look at the buildings and places that have made scientific history.

There are plenty of opportunities to get away from the city streets for a quieter amble too. Both Shakespeare's Way and the Thames Path pass through the centre of Oxford and places such as **Port Meadow** to the northwest provide acres of peace. My choice every time would be to visit **Christ Church Meadow**. It's right in the very centre, so you can combine bustling city sightseeing with quiet riverside contemplation without having to travel too far to reach it.

Tourist information centre

Oxford Tourist Information Centre 15–16 Broad St &01865 252200
🖱 www.visitoxford.org. Here you can book accommodation, tours and tickets for events in Oxford.

Accommodation

Malmaison Oxford 3 Oxford Castle, New Rd &01865 268400
🖱 www.malmaison.com. Your chance to 'do time' in what was once the Norman castle adapted into Oxford Prison. The beds are more comfortable, the bathrooms considerably more than a bucket in the corner, but you still get to stay in the same cells. It's all a bit more chic now: the brasserie retains the original features of this prison and the al fresco terrace was once the exercise yard. Expect the food to be a good deal more pleasurable than it once was.

Oxford University 🖱 www.oxfordrooms.co.uk. Oxford University is made up of 38 collegiate colleges and when the students have gone home for the holidays, the colleges are open to guests. It's a unique opportunity to stay in historic surroundings, eating in grand college halls and wandering college gardens without having to spend several years studying. Rooms may or may not be basic, with or without en-suite facilities, but all are booked as B&B. Many colleges offer additional privileges such as the use of sports centres or tennis courts and visits to areas generally not open to the public. The colleges include Balliol, Trinity, Magdalen, Keble, Jesus and St Anne's among others.

Old Parsonage Hotel 1 Banbury Rd &01865 310210 🖱 www.oldparsonage-hotel. co.uk. Small privately owned boutique hotel in beautiful 17th-century building, 5 minutes' walk from the city centre. Tastefully furnished, offering 30 individually decorated bedrooms, a restaurant, cosy bar and 3 terraces for dining outdoors or listening to the summer jazz 'concerts' every Friday evening. Very good food – *the* place for a quiet afternoon tea.

Food and drink

Oxford is a cosmopolitan city and you can buy sushi or tapas just as easily as you can bangers and mash. The **Cowley Road** is where you'll find an eclectic mix of restaurants from many nations while small enclaves such as **Summertown** and **Jericho** each have their own collection of restaurants and bars characterising their location. Afternoon tea in the Randolph, an Oxford institution, sits equally with intellectual chat in one of the many town pubs.

Cafés and restaurants

Ashmolean Dining Room Ashmolean Museum, Beaumont St &01865 553823
🖱 www.ashmoleandiningroom.com. Oxford's first rooftop restaurant, with terrace and views towards Boars Hill. Rustic, European dishes using seasonal ingredients.

The Big Bang 124 Walton St ☎01865 511441 🖱www.thebigbangrestaurants.co.uk. Opened in 2005 by Max Mason in Oxford's Jericho district, this sausage and mash restaurant has quickly become a classic scooping many local and national awards for both its food and its ethics on sustainability and use of local produce. They use top-quality sausages, including the Oxford sausage, and ingredients are sourced within 40 miles; the beer is local too..

Café Loco 85–87 St Aldates ☎01865 200959 🖱www.goingloco.com. Great place to begin the day with breakfast plus light lunches and afternoon teas – opposite the entrance to Christ Church Meadow. Inspired by *Alice in Wonderland*, it has a large mural of the Mad Hatter's Tea Party.

G & D's Ice Cream 🖱www.gdcafe.com. Oxford's own boutique ice-cream parlours. George & Davis in Little Clarendon Street is where it's all made. Then there is also George & Danver in St Aldates and George & Delilah on the Cowley Road. High-quality ice cream using natural ingredients and made in Oxford.

Georgina's Coffee Shop Avenue 3, Covered Market ☎01865 249527. One of my favourites. Bohemian décor – old film posters 'wallpapered' on the ceilings, rustic pine tables and chairs – nothing matches – and chalked blackboards on the walls. Enjoyably hearty food and snacks and huge vats of tea and coffee. Popular place but easy to miss – upstairs above 'Brothers'. Look for the bright pink staircase and powder blue windows.

The Nosebag 6–8 St Michael's St ☎01865 203222 🖱www.nosebagoxford.co.uk. My other main favourite, this serves a more substantial lunch than Georgina's. Large portions of hot, wholesome dishes or choose from the giant bowls of salads to create a plate, alongside enormous slabs of quiche. Fantastic homemade cakes and puddings too. Very popular. Sit at long refectory-style tables with whoever else happens to be sitting there. All the crocks are from Russell Collins Pottery in Hook Norton.

Pierre Victoire Bistrot 9 Little Clarendon St ☎01865 316616 🖱www.pierrevictoire. co.uk. Tiny, authentic, French-owned bistro serving classic, hearty dishes such as *moules marinière* and *tartiflette*. Set menus are very good and inexpensive.

Vaults Garden Café University Church of St Mary the Virgin, Radcliffe Sq ☎01865 279112 🖱www.vaultsandgarden.com. Come here just for the location – a quiet garden overlooking the Radcliffe Camera, or tuck down in vaults of the University Church. Wholesome food using organic and Fairtrade produce. Much of the food is sourced from nearby farms.

Pubs

Eagle and Child 49 St Giles ☎01865 302925. Historic pub owned by St John's College. This is where the Inklings writers' group, which included C S Lewis and Tolkien used to meet.

Lamb and Flag 12 St Giles ☎01865 515787. Another literary institution that has been popular with students for decades. Thomas Hardy's *Jude the Obscure* was reputedly written here.

The Morse Bar Randolph Hotel, Broad St ☎0844 8799132. Many an episode of Morse has the Inspector puzzling over his crossword in this bar. The cosy, wood-panelled bar with roaring log fire is more of a comfortable living room than town-centre pub. The bar still features regularly in episodes of the TV series *Lewis*.

Perch Inn Binsey Ln ☎01865 728891 🖰 www.the-perch.co.uk. A 17th-century thatched pub in Binsey. Traditional Englishness combined with French cuisine. One of the best pub gardens I know.

Trout Inn 195 Godstow Rd, Wolvercote OX2 6PN ☎01865 510930 🖰 www.thetroutoxford.co.uk. It takes a little effort to get here but it's worth it. Frequented by many authors over the years including Lewis Carroll, C S Lewis and Colin Dexter, it has a superb location with large terrace on the banks of the Thames. Another of Inspector Morse's haunts. My pick of the pubs.

Turf Tavern St Helen's Passage ☎01865 243235. A 13th-century pub often teeming with university life. Well hidden off the main streets it's very much a drinking pub with hearty snacks. The bars are tiny, low-beamed ceilings catch the tallest of folk unawares and the courtyards are cosy, but this is the pub for lovers of real ale.

White Hart Inn Wytham OX2 8QA ☎01865 244372 🖰 www.thewhitehartoxford. co.uk. Very cosy pub in the tiny village of Wytham, 3 miles from Oxford, but accessed from the city centre via the Thames Path. A secret hideaway.

North of Queen Street and west of Cornmarket Street

My starting point is the **Carfax Tower**, at the crossroads of the four main streets in Oxford. Its name is derived from the French for crossroads, *carrefour*, and it's a good thing to climb the tower's 99 steps to get some bearings. There are so many 'dreaming spires' that they tend to blend into a confusing mishmash until you begin to recognise certain landmarks – the slender cupola of Tom Tower of Christ Church, the dome of the Radcliffe Camera, the spire of St Aldates Church or the pinnacled tower of Merton College Chapel.

The Carfax Tower is all that remains of St Martin's Church, the main body demolished to make way for road widening at the end of the 19th century. On its east façade, facing the High Street, is the church clock, accompanied by two 'quarter boys' who chime the bells every quarter-hour.

From the top you can make out the north-facing **Cornmarket Street**, one of Oxford's main pedestrianised shopping streets where buskers vie for attention and where Shakespeare's Way continues on its trek from Stratford-upon-Avon to London. Hidden away from the bright lights of the shop windows is the **Painted Room** on the second floor of 3 Cornmarket Street. In the 17th century, this was the Crown Tavern, owned by John Davenant and his wife, who were friends of Shakespeare. The playwright would stay here on his journeys to London, and became the godfather (rumour has it actually the father) of the Davenants' son, William. You can visit the Painted Room to look at the 16th-century wall paintings 'hidden' behind some early 17th-century oak panels, themselves covered in very early rich red wallpapers. But the room is part of the offices now occupied by Oxford Aunts, so it is necessary to book a visit in advance (Monday to Friday only) by phoning 01865 791017.

Oxford Open Doors

Most of Oxford's museums are free to visit. The main colleges are not. But a great weekend to visit Oxford is Oxford Open Doors (*www.oxfordopendoors.org.uk*), usually held the second weekend of September, when many places around the city open their doors for free, including Christ Church and Magdalen colleges. There are lots of places that open specially for the weekend too, which are otherwise closed to the public and many events are also put on, such as free narrowboat trips on the Oxford Canal – very popular – and guided tours or talks that give an inside knowledge about a building or park.

Other gems concealed behind closed doors are in the **Oxford Union** just off St Michael's Street. The union is one of the world's most prestigious debating societies where prime ministers, heads of state, world leaders and internationally recognised stars have spoken, often on controversial issues. Its debates are only open to members but visitors may enter to look at the Pre-Raphaelite murals that adorn the walls and ceiling of the old library. Painted between 1857 and 1859 by Dante Gabriel Rossetti, William Morris and Edward Burne-Jones, the paintings depict scenes from the Arthurian legends.

North of the Oxford Union and running parallel with the pedestrianised St Michael's Street is **George Street**. The street is home to both the New Theatre where major West End productions are performed and also the Crisis Skylight Centre (formerly the Old Fire Station Studio), a more modest community theatre and arts centre space. In between is the Odeon Cinema, arguably one of the ugliest buildings in the city but opposite is the far more attractive faculty of history, with elegantly carved ornamental stonemasonry, pretty clock and gabled façade; this was once Oxford's High School for Boys where former pupils included T E Lawrence ('Lawrence of Arabia') and Ronnie Barker.

Gloucester Green, the square where two soldiers from the Levellers were shot for opposing Cromwellian forces in 1649, is accessed off George Street. The square is in need of an update but houses a Thursday antiques market and a farmers' market on the first and third Thursday of every month. There's a separate exit and entrance that leads onto Beaumont Street, where the Oxford Playhouse and its offshoot the Burton Taylor Studio Theatre put on more serious drama and community-based entertainment than the blockbusters offered at the New Theatre. Oxford, of course, is known for producing many top-class comedians and actors through the **Oxford Revue**. Past members include Michael Palin, Dudley Moore, Rowan Atkinson, Richard Curtis, Alan Bennett, Ian Hislop and Al Murray. You're likely to be able to catch potential new stars from the current membership at the Burton Taylor Studio.

Next to the Oxford Playhouse is the grand-looking **Randolph Hotel**, the largest and most prestigious hotel in Oxford and a place that was frequented by the fictional Inspector Morse. 'The Morse Bar' in the hotel has been named in his honour. Opposite the Randolph is the **Ashmolean Museum** (*01865 278002; www.ashmolean.org; open Tue to Sun and bank holiday Mon*), which was the first museum in the world when it opened in 1683 and, following a major redevelopment, doubled its display space in 2010. The museum has thousands of exhibits, and is renowned for its collections from ancient Egypt and Greece as well as important works of art. My favourites are the displays from Mughal India in the Asian Crossroads Gallery and the paintings by Pissarro in the Western Art Gallery. You'd have no problem to spend all day in the museum to cover all five floors of displays but I found the signage throughout the building somewhat bewildering (the direction boards are placed a different way round from those laid out in the floor-plan booklet) and it can take quite some time if you're looking for specific works. On the up side, the museum is free to enter and there are many free or low-cost activities that bring the collections to life.

The east façade of the Ashmolean runs along **St Giles**, the widest boulevard-like street in the city, adorned by magnificent university college buildings built with those dream-like qualities that Matthew Arnold referred to – St John's College on the east side and Blackfriars, on the west, home to a community of Dominican friars. St Giles, the patron saint of the poor, has a church dedicated to him at the northern end of the road where the Woodstock and Banbury roads converge. The St Giles Fair is held along the full length of the street every September, shortly after St Giles Day, and is one of the largest fairs in the country. Though not traditionally a hiring fair, it falls conveniently in line with the timing of other Mop Fairs held around the Cotswolds.

St Giles provides the eastern edge for an area of Oxford known as **Jericho**. Formerly the quarter where print workers lived and threatened with demolition in the 1960s but fortunately saved, this has always had a unique character and in recent years has become a trendy part of town, occupied by chic eating houses such as Raymond Blanc's Brasserie Blanc on **Walton Street**, where the great chef himself is often to be found eating Sunday lunch. Walton Street is also home to the enormous, in both square footage and stature, Oxford University Press and the world's most famous dictionary. Though the *Oxford English Dictionary* is a relatively new addition – the first edition began publication in 1884 – Oxford has had a long tradition with publishing, producing books long before printing presses were introduced. Indeed, the city was hot off the mark with 'modern' technology, printing its first book in 1478, only two years after William Caxton set up the first British printing press.

Joining Walton Street with St Giles is one of my favourite shopping streets in Oxford, **Little Clarendon Street**. So much quieter than the busy main streets, it's full of little restaurants, bistros and bars and some appealing independent shops as well as the admissions centre for Oxford University should you wish to 'discover' the city over a number of years.

The area of Jericho extends to the **Oxford Canal**, one of the oldest canals in England, stretching 77 miles from Oxford to Coventry. Beginning at Hythe Bridge, it joins the River Thames just 200 yards north at Isis Lock, meaning boats

Mop Fairs

Fairs are held nationwide but the Cotswolds, with its large rural population, held a significant number of Mop Fairs. With a tradition that goes back several hundred years, mops were essentially recruiting grounds. Farm labourers, craftsmen and servants, having finished their current employment at the end of the harvest would look for new employment in October, around Michaelmas. They would carry with them a tool to signify their trade, and those without skills would carry a mop.

Employers would also visit to arrange terms with new employees, who would be provided with a token of money as a down payment. This was spent on the games, activities, food and drink at the fair.

Today, the traditional aspect of recruitment has gone, but the funfairs remain, always around Michaelmas. From St Giles in Oxford, the fair splits and heads off to Banbury, Chipping Norton, Cirencester and Stratford-upon-Avon.

can travel from London to the north of England direct. You can walk the full length of the canal or simply stroll along the towpath from Hythe Bridge up to Isis Lock. Self-drive day trips on the canal are possible to Oxford from the canal centre (*www. oxfordshire-narrowboats.co.uk*) at nearby Thrupp. The trip takes seven hours with no time in Oxford but it provides a gentle day's escape from the city bustle.

North of the High Street and east of St Giles

To Oxonians, the High Street is simply known as **The High**, a street bordered by shops for the first few yards from the Carfax Tower before being lined with the silk of smooth, honey-stoned college buildings. The area north of the High Street is one of the most concentrated university areas in Oxford, with some of the best-known colleges such as Brasenose, Jesus, Queen's, New College, Balliol, Trinity and All Souls, along with the most familiar university landmarks – the Radcliffe Camera, the Bodleian Library and the Sheldonian Theatre.

This is the best quarter for walking, with plenty of car-free streets, where you can glance at the magnificent architecture, craning your neck to look at the numerous grotesques and gargoyles that hang from the walls like impious schoolboys. Take a look at Turl Street – though you may find some drunken, 'witty' student has altered the street sign, transforming the 'l' to a 'd' after a late night out – Brasenose Lane or Ship Street that leads to **St Michael at the North Gate**, on the corner of Cornmarket Street. Another of the city's lookout posts, the rickety stairs of the Saxon church tower can be climbed, past the giant hanging bells, for views above the rooftops. You'll discover some 250-year-old maintenance work too, in the form of the lead roof patched with the date 1765.

The Covered Market

Oxford's Covered Market is special. Accessed off The High, Cornmarket Street and Market Street, it's full of cosy cafés and tiny independent boutiques selling interesting things. Most of all though, it remains a food market where the same family butchers have been trading for generations, where fruit and vegetables really are fresh and where you can buy food that has genuinely been produced in Oxford. Products such as the Oxford sausage with its illustrious centuries-old history, Oxford Blue cheese, Oxford Sauce with a kick that will send you flying over college roofs and Oxford Marmalade, sadly the only one now outsourced from other parts of the country. Look out for the market's famous Cake Shop too; where cake artists shape and decorate the cakes in the window.

One of the narrowest streets to wander in this area is the winding Queen's Lane that leads to New College Lane and Catte Street. Crossing the two is the **Bridge of Sighs** joining the old and new quadrangles of Hertford College. So called because of its supposed similarity to the Venetian Bridge of Sighs (it actually resembles the Rialto Bridge more closely), Oxford's Bridge of Sighs official title is actually Hertford Bridge. It's a recent addition to the city's architecture – spanning the street only since 1914.

Though, to me, nowhere more epitomises how special learning in Oxford is than **Radcliffe Square**, with the well-dressed entrance to Brasenose College on the west side, the ornamented gilt gates entering the other world of All Souls College to the east, the University Church spreading itself between the square and The High, the mesmeric matter of the Bodleian Library to the north and in the centre, encompassed by iron fences, the **Radcliffe Camera**.

Although closed to the public, the Palladian building is one of the most iconic landmarks of Oxford and, once a science library, is now used as a part of the **Bodleian Library** (*www.bodleian.ox.ac.uk*). Wandering around Radcliffe Square, you'll unwittingly find yourself in the sacrilegious act of walking all over books. For the Camera and the Old Bodleian Library (the New Bodleian Library is 'across the road' on Broad Street) to the north are linked underground and much of the library's storage areas lie under the Square. One of the greatest research libraries in the world, it is also one of a handful entitled to receive a copy of every book published in the UK; it now stores over 8 million volumes on 110 miles of shelving.

Visitors are allowed to visit the Old Bodleian Library, which includes the Divinity School, the university's oldest teaching and examination room, dating back to 1427. Entrance to the Schools Quadrangle, the courtyard in the centre of the Old Bodleian Library and the Exhibition Room, where regular displays are held, are free but you can take a 'behind-the-scenes' guided tour of other areas within the library, worth every penny just to see the vaulted ceiling, as intricate as a lady's lace fan, in the Divinity School.

South of Radcliffe Square is the **church of St Mary the Virgin**, and as the spiritual heart of the university, otherwise known as the **University Church**. I love its interior for the intricacy of the glass windows and the finely carved choir stalls in the chancel, riddled with woodworm. If your legs will climb the 127 steps, the top of the tower provides one of the best views of Oxford.

John Radcliffe, a scholar and benefactor to the university (hence the Radcliffe Camera) and the royal physician to William and Mary (hence the John Radcliffe Hospital and the Radcliffe Infirmary), is buried in the church but of more historical note is the use of the church in 1555 for the heresy trials of the bishops Latimer and Ridley and Archbishop Cranmer during the Reformation. Becoming known as the Oxford Martyrs, the trio were burnt at the stake just north of the city walls, now **Broad Street**. A cross set into the road here marks the location; the Martyr's Memorial in Magdalen Street, at the western end of Broad Street, commemorates the event.

Broad Street is also the location of the first ever Oxfam charity shop, opened in 1948 and still running today, and the famous bookshop, **Blackwell's** (*www.blackwell.co.uk*). Indeed Broad Street is home to no fewer than four Blackwell's bookshops – the main store, Blackwell's Rare Books, Blackwell's Music and Blackwell's Art and Poster Shop. Every one of them has hours of browsing potential.

Broad Street's other notable resident is the **Sheldonian Theatre**, the first major work of Sir Christopher Wren. It's used as the university's ceremonial hall when gowned students process towards matriculation, when they are formally admitted to the university and upon graduation. At other times of the year it's open to the general public for a quick, fleeting visit or, better still, for one of the many concerts held there. The cupola is another rooftop viewing point.

Outside the Sheldonian Theatre, and the neighbouring **Museum of the History of Science** overlooking Broad Street, 13 emperors stand guard – or rather cast a watchful eye – for it is only their bearded heads that are *in situ* sitting upon pillars. They do not represent any individuals, but each one sports a different-looking beard.

Walk down Parks Road, which runs parallel with St Giles, and you'll find the medieval and classical architecture dressed in local soot-tinged Cotswold stone changes to Victorian Gothic brick. Much of the science faculty is based around here, as is **Keble College**, named after the Reverend John Keble who was Professor of Poetry at Oxford and a curate several miles away at the tiny church in Eastleach Martin (see page 120).

Two of the best museums owned by the university are opposite, the **University Museum of Natural History** (*www.oum.ox.ac.uk*) and the **Pitt Rivers Museum** (*www.prm.ox.ac.uk*). Both are free to enter and are a big hit with children. The Museum of Natural History is a fabulous building. Internally, the roof and ribs of the building are as skeleton-like as the exhibits it shelters. Marble busts and figures of eminent scientists such as Darwin, Aristotle, Galileo and Newton peer down upon you from among the arches as if to say, 'Don't you know anything?' There's a portrait of the Oxford dodo to the left of the main entrance and, elsewhere in the museum, information about the pigeon-like bird, where it came from and how one came to be in Oxford – and how European explorers and settlers aided its extinction. You can also watch live camera pictures of swifts nesting in the museum tower, a part of the Oxford Swift Research Project.

The Pitt Rivers Museum provides a dramatic change from the light and lofty Natural History Museum, through which it's accessed. Very dark, it is like entering Granny's attic, and is likeably old-fashioned. Three floors are stuffed full with over half a million artefacts and objects from around the world – anything from a totem pole to an ivory salt spoon, a knuckleduster to an old typewriter. Visitors are provided with torches to peer in the cabinets and anywhere else that objects from the anthropological collection are crammed. Children love the whole feel of the museum and there are many family events and activities planned throughout the year. But there is far too much to take in over one visit, so it's an idea to explore a couple of themes at a time.

If when you leave – or when you arrived – the two museums, you wonder what the giant footprints at the entrance are, they are those of a Megalosaurus, replicated from the 190 feet of footprint tracks found in a limestone quarry at nearby Ardley.

Wrapped around the north and east of the museums are the **University Parks**. With 70 acres of beautifully landscaped grounds on the western bank of the River Cherwell they include many sports pitches for the university and a colonial-looking timber cricket pavilion. In amongst though are specimen trees, flower borders, paths and public areas for informal games and activities.

As the River Cherwell curves around to form an ear shape on its way to meet up with the Thames, the ear is filled in with the grounds of **Magdalen College**. This is undoubtedly one of the most beautiful of the Oxford colleges and the public are invited (for a fee) to walk through the grounds and the deer park – all very surreal in the centre of a city. In spring the meadow is smothered with Oxfordshire's county flower, the snakeshead fritillary. Don't miss a chance to listen to the famous Magdalen College Choir sing, either at one of the seven chapel services in which they appear or on May Morning when, steeped in tradition, the choristers climb to the top of the Great Tower at the college and greet the morning sun with their singing.

South of the High Street and east of St Aldates

St Aldates is one of the busiest streets in Oxford, it being one of the main arteries leading into the city and is lined with bus stops every few yards. At the top, close to the junction with the High Street is the imposing town hall and inside, the free-to-enter **Museum of Oxford** (*01865 252761; www.museumofoxford.org.uk; open Tue* *to Sat*). This provides plenty of history: the importance of the city's location; the story of Frideswide, the Saxon princess and her connection to the city; the rise of the colleges as religious institutions, first University, Balliol and Merton, then New College in 1379; the 'Town and Gown' riots at the terrific-sounding Swindlestock Tavern in the 14th century; the rise of publishing; the base for Charles I during the English Civil War; and more recent industrial developments such as the birthplace of the British car industry under William Morris (the Lord Nuffield William Morris, not he of willow-leaved wallpapers fame), a trade that continues to grow with the construction of the Mini at Cowley, albeit under German owners. There's also a permanent exhibition on the real-life Alice in Wonderland.

Below the town hall, the vast expanse of **Christ Church** college begins, the slender cupola of the Tom Tower a giveaway to its presence. The tower is named after Great Tom, the bell within that resonates across Oxford 101 times every night at 21.05. Originally it was to signal for students to return to college for the night, now it's more likely waking any slumbering sloths from their daydreams ready for a night out. The timing is significant, the five-minute time delay is equivalent to 21.00 'Oxford Time', being west of the Greenwich meridian.

Built by Sir Christopher Wren, the Tom Tower hangs over Tom Gate, the main entrance to Christ Church College. The entrance for visitors to the college, including the Great Hall, which provided the inspiration for the set of Hogwarts Hall for the Harry Potter films, Christ Church Cathedral or the Christ Church Picture Gallery with its collection of Old Masters is through the wide decorative gates just to the south of the college.

These gates take you into Christ Church Meadow, accessed along the Broad Walk, one I would single out above all others in Oxford – an Arcadian idyll in the centre of a bustling city. From the gates are the most famous views of Christ Church College and the cathedral across the carefully tended and colourful Memorial Garden. The Broad Walk cuts a straight line between the meadow and Merton Field to the River Cherwell. Linking up with the Broad Walk is the Dead Man's Walk that skirts Christ Church, Corpus Christi and Merton colleges, so named because it was the route taken by coffins to the Jewish cemetery – now the Botanic Garden – in the 13th century. But take the time to turn off the Broad Walk down the New Walk, another avenue of shady trees, past the longhorn cattle that graze the meadow towards the Thames and you'll come to a more peaceful world.

Oxford has two rivers, the **Thames** and the **Cherwell** (pronounced 'charwell'). The pair meet at the southeastern tip of Christ Church Meadow. Except that in Oxford the Thames is locally known as the **Isis**. On a small island between the Thames and the Cherwell 'delta' the Oxford University boathouses line up like soldiers. There are no names, only the college crests to distinguish one from another. It's where sweat and the tears of elation or despair are absorbed by the river's might.

Don't ask me why, maybe it was just a nice sunny day and the river was calling, but when I last visited, I suddenly felt the urge to take out a boat – and row downstream as if my life depended on it, feeling the wind whistle past and the

Lewis Carroll and *Alice in Wonderland*

No author was actually called Lewis Carroll: this is the pseudonym of Charles Lutwidge Dodgson. The Latin for Charles is Carolus, thereby Carroll, while Lutwidge translates as Ludovic, or Lewis when anglicised, hence Lewis Carroll.

Charles Dogdson both attended and taught mathematics at Christ Church College. The college is significant in the lives of both he and Alice Liddell, upon whom his book is based; Alice's father was Dean of Christ Church and a very good friend of Charles Dodgson. The mathematician would take Alice and her siblings for frequent rowing trips and picnics on the Isis, telling bizarre stories as they travelled. 'Alice's Adventures Under Ground' was born from this, and was later published as *Alice's Adventures in Wonderland*.

There are many places and features around Oxford that crop up in Lewis Carroll's books such as the Oxford dodo. The Great Hall in Christ Church College houses portraits of both Henry Liddell, Alice's father, and Charles Dodgson plus an 'Alice' window depicting Alice Liddell, the dodo and other Wonderland characters. The St Catherine Window in the cathedral, created by the Pre-Raphaelite artist Edward Burne-Jones, is dedicated to Alice's sister Edith who died while living in the city.

Alice's Shop, opposite the entrance to Christ Church Meadow on St Aldates, stuffed with Alice memorabilia today, was the sweet shop where the little girl would buy her favourite barley sugars.

splash of water. The Isis here has this kind of effect on people. To see the boathouses busy, you need to be there for early morning training, or during the Torpids and Summer Eights racing weeks in early March and May, when much of Oxford lines the riverbanks of the Isis to cheer on the college teams.

One of the vintage views of Oxford is from the top of the little bridge that crosses the Cherwell to the boathouses. With the cattle of Christ Church Meadow grazing the foreground, the spires and towers of numerous colleges and churches and the dome of the Radcliffe Camera prick the skyline. A favourite spot of mine is a quiet bend in the River Cherwell just behind the boathouses at the very tip of Christ Church Meadow. Many tourists don't make it this far and, with the bells of the cathedral melodiously singing in the distance, the whispery seed heads from the thistles that line the meadow seem to float off on a journey as if to impart a city's wisdom and knowledge around the world.

The meadow path along the banks of the Cherwell, being the furthest from the entrance gates at St Aldates, is one of the most pleasant places in Oxford for a summer picnic or a winter walk. Your lunchtime entertainment might be the hilarity of watching punts slide sideways as the inexperienced try to grasp the knack of punting, frequently finishing up with their pole stretched between two branches of a riverside tree. A leisurely punt along the Cherwell is as much a part of river life in Oxford as serious rowing. You can hire punts – or rowing boats if oars rather than slippery poles are your thing – from the boathouse at Magdalen Bridge (*www.oxfordpunting.co.uk*), accessed off the High Street. Punts can also be hired from the **Cherwell Boathouse** (*www.cherwellboathouse.co.uk*), just north of the University parks.

If a skipper taking control is more orderly, larger boats ply up and down this southern stretch of the Isis. Salters Steamers (*www.salterssteamers.co.uk*) run short trips from **Folly Bridge**, southwest of Christ Church Meadow, to Iffley Lock downstream or two-hour trips to Sandford and Abingdon.

Butting up to the Cherwell is the university's **Botanic Garden** (*www.botanic-garden.ox.ac.uk*), fit for any season and open all year round. Botanical family collections are grouped in large, rectangular borders and there are collections grouped by geography too. With over 7,000 different types of plant concentrated in just over four acres, it's the most compactly diverse collection of plants in the world, as well as being Britain's oldest botanic garden. One thing you'll not fail to miss is the impressive specimen *Pinus nigra* (black pine) tree with its stubby trunk and branches that twist and curl their way to the heavens. However, it's the second half of the garden, through the giant stone pillars, that I find more exciting. Less formal, it has paths curving around orchards and beanpoles, water features and borders exploding with colour from spring to autumn. And ferns, alpines, palms and tropical lilies the size of tractor tyres shelter from Britain's unpredictable weather in the greenhouses close to the river.

The Botanic Garden is accessed from the High Street close to Magdalen Bridge. As you wander west back along The High, the road very gradually curves round, and you'll come across some of the best views of the street towards Queen's College, All Souls and the University Church with the Radcliffe Camera behind. You'll also pass the university's examination school where intricately carved, gowned and mitred figures are recessed into the wall. It's where many students finish their final days in Oxford, and there is nothing quite so daunting or nerve-jangling as trying to finish an exam paper on time with the painted eyes of university dignitaries peering down on your every thought and scrape of the pen.

South of Queen Street and west of St Aldates

From the Carfax Tower, Queen Street runs due west and is taken up with big chain stores. There are quiet streets in this quarter though to amble along – Rose Place, St Ebbe's and Brewer Street are all worth a walk but are not at the top of the list of places to visit if you are short of time. In fact, this whole quarter is more about everyday Oxford filled with modern shopping centres, car parks and the busy inner ring road and less about the historic city, with the exception of the picturesque **Pembroke College** and its sunny rose-clad courtyard.

Another to seek out is **Modern Art Oxford** (*www.modernartoxford.org.uk*).

There are no permanent collections here, but a large open space that puts on regular exhibitions of modern and contemporary work as well as talks, guided tours, live music performances and film screenings.

Out of line with all the historic buildings is the more futuristic-looking **Oxford Ice Rink** on the Oxpens Road (the inner ring road) where regular ice-related activities take place including matches played by the Oxford City Stars Ice Hockey Team. It's perhaps not quite the New Jersey Devils or the Toronto Maple Leafs but it may be a welcome distraction from all the history and tradition of the university.

Queen Street becomes New Road as it turns northwest and it's here that you'll find the remains of **Oxford Castle** (*www.oxfordcastle.com*). Once a royal motte and bailey stronghold – the mound is still evident – and the city's prison, the whole space was regenerated in 2006. It now houses the boutique Malmaison hotel (see page 146), several eateries and a visitor attraction, **Oxford Castle Unlocked**, revealing the history of the site. Visitors can climb the Saxon tower of the former city defences, descend into the crypt and experience the confines of prison life. Various events take place throughout the year including spine-tingling after-dark castle tours, a ghost festival and, on a lighter note, Oxford's Christmas market.

Across the Oxford Canal, where New Road becomes Park End Street, is the austere-looking brick **Jam Factory** (*www.thejamfactoryoxford.com*). Now an arts centre, restaurant and bar, it was once where the famous Frank Cooper's Oxford Marmalade was produced at the beginning of the 20th century, after the business run by him and his wife grew out of premises on the High Street. The arts centre puts on exhibitions specifically of Oxfordshire-based artists. Various art groups and classes also run from the historic factory rooms.

Oxford's outskirts

Sometimes the world of academia and streets filled with ancient institutions can begin to feel slightly claustrophobic and the need to escape bombards the mind. **Summertown** is a vibrant suburb to the north of Oxford with its own community feel and collection of shops and restaurants. It still retains the buzz of city life but without the glut of historic buildings. Alternatively visit the multi-cultural **Cowley Road** and head off to the **Mini Plant at Cowley** where the bodywork of the Mini car is manufactured, a 'sample' decorating the factory roof as if perched ready for some kind of *Italian Job* stunt. It's all quite noisy – the main Oxford bypass shoots overhead but there are windows into the factory where you can watch the process. There are possibilities to take a tour of the Oxford plant if pre-booked via www.mini-production-triangle.com.

To the east of the city is **Shotover Country Park**, where 289 acres of hillside can be explored. With views over the city from the hilltop, bracken-covered slopes sit side by side with ancient woods – it was once part of the royal forest of Shotover – flowery meadows, marshes and ponds. Celandines, bluebells and ox-eye daisies rub shoulders with butterflies, song thrushes and muntjac deer. The three waymarked trails all begin from Mary Sadler's Field, near the free car park at the hilltop entrance, plus an extensive network of other paths. A 20-station orienteering course is marked out around the park too – look out for the red and white marker posts. To reach the park using public transport, catch the 10 Stagecoach bus from the High Street in the city centre; get off at the Corner House pub at the end of Slade Road, walk down Horspath Driftway and cross the Eastern Bypass at the pelican crossing, entering the park close to the bypass and Brasenose Wood, a Site of Special Scientific Interest.

The other high point, to the southwest of Oxford, is **Boars Hill**, where Matthew Arnold wrote about Oxford's dreaming spires. His poem attracted many people who built houses there to take advantage of the view he described, and the view disappeared. **Jarn Mound** was built by hand to retrieve the vista across the land on the north side of the hill, which is now owned by the Oxford Preservation Trust, an organisation similar to the National Trust specifically for Oxford. The trust also owns other areas of Boars Hill including Abraham Wood, with public access.

Though perhaps Oxford's most celebrated outlying area is the low-lying **Port Meadow**, adjoining Wolvercote Common. The 300 acres of riverside common land is a popular strolling ground, accessed at its southern end from Jericho close to the city centre and at its northern end from Wolvercote, where the popular Trout Inn tucks up against a spur of the River Isis (Thames). The Thames Path gives distant views of Oxford's roofline to the south and the remains of **Godstow Abbey** to the north. The shallow spur of the river by the Airmen's Bridge just west of Lower Wolvercote makes this part of the water meadow a popular place for bathing, especially as it has a picnic area and a free car park.

It was this section of the Isis, alongside Port Meadow, that Lewis Carroll and his young companions – Alice Liddell and her sisters – rowed one summer's day. During the trip the story that would become *Alice's Adventures in Wonderland* was created. Oxford River Cruises (*www.oxfordrivercruises.com*) run boat trips along this stretch of the river, including a 'Mad Hatter's Tea Party' on board, from the Perch Inn at the tiny village of Binsey. Lunchtime picnic trips and straightforward sightseeing trips alongside Port Meadow are offered too.

One final hideaway, only a mile west of Port Meadow is the tiny village of **Wytham**. It was a tradition before the age of the car for residents of Oxford to drive out from the city with a pony and cart for strawberry teas at Wytham. The village is owned mostly by the University of Oxford today – Wytham Great Wood, on the hill behind, is a large ecological research 'laboratory' for the study of birds. Tucked over the little Wytham stream with its handsome manor house and church, the village is worlds apart from city life. The little village shop includes a tea garden where the tradition of having a strawberry tea continues. Opposite is the cosy White Hart Inn, with a very pleasant walled garden surrounded by the woods. You can walk to the village from the city using the Thames Path or by crossing Port Meadow and walking the last few yards along the quiet road from the Trout Inn.

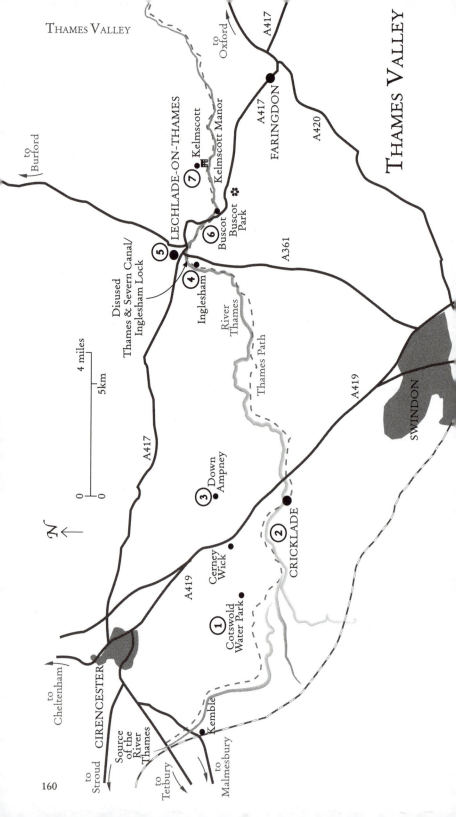

THAMES VALLEY

to Oxford

A417

FARINGDON

A417

A420

Kelmscott

Kelmscott Manor

⑦

LECHLADE-ON-THAMES

Buscot
Buscot Park

⑥

A361

⑤

Disused
Thames & Severn Canal/
Inglesham Lock

④

Inglesham

River Thames

Thames Path

to Burford

4 miles

5km

A417

A419

③ Down Ampney

N

SWINDON

A419

Cerney Wick

② CRICKLADE

① Cotswold Water Park

to Cheltenham

CIRENCESTER

to Stroud

Source of the River Thames

Kemble

to Tetbury

to Malmesbury

7. THAMES VALLEY

Where do you immediately think of as the Thames Valley? Reading, Goring, Marlow or Windsor perhaps? The phrase has been usurped to represent a particular region between Oxford and London for politics, policy and organisation. How about Kemble, Cerney Wick or Inglesham? The true Thames Valley begins in rural Gloucestershire, 53 miles west of Oxford.

It's hard to imagine the source of the Thames being anywhere other than where it actually is, but the debate over its location has divided opinion for many years and was even discussed in the House of Commons in 1937. Officially, the Thames Head is close to the Fosse Way between the villages of Coates and **Kemble**, a mile south of Cirencester. It remains dry for most of the year – I've never seen it so much as trickle from the ground here in many years – while the source of the River Churn, at Seven Springs southeast of Cheltenham, could actually be the Thames's true source. It never dries up and, being longer to the confluence than the Thames, should theoretically be the main river.

It would be a brave soul to suggest change either to its route or its name now. The Thames is a part of the British psyche. From the river's gentlest of beginnings, it seeps through the village of **Ewen** before winding through the old gravel pits that more recently have become the **Cotswold Water Park**. It soon gains water and is most definitely a reasonable stream when it reaches the edge of **Cricklade**, the first town on its journey. From there the river passes through flat open countryside with few villages to get in its way as if with a burning desire to become larger, fuller and more self-confident once the tributaries of the Coln and the Leach add to its stature. By the time it passes through **Lechlade-on-Thames**, the first town to bear its name, the river is navigable. Small marinas appear and the first of the locks, **St John's Lock**, is just east of the town where the reclining figure of **Old Father Thames** proudly watches over his adolescent child. Both Cricklade and Lechlade are Cotswold gems that often get overlooked by tourists concentrating on the big-name towns.

Within a few miles the river has all but left its Cotswold roots behind, passing through open vales rather than a valley lined with hills. Only when it comes close to Oxford does it show any signs of being a Cotswold river again passing by suitably Cotswold-esque architecture, but by now the river has grown up, it has left its youthful home behind and it continues its 215-mile journey to the North Sea as an adult responsible for grown-up boats and beautifying the grounds of dazzling, upmarket riverside properties. This chapter focuses solely on its youthful beginnings, until just east of Lechlade, when the river passes by the **Buscot Estate** and **Kelmscott Manor**, the home of William Morris.

Getting there and around

Trains

The only railway station hereabouts is at Kemble, though with this being right on the western edge, the station at Swindon is closer to some of the places mentioned in this chapter (Lechlade, Buscot and Kelmscott). **First Great Western** (*www.firstgreatwestern.co.uk*) operates trains from London, the southwest, Wales and the north via Birmingham New Street to Swindon. The station at Kemble is a spur between Gloucester and Swindon, so changes at either of these stations are likely. Kemble is the best station for walks close to the source of the river, along the Thames Path.

Buses

A frequent (at least hourly) bus service runs between Cirencester and Swindon stopping at South Cerney and Cricklade, while Lechlade is a stop on the Swindon to Fairford route. Cirencester and Lechlade also link up. However, as these bus services tend to stick to the main roads, outlying villages are less well served. A bus service from Cirencester to Tetbury and Malmesbury stops at Kemble, useful for those wishing to reach the source of the Thames or walk along the Thames Path.

Cycling

The Sustrans National Cycle Route 45 runs from Cirencester to **Cricklade** and from South Cerney, 2½ miles south of Cirencester; it's entirely traffic-free, using a disused railway line and passing through the **Cotswold Water Park**. It's all very flat and easy wheeling.

Elsewhere in the water park, cycling is useful for getting from A to B but the landscape is not particularly conducive to a really scenic bike ride, as most of the lakes are surrounded by tall hedges. In essence this locale is not the finest for bike rides.

Bike hire

Go By Cycle Tall Trees, Water Lane, Somerford Keynes GL7 6DS ℡07970 419208 ◌⏚ www.go-by-cycle.co.uk. Bike hire including all-terrain bikes, child bikes and cycle trailers, tag-alongs, tandems and tricycles. Helmets included in the hire. Hourly, daily or weekly rates.

Walking

The obvious choice here is the long-distance **Thames Path**. Approximately 35 miles of the 184-mile footpath run through this locale; this makes a good walking weekend, by breaking the journey into two and stopping at Cricklade and Lechlade or Kelmscott.

Accommodation

Log House Holidays Poole Keynes GL7 6ED ☎01285 770082
🖰 www.loghouseholidays.co.uk. A choice of 6 traditional Finnish log cabins right on the shoreline of a private and secluded 100-acre lake within the Cotswold Water Park. The whole site is a designated Site of Special Scientific Interest because of its importance to wildlife conservation. Sleep from 4 to 8 people. Each log cabin is in its own secluded location and has an outdoor hot tub. Rowing skiffs are provided for access to the lake. Wood-burning stoves for winter cosiness too.

Manor Farm Kelmscott GL7 3HJ ☎01367 262620 🖰 www.kelmscottbandb.co.uk. A 17th-century farmhouse owned by the National Trust on a 315-acre working arable and livestock farm that is run by the Horner family. A hearty breakfast uses produce from the farm and that of their neighbours. Very friendly hosts. Children welcome.

Red Lion 74 High St, Cricklade SN6 6DD ☎01793 750776
🖰 www.theredlioncricklade.co.uk. Just yards from the not-very-large Thames, B&B accommodation in this old pub with plenty of character. Five bedrooms available are situated in an annexe, away from the bar areas. Two rooms are 'dog-friendly'. Good bar and restaurant food.

The source – Kemble and Ewen to Cricklade

I remember once, as quite a young girl, being driven past the vast RAF airfield at Kemble and, in one of those naive excitable childhood moments without concept of monetary value, wanting to buy it because I was told that it was threatened with closure and the Red Arrows display team, with which I was fascinated, would have to leave their base. The airfield was worth millions and I probably had little more than 50 pence pocket money saved.

The airfield has been renamed, rather grandly, as Cotswold Airport and is now used by corporate jets looking to avoid the queues at major airports. It's also a graveyard for decommissioned jumbos and from several miles away you can't help but notice the enormous tail fins of these monsters sticking up from the treeline. You pass right by the airfield on the Fosse Way.

But to view some aircraft up close, visit the **Bristol Aero Collection** (*01285 771204; www.bristolaero.com*), which preserves and exhibits many of those created by the famous Bristol Aeroplane Company. On display are aircraft including a Harrier 'jump-jet', the fighter jets used on aircraft carriers until they were decommissioned in 2010, engines, missiles and spacecraft.

The source of the Thames is a few fields away from the airfield's perimeter fence. It's hard to tell simply by driving along the Fosse Way from Cirencester to Kemble that you are close to the source. There's no water. Barely even a snake of sunken ground that suggests a river, and no sign or large arrow on the roadside that says, 'Source of the River Thames – this way'. Its official source is northwest of the Fosse Way, a mile from Cirencester in a far-flung meadow that you can reach only on foot. No car park, no fanfare, just a stone marking the spot.

The countryside is gentle and relatively flat here. The river, what there is of it now, bypasses the modernised village of Kemble, expanded owing to its proximity to the railway, and the linear village of Ewen. It's barely recognisable as a stream until it reaches the Cotswold Water Park.

① Cotswold Water Park

Covering over 40 square miles of countryside, the Cotswold Water Park (*www. waterpark.org*) was once an area buzzing with heavy industry, extracting sand and gravel; there are still a few active quarries operating. Since the 1890s, when the first pits were dug to provide ballast for railway line construction (in the 1960s aggregate from here was also used to build the M4 motorway), more than 150 lakes have been created. Owing to the high water table, any hole that was dug greater in depth than 12 inches would rapidly fill with water. Early forms of extraction would leave gravel behind beneath the water surface but the methods used have ultimately created havens for aquatic plants and a great habitat for insects, feeding bats and nesting birds. With relatively shallow, uneven-bottomed lakes that have irregular shorelines and several islands, much of the park looks like a natural part of the landscape rather than something entirely manmade.

However, don't expect to see much of the park simply by winding the car window down while driving along the roads that criss-cross between the lakes. Most lakes are surrounded by dense trees, and you'll see little of them without walking, cycling or, better still, getting onto the water. Each lake has a distinct 'use'. Some are used simply as a scenic backdrop to holiday lodges and houses, accessed only by residents. Others are specifically for various watersports such as sailing or for angling. But there are many lakes left to nature for migrating birds and wildlife projects that attract endangered species such as the water vole.

There are two sections to the water park – one between Fairford and Lechlade known as the eastern section, while the western section, the larger of the two, is concentrated around the villages of South Cerney, Somerford Keynes, Ashton Keynes and Cerney Wick.

For many visitors to the area, the first stop is the Cotswold Water Park **Gateway Centre**, close to the A419. Centrally located between the two sections of park, it is like the nerve centre and is a useful stopping point to pick up free maps of the area, use the facilities and sit in the rather pleasant eco-friendly green oak-framed building overlooking one of the lakes. Within the centre is the skull of a woolly mammoth that was found in a quarry during excavations in 2001 at nearby Ashton Keynes. There's a convenient but ordinary café on site too – though the views across one of the lakes are idyllic – and a very good, large branch of the Cotswold Outdoor chain, useful for picking up outdoor activity clothing and gear.

Numerous footpaths cut between the lakes too, including the Thames National Trail, so there are plenty of opportunities to create a circular walk lasting a few hundred yards or several miles. One of the most pleasant is a simple walk around the **Neigh Bridge Country Park** in the west of the western section, close to the village of Somerford Keynes. It's an easy stroll along a path that surrounds one of the more secluded lakes and there are large lakeside areas suitable for picnics. It's also one of the best places in the water park to view wildlife. There's plenty of birdlife on the water, with winter migrants and spring breeders, but in the summer it is the grass that is awash with electric blue damselflies, which have really taken to the area. If driving, the free car park for Neigh Bridge is accessed off the main arterial Spine Road.

Other places to spot wildlife within the western section of the park include Lower Moor Farm Nature Reserve, Shorncote Reed Bed, Coke's Pit Nature Reserve and Swillbrook Lakes Nature Reserve, the last a place to listen to the singing nightingales. The Cotswold Water Park Trust (*www.waterpark.org*) is responsible for the conservation of the area, working to improve biodiversity. The trust organises events throughout the year including wildlife walks with field officers, introductions to birdwatching (see www.surfbirds.com/blog/cotswoldwaterpark for a detailed blog, set up by the society's biodiversity officer Gareth Harris, on what birds to see where and when), fossil hunts and wildlife talks by distinguished speakers.

While walking, look out for several sculptures dotted throughout the whole of the Cotswold Water Park, the most prominent being the *Reed Hide*, made from rammed earth, oak and woven hazel. It overlooks a large heronry on the edge of Cleveland Lakes and is only accessible on foot either along the Thames Path, close to the hamlet of Waterhay or along the disused railway line from Wickwater Lane. The locations of all the water park's sculptures, part of a public art project 'Access and Art' to encourage walking in the area, are shown on an interpretation panel at the Lakeside Recreation area along Station Road, between the **Gateway Centre** and **South Cerney**.

Food and drink

Butts Farm Shop South Cerney GL7 5QE ☎01285 862224 🖥 www.thebutts farmshop.com. Farm shop selling the highest-quality meat from the rare breeds of animals that are kept on the farm, including Cotswold lamb. Farm visits Feb to Oct.
Wild Duck Inn Drake's Island, Ewen GL7 6BY ☎01285 770310
🖥 www.thewildduckinn.co.uk. Classic country-inn ambience with low, beamed ceilings, timber floors, wood settles and gentle lighting. The walls are filled with oil paintings. Bar and restaurant menu using organic and locally produced fare. Vegetarian options and plenty of daily specials. Canopied, leafy courtyard garden for dining outside. Accommodation.

Activities within the Cotswold Water Park

Adventure Zone Lake 32 ☎01285 861202 🖥 www.adventure-zone.co.uk. Adventure

Bringing back the water vole

Far from being just a leisure landscape for the benefit of people keen on watersports, the Cotswold Water Park is of enormous importance to the wildlife population too. The Cotswold Water Park Trust, a non-profit-making environmental body, puts an immense amount of work into ensuring that the area is beneficial to all. Working with mineral companies, farmers and local councils, the society has created a new biodiversity vision for the water park, the 'Head of the Thames Project', to ensure a healthy 14-mile wetland corridor for wildlife, from the river's source to Lechlade.

There are many biodiversity projects continuing in the park, working to maintain healthy numbers of birds, bats, dragon and butterflies and other water creatures. In particular are two projects that caught my eye. One is the reintroduction of native **beavers**, which became extinct from Britain in the 17th century but who are now colonising the private Lower Mill Estate in the water park. You can take yourself on a self-guided walk to see the area where they live or book one of the informative guided walks.

The other project is to reverse the drastic decline in the number of water voles (think Ratty from *The Wind in the Willows*), a creature that has become close to extinction in certain parts of the country and whose numbers declined by almost 50% along the Thames within five years during the 1990s. In April 2008 the water vole became fully protected under the Wildlife and Countryside Act 1981. Gareth Harris, the Biodiversity Field Officer for the Cotswold Water Park, explained their work: 'In 2002 we set up a project to prevent the further decline of the water vole in the Cotswold Water Park. Changes in land management practice and the release of the American mink into the wild had devastating effects on the water vole population. Mink will eradicate whole colonies of water voles within weeks, which also has a huge impact on waterbirds too.

activities for children and parents including sailing, windsurfing, canoeing, raft-building, problem-solving and bushcraft.

Cotswold Country Park and Beach Spratsgate Ln ☎01285 868096
🖰 www.cotswoldcountrypark.com. Situated around large lakes, the park includes the UK's largest inland beach. Lakeside barbecue hire.

Cotswold Forest School ☎0845 0941 949
🖰 www.cotswoldforestschool.co.uk. Five acres of native woodland used for exciting outdoor activities, aimed particularly at children, such as woodland survival skills, camp craft, den-building and woodland art. Workshops last for one day. Expect to get grubby.

Head 4 Heights ☎01285 770007
🖰 www.head4heights.net. Aerial adventure centre with climbing, jumping and swinging activities. For ages 5 years to adult. Individual activities may be booked separately or book a combined ticket to perform several challenges. Open to the general public every weekend and daily during school holidays Apr–Oct.

'So following several surveys that established we had a problem with mink, we spent eight years bringing their numbers under control. Only once the mink population had gone, could we address the issues of a suitable habitat for the water voles. It was not until September 2010 that we had monitored a full year without mink.'

Gareth continued, 'Water voles breed very well and if the conditions are right, they will colonise. We have not, therefore, had to purposely reintroduce any water voles as they are returning by themselves gradually, but we are continuing to make small-scale improvements to their habitat. We need to ensure that the water voles populate a continuous habitat with no more than a kilometre between colonies. This means they can breed successfully and prevent individual colonies from becoming isolated, potentially putting them at risk from predators.

'The presence of water voles indicates a healthy landscape. If you can get the habitat right for water voles, many other species benefit too. In addition to colonising the water park again, water voles are increasing well in the Thames tributaries such as the Churn and the Coln [see pages 128 and 121] rather than the Thames itself, which floods too quickly, causing problems for the creatures that need to escape to ditches and hedgerows. However, exceptions to this are colonies at Lechlade, where, having not been spotted for many years, water voles have been seen on the banks of the Thames opposite Riverside Park. Another good place to spot water voles is at Bibury where, unconventionally, they are living in dry-stone walls.'

Visitors to the Cotswold Water Park can take guided walks with Gareth and other members of the biodiversity team, who will provide a fascinating insight into the ecology of the park and their work. Alternatively, you can become a volunteer ranger, helping with environmental work in the park such as planting hedges, clearing reed beds or coppicing willows. A programme of work and dates is available on the Cotswold Water Park website.

Watermark Fisheries Wildmoorway Lane ☎01285 862680
🖥 www.watermarkfisheries.com. Coarse and game fishing across 12 lakes providing over 300 acres of water as well as river trout fishing. Day and 24-hour tickets available on site from the Tackle Den.

WMSki The Watermark, Spring Lake, Station Rd ☎0845 895 9000
🖥 www.wmski.com. Introductory courses in both boat and cable waterskiing plus wakeboarding and fun inflatable water rides. Children's introductory waterskiing mornings too.

② Cricklade

Cricklade's Latin motto, derived from a 12th-century text on English history, is *in loco delicioso*, or 'in a delightful place' and I wouldn't disagree.

For a town so small its history is significant: it was created by the Anglo-Saxons as a fortified burgh for King Alfred to protect Wessex. Only 'North Wall' at the northern end of the High Street acts as a reminder of the town's defences. The town had its own royal mint, and coins from Cricklade, having been paid to the Vikings as ransom to prevent attacks, are in museums across Scandinavia.

Cricklade's High Street is a delight, a concoction of ageing stone and rendered buildings dating from the 15th century encompassing houses, shopfronts and old coaching inns. Wander up Church Street, west of the High Street, and you'll pass the Jenner School, with gabled windows in typical Cotswold style. It's best viewed from the churchyard at the rear where grass lawns show off the old school's stone façade to best advantage.

Allow time to take a look at St Sampson's Church too. There's a tiny stained- glass window on the wall of the South Isle that is so vibrantly scarlet red that I thought it had been lit from indoors. I found the lead panels, removed during repairs to the roof in 2009 and exhibited in the church, really fun. On them are graffiti etched into the lead dating back to 1776, with drawings of shoes, hands that have been initialled by their artist, ships, rifles, a small bird and the elevation of a house.

One of the best places to view the church and its dominating bell tower in relation to the rest of Cricklade is from **North Meadow**, aptly, just north of the town and a short walk from High Bridge at the top of the High Street, and designated as a National Nature Reserve and a Site of Special Scientific Interest.

This traditional and ancient water meadow usually floods in winter, when nutritious minerals from the river are washed over the ground, creating perfect fertile ground for many wild flowers and grasses. It has been managed in the same way for centuries, with a hay crop taken in summer to provide winter fodder and then grazed by livestock that nibble down the tougher grasses allowing space for next year's wild flowers, in turn bringing out bees, butterflies, dragonflies and many hedgerow birds. But the meadow's most distinguishing feature is that it has the largest number of snakeshead fritillaries anywhere in the UK, representing 80% of the total fritillary 'population' and attracting crowds of people who come to walk among these delicate flowers.

The best time to see the fritillaries is during the second and third weeks in April, when the reserve manager takes guided walks through the flowers. You can find out exact dates and times, and book a walk, by phoning 07795 316191. However, the 110-acre meadow is extremely attractive at any other time of year. To enjoy its beauty and differing characteristics, such as the riverside, pollarded willows or reed beds, three walks of varying length are marked out.

The main entrance to North Meadow is from the B4553, north of Cricklade. Cars should not be parked in the entrance but in the lay-by 100 yards north. Better still is to walk from the town centre, using either the Thames Path heading west or via the short public footpath just north of High Bridge crossing the Thames.

Food and drink

Red Lion 74 High St ☎01793 750776 🖥 www.theredlioncricklade.co.uk. Two menus for the bar (including chunky sandwiches, soup, ploughman's and sausage and mash) and restaurant (such as steak pie, pheasant or slow-cooked pork). Lots of beers from different microbreweries in the UK and abroad that rarely make it into large town pubs. Close to the Thames, it's a good base from which to set off for North Meadow National Nature Reserve.

North of the river – the Ampneys

Unlike its Cotswold tributaries that frequently run through steep-sided valleys, the course of the Thames drifts through large, flat water meadows. Four miles to the north of the river is a small cluster of villages, the Ampneys – Ampney Crucis, Ampney St Mary and Ampney St Peter. Put together they make an interesting detour from nearby Cirencester. Ampney Crucis is the largest of the three villages but of note is Ampney St Mary and its separated church. The village, though centuries old, is modern by comparison with its 12th-century church. In 1349 the Black Death hit the original village hard and a new settlement was built a mile from the church. Nothing remains of the original village except the church standing alone by the side of Ampney Brook, a tiny tributary of the Thames. Known locally as the Ivy Church for the simple fact that it was covered with this creeper until restoration in 1913, the building has remained virtually unchanged. Its medieval wall paintings are remarkably well preserved.

Food and drink

Red Lion Ampney St Peter ☎01285 851596. Close to the A417 between Ampney St Peter and Ampney St Mary, a 2-room pub that time forgot. Hatch bar with just 2 ales and only the 3rd landlord in a century. Very traditional with log fires and no food. Very friendly. Very limited opening hours – Fri to Mon evenings and Sun lunchtime.

③ Down Ampney

While it retains the 'Ampney' name, the village of Down Ampney is three miles from its other namesakes, and is much closer to the Thames. It is also better known than its counterparts for being the birthplace in 1872 of the celebrated English composer Ralph Vaughan Williams. His father was vicar of All Saints', Church and Ralph was born at the Old Vicarage, a handsome house right in the centre of the village.

The church, where his father preached and is buried having died just three years after the composer was born, is tucked away from the main part of the village in a very pleasant spot surrounded by parkland and fields. In the bell tower is a superb exhibition about the life of Vaughan Williams created by the RVW Society and opened by the composer's widow in 2001. In dedication to his place of birth, Vaughan Williams named the hymn tune for 'Come down, O love divine' after Down Ampney.

Whenever I visit the church, I feel an affinity with the village. My grandfather was a friend of Ralph Vaughan Williams and he conducted much of the composer's music at concerts. Just before my grandfather died he presented me with a treasured signed photograph of the composer.

Hugh the Drover – a Cotswold opera

Ralph Vaughan Williams was most noted for his dedication to the collection and preservation of traditional English folk song, searching for music that would otherwise have been lost because of its oral traditions. His love of the countryside and the incorporation of traditional melodies within his own music, led him to write his first opera, *Hugh the Drover*. A story about English life in 1812 and a love-at-first-sight relationship, it is the only opera ever to be set in the Cotswolds and includes typical Cotswold scene-setting at a fair.

Begun in 1910, it was not finished until after World War I, when Vaughan Williams had witnessed the horrors of war on the front line in France, and subsequently amended. It was thought that his completion of a simple romantic tale using the English folksong traditions that he so loved was a therapeutic cleanser for all that he had seen. The first public performance of *Hugh the Drover* was in 1924 by the British National Opera Company, conducted by Malcolm Sargeant.

Ralph Vaughan Williams died in 1958 and was buried at Westminster Abbey. His funeral included the hymn tune 'Down Ampney'.

Postscript, by Tim Locke, Bradt editor and author:

As I was editing this book and writing my own *Slow Sussex and South Downs National Park*, I had the Cotswolds very much on my mind as I performed in a New Sussex Opera production of *Hugh the Drover*. It hadn't been produced professionally in London for half a century, and despite some shortcomings of the libretto it wasn't that obvious why: the music is lusciously folksy and appealing (complete with market traders' cries which the composer had collected on his travels), representing Vaughan Williams at his most radiantly lyrical. Set in 1812 at the height of the Napoleonic War, it tells the story of Cotswold villagers full of xenophobic hatred of the French, and an astonishingly set boxing match to decide whether Hugh or John the Butcher should win the hand of Mary. Morris dancers make a brief appearance before the drover himself appears: Hugh collects horses (presumably from the Welsh hills) for the army; after arrest on a false charge of being a French spy he is about to be taken to Gloucester prison to be executed when all comes right for him in the end. While the opera most certainly belongs to a music tradition of pre-1914, nearly a hundred years after it was begun it may well come back into fashion as we can appreciate the qualities of this charming period piece. It has been well recorded by Hyperion.

Though it is a there-and-back walk to a tiny lake-filled copse, take a few moments to wander along the tree-lined bridleway from the churchyard entrance. It's a very pleasant walk through fields and small pockets of woodland and crosses the end of the disused RAF Down Ampney Airfield, which once hummed to the throaty sound of old Dakotas and played a significant part in both Operation Market Garden at Arnhem and D-day. The Arnhem Memorial Window, an unusual stained-glass picture in the church illustrating a Dakota aircraft, commemorates the troops who were deployed from the airfield to Operation Market Garden.

Inglesham to Kelmscott

The Thames drifts east through open countryside past the villages of Castle Eaton and Kempsford and then takes a sharp turn north to meet with its tributary the River Coln at **Inglesham**. This is half a mile southwest of **Lechlade-on-Thames**, the first settlement downstream to take the name of the river, and where the Thames becomes truly navigable. Boats begin to appear, with the first of the river's locks, St John's Lock, just east of the town.

The river's route is no less winding than elsewhere though, curving through some of the flattest ground in the Cotswolds past the Buscot Estate and the tiny dead-end village of **Kelmscott**, where the Victorian designer William Morris once sought out a secluded hideaway house for a home.

④ Inglesham

There are two parts to Inglesham – Upper Inglesham that's split by the very busy A361 and simply Inglesham, north of its neighbour, and the part that I'd like to focus on. There's very little here, just a few surviving buildings from a medieval village 'protected' by a bend in the River Thames, but it's an important place nonetheless. Drive too fast along the A361 south from Lechlade and you'll miss the inconspicuous turning to the one access road; a tiny wooden sign points in the direction of a remote 13th-century church.

St John the Baptist Church, with Saxon origins, is significant though. A series of remarkable medieval wall paintings – and the church itself – is likely to have crumbled to dust but for one man, William Morris. In 1887 he discovered the church in a state of disrepair, fell in love with the building and vowed to restore it. The restoration project was one of his first after having founded the Society for the Protection of Ancient Buildings, an organisation still extant that is based upon Morris's principles to restore 'old and interesting' buildings in a sympathetic way, using appropriate, traditional materials.

Rather than arrive by car – there is no official parking and the road is extremely narrow – the most appealing route is from Lechlade, crossing ancient water meadows using the Thames Path, which passes the entrance to the church.

The Cotswold canals – a restoration project

In the 18th century two canals, the **Thames and Severn Canal** and the **Stroudwater Canal**, were built to create a 36-mile stretch of waterway that linked up the rivers Severn and Thames. It made a formidable and important journey for goods to be transported from towns on the Severn to London. Merging in Stroud, the pair became known as the Cotswold Canals.

The Stroudwater was the first to be built, between 1775 and 1779, with the Thames and Severn Canal completed a decade later. But the River Severn is considerably lower than the Thames and a flight of locks was required to reach the summit at Daneway, near Sapperton (see page 184), where one of the longest canal tunnels in Britain was built.

The Cotswold Canals were an incredibly important and busy thoroughfare for goods but competition from the railways during the latter half of the 19th century caused decline and by 1927 the Thames and Severn Canal was closed followed shortly after by the Stroudwater. With the canals neglected they soon became derelict.

Today restoration is uppermost in the mind of the Cotswold Canals Trust (*www. cotswoldcanals.com*), which owns parts of the canal including Inglesham Lock, considered the gateway to the Cotswolds from the Thames. The aim ultimately is to restore the full length of both canals, using volunteers to clear undergrowth, rebuild locks and repair walls. Liz Payne, chairman of the Cotswold Canals Trust, explained 'Volunteers can approach us through the website or by dropping into one of our visitor centres at Wallbridge in Stroud and at Saul (open every weekend). We really need enthusiastic people to maintain and restore locks and even run boat trips that help to generate income to keep the restoration project going.'

Another intriguing building close to the tiny village, is at **Inglesham Lock** (which you would pass if using the Thames Path to the church). Close to where the River Coln meets the Thames, there is the entrance to an old, disused canal. This was the Thames and Severn Canal, a waterway that helped to join the two mighty rivers together until 1927. Inglesham Lock is the point at which river and canal met and by it is the **Round House**. The unusual dwelling, built in 1790, was lived in by the canal lengthman who would manage the lock and the first stretch of canal. Horses were stabled on the ground floor while the ingenious inverted roof (providing it didn't leak) collected rainwater for domestic use. It is one of five lengthman's round houses along the disused canal with others at Coates, Chalford, Cerney Wick and Marston Meysey.

Inglesham Lock is one of the most scenic spots in this locale and should be even more so in years to come. The **Inglesham Lock Restoration Project** (*www. inglesham.org.uk*) aims to restore the lock and is appealing for both funds and volunteers to help clear the canal bed, reface the lock chamber wall and install new lock gates. The tiny bridge needs repairing too.

⑤ Lechlade-on-Thames

Lechlade possibly gets overlooked by mass tourism even though the A361 from Burford to Swindon passes straight through, meeting with the road from Cirencester to Faringdon. But that in itself, together with the Thames, shows the town's importance as a trading post with a fascinating history. And today, there are some very quirky shops to nose around.

There is, albeit buried, evidence of Bronze Age, Iron Age, Roman and Saxon living within the vicinity but much of what you see today, especially around the High Street and the Market Square, is elegant town houses built using the wealth created by the town's trade. The Salt Ways from Droitwich ended in Lechlade with the salt then loaded onto boats to be shipped down the Thames to London. The ancient drovers' road, the Welshway, also arrived at Lechlade where livestock were either sold off at one of the markets or, like salt, shipped down the river to London.

Indeed as a highway the Thames was as important to the town as any of the converging roads. The river was dredged, deepened and widened downstream from Lechlade as early as 1235 to allow London barges to pass. The riverside wharves were busy loading stone, cheese (made around Cricklade) and corn bound for the capital and other major cities such as Bristol and Liverpool via the Cotswold canals. Anglers, pleasure boats and swans now use the river.

The charming 12-seater *Inglesham* launch provides 30-minute trips, between April and September, from the **Riverside Park**, just south of Lechlade on the opposite side of the Thames. These are run by the Cotswold Canals Trust, and money raised from the river trips goes towards the restoration of Inglesham Lock. If you prefer to spend longer enjoying the river, Canadian canoes and kayaks can be hired from Lechlade Angling and Outdoor Pursuits, next door to the Riverside Inn. Other than standard hourly and day hire, you can book a **Canoe Mini Break** where your canoe is delivered to Cricklade or Castle Eaton and you navigate the section of the river that boats can't access, down to Lechlade.

Spanning the Thames, **Ha'penny Bridge** was built in 1792 when a halfpenny was the toll levied from the small square tollhouse on the Lechlade side. Cattle and people were charged in addition to carts.  From the Riverside Park next to the bridge you can get a very attractive view of the town, with the wharf, the bridge and the spire of St Lawrence's Church; this is a prime picnicking spot and the place to pick up the Thames Path to Inglesham. Views to the west incorporate the sight of Inglesham Church in the distance, across the meadows.

Lechlade celebrated 800 years of market status in 2010. The weekly market that once thrived on the through-trade has long gone but a farmers' market still takes place on the third Thursday of every month and the brick façade of the New Inn – one of the few brick buildings in the centre of town

– still sports the archway through which stage and mail coaches would start their journey to London.

In the corner of the Market Square is the majestic **church of St Lawrence**, its spire a landmark for many miles. The church was originally known as St Mary but Catherine of Aragon, whose estate included Lechlade Manor, insisted that it be renamed after a saint from the Spanish region of Aragon. A pomegranate, Catherine's symbol, is carved into the huge church door. It was the poet Percy Bysshe Shelley who wrote most notably about Lechlade. He was so taken with the church that in 1815 he wrote 'A Summer Evening Churchyard: Lechlade, Gloucestershire' while staying at the New Inn. The path through the churchyard is known as **Shelley's Walk**, from where you can take a fine circular walk out of town. My preference is actually to start from Ha'penny Bridge and walk east along the Thames Path until you reach the Trout Inn close to St John's Lock, then return using the ancient raised causeway across the water meadow just north of the Thames, where you'll gain superb views of the church spire, finally reaching Shelley's Walk.

St John's Lock and Old Father Thames

Half a mile east of Lechlade is **St John's Lock**, the first lock on the navigable stretch of the Thames. The lock takes its name from the medieval priory dedicated to St John the Baptist that once stood where the Trout Inn is now. Close by, St John's Bridge, built in 1229, was one of the first bridges across the Thames to be built outside of London.

Overseeing the lock is **Old Father Thames**. The reclining figure, shovel swung over his shoulder, was commissioned for London's new Crystal Palace Exhibition in 1854. Bought by the Thames Commissioners following the exhibition, the old man was placed at the source of the river until being relocated to St John's Lock.

Following the flow of the Thames, half a mile from St John's Bridge is **Cheese Wharf**, a 180-degree loop in the river close to which warehouses, in the early 19th century, stood brimming with cheese from north Wiltshire and Gloucestershire. Between two and three thousand tons of cheese were sent down the Thames to London annually. The warehouses are gone and there's enough space to pull off the road to stop: it's a very pleasant place to watch ducks dabbling by the shallow banks of the river.

Food and drink

Colleys High St ℂ01367 252218 🖰 www.colleyslechlade.co.uk. Great place for café-style lunches or more lavish dinners taken from a set 4-course menu. There is only one sitting per night. Menu changes fortnightly.

Crown Inn High St ℂ01367 252198 🖰 www.crownlechlade.co.uk. Home to the Halfpenny Brewery, the town's first microbrewery. A drinker's pub, simple food (ploughman's and Sunday roasts) is served only at weekends.

Riverside Inn Park End Wharf. Pub garden overlooking the Thames, Riverside Park and Ha'penny Bridge. Watch the swans don't nick your sandwiches!

Richardson and Amey Nature Reserve

Lechlade is still considered to be within the boundaries of the Cotswold Water Park with many former gravel pits making up this eastern section. The lakes are most noticeable just to the north of Lechlade, spreading from the Burford road. One of these, west of the Burford road and accessible from the roundabout on the very edge of town, is the Richardson and Amey Nature Reserve. Managed by Gloucestershire Wildlife Trust, the two very shallow lakes, surrounded by willow, are full of resident and migrating birds such as kingfishers, widgeon, teal and great crested grebes. A bird hide helps you view the activity on the northern lake while a nature trail around the crescent-shaped southern lake provides a quiet, scenic spot. Dragonflies are a sight in summer too, and orchids have colonised the gravel scrub.

Trout Inn St John's Bridge ☎01367 252313 🖥 www.thetroutinn.com. Popular pub half a mile from Lechlade close to St John's Lock. Regular live music including the Lechlade River Folk (🖥 *www.riverfolk.co.uk*), a community-based music session where anyone can turn up and sing or play an instrument.

Shopping

Anthony Hazledine 6 Burford St ☎01367 253871 🖥 www.anthonyhazledine.com. A really unusual selection of antique rugs, textiles and tribal art from around the world laid out in a homely atmosphere.

The Christmas Shop High St ☎01367 253184 🖥 www.thechristmasshop.org. It's Christmas all year round in Lechlade, at least in this shop. Far from being tacky, the shop is full of traditional and unusual items, mainly handcrafted in wood, porcelain, pewter and brass.

Lechlade Angling & Outdoor Pursuits Park End Wharf ☎07900 154 098 🖥 www.lechladeanglingandoutdoorpursuits.co.uk. Dave Orrie, the very friendly owner, has over 60 years of experience fishing in the area and is the man to talk to about fishing the Thames at Lechlade. New and secondhand tackle, plus baits in stock. Canoe hire.

Old Ironmongers Antiques Centre 5 Burford St, Lechlade ☎01367 252397. My little secret – I don't really want to give it away! A fascinating shop that is crammed full from floor to ceiling with bits and bobs that cannot fail to interest. From old furniture and period house fittings to old woodworking tools, advertising hoardings, uniforms, traditional pottery and bottles, plus cabinet after cabinet of knick-knacks. It's the sort of tightly stashed place where carrying a large bag might knock something over as you swing round to browse.

⑥ Buscot Park

Three miles east of Lechlade, Buscot Park (*0845 345 3387; www.buscot park.com; open Apr to Sep*), owned by the National Trust, remains the family home of Lord Faringdon who lives in and administers the house and grounds. The house therefore feels alive and, despite the opulence and grandeur of the architecture and interior design, there are personal touches. Not least in the Faringdon Collection, a significant portfolio of art, furniture, ceramics and *objets d'art*, which is displayed in the house and to which Lord Faringdon continues to add with contemporary works. The collection includes artwork by Rembrandt, Reynolds, Rubens, Van Dyck and Murillo but, perhaps of greatest importance given the proximity of the estate to Kelmscott, is the representation of 19th- and 20th-century British art, in particular some Pre-Raphaelite masterpieces: Edward Burne-Jones's famous series *The Legend of the Briar Rose* hangs on the walls as does Rossetti's portrait of *Pandora*.

Outside, paths through the parkland and pleasure grounds fan out towards two large lakes. Fishing is allowed but day tickets must be bought in advance from Cotswold Angling (*01793 721173*). Each path creates an intriguing vista, pulling you further into the pleasure grounds, where themed gardens and sculptures break up the asymmetrical lines. I particularly enjoy the Swinging Garden, an intimate roundel like an oasis among the trees, lined with swing seats for gentle contemplation. And I look forward to returning over the years to watch the newly planted avenue of monkey puzzle trees develop. However, my children, obsessed with swimming, believed that the elongated formal water garden, created by the celebrated garden designer Harold Peto, would make a fabulous two-lane training pool for swimming lengths!

While the currents of the river should not be underestimated, it's the Thames at **Buscot** that makes the better swimming, the weir pool in particular being a renowned spot for a refreshing outdoor dip. The National Trust also owns this tiny one-street village with a mix of tantalisingly attractive brick and Cotswold stone houses. The river and its southern watermeadow forms a natural development barrier; you must park in the small car park provided in the village and walk the hundred yards or so to the river.

The tempestuous noise of **Buscot Weir** is therapeutically energetic. You can stand on a small bridge directly above the weir and watch the frothing foam just beneath your feet, a fearsome reminder of the power of water. It's hard to talk above the natural noise so it's best simply to watch in awe. However, there's something equally refreshing about moving away to the quietness of the nearby weir pool and riverside picnic area. This whole stretch of the Thames is strikingly scenic and deserves savouring slowly. Turn left from the weir pool along a riverside footpath and you will come to Buscot Church, separated from the remainder of the village. Virtually on the banks of the river, the church is renowned for its very attractive stained-glass windows designed by Edward Burne-Jones. The figures in both *The Good Shepherd* and *Faith, Hope and Charity* are noticeably in the Pre-Raphaelite style.

In the middle of the river, where the pumping station stands, is **Brandy Island**. A distillery to turn sugar beet into brandy was built here in 1869 when the tycoon Robert Tertius Campbell owned the estate. Initially a success, the business ultimately failed and the distillery was pulled down just ten years later but the name Brandy Island has stuck ever since. Despite it being in such a historical part of the river – with many connections to the Pre-Raphaelite movement – as well as being so attractive, Brandy Island is once again under threat of development and there is an ongoing campaign (*www.savebuscot.com*) for the land to be bought by the National Trust and placed back under the wing of the Buscot Estate where it once belonged.

Turn right by Buscot Weir and you can follow the Thames Path for two miles to find another church with Pre-Raphaelite connections, at the site of the deserted village of **Eaton Hastings**. The windows here were designed by William Morris, Ford Madox Brown and again, Edward Burne-Jones. They were all installed by William Morris's interior design business, Morris, Marshall, Faulkner & Co, latterly Morris & Co.

I love this stretch of the Thames between Buscot and Eaton Hastings, where the only noise comes from an occasional swan gliding into land on the swirling water and the odd plop of some mythical creature in amongst the river weed. Teasels are splashed with the pink of rosebay willowherb and vetch, and willows droop over the riverbanks.

It's believed that one of the most famous of William Morris's designs, 'Willow Bough', was inspired by walks in the area from his home at nearby **Kelmscott**. A four-mile waymarked circular walk from Buscot Weir, the **Willow Walk** (follow the signs with a willow leaf), makes the most of the Thames Path and other local footpaths through water meadows north of the river. It passes through the village of Kelmscott.

Food and drink

There is a tea room at Buscot Park but my pick is one in the village of Buscot itself.

Buscot Tea Rooms 6 Buscot 📞01367 252142. Tiny tea shop in the centre of the village serving good freshly prepared snacks (quiche, ploughman's, sandwiches) and superb cakes and cream teas. Pretty tea garden too. Laura Curtis, the landlady, is very friendly and a mine of local information. Open 6 days a week (closed Mon) Apr to Oct and weekends only Oct to Mar.

⑦ Kelmscott Manor and Kelmscott

Just yards from the north bank of the Thames, 1½ miles east of Buscot is Kelmscott, another 'secluded' village in remote farmland. William Morris, the craftsman central to the Arts and Crafts Movement, believed the village to be 'heaven on earth' when he first discovered it. He chose **Kelmscott Manor** (*01367 252486; www.kelmscottmanor.co.uk; open Apr to Oct every Wed plus 1st and 3rd Sat*) as a summer house to get away from the stresses of his successful but busy interior design business and London life. At first he merely rented the notably homely manor (actually a farmhouse), with his artist friend, the Pre-Raphaelite painter Dante Gabriel Rossetti. Rossetti felt that the property and the surrounding countryside were ideal for painting in; his studio together with his paintbox and squeezed-out tubes of paint, can be seen on the upper floor. But his attentions towards Morris's wife, Jane, created friction and Rossetti moved out. Ultimately, William Morris bought the property outright and he created a family home.

Morris loved the house for its pureness – it had been virtually untouched since its building in 1600. He found not just peace and sanctuary from the village and the countryside but inspiration, and much of his work, both in the house and throughout his world-famous designs, shows evidence of this. His designs seem much more meaningful having seen his house and the environment within which he chose to live his life.

I find the house soothing because it is so evidently a creative family home with almost every aspect worked upon or created by a family member or a friend. Furniture, rugs, bedspreads, embroideries, paintings, wall hangings are all personal. There are Pre-Raphaelite paintings on the walls by his friends Rossetti and Burne-Jones, and tapestries by his daughter May, one of the finest embroiderers of her generation and a celebrated craftswoman in her own right. Cushion covers are the work of his wife and daughter, the wallpaper the work of Morris himself. Every room of the house shows artistic expression and a love for the building.

The gardens are no less inspiring. There is nothing grand or formal about them; they make a very restful place to stop for a while where sunny glades and courtyards, alluring pathways through the undergrowth and hidden corners beneath shady fruit trees can be found.

The main car park for visitors is approximately ten minutes' walk from the manor, though the most evocative first glimpse of the house is arriving on foot from the Thames. A 180-yard footpath links the two.

William Morris, his wife and two daughters are all buried in the churchyard in Kelmscott, his grave like a giant Cotswold stone ridge tile. Morris helped to restore the church and his fabric is used in the altar while kneelers are derived from his *Strawberry Thief* design.

Food and drink

Plough Inn Kelmscott ☎01367 253543. Useful stopping point for those visiting Kelmscott Manor or walkers on either the Thames Path or the Willow Walk. Very attractive pub. Classic pub grub at lunchtime and more extensive evening menu.

Stable Restaurant Kelmscott Manor. Within the farm buildings at William Morris's home, a comfortable restaurant and glorious courtyard for wholesome lunches and teas, using produce from the gardens and nearby farms.

8. THE SOUTHERN COTSWOLD SCARP AND FIVE VALLEYS

While the northern and eastern areas of the Cotswolds are cosy, gentle and lay claim to soft undulations, the southern Cotswolds are rugged, raw and wild. Sharp escarpments and gorge-like river valleys twist and bend with absurd frequency, where cold winds are funnelled and fogs linger. In between the contorted valleys and giant beech woods, high ground amasses creating rough commons, superb for bracing walks and views.

There's an edgier feel to the area too. Where the softer wolds of the northern Cotswolds illustrate a rural heritage of growing sheep and selling wool with the odd farmstead and squire's manor house dotted across the countryside, here is the corresponding industrial landscape. Cloth mills, originally powered by the area's fast-running waters, lined the valley floors and, with the escarpments so steep builders had nowhere to go but up. Consequently the houses of the workforce, cling limpet-like to the valley sides.

Having skirted around Cheltenham, the western escarpment continues to run south from **Crickley Hill** towards **Stroud** and then on towards **Dursley** until it reaches the graceful city of Bath. This section of the escarpment has some of the most dramatic views in the Cotswolds, over the Severn Valley and into Wales.

In the hinterland, the area around Stroud is known as the **Five Valleys**. Synonymous with the cloth industry, each of the five valleys follows small streams; to the east there are further valleys, unconnected to the cloth industry, that are completely dry. There are no giant rivers here. North of Stroud is the **Painswick Valley**, its western ridge making up a part of the main Cotswold escarpment. Northeast is the **Slad Valley**, made famous by the author Laurie Lee, who lived there for much of his life.

To the east is the **Frome Valley**, otherwise known as Golden Valley when it edges ever closer towards Stroud and, like a northerly spur from it, the **Toadsmoor Valley**. Running due south of Stroud is the **Nailsworth Valley**. At first it is as steep as its neighbours but gradually the land begins to flatten and the odd barbed spur escapes such as at **Woodchester** to the west and towards Avening and **Tetbury** to the east.

The area of the Five Valleys is utterly unique in Britain. I find the whole landscape bizarre and intriguing, curious and beguiling, almost alien. As one who lives in the more open wolds of the Cotswolds to the east, I even find the valleys slightly claustrophobic. I love visiting – and yet I'm glad to escape to the high ground of **Minchinhampton** and **Rodborough Common** or to stand on top of the escarpment and breathe in great gulps of air.

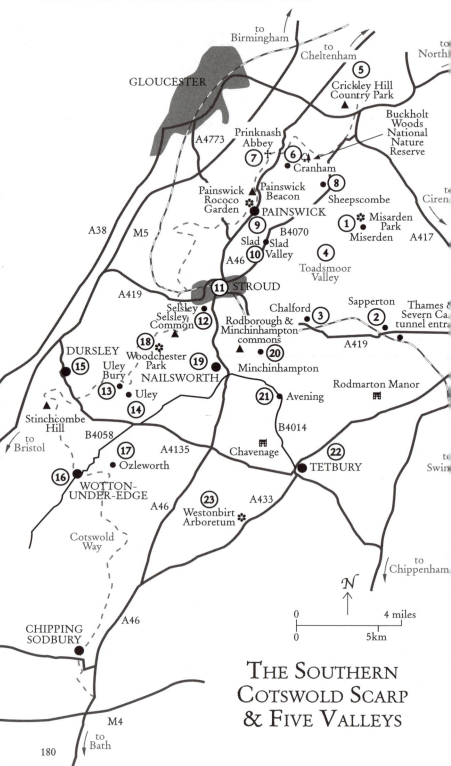

THE SOUTHERN
COTSWOLD SCARP
& FIVE VALLEYS

Getting there and around

Trains

The only main railway station in the locale is at Stroud. **First Great Western** (*www.firstgreatwestern.co.uk*) operates services from London Paddington via Swindon. From the southwest and Wales, services are via Gloucester. Trains from Birmingham and the north are operated by **Cross Country Trains** (*www.crosscountrytrains.co.uk*); a change at Gloucester is required.

A local train service, also operated by First Great Western, runs to the Cam and Dursley station from Bristol and Gloucester. The station is actually three miles from the centre of Dursley.

Buses

As one of the main meeting points, most bus journeys in the area begin and end in Stroud. Regular services operate from Stroud to Cheltenham along the Painswick Valley, to Nailsworth, Tetbury and Dursley. There are only limited services along the Frome Valley, with most daily buses stopping at Chalford. An hourly service operates from Gloucester to Dursley and from Dursley to Bristol via Wotton-under-Edge.

Most buses keep to the main roads, so alternative modes of transport are essential for finding those out-of-the-way places.

Cycling

There's no getting away from it, cycling is hard work in this area unless you stick to the valley floor, but you would be denying yourself some of the most dramatic of Cotswold scenery to do so. The Sustrans **National Cycle Route 45** provides traffic-free cycling through Golden Valley and the Nailsworth Valley. The six-mile **Stroud Valleys Trail** uses a section of the route from Stonehouse, west of Stroud to Nailsworth.

Guests are welcome to join members of the **Stroud Valley Cycling Club** (*www.ctcwest.org.uk/stroud*) for their weekly bike rides. The Saturday and Tuesday afternoon rides are generally more relaxed, with some of the trips on other days for hardened cyclists. Rides on the first Sunday morning of every month are the easiest, designed for inexperienced cyclists and on relatively easy terrain. There are summer evening pub rides too.

The **Stroud District Cycling Map**, available from tourist information centres, grades all the roads in the area according to their suitability for cycling.

Bike hire and repairs

The Bikeworks Frogmarsh Mill, South Woodchester ☎01453 872824 www.thebikeworks.co.uk. Sales and repairs.

Noah's Ark Bourne Mills, Brimscombe ☎01453 884738 www.noahsark.co.uk. Mountain-bike sales and repairs.

Thames & Cotswold Cycles 21 Church St, Tetbury ☎01666 403490. Hire of road and mountain bikes.

Walking

The continuation of the Cotswold Way is naturally the focal point for walkers here as it utilises the full length of the western escarpment for stunning, far-reaching views. But there are plenty of opportunities to pick a short stretch of the long-distance route for a there-and-back walk – look at the scenery to the west walking one-way, and to the east on the way back, because you won't want to miss any of it. My recommendation would be on sections around **Crickley Hill**, **Painswick Beacon** or **Hawkesbury**. Alternatively there are now several circular graded walks that use some of the most scenic parts of the Cotswold Way. As designated waymarked walks, full instructions for them can be downloaded from the National Trail website (*www.nationaltrail.co.uk/Cotswold*). Five of these walks are within this locale, with each one graded for ability and no more than four or five miles in length.

Off the Cotswold Way, some of the best walking is on **Selsley**, **Rodborough** and **Minchinhampton commons**, southeast of Stroud. They provide space and give bird's-eye views of the landscape and how the valleys interconnect. Most of this of course is hill-walking; my pick of the valleys is the **Frome Valley** around **Sapperton** and **Daneway**. You can easily add this on to the flatter sections of ground east of Sapperton where Sapperton Park and the extensive Bathurst Estate provide some very peaceful woodland walks.

Accommodation

Cotswolds88 Hotel Kemps Ln, Painswick Gl6 6YB ☎01452 813688
🖥 www.cotswolds88hotel.com. An intimate boutique hotel that's chic and stylish and has something of a cult following. Seventeen rooms, many with a view of the Painswick Valley, are all individually furnished. Organic and local ingredients are used in the restaurant and there's a cooking school on site, with courses tutored by the head chef.

Cotswold Yurts Westley Farm, Chalford GL6 8HP ☎01285 760262
🖥 www.cotswoldyurts.co.uk. Four yurts tucked into sunny glades amid ancient beech woods on a 75-acre farm that uses sustainable methods of agriculture. Traditional hay meadows and ancient woodlands lie all around and are there for guests to explore. Cosy rugs, full double beds, wood-burning stoves and even a roll-top bath make this far from camping. Each has its own compost loo too, although there is a flushing loo and showers in the nearby barn. All of the yurts have been handcrafted on the farm. Very romantic and secluded hideaways.

Tourist information centres

Nailsworth The Old George, George St ☏01453 839222.
Stroud George St ☏01453 760960.
Tetbury 33 Church St ☏01666 503552.
Wotton-under-Edge The Heritage Centre ☏01453 521541.

The Frome Valley (Golden Valley)

The River Frome bubbles from the ground a good way northeast of Stroud, close to the village of Brimpsfield and the old Roman road, Ermin Way. It flows due south for six miles past the villages of Miserden and Edgeworth, collecting riverlets from other dart-like valleys on its way. At Sapperton the river changes course, turning west towards Chalford, where the Frome Valley becomes better known as the Golden Valley, so called because of the money generated by the processing of wool. At the peak of production, in the 19th century, the Frome powered 150 mills. Some are still evident today in the steep-sided valley, though used as shops, warehouses and dwellings, in what was once a teeming hub of industry. Two of the prettier villages at the end of the valley closest to Stroud are **Thrupp** and **Far Thrupp**, partway up the northern hillside, with views across to Rodborough Common.

① Misarden Park and Miserden

Why Misarden Park comes to be in the village of Miserden and how or why the change of vowel came to be seems to be a mystery. But regardless of spelling or pronunciation, the estate-owned village is perhaps the most attractive in the whole of this locale, perched on top of the extremely steep valley and looking across to Warren Hill, Fishcombe Bank and right along both the Frome Valley and its thickly wooded neighbouring spur.

Miserden is a village that you have to get to rather than pass through. But once there, numerous footpaths take you to the point where the two valleys unite, and from which you can make several very enjoyable streamside and woodland walks, or head to the more southerly village of **Edgeworth**, where you can walk through one of the most delightful sections of the Frome Valley. For just a few pounds you can be taken on a guided walk around the hills and valleys of Miserden followed by lunch at the **Carpenter's Arms** (*01285 821283; ring the pub to find out dates and times of walks*) in the village. The pub serves cream teas all day too.

One of the main reasons for going to the village though is to visit **Misarden Park Gardens** (*01285 821303; www.misardenpark.co.uk; open Apr to Sep, Tue to Thu*). While the striking 17th-century Cotswold stone manor house, with external additions by Sir Edward Lutyens, is closed to the public, the gardens provide sublime vistas of the house and the valley over which it looks. There are areas of the valley, including the Misarden Park Lake, otherwise closed to the public that are available to visitors.

I find this one of the most beautiful of all Cotswold gardens, in the most tranquil of settings. The last time I was there it was pouring with rain but the spectacle really lifted the spirits and I noticed that, despite being late in the summer season, the garden was still filled with colour at a time when other gardens were not. I got chatting to the owner of the very good plant nursery next door (where you can purchase many of the plants found in the garden) who mentioned that the long, wide traditional borders were completely replanted three years ago with the aim of providing long-term colour. This continues right into early autumn when the leaves of the specimen trees begin to change their hues on the lower slopes.

② Sapperton, Daneway and Frampton Mansell

Of the three villages, **Sapperton** and **Frampton Mansell** stand on the hillside above the Frome Valley while the tiny hamlet of **Daneway**, no more than a pub and a couple of houses, sits on the valley floor between the two. This trio make an excellent combination to visit together, with plenty of opportunities to walk between the three. Sapperton in particular is a walker's dream. On the southern side of the valley, now that the river has turned a corner, there are superb views from the village over the valley below, which is crammed with beech trees.

A picturesque, short trek is between the **Bell Inn** in Sapperton and the riverside **Daneway Inn**, next to the Daneway Bridge. Decide whether you wish to begin at the bottom and do the appreciable climb to Sapperton first before supping a pint overlooking the valley or whether to take the downhill leg first and summon up the energy for the return climb in the Daneway Inn by the banks of the Frome.

An alternative, longer two-pub walk without a hefty climb is from the Bell Inn at Sapperton to the **Tunnel House Inn** near Coates, following the course of the Thames and Severn Canal using the **Macmillan Way** through Hailey Wood. For Sapperton is where the disused Thames and Severn Canal (see page 172), having followed the Frome Valley from Stroud, turns a corner to meet up with the section of canal that uses the Thames Valley to Lechlade. But to link the two sections it was necessary to build a tunnel between Sapperton (or actually Daneway being on the valley floor) and Coates. Completed in 1789, the **Sapperton Tunnel** was at that time the longest canal tunnel and, at 3,817 yards, remains the third longest in Britain today. In places the tunnel is 200 feet below ground level; the section of the Macmillan Way runs above much of the course of the tunnel.

The Tunnel House Inn, originally built to accommodate the workers building the canal, sits in the middle of nowhere just yards from the classical-designed portal at the tunnel entrance. Another, less ornamental portal is at the Daneway entrance to the tunnel. Further walks along the canal towpath can be accessed from the Tunnel House Inn but be careful when walking with young children as the empty canal is deep and the sides sheer.

A short walk in Sapperton

Much of Sapperton and the surrounding land is a part of the vast Bathurst Estate. My pick of possible short walks around the village uses the **Broad Ride** and is two miles long. As its name suggests it's a wide avenue, as straight as a ruler, which, if you followed for its full five-mile length, would deposit you in the centre of Cirencester. The grass is often long so boots or stout shoes are advisable.

Turn left out of the Bell Inn at Sapperton and walk through the village to the T-junction opposite Sapperton Lodge. Turn right and in 50 yards turn right down Broad Ride, which is signposted as a bridleway. Continue along the Broad Ride, through open parkland and crossing a quiet road, for three-quarters of a mile. You'll begin to get views over the Frome Valley. As the Broad Ride finishes, with dense woods in front of you, turn right along the narrow lane. At the crossroads, go straight across into the village, past the school on your left. With the church on your left, turn right to return to the Bell Inn.

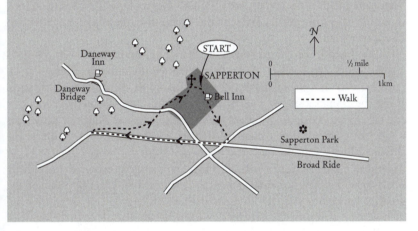

Food and drink

Bell Inn Sapperton GL7 6LE ☎01285 760298 🖥 www.foodatthebell.co.uk. A friendly pub in the heart of the village with a very pretty front garden providing good views. A good base from which to walk. Very good food with British classics. Children welcome at lunchtimes but no-one under the age of 10 allowed in the evenings.

Crown Inn Frampton Mansell GL6 8JG ☎01285 760601 🖥 www.thecrowninn-cotswolds.co.uk. Good-looking Cotswold-stone pub and front garden with incredible views over the Frome Valley. Cosy inside too with log fires and very good gastro-pub food. Accommodation.

Daneway Inn Daneway GL7 6LN ☎01285 760297 🖥 www.thedaneway.com. Very traditional riverside pub with simple but nourishing lunchtime and evening food (pies, sausages, lasagne, etc). Secluded, 'wild-camping' campsite (tents only) 200 yards down the valley among the trees.

Tunnel House Inn Coates GL7 6PW ☎01285 770280 🖰 www.tunnelhouse.com.
Deservedly popular pub on its own, down a half-mile drive and next to the Coates
portal of the Sapperton Canal Tunnel. Views across the fields and a camping meadow
outside, plus lots of walks along the old towpath and into Hailey Wood. Inside, rustic
atmosphere with sofas, candles, old advertising signs and a stay-all-day atmosphere.
Open daily from 11.00. Good food – from light bites and pub classics to some more
inventive dishes. A great place for children, the pub is reached on the Tarlton to Coates
road, between the railway and disused canal.

③ Oakridge and Chalford

There are just three crossing points over the Frome between Sapperton and Chalford.
All the roads running along the valley and across the river are incredibly narrow,
often single track, but they provide a constantly changing view. I approached
Oakridge and Chalford by crossing the ancient Daneway Bridge and taking a
short driving tour up through the enchanting beech trees of Hillhouse Wood to
Waterlane and then descending into Oakridge. This route gives a different outlook
above the valley rather than arriving in the villages from the main A419 Stroud to
Cirencester road.

Chalford and its conjoined neighbour, France Lynch, have oft been described
together as an alpine village. A touch over the top, for although steeply sloped,
timber chalets on rocky mountains it's not; Chalford has a character quite unique.
While the old block-shaped mills of yesteryear, with their symmetry of windows
and tall chimneys that poke just above the road line, spread along the valley floor
– now the Golden Valley – confined weavers' cottages are crammed against the
cliff-like hillsides. Cars need to breathe in to ride down the warren of tiny lanes, no
wider than a sheet of cloth – even the High Street struggles with two cars side by
side. Chalford is made for walking, not cars, if your calf muscles will withstand the
gruelling hill-climbs. Life, one imagines, must have been tough for the weavers and
their donkeys that plied the hillsides carrying materials. Rack Hill, in the centre of
the village, is where the cloths were spread out on racks to dry.

There are walks along the towpath by the disused canal and at Chalford Wharf,
just below the church, one of the five round houses along the Thames and Severn
Canal that were used as a lengthman's cottage. As a private residence, this one is
particularly well preserved.

④ The Toadsmoor Valley

Residues of old mills lie along the Toadsmoor Valley, a pencil-thin gorge with little
more than the width of the road that winds down it for space. The valley runs north
to south, like a spoke off Golden Valley. So tight-knit and secluded, it is secretive
and intriguing with plenty of good walks through the beech woods on its western
slopes, which waft with the smell of wild garlic in early summer.

At the head of the valley is **Bisley**, a charming village that, before the wool trade,
was more important than Stroud or any of its neighbours. The town has a bizarre
story to tell: the legend of the Bisley Boy. In 1542, Henry VIII came to visit Over

Horseback through the Frome Valley

An entirely different outlook altogether is from the saddle of a horse. **Totally Trekking** (*01285 710568; www.totallytrekking.co.uk*), based in Far Oakridge, provide peaceful horse treks through the Frome Valley countryside, exploring quiet lanes and bridleways. Customers can choose for how long and where they wish to ride – on or off road with options to stop for a pub lunch or a canter across the fields. Any ability and age (although children must be over the age of four years) is catered for. Explained Neil Winstone, 'My wife Jan leads the treks and can literally lead the horse with a rein for inexperienced riders. People love to explore the villages around here and enjoy the slow pace that a gentle ride brings, so a popular choice is a circular route linking Oakridge with France Lynch, Bournes Green, Waterlane and Far Oakridge'.

Court, reputedly a royal hunting, lodge where his daughter Elizabeth was staying. While Henry was out hunting, the young princess fell ill and died. Rather than explain the tragic event to the king, courtiers buried her swiftly and substituted a like-for-like 'replacement' with red hair, except that the 'new' princess was a boy. It's believed that's why the Queen never married, went bald and requested that no post-mortem should be carried out on her body upon death! In a later twist, a Reverend Thomas Keble confessed that during restoration work to Over Court in 1870, he found a stone coffin with the remains of a little girl in Tudor dress and, respecting the original story, ordered the remains to be buried secretly once more.

Queen Elizabeth indeed once owned the house, which still stands in the village, as so many properties did once belong to the crown, but that is about the closest link. The Gothic writer Bram Stoker wrote about the legend/hoax in his book, *Famous Impostors*.

The Painswick Valley and the Slad Valley

The lie of the land north of Stroud looks like a part of the left hand: if the Painswick Valley is the index finger, a tiny spur around Sheepscombe is the knuckle and the Slad Valley is the thumb.

Having bypassed Cheltenham in a ring, the main Cotswold escarpment turns south and you begin to get spectacular westerly views from **Crickley Hill**, **Barrow Wake** and **Cooper's Hill**. The Painswick Valley proper begins in **Buckholt Wood**, a beechwood nature reserve of national importance and the source of the tiny Painswick Stream. Further views are obtained from the next high point, **Painswick Beacon**, followed by the exquisite town of **Painswick**. Opposite is the knuckle, where **Sheepscombe** is enveloped by further significant beech woods.

Below Sheepscombe is the thumbnail, the head of the Slad Valley and roughly on the thumb joint, the village of **Slad**, the location of Laurie Lee's autobiographical *Cider with Rosie*. The two digits are webbed as well, for there is little between the valleys, each one pushing against the other.

⑤ From Crickley Hill to Cooper's Hill

Crickley Hill is one of the best places in the Cotswolds to see the strata of oolitic limestone; the hill cliffs have the thickest section in Britain of pea grit, a particular kind of poor-quality limestone that is made up of pea-like nodules brimming with fossils. The area around the hill is a country park with beech and oak woods, grassland, old quarries and an archaeological site where 5,000 years of occupation are exposed, featuring a Neolithic causewayed enclosure and an Iron Age hillfort. Five circular trails from the car park are waymarked, variously including the hillfort, the parkland, a short trail for families, the scrubs or the steepest section of the park on the edge of the escarpment.

Just south is **Barrow Wake**, a viewpoint and picnic spot designated as an SSSI with some of the finest views across to the Malverns, and across to Crickley Hill, where you can see the limestone strata of the cliffs even more clearly. Right on the edge of the escarpment, it's a windy spot and the slopes are inevitably steep but there's plenty of flora and fauna enjoying the limestone grassland. The area is named after an Iron Age burial chamber discovered by quarry workers at the end of the 19th century.

As the escarpment continues south, grassland turns to dense woodland, in particular filled with beech trees, for which this part of the Cotswolds is most renowned. Witcombe Wood covers much of the escarpment as it folds around to create a crescent shape towards Cooper's Hill. To see how the scarp curves round, follow the road from Little Witcombe to **Great Witcombe Roman Villa** (*free access; unstaffed*). Here, partway up the ridge and below the Cotswold Way, are the remains of a once-grand house and bathhouse built around AD250 within a large country estate. Little is left – just the low-lying outline of some of the walls, but it is a contemplative place to take in the surroundings: villa sites were often chosen for their views, and this has steep pastures and woodlands as a backdrop, with Gloucester, villa town of Roman origins, in the near distance. There is a small car park for the villa but the remaining 150 yards must be made on foot.

The line of high ground continues to **Cooper's Hill**, facing north right on the end of the crescent before the escarpment takes a dramatic turn south. It's one of the most jaw-dropping points of the Cotswold ridge. If the gradient of the escarpment were not steep enough, Cooper's Hill then appears to sit on top, with a 1 in 2 incline beneath. As this is common land, you are entitled to walk on the hill – and the Cotswold Way passes along its foot – but what is all the more remarkable is that hundreds of people, who one can only assume must be bordering on insanity, throw themselves down this slope to chase after a giant wheel of Double Gloucester cheese. The annual **cheese-rolling** event, which takes place every spring bank holiday at the end of May, is a highlight of the quirky Cotswold calendar. But you simply cannot appreciate the gradient of the hill, or the feat that the participants put themselves through, without standing at the top or bottom of the hill and gazing in awe.

Getting to Cooper's Hill at any time of year is tricky. There is a tiny car park along the narrowest of single-track roads off the A46 from Brockworth, and up a steep incline up the side of the escarpment. The best access route is on foot, along the Cotswold Way.

Food and drink

Air Balloon Crickley Hill, Birdlip GL4 8JY ☎01452 862541 🦉 www.airballoon-pub-gloucestershire.co.uk. Not the quietest of locations, situated at the junction of the main A417 road to Gloucester and Swindon but a convenient stop for walkers on the Cotswold Way or those visiting Crickley Hill or the surrounding area. Food served from midday until late evening.

⑥ Cranham

South of Cooper's Hill and running east to west, sandwiched between the A46 Cheltenham to Painswick road and the Birdlip to Bisley road is **Buckholt Wood**. The lie of the land appears not to know which way to turn, darting this way and that. The wood is of international importance, demonstrating some of the finest ancient beech in Europe and making up a part of the **Cotswold Commons and Beechwoods National Nature Reserve**. The wood is a joy to wander through – even if some of the paths are steep – a chiaroscuro of wide tracks and light-filled open woodland, against dense shades of bottle green. On its floor are bluebells in spring and rare orchids in summer, spiders and snails found only in ancient woodlands and rare butterflies such as the white admiral.

Adjoining the woods is **Cranham Common**, also part of the national nature reserve. The 48-acre piece of hillside is classic unimproved limestone grassland, grazed using traditional methods and issuing cowslips in spring, orchids in early summer and later in the year, knapweed, harebells and wild thyme. You may come across the rare rufous grasshopper, a very localised species with distinctive white-tipped, club-shaped antennae, or hear the skylarks singing above your head. It's an ideal place for a picnic – I've particularly noted a bench on the single-track road that crosses the common and connects the two parts of **Cranham** village. It's one of the best spots to view the autumnal changing colours of Buckholt Wood.

⑦ Prinknash Abbey

West of Buckholt Wood, tucked into the escarpment, is Prinknash Abbey (*www. prinknashabbey.org*), accessed off the A46 Cheltenham to Painswick road. The abbey is no longer used by the Benedictine order, the 12 remaining monks who lived and worked there having moved to St Peter's Grange, a tranquil medieval manor house in the grounds of the estate. However, open to the public is the Monastery Shop and Café (*closed Mon and Tue*) selling monastic gifts and items made by the monks

Cotswolds Grazing Animals Project

A lack of traditional grazing by animals over the years allows coarse grasses and scrub to take over an area of land, which prevents low-lying grasses, herbs and many of the limestone-loving flowers from peeking through and regenerating. These flowers, herbs and mosses, often unique to the Cotswolds, also flourish on poor, brashy soils so they do not thrive on pastures, or 'improved' grassland, that have been enriched by fertilisers or pesticides.

A partnership between the National Trust and Natural England is gradually restoring, conserving and enhancing chunks of the unimproved limestone grassland that makes the Cotswolds so unique. The **Cotswolds Grazing Animals Project** is placing cattle on 20 to 30 sites that require traditional grazing methods to keep the scrub under control. Explained Paul Rutter, the National Trust's Countryside Manager for Gloucestershire, 'Traditional grazing methods are essential to maintain a healthy grassland and it's the only way that some SSSIs are allowed to be managed. Sheep are not always the most appropriate to restore the land so we have selected two British breeds of cattle that require conserving in their own right and which are incredibly hardy so they can remain outdoors all year round. Both the National Trust and Natural England own the conservation herds of Welsh Blacks and Belted Galloways, which we are using as bulldozers to help flatten the scrub and allow more sensitive plants to come through. These breeds like the unimproved grassland, which is not too rich for their palate.'

Places where you are likely to see these cattle grazing are at Crickley Hill, Haresfield Hill, Cranham Common, Sheepscombe and, in particular, Rodborough and Minchinhampton commons. A limited supply of the very tasty beef is available every autumn to purchase, sold direct to the public in ten-kilogram boxes, containing a selection of cuts. The boxes must be pre-ordered (*01452 810058; Cotswoldgrazing@nationaltrust.org.uk*) in advance and collected from the NT's office at Ebworth, near Sheepscombe.

(Prinknash is apparently famous worldwide for its incense) together with books. It's housed in a not very spiritual-looking building, an old 1970s office block, with classic polystyrene ceiling tiles and fluorescent lights, that was once used by the Prinknash Pottery. But don't let that detract you from visiting: the café, serving delicious cakes, biscuits, breakfasts and lunches all made on the premises, has a restful quality, playing recordings of gentle monastic chants and with easy chairs where you can sit quietly and read. On the walls are watercolour pictures of local scenes, the work of the monks. You can visit the Prinknash Abbey Watercolour Gallery too, showing additional works of art with originals and limited edition prints for sale. Visits must be made by appointment with Father Stephen Horton (*07722 501382*) who runs the gallery.

A monastic exhibition details the lives of the monks at Prinknash, a day that begins at 04.40 and with seven calls to prayer. In between, work involves the blending of incense – the oldest incense-blenders in Europe still operating – tending the walled kitchen garden and making cider in season from the apples that grow on the estate.

In the monastery garden, a woodland workshop has been set up by Cotswold Woodland Crafts (*01453 753452; www.cotswoldwoodlandcrafts.co.uk*). They have developed a series of one- and two-day green woodworking courses for all abilities from novice to expert on trug-making, traditional chair-making and green woodcarving. All the tools and equipment are supplied, including a constantly burning fire for steaming and bending wood.

Prinknash Pottery

Clearly an artistic bunch, the monks here founded Prinknash Pottery in 1942 when they discovered a seam of clay during building work on the estate. Their distinctive red earthenware gained high regard but the pottery at Prinknash closed in 1997 when the company was sold. Their work is now highly collectable.

⑧ Sheepscombe and Painswick Beacon

If you want to survey Painswick from afar before heading into the town, there are two places from which to do it. The first is the road to **Sheepscombe**, to the northeast, and on a valley nodule. A tiny stream splits the pretty village, with houses on both hillsides. From there you can take walks into the vast surrounding beech woods that are part of the Cotswold Commons and Beechwoods National Nature Reserve. Laurie Lee, in *Cider with Rosie*, describes how his Uncle Charlie helped to plant some of these woods.

The second is **Painswick Beacon** to the north of the town. An area of common land, this high point is ideal for walking, filled with scrub and woodland, native juniper bushes (which are in national decline), wild flowers and butterflies. And in contrast to the beech woods, the beacon is covered with a good mix of pines, chestnut, ash and field maple. Having been quarried years ago, the ground is lumpy and intriguing – you never know quite where the next view is coming from. The official beacon is on top of an Iron Age hillfort, the ramparts of which are remarkably clear. Views from here are quite something, over Painswick, Haresfield Hill (another of the Cotswolds high points) and westwards over the Severn Vale. From the beacon you begin to realise just how vast an area (by English standards) Buckholt Wood and the beech woods around Sheepscombe occupy. There's a golf course at Painswick Beacon too and one of the greens fits snugly into the hillfort's ring as if to protect the golfers from marauding armies of hill-walkers. Actually, the defences have already been breached, as a footpath runs right through the middle.

Food and drink

Butcher's Arms Sheepscombe ☎01452 812113 🐝 www.butchers-arms.co.uk. On the north side of the valley, very much a traditional village pub with simple food and bar snacks. Good views.

⑨ Painswick

Approaching Painswick on the road from Cheltenham, it's as if the church spire of St Mary's is piercing the tarmac in front of you. A surreal entrance down New Street ('new' in 1428), a composé of fine Georgian façades and chimneys galore, you begin to appreciate just how special this bite-size town is, perfect for exploring in an afternoon.

The absolute must-visit is the churchyard, celebrated for the significant number of, sadly crumbling, chest tombstones and the 200-year-old lollipop yew trees, which legend says will always remain at 99 in number. Inside the elegant church, along the north aisle, are the graffiti of a disgruntled Puritan soldier who, in 1643, was imprisoned here during a disastrous English Civil War siege of the town. Charles I had his headquarters in the adjacent court house for some time.

This is a town to look out from, with views of the more open valley hills to the east from many of the attractive streets such as Hale Lane and the memorably named Tibbiwell. But of most significance to the town is how it has been adopted as a centre for the contemporary Arts and Crafts movement. Art and crafts are evident throughout the town with many interesting little shops, but no more so than at the **Guild Gallery**, home of the **Gloucestershire Guild of Craftsmen** (*Painswick Centre, Bisley St; 01452 814745; www.guildcrafts.org.uk*). Within the walls are permanent studios and exhibitions where you can view, talk to and watch the artists and craftsmen working. Buying or commissioning work is of course desirable too! In addition to the permanent exhibitions, the guild holds a popular annual Summer Show.

Painswick Rococo Garden

A half-mile walk from the town centre, Painswick Rococo Garden (*01452 813204; www.rococogarden.org.uk; open daily Jan–Oct*) is acknowledged as one of the finest examples of Rococo theatricality left in Britain. Still being restored to the way it looked in its flamboyant heyday, the various follies and architectural delights from

which to enjoy numerous vistas create an atmosphere that you're unlikely to find anywhere else in the Cotswolds. A circular walk is best to appreciate all the nuances of the garden. Snowdrops smother the woodland banks in January and February, replaced by carpets of naturalised cyclamen later in the year.

I visited in pouring rain and had the garden to myself. While I may not have lingered so long over the scent of a rose, the follies became more purposeful and I began to appreciate their being and how they fit into the structure of the garden. By their very nature, follies of course have no purpose other than decoration. That was not the case here, with the Red House originally used for afternoon tea (and to shelter from the rain on my part). But this romantic hideaway at the top of the garden is very popular as a wedding venue today.

Food and drink

Royal Oak St Mary's St ☎01452 813129 🖥 www.theroyaloakpainswick.co.uk. Very good, British fare served all day, including morning coffee and afternoon tea and well-kept beer from the Stroud Brewery. Comforting surroundings with wood-panelled bars and huge log fires.

St Michael's Restaurant Victoria St ☎01452 814555 🖥 www.stmichaels restaurant.co.uk. Small restaurant in a listed building with informal lunches and chic dinners. British/European menu using seasonal produce. Closed Mon and Tue.

⑩ The Slad Valley

Like its neighbours that make up the Five Valleys, the Slad Valley once bustled with cloth mills until 1820. The evidence has largely gone and the hillsides around the playful Slad Brook have returned to a rural idyll.

While the outskirts of Stroud are pushing their way up this short valley, the only other settlement is the ribbon village of **Slad**. This is where the poet Laurie Lee spent his Edwardian childhood and where his autobiographical book *Cider with Rosie* is based. He is also buried in the village churchyard and, prior to his death, was a familiar figure in the area. Despite the prolific attention that's given to his life and work, surprisingly there is no museum or even exhibition to look at in the village; instead you need to visit Stroud, where a tiny corner of the Museum in the Park (see page 194) is given over to the author.

One of those books that seemed to be forever on the exam syllabus in schools, I refused to read *Cider with Rosie* for many years. Finally picking up a copy a year ago, I could read it without the need to dissect every sentence structure and appreciate Laurie Lee's sublime descriptions of the countryside around the Slad Valley. He depicts it like living in a 'bean-pod'. Visit this valley and you'll understand exactly what he means.

Food and drink

Woolpack Inn Slad ☎01452 813429 🖥 www.thewoolpackinn-slad.com. The pub immortalised in *Cider with Rosie* and a haunt of Laurie Lee in adult years. A traditional Cotswolds pub for both drinkers and diners. Good food with interesting menu. Stunning views from the rear garden.

⑪ Stroud

You only need to see how the Five Valleys all come together to realise that Stroud has, for centuries, been an important meeting point. It developed late, by comparison with other Cotswold towns, not surprisingly owing to the inhospitable landscape before any forms of transport became available.

Today it thrives on being different and has carved a niche for itself as a bohemian place, shunning large chain stores and embracing the independent ones. The weekly **farmers' market** – held every Saturday – is first rate, and one of the first ever to be introduced in the UK at the beginning of the renaissance for good, local food. Organic and fresh, local produce abounds throughout the town.

Stroud's rise came as the centre for the cloth-making industry and while this may have waned, there are at least some mills remaining. But the contemporary Arts and Crafts movement, in particular textiles, is important here and pride in locally made goods is huge. **Made in Stroud** at 16 Kendrick Street (*01453 840265; www.madeinstroud.co.uk*), set up by the same couple who set up the farmers' market, is one of the most popular shops in town, selling craftwork and gifts that are locally made.

But, aside from shopping, my favourite place to visit in Stroud is the **Museum in the Park** (*01453 763394; www.museuminthepark.org.uk; closed Mon and all Dec*). Set up in a 17th-century mansion house that was built by a wealthy clothier, it's a fascinating museum that provides a potted history of the Stroud valleys in addition to an art gallery and regular exhibitions. Free to enter, it's well-attuned to families, with children's discovery trails and child-friendly displays.

Inside you can really get to grips with the history of the cloth industry; how Stroud, and nearby Dursley, became famous for making broadcloth, a heavy felted fabric that was used for regimental soldiers' uniforms, the covering of billiard tables and more recently tennis balls. Much of the cloth was dyed with strong colours that became known as 'Stroud Scarlet', the classic colour for a soldier's uniform, 'Uley Blue' and 'Billiard Table Green'. But by 1900 only 20 mills had survived and by the end of the 20th century only one major manufacturer remained. Stroud was also the birthplace of the lawnmower, inspired by the rotary shearing machines used to cut the surface of cloth in the local mills.

The **Stroudwater Textile Trust** (*www.stroud-textile.org.uk*) is committed to keeping the textile traditions of the area alive, organising textile events, preserving historic machinery and providing courses on weaving, felt-making and dyeing. They also organise a series of mill visits between April and September each year, where you can watch – and have a go at – some of the processes required to make cloth.

Food and drink

Stroud **Farmers' Market** takes place every Saturday but there's also an **organic market** held every Friday and Saturday in the Shambles Market, off the High Street.

Star Anise Arts Café Gloucester St ☎01453 840021 🖰 www.staraniseartscafe.com. Town-centre café specialising in nutritional food with a philosophy to use wholesome, organic and local, seasonal produce. Includes organic beers and wines too. The walls are covered with the artwork of local people and Saturday mornings include storytelling for children.

Woodruffs Organic Café 24 High St ☎01453 759195 🖰 www.woodruffsorganiccafe. co.uk. Mainly vegetarian menu with plenty of options for allergy sufferers. Good, wholesome and appetising food with plenty of choice. Vegetarian cookery evening classes too.

The Cotswold Scarp – the dry valley?

Southwest of Stroud the landscape has a very special quality. This is a continuation of the Cotswold ridge but there is no way of finding uniformity at any point. The ridge meanders like an ageing river, except that there is no river, at least not of any note or length. And within these meanders are knuckles of miniature valleys clustering together.

Every so often prominent hills such as **Downham Hill** and **Cam Long Down** are dotted about, the effects of land slippage when the crust of the Cotswold ridge was tilted up onto its side millions of years ago.

⑫ Selsley to Uley Bury

Leaving Stroud on the B4066 to Dursley requires an instant and dramatic climb, passing through the village of Selsley, on the cusp where the Nailsworth Valley and the Cotswold escarpment meet. Particularly noticeable in the village is the French-looking saddleback tower of All Saints' Church, which catches the sunlight at a time when the surrounding hills are in shadow. The stained glass here was one of the first major commissions granted to William Morris. Windows include the work of Morris together with his Pre-Raphaelite friends, Dante Gabriel Rossetti and Edward Burne-Jones. Each artist designed one of the three triptychs on the south side of the nave while the rose window, above the west door, is the work of Morris himself.

From Selsley the main road actually runs a part way up the westerly hillside of the Nailsworth Valley, and to its west is **Selsley Common**. At the centre of the common is the top of the ridge that divides this valley from the western edge of the Cotswold escarpment.

Selsley Common is an SSSI, and rich in the wild flowers – and therefore birds and butterflies – most associated with the limestone grassland of the Cotswolds. Formerly quarried, the land dips and rises and, owing to the natural curve of the land, you get one view disappearing as another arrives. Yes, there are views over the Severn Vale and the Forest of Dean but what's best about the common are the views over Stroud and some of the other valleys, the walks and the picnicking opportunities, despite the often windy conditions.

Beyond the common are Pen Hill and Pen Wood, filling a loop in the distorted ridgeline and, on the other side of the road, the home of the **Bristol and Gloucester Gliding Club** (*www.bggc.co.uk*). On a fine day, you'll see the gentle, giant gliders whistle overhead but you can have a go too. Close to the edge of the scarp, it's the perfect place for gliding, the pilots (members of the club include world and European champions) using the warm currents that rise off the ridge for soaring. Trial lessons provide a 15- to 20-minute soar with a fully qualified instructor above the Cotswold Scarp, arguably the best way to see it – and you'll get to take hold of the controls too.

There's a picnic area at the 778-foot-high **Coaley Peak Viewpoint**, with the scarp dropping like a thunderbolt below. While munching on a sandwich, you can easily make out Sugar Loaf Mountain in Wales and the Malverns. On this site is **Nympsfield Long Barrow**, an exceptionally fine example of a Neolithic chambered tomb, which is in the shape of a cross despite being pre-Christian by five thousand years. When excavated, the communal grave was found to contain the skeletons of 17 men, women and children and was possibly used for the ritualistic sacrifice of animals too. **Hetty Peglar's Tump**, one mile south, is another fine example and still roofed. At 120 feet long and 84 feet wide it's big enough to crawl into. There is no parking at the tump so to reach it, park at Coaley Peak Viewpoint and walk along the Cotswold Way.

⑬ Uley Bury

Making the most of a promontory between the edge of the scarp and knobbled valley is the scheduled ancient monument of Uley Bury. The large, 32-acre Iron Age hillfort once was home to an industrious farming community that made woollen cloth and early coinage. As a prime example of unimproved grassland, the terraced structure is grazed using traditional methods to stop the encroachment of trees and walkers are not allowed in the centre. But you can walk the full distance around the mile-long ramparts using the circular bridleway for unmitigated views.

I took a walk there recently and, in addition to the profusion of common blue and gatekeeper butterflies and coppery gold damselflies, was particularly struck by the views over the Severn Vale on the northwest side and those over the Ewelme Valley to the southeast. But by far the most captivating aspect is the short stretch of rampart facing the southwest. My map was all but blown away, and my children and I struggled to stay upright on the edge of the rampart as the wind hits this projecting side of the escarpment hard. But the views over the landmark hills of Downham Hill (or Smallpox Hill locally), Cam Long Down and Peaked Down towards **Stinchcombe Hill** were out of this world. I don't know what it is about these protruding luscious green hummocks in an otherwise relatively flat landscape below the escarpment, but I fell in love with them instantly. We met an elderly man on the tip of the bury who had lived in the area for years. He described how in springtime these mounds become highlands as the mist envelopes the valley: 'The tops peek out and the mist swells up and down like the ocean.' This southwest corner of Uley Bury he described as having 'one of the finest views in England'. I agree.

To visit Uley Bury you can park at the northeast entrance, where you can also pick up paths to visit the very steep **Coaley Wood**, owned by the Woodland Trust. This is an alternative route to visit Hetty Peglar's Tump too.

⑭ Uley and Owlpen Manor

The village of **Uley** sits in the Ewelme Valley, a stubby valley upon the eastern side of the Cotswold escarpment. The knobbly contours of the land ambling in and out create a series of plump, green cushions, fringed with woodland. The village is strung along the Stroud–Dursley road and is made up of many fine clothiers' houses in typical Cotswold style. Like its counterparts, this valley was caught up with the boom of the cloth-making industry, and Uley Blue cloth, used for military uniforms, was unrivalled from the 17th to the early 19th century. Today the village is better known for its brewery, producing ales such as Uley Bitter and Hogshead, using water from the Cotswold springs that feed the Ewelme.

A mile to the east of Uley, tucked into a secret spur of its own, is **Owlpen Manor** (*01453 860261; www.owlpen.com; house closed, gardens open May to Sep, Mon, Wed and Thu*). Known as one of Prince Charles's favourite places in England, the beauty of the Owlpen estate defies words. Its location is so hidden you cannot see it from Uley Bury, despite the 'whole' of the Ewelme Valley being laid out before you. The Tudor manor house is an architectural gem that was left untouched for centuries until sympathetic restoration began early in the 20th century during the Arts and Crafts Movement. The house is currently undergoing further restoration and will therefore remain closed throughout 2011.

The gardens, however, are open and, like the house, have received acclaim from many of Britain's greatest garden designers like Vita Sackville-West and Gertrude Jekyll. Of historical importance, it's the most complete garden of the Stuart period open to the public, containing seven formal hanging terraces together with further additions made by the present owners along 'old English' traditions. Box parterres, immaculately clipped hedges and moss-lined stone walls frame borders rich with colour. Visitors can wander through the idyllic estate-owned village and peaceful valley too, with miles of walks through the surrounding beech woods.

Food and drink

Old Crown Inn 17 The Green, Uley 📞01453 860502 🍺 www.theoldcrownuley.co.uk. Traditional country pub on the village green at the top end of the village. Serves ales from the Uley Brewery plus guest beers and simple fare – jacket potatoes, cottage pie and the like.

⑮ Dursley and Stinchcombe Woods

Dursley is an extraordinary Cotswold town in that it doesn't have that typical look or quaint charm so connected with the towns of the north Cotswolds. A refreshing change, it's made up of buildings in a mixture of styles, ages and materials. Sitting in the Cam Valley, to the east of and beneath **Stinchcombe Hill**, it is really the conjoined triplet of both the larger town of Cam to the north and Woodmancote to the south, sandwiched between the two.

First and foremost, Dursley has always been an industrial town, initially in the woollen industry and the manufacture of cloth and more recently as the home of the Lister engine. Neighbouring Cam retains one of only two cloth mills with any major output in the whole of the Stroud area, the other at Lodgemore Mills near Stroud. The two mills are linked, owned by the American company Milliken, weaving and dyeing the cloth used to cover snooker and billiard tables, and tennis balls for major championships around the world, including Wimbledon.

Parsonage Street, Dursley's main, pedestrianised shopping street down which the Cotswold Way runs, has been taken over by a plethora of charity shops and low-cost supermarkets but remains endearing nonetheless. Dursley's most iconic building is the pillared Market House, built in 1738, now used as the town hall and the location for the monthly farmers' market. An interesting little **Heritage Centre** (*open Tue, Thu, Fri, Sat 10.30 to 12.30; entrance free*), opposite the Market House, gives a thousand years of history and showcases many locally made objects from the town's industrial past.

Southwest of Dursley is **Stinchcombe Hill**, a protruding limb of the Cotswold escarpment. Its rim is lined with woodland but the top is a windy wilderness, used partly by the Dursley Golf Club and by walkers on the Cotswold Way, which skirts around the edge. In my view it's a must-visit place if you're in this part of the Cotswolds; a long, narrow road takes you from Woodmancote to the centre of the hill – don't park in the first car park that you come across, near the clubhouse, as it's for members of the golf club but continue until the road stops where there's a second, public car park. A circular walk around the rim of the down-like, unevenly shaped hill will provide astonishing if wind-blown views, particularly at Drakestone Point, one of the most westerly points of the Cotswold escarpment. But close to the golf clubhouse, the Cotswold Way passes right by a very pretty triangular green, perfectly sheltered for a picnic.

A mile from Stinchcombe Hill, approached along the same narrow road, is the predominantly beech **Twinberrow Wood**. During the winter there are glimpses of Dursley below but in spring the woodland floor comes alive with bluebells and wild garlic. Within the wood, a **Sculpture and Play Trail** aimed at encouraging more people to visit and particularly to develop imaginative play among children. The various sculptures and artwork that crop up along the trail have been created by many different community groups and organisations such as the Girl Guides, a nearby residential care home (where the residents have provided some fascinating stories from their own childhood memories of visiting the woods, displayed on the trail), an art group and local schools. There are activities too, such as the 'Friendship Circle': simple enough, you sit on logs and talk to one another, sharing a woodland story. A proportion of the trail is accessible to wheelchairs and pushchairs.

Food and drink

Old Spot Inn Hill Rd, Dursley ☎01453 542870 🖥 www.oldspotinn.co.uk. Has gained a national reputation for its wide selection of real ales, in particular those of the nearby Uley Brewery, but remains popular with locals too. Useful for the Cotswold Way, which passes by the entrance. Hearty home-cooked food.

⑯ Wotton-under-Edge and North Nibley

As its name implies, **Wotton-under-Edge** sits at the edge of the Cotswold escarpment. Yet its position is not quite that simple, for it also spreads up the hillsides of the small Tyley Valley that runs at right angles to the escarpment, the pair crashing into one another right beneath the feet of the town. You'll realise during any exploration that you are constantly walking up or down a hill.

Like Dursley, Wotton is not picture-postcard stuff, but a working town with a welcoming spirit and a mix of architectural styles. In the centre is the little stream that flows down the valley, once used by dyers to change the colour of broadcloth. For Wotton too was completely taken over by the woollen industry from the 13th to the 19th century and was originally one of the most important woollen towns in the area. Women would spin the wool while the men wove the yarn into cloth – there's a string of weavers' cottages on the Culverhay, close to the parish church. But the town's woollen demise came when it couldn't compete with the mills around Stroud.

Long Street and the High Street, to the west of the stream, are the main shopping areas, with plenty of interesting independent shops, the impressive Tolsey Clock erected in honour of Queen Victoria, and eateries to occupy a wander. But head down Market Street, off the High Street, and you'll come across three buildings of note. The first is the town hall, where the farmers' market takes place on the first Saturday of every month and Wotton's 'Town Hall Teas'.

Next door is the **Electric Picture House**, an intimate 100-seat cinema run by the community with volunteer helpers, showing both popular and unusual films in state-of-the-art digital format. It's a cinema like no other and is certainly worlds apart from the multiplexes. Next door is the **Heritage Centre**, a tiny building crammed full of interesting bits and pieces. Again run by volunteers, it's free to enter. You'll really get to grips with the history of the area there. Have a look at the exquisite 3D fabric map of the town, made by the Women's Institute in 1979. Also in the centre are leaflets on numerous local walks, including three 'Mill Walks' of two, five and seven miles long, pinpointing the remains from the woollen industry along the way.

Town hall teas

Every Sunday from April to October (14.30 to 17.00) Wotton's town hall is taken over by local community organisations that put on a spread of homemade cakes and refreshments to raise funds for various causes. Having run for many years, the teas are proving ever more popular, attracting people from afar.

Elsewhere look out for the **Perry and Dawes Almshouses**, built in 1630 along Church Street. Accessed through an archway, there's a very pleasant little grass courtyard where you can sit and the sweetest tiny chapel to visit. Inside, two stained-glass windows draw the eye – a tiny commemorative window made in 2005 that's filled with daffodils and roses, and the other showing the town's dependence upon sheep, wool and the clothing trade.

Approaching Wotton-under-Edge from Stinchcombe, you pass through the village of **North Nibley**. It's no more or less remarkable than any other village but on the hillside above is the **Tyndale Monument**. At 111 feet tall, the tower can be seen for miles around – including from Stinchcombe Hill – and was built in memory of William Tyndale, the first translator into English of the New Testament in 1525. Though born in North Nibley, Tyndale was strangled and burned at the stake in Belgium for heresy upon the orders of Henry VIII. However, in 1540, just four years after Tyndale's death, his work was used as the basis for four translations of the Bible, including the king's official 'Great Bible' and in 1611 the King James version, still in use today. The monument is accessed up a steep path just to the south of the village.

To the northeast is **Hunts Court Garden** (*01453 547440; open Tue–Sat except Aug*), a little-known 2½-acre garden used as a living showcase for the attached nursery, which specialises in traditional old-fashioned roses. With a backdrop of the wooded escarpment, it has over 450 varieties of old roses together with a large collection of penstemons and hardy geraniums and is particularly worth a visit during June and July.

Food and drink

Long Street has a really good selection of everyday shops and places to eat or buy food. My pick of the bunch includes the **Harvest Store**, a greengrocer and deli selling fresh fruit and vegetables from the area plus fresh fish and local cheese – all well presented. **Wotton Coffee Shop** and the **Singing Teapot** are two good places to stop for a quick bite or a leisurely drink.

Wotton Farm Shop Bradley Rd ☎01453 521546 🖥 www.wottonfarmshop.co.uk. Superb farm shop selling home-grown (from the farm) fruit and vegetables in addition to other produce from the county. The butcher prepares cuts from animals reared on the farm and the on-site kitchen cooks cakes, pastries, soups, ready meals and makes ice cream.

⑰ Ozleworth and the last of the Cotswold Scarp

Parallel with the Tyley Valley, at the bottom of which is Wotton-under-Edge, a neighbouring valley spreads similarly from the northeast and pushes against the western escarpment. Likewise, there's a tiny stream that cuts through this quiet and secret valley, barely touched by human habitation, with the undulating hills either side appearing like soft, green pillows just as at Uley and Owlpen. And one tiny lane carves its way along the Ozleworth Bottom valley floor and up the steep bank to Ozleworth. This miniscule hamlet consists of little more than three or four modest houses and **Ozleworth Park**, surrounded by parkland and 12 acres of handsome gardens with neat box-enclosed parterres. Though privately owned, the gardens are opened to the public on several days during the summer in aid of charity. But within the park grounds, and accessible all year round, is **St Nicholas of Myra Church**. You cannot get near with a car but must walk (or ride) along footpaths and bridleways to reach it. Wonderfully atmospheric, tucked against the side of one of the most unspoilt valleys in the Cotswolds, in a walled garden and surrounded by parkland, this tiny, squat building exudes a sense of peace. It has an unusual hexagonal tower of irregular proportions; no two walls are the same width. It's most noticeable from inside when you gaze up to the tower ceiling.

At the top of the valley ridge, and best accessed from Wotton-under-Edge, is **Newark Park** (*01793 817666; www.nationaltrust.org.uk; open Wed/Thu from Mar to Oct plus weekends from Jun to Oct*), owned by the National Trust. As a Tudor hunting lodge and later expanded into a Georgian country house, Newark Park has plenty of history, but its glory is its location overlooking this wild but luscious-green and partly wooded valley. A series of permitted walks through the estate, including former deer parks, allows you to explore this otherwise inaccessible part of the valley, devoid as it is of public footpaths.

Ozleworth Bottom is almost the last of the extended valleys running at right angles to the western ridge. From here, the Cotswold escarpment compresses itself into a thin band that runs due south, passing the tiny villages of Hawkesbury, Horton and Little Sodbury and Old Sodbury. The little lanes that follow the ridge between the villages provide some spectacular westerly views, if not a little surreal to be seeing the large expanses of Bristol and Yate close by.

One of the best outlooks is from the **Somerset Monument**, close to the village of Hawkesbury Upton. Not dissimilar to the nearby Tyndale Monument, it was erected in 1846 in memory of General Lord Robert Somerset, a soldier whose ancestral home was at nearby Badminton (see page 219) and who had a distinguished military career fighting at the Battle of Waterloo.

Chipping Sodbury is the last of the Cotswold towns along the ridge – or actually sitting just below the ridge – before Bath. As 'chipping' was a word that meant 'market', unsurprisingly Chipping Sodbury was an important market town during medieval times and a meeting point on the Bristol to London road. While the town has expanded over the years, joining up with the town of Yate, the very wide main street through Chipping Sodbury, aptly named Broad Street, remains extremely attractive with a mixture of Cotswold stone and neatly painted buildings.

The Nailsworth Valley

Stroud spreads down the first mile of the Nailsworth Valley, sandwiched between Selsley and Rodborough commons. The Nailsworth Stream lines the valley floor, once marshland so early inhabitants stuck to the steep valley sides. Villages such as **Woodchester** and the town of **Nailsworth** have only really developed since the 17th century when the woollen industry took off here.

On the eastern slopes tiny villages, all connected to the cloth industry, hug the steep hillside. It's as if everything is in miniature here – tiny, terraced former weavers' cottages line the narrowest of lanes. You can make a very picturesque day out by linking together hamlets such as Littleworth, Amberley, Theescombe and Watledge, where the poet W H Davies, whose poem began the introduction to this book, spent his final years. Walking constantly on the slope can be tough, but the roads are sufficiently narrow and twisty that you have to go slow either when driving (small cars required) or cycling. Make the most of the requirement to be unhurried and soak up the views as you progress from village to village.

To the west, two further tight-knit valleys run at right angles to the Nailsworth Valley. The wooded **Woodchester Park** fills up the more northerly of the two while the Newmarket Valley just below remains totally naturalised with no roads along its floor and just the village of Nympsfield at its western end for habitation.

⑱ Woodchester Park

To the northwest of Nailsworth is Woodchester Park, a lost 18th- and 19th- century landscape park that takes up most of a steeply sided valley. For 200 years, until the mid-19th century, the park was the seat of the Ducie family who designed and constructed the landscape park around their home, since demolished. It included formal gardens and large fishponds as well as carriage drives providing panoramic views over the estate. During the late 19th century the estate, under new owners, was planted up to trees, which have now matured creating a new wooded park but this was not the Ducie's original intentions.

The National Trust now owns Woodchester Park and visitors can wander through the 400-acre estate all year round, free of charge. The trust is performing a gradual restoration of the park, thinning out some of the plantations to create the vistas that there once were.

It is an idyllic place, regardless of tree count, to go for a walk, either through the shaded beech woods, annually filled with bluebells and wild garlic, or through the more open glades and pastures alongside the string of five lakes created by the Ducie family. Their enchanting boathouse, built in the early 19th century and used by the family for picnics and boating parties, was restored in 1998.

The trust has created a series of walks throughout the estate – you can pick up a leaflet at the car park, accessed off the B4066 Stroud to Dursley road – but my favourite is the 3½-mile circular Boathouse Walk that makes the most of the vistas from both the lakes and woods. Although manmade, the lakes are most attractively naturalised in appearance. On a recent summer walk there, when iridescent

The Woodchester Mosaic

A Roman villa once stood at Woodchester and in 1693 the Orpheus Pavement was discovered close to the village, the largest and most detailed mosaic this side of the Alps. The mosaic, which dates from AD325, is still *in situ*, buried in a churchyard, but has not been uncovered since 1973 when the village struggled to cope with the hordes of tourists that came to look. A decision was taken then never to uncover the mosaic again.

Instead, two local brothers began ten years of painstaking work to create a replica mosaic, containing 1.6 million pieces and measuring 2,200 square feet. In 2010, the replica lost its 'permanent' exhibition space at Prinknash Abbey and was sold at auction to an anonymous, private buyer. Its whereabouts are sadly now a mystery. It's a stark possibility therefore that neither the original nor the replica may ever be viewed again.

dragonflies in number were fluttering like leaves from the trees, we were passing the dappled water of 'Middle Pond' when my young daughter suddenly leapt in the air crying, 'What's that?' I glanced to where she was pointing, half expecting to see some mythical monster rising from the deep. Instead it was a shoal of enormous finned fish, gliding silently around their watery world, completely ignoring an angler's line waiting patiently further down the lakeside.

Woodchester Mansion

Hidden among the trees in this secluded valley, a mile from any road, is one of the most secret of houses, the 19th-century Victorian Gothic **Woodchester Mansion** (*01453 861541; www.woodchestermansion.org.uk; open Sat and Sun, Easter to Oct; not National Trust owned, so National Trust members must pay to visit the house*). To me, it's also one of the most memorable houses in the whole of the Cotswolds, indeed Britain, made all the more special because it will never be completed.

Woodchester Mansion has no glass in the windows, limited staircases and barely any floors. It is not a derelict ruin though the masterpiece was mysteriously abandoned mid-construction in 1873. The listed building, completed externally but not internally, is an extraordinary architectural exhibit, the craftsmanship second to none and your imagination is required to finish the house. Doors lead nowhere, fireplaces hang in mid-air and the timber scaffolding of Victorian builders remains in place.

Intricately carved corbels, butted against the walls, stand ready to receive vaulted ceilings that never materialised, Gothic arches are part-finished and the marks of the builder's pencil are poised for a non-existent completion. Time really does stand still here.

Only one room was ever finished and to a lower standard of work not seen anywhere else in the house. It was hurriedly completed to receive a dignitary that unexpectedly accepted an invitation to visit. It makes the remaining abandonment all the more poignant. But the roof of the house is occupied now – by two nationally important colonies of bats recorded in the hundreds. Live footage of both greater and lesser horseshoe bats can be seen from the webcam in the Bat Room.

Various events and children's activities are hosted regularly throughout the summer, both in connection to bats and Victorian history. Like the park, access to the house is from the B4066 Stroud to Dursley road, close to the village of Nympsfield. Visitors may walk the mile from the car park to the house or use the free minibus.

Food and drink

There are no facilities at Woodchester Park. Woodchester Mansion has a small tea room in one of the uncompleted rooms but it can get very busy. The Rose and Crown at Nympsfield is the nearest place to eat otherwise.

Old Fleece Woodchester ☎01453 872582 🖰 www.food-club.com. One of a small group of superb eating venues in the area. Wood panelling and timber floors make the old inn warm and inviting. A mix of British and continental food on the menu with plenty of choice for light meals or something more substantial.

Ram Inn Station Rd, South Woodchester ☎01453 873329. Known for its selection of cask ales, particularly from local breweries in Stroud and Uley. Simple food menu too.

Rose and Crown Inn Nympsfield ☎01453 860240 🖰 www.theroseandcrowninn.com. A 17th-century Cotswold stone pub that was completely refurbished in 2010. Popular with locals. Simple food such as pies, soup, sandwiches and Sunday roasts can be eaten in the bar or restaurant – same menu in both.

⑲ Nailsworth

Of all the towns in the Five Valleys, I find Nailsworth the most rewarding. It has an industrial heritage, in both wool production and quarrying stone, and yet retains the Cotswold charm and good looks seen in the towns of the north Cotswolds. The stone is much paler here than in the north and east, and was often quarried underground rather than in open pits. Its quality was renowned, coming out of the ground in large blocks that was good for carving, used in stately homes and even the Houses of Parliament, while the rubble was used to build the quaint weavers' cottages on the hillsides.

But Nailsworth is better known for its mills – 12 in total dotted along the valley, each one used for a different process of woollen cloth manufacture. Like the mills of Stroud, it was most closely associated with producing the West of England cloth for military uniforms, lengths of scarlet-dyed material regularly seen stretched out to dry on the valley slopes. All the mills have either been demolished or changed to other uses today but **Dunkirk Mill** on the northern edge of town is a good surviving example. It's now used for residential flats but next door is a museum, run by the Stroudwater Textile Trust, in which you can see Gloucestershire's largest working waterwheel, still driving traditional textile machinery. **Egypt Mill**, close to the town centre, is used as a hotel and restaurant where you can see the two waterwheels, while **Days Mill** still stands right in the centre of Nailsworth, along the old market street.

For its size, Nailsworth has an impressive mix of independent shops and places to eat. The open nature of Old Market and the Town Square running parallel with Fountain Street, the main thoroughfare, doesn't make the town feel closed in. And yet the hills are never far away, with Minchinhampton Common just to the east, the road climbing up the hillside from Nailsworth known locally as 'the W', indicating the number of sharp hairpin bends required to reach the top. Alongside is the **Nailsworth Ladder**, an even steeper footpath that links the town and the common, with a gradient of 1 in 2¼ in places.

Food and drink

Foodies are spoilt for choice in Nailsworth with great delis for picnic goodies, gastro pubs, cosy restaurants and more upmarket dining.

Britannia Inn Cossack Sq ☎01453 832501 🖰 www.food-club.com. One of 5 pubs and restaurants owned by the Food Club, each place bursting with individual character. Britannia is a town centre bar in a former manor house with log fires and snugs. Watch as stone-baked pizzas are cooked alongside other continental fare. Good front garden to watch the world go by.

Egypt Mill Bridge St ☎01453 833449 🖰 www.eqyptmill.com. Superb location on the banks of the Nailsworth Stream, Egypt Mill was once used for cloth manufacture; there's a small, rear terrace overlooking the stream. Watch the two 'working' waterwheels as you eat in the comfy restaurant with flagstone floors, beams and sofas. Accommodation.

Tipputs Tiltups End, near Nailsworth ☎01453 832466 🖰 www.food-club.com. Another winner from the Food Club clan, in an old coaching inn and barn, full of character. Very good food, everything homemade, with plenty of variety on the menu. This is 1½ miles from Nailsworth town centre on the Bath road; Tiltups End is so named because overladen carts travelling from Nailsworth to Bath would tilt-up while trying to climb the escarpment.

Wild Garlic Restaurant Cossack Sq ☎01453 832615 🖰 www.wild-garlic.co.uk. Everything is handmade on the premises, from fresh pasta to chocolates, ice cream to bread. Quality of produce and flavour is of the utmost importance to the owners, who try to source all their ingredients from the Cotswolds and southwest of England. Accommodation too.

William's Fish Market and Food Hall Fountain St ☎01453 832240 🖰 www.williamsfoodhall.co.uk. You can't help but be drawn into this shop and café, such is the sight of fresh food through the plate-glass windows of this timber-framed building right in the centre of Nailsworth. Choose from the deli, sumptuously fresh fish and meat counters for take-out treats or eat in the Oyster Bar, naturally specialising in fish but with plenty of other options.

The commons and skinny valleys

At Nailsworth, the Nailsworth Valley actually splits into two further valleys running southwest to Kingscote and southeast towards **Avening** where it begins to curve north towards Cherington and Aston Down. These are the feeder streams for the Nailsworth Stream, ultimately flowing into the River Frome at Stroud. Having curved around to all but meet up with the Golden Valley in the north, an area of high ground is encapsulated, creating **Minchinhampton** and **Rodborough commons**.

Southeast of the Nailsworth Valley the land remains gently undulating in the main, nothing like the gouged-out landscape of the Five Valleys. Except that, here and there are sudden reminders – or pre-empters – of these dramatic escarpments and valleys, where pencil-thin, elongated relations suddenly flare up among the hills. One such dry valley begins close to Kemble, near Cirencester, and runs southwest to **Tetbury**. The main Cirencester to Bath road follows its course. A similarly dry valley runs through the **Westonbirt Estate** towards Tetbury, finally picking up water just before entering the town.

⑳ Minchinhampton and Rodborough commons

Between the Nailsworth Valley and Golden Valley, the land rises sharply with Minchinhampton Common and Rodborough Common, closer to Stroud, keeping the pair apart. They are very popular with walkers and picnickers for the views over the Five Valleys but, owing to the lie of the land and the distance between viewpoints, you'll never see everywhere all at once. Head to the west side of **Rodborough Common** to look over Stroud, the Painswick Valley and Selsley Common, and the east side for a view of Golden Valley overlooking Thrupp and Brimscombe. The west side of **Minchinhampton Common** gives the best views of Nailsworth while from the east side you can see up the Toadsmoor Valley and further along the Frome Valley. From up here you get the sense of how tightly compact all of these valleys are.

The commons are superb for walking and, as common land, you can walk pretty much anywhere you like. But these are some of the best examples of the Cotswolds unimproved limestone grassland where cows roam free, and consequently some of the best places to view the accompanying wild flowers, including 13 species of wild orchid, and varieties of butterflies (I spotted six different species in a short space of time on my last visit) rarely seen in gardens these days. For alternative but equally pleasing views of the Golden Valley take a ride along the tiny lane between Swellshill and Butterow, via Bagpath. The road has been designated as a Quiet Lane, a legal status that affords walkers,

Gifford's Circus

If you think of 'the circus' as huge big tops, impersonal arenas and depressed elephants, think again: Gifford's Circus (*0845 459 7469; www.giffordscircus.com*) is different. A truly traditional show that turns up on village greens and commons in and around the Cotswolds, this is an intimate and unashamedly old-fashioned extravaganza, a tiny ring in a tiny tent with rickety wooden benches where you'll have the night of your life. Each show is both visually attractive and electrifying. For children and adults alike it is utter, spine-tingling magic.

The traditional atmosphere is intensified with the burgundy-and-gold show wagons that surround the tent too – you buy your programme and bag of sweets from a costumed seller in a painted caravan. And during the interval the Tea Tent sells homemade cakes, locally made Cotswold ice cream and proper tea, all from appropriately patterned Emma Bridgewater crocks. Circus Sauce, the show's 42-seat travelling restaurant, pops up in a tent near the main top, where the audience can enjoy a spectacular starlit circus dinner with the artistes after the show, an attraction in its own right with fresh and local ingredients used for the three-course meal.

Each summer brings a new and totally unique show full of musicians, jugglers, clowns, acrobats and wirewalkers performing breath-holding stunts. Explained Nell Gifford, who owns the circus with her husband Toti, 'There's a whole team that works on each production. I'm the artistic director along with my husband, then there's a music director and a choreographer and producer. I tend to write the material for the show and we always aim to create outstanding quality shows for a rural audience. We're from the area, we live in the area and Gifford's Circus is very much a part of the Cotswolds.'

cyclists and horseriders as much right to be there as cars. There's no room for speed, this is a road to enjoy slowly.

From the common you can quite easily walk to **Minchinhampton**, a quiet old market town on the eastern edge of the hilltop. Its streets and buildings, including the arched Market House, are very enticing and the High Street is a heady mix of Cotswold gables and Georgian façades with barely a modern intrusion in sight. Peeling off along West End, you'll come across 'West End Stores', an old shop window filled with vintage motorcycle paraphernalia.

Opposite the old shop is the entrance to a tiny public footpath. Utterly intriguing, it has high stone walls on either side and miniature bridges under which you need to duck to continue on your way. The short footpath leads round to Well Hill, from where you get great views of Gatcombe Wood, a part of the Gatcombe Park Estate where Princess Anne lives and which is also home to the annual Gatcombe Horse Trials.

Perhaps the most striking of Minchinhampton's buildings is Holy Trinity Church in Bell Lane. The church tower is like a truncated cone topped with a coronet, although its design is not the original idea. The tower has a square base and should have remained square to the top but cracks began to appear as it was being built and so changes to its shape and appearance were necessary. Inside the church are a number of eye-catching brasses that you can take rubbings of for 50p; bring your own supplies of paper and crayons.

Food and drink

For such a small town, Minchinhampton is very well endowed with good places to eat or buy food. Taylor's butcher's on The Cross is revered by locals for miles around, and a country market sets up every Thursday at the Market House. And don't forget to stop and buy an ice cream from Winstone's, in between Rodborough and Minchinhampton commons, when out for a walk: the family have been making delicious ices since 1925.

Amberley Inn Amberley GL5 5AF ✆01453 872565. On the west side of Minchinhampton Common, overlooking the Nailsworth Valley. Warm ambience with good food and a choice of bar or restaurant menus. Accommodation.

Bear of Rodborough Rodborough Common GL5 5DE ✆01453 878522 ✆ www.cotswold-inns-hotels.co.uk. Right on top of the common with commanding views. Dine in the Box Tree Restaurant, take afternoon tea in the cosy lounge or have a drink and a 'bar meal' (gastro-pub food) in the Grizly Bar.

The Kitchen High St, Minchinhampton ✆01453 882655 ✆ www.thekitchenminchinhampton.co.uk. Family-run café and tea room where all the food, from cakes and biscuits to pâtés and chutneys, is made on the premises. Their ingredients really are sourced from local producers too. Very popular with locals. Open Tue to Sat.

Old Lodge Minchinhampton Common ✆01453 832047 ✆ www.food-club.com. Part of the Food Club group of local pubs and restaurants, sublime food in convivial surroundings and delightful gardens overlooking the common.

Ragged Cot Cirencester Rd, Minchinhampton ✆01453 884643 ✆ www.theraggedcot.co.uk. Half a mile east of Minchinhampton, a country pub with food that makes the most of the farms and local food producers, using organic whenever possible. Try the popular Saturday brunch for something different.

Sophie's Café Restaurant 20 High St, Minchinhampton ✆01453 885188 ✆ www.sophiesrestaurant.co.uk. In a listed Georgian building. Uses locally sourced organic produce to cook simple, rustic French food (Sophie is from the Basque region of France). The wine list is selected personally from French vineyards – her husband spends the summer out in France selecting them.

Woefuldane Organic Dairy Market Sq, Minchinhampton ✆01453 886855 ✆ www.woefuldaneorganics.co.uk. Run by Jonathan and Melissa Ravenhill, the dairy stocks organic cheeses, milk and other dairy produce all sourced from the Ravenhills' small, organic farm half a mile from the shop. Member of the Specialist Cheesemakers Association. Open Tue to Fri and Sat morning.

㉑ Avening, Cherington and Rodmarton

Across the **Avening Valley** south of Minchinhampton is **Avening**, a hilly mill town at the extremities of the cloth-making area. A thousand years ago it was owned by a Saxon nobleman who rejected the advances of a young girl in Flanders. She, Matilda, went on to marry William the Conqueror, and in so doing was able to inflict revenge on her former suitor by confiscating his estate. Feeling remorse upon the nobleman's death, she requested that the church at Avening be built. It's one of the fine buildings that you can still see today, along with some of the old mills and the handsome houses of the mill owners.

At the far end of the valley is the tiny village of **Cherington** where the feeder springs for the Avening Stream run through Cherington Pond on their way to the cloth mills. The pond was built in the 18th century to provide fishing for the manor house but today, in amongst woodland, it is a quiet nature reserve. A public footpath runs around the pond, from which you can create a short circular walk along a part of the valley and back to the village.

Rodmarton Manor

Approaching Rodmarton Manor (*01285 841253; www.rodmarton-manor.co.uk; see website for variable opening days and times*) through the entrance gates, and finding the many-gabled house curving around a courtyard, you would be forgiven for believing that it had stood there for centuries. But you'd be wrong. The house in fact, dates back only to 1909 when it was built at the request of the Biddulph family, who still reside there today. Ernest Barnsley, a well-known figure in the Arts and Crafts Movement and who was responsible for much of the Arts and Crafts buildings in nearby Sapperton (see page 184), led a group of craftsmen, taking 20 years to complete the house using traditional skills in woodwork, metalwork, needlework, painting and gardening. It was one of the last country houses to be built in the traditional style using local materials and local craftsmen, and when all the work was done by hand.

But the work didn't stop there, for once the house was built, it was furnished in the Arts and Crafts style too, with all the furniture and furnishings made by eminent craftsmen, much of it in the workshops at Rodmarton. All this craftwork remains in the house. But despite the extraordinary amount of notable artwork, it is still, refreshingly, a very much 'lived-in' house.

I found it a joy to wander through. On my visit there were seed packets on the floor, the toys and birthday cards of a grandchild scattered by the fireplace and family pictures anywhere they could be displayed. I'd creep gingerly into each room as if expecting to suddenly intrude on someone's day but the informality – and clearly illustrated love of living in the house – made it feel all the more special.

Outside the eight-acre gardens are uplifting too. Originally designed as a series of rooms, each has a unique feel, while retaining the overall character of the garden. Traditional cottage plants mix with chiselled topiary and mossy stone walls, wide borders and pathways draw the visitor to some other 'room', and then another. Losing your bearings is quite likely with all the pathways and hedges, so find a focal point on the house and stick with it.

㉒ Tetbury

The very yellow Market Hall, antiques and the Prince of Wales are always my immediate thoughts when I think of Tetbury, a town that in 1633 was 'given' to its inhabitants by the then lord of the manor and a delegation of seven feoffees, or trustees, accountable to the townsfolk, were appointed to look after property.

Though less authoritative than they once were, feoffees still perform some duties around the town including looking after the magnificent, sunflower-yellow Market Hall, built in 1655. For, like other Cotswold towns, Tetbury made its wealth through the wool trade with a prospering market taking place since the 12th century, at first in The Chipping, but later in and under the pillared **Market Hall**. It remains the most prominent building in town, with its distinctive illuminated clock and colourful floral displays.

Other prominent buildings in town include **St Saviour's Church** on the Avening road, a medieval-style Victorian building with an unusual roofline for the area and the thickest of Cotswold stone roof tiles. It was built for the poor of the parish who could not afford to pay for seats in Tetbury's other church. In 1975 the building was struck by lightning, damaging the roof and bringing the weathercock crashing to the ground. Inside was found a poem, dated 26 June 1848, by the maker William Sealy:

> *Will'm Sealy Made this Cock, The wind that blew will make it work, The place where it is to stand, The Lord preserve it with His Hand.*

Records show that Sealy was a working smith in business in the Market Place as an ironmonger, brazier and nail manufacturer.

St Mary's Church has a spire that can be seen for miles around. Built in 1781 the church has an elegant Georgian interior with panelled galleries, box pews and grand slender columns. It also has a modern, yet fitting, entrance that catches you unawares with contemporary paintings and 'Magnificat' in giant gold lettering above the

Woolsack races

Every spring bank holiday Monday, Tetbury revives an old tradition of gruelling hard work when men and women – originally the competition was just for men to demonstrate their masculinity – compete in the Woolsack Races. The location is **Gumstool Hill**, where fraudulent traders received a watery punishment at the ducking-stool. Competitors race from the Crown Inn at the top of the hill to the Royal Oak at the bottom carrying a bag of wool on their shoulders, weighing a staggering 65 pounds. But that's not the half of it, for they then pass the bag to a team member who must climb back up the hill – with a gradient of 1 in 4 in places – still carrying the sack. A plaque in the wall close to the Crown Inn marks the start and finish line.

Highgrove

A mile south of Tetbury is Highgrove, the private residence of HRH the Prince of Wales and the Duchess of Cornwall. For many years the prince has opened up his beloved gardens, developed and maintained enthusiastically embracing organic principles, to visiting community groups but now the general public may visit too. Guided tours of **Highgrove Gardens** (*020 7766 7310; www.highgrovegardens.com*), available from April to September on weekdays only, must be booked in advance and all proceeds go towards the prince's Charities Foundation. I thoroughly recommend a visit. The gardens are the Prince's passion in which he has a direct hand both in the design and the work. They are a personal reflection of joys and beliefs.

door. Look, too, for the small exhibition in the church of old photographs. There are some wonderful pictures of the church spire being taken down and rebuilt in 1890, with some very dodgy-looking wooden scaffolding that doesn't look as if it would pass 'health and safety' today.

St Mary's has also made efforts to create a wildflower haven right in the centre of town, having planted the churchyard with 300 English bluebells, hundreds of snowdrops, carpets of cyclamen and many perennial wild flowers. It provides a tiny retreat from the bustling shopping streets, where antique and interior design shops play a prominent role, particularly down Long Street.

Long Street is also the address for HRH the Prince of Wales's flagship **Highgrove Shop** (*01666 505666; www.highgroveshop.com*), a very popular destination among visitors to the town. Inside is the Highgrove Collection of gifts, with every product inspired by some aspect of the house or gardens on his private estate.

For another address that has less of a waiting list to visit, **Chavenage** (*01666 502329; www.chavenage.com; open May to Sep on Thu and Sun afternoons*), just to the west of Tetbury, is not to be rushed. The Elizabethan house is very good looking from the outside, with its mottled Cotswold stone simplicity, but inside is full of stories to tell. David Lowsley-Williams, the owner who guides you around, is a very good raconteur, telling you about the lives of the people who have lived there and those who have visited, including a happy monk from a bygone age who apparently kneels at the altar of the little chapel occasionally.

Food and drink

With so many top-quality farms and food producers in the area, it's not difficult to find fresh, local food here. For a picnic area and pleasant out-of-town walk along a miniscule valley, head to Preston Park, next to the old railway station, accessed from The Chipping.

Hobbs House Bakery 20 Church St ☎01666 504533 🖥 www.hobbshousebakery. co.uk. Traditional bakers, passionate about making real, artisan breads (as opposed to the 'plastic' variety found in supermarkets). Sandwiches made to order, handmade

patisseries and some of the best coffee in the Cotswolds. Useful for picnic provisions.
Snooty Fox Market Pl ☎01666 502436 ✆ www.snooty-fox.co.uk. Overlooking the
Market Hall, with pavement tables outside and a warm, comfy lounge-like bar inside.
Restaurant serving classic British food; a creative menu.
The Veg Shed Duchy Home Farm, Cherington Lane GL8 8SE ☎01666 503507.
The place to buy fresh, organic, seasonal fruit and vegetables, grown on the farm
owned by HRH the Prince of Wales. Open every Wed, Fri and Sat.

㉓ Westonbirt Arboretum

Most intriguingly, the layout at Westonbirt Arboretum (*01666 880220; www.
foresty.gov.uk/westonbirt; open daily*) is registered as a Grade I Historic Landscape
of International Importance. Robert Stayner Holford, one-time owner of the
Westonbirt Estate, began to plant trees in the 1850s and laid out the grounds
using a blueprint known as the Picturesque Landscaping Style, the argument
being that the best way to improve a landscape was to apply the principles of
painting. The collection, of course, has been added to and extended, but you
can still make out those principles in the Old Arboretum, with disappearing
perspectives in the long, stately avenues that look towards Holford's mock-
Eliabethan mansion, colour against the skyline and vistas.

Yet the area around Westonbirt has something unique in the Cotswolds. Split
by a small, dry valley, the arboretum has two contrasting areas, as it sits on two
differing soil types – the alkaline limestone to the east of the valley, where the
Old Arboretum is, and to the west, an acidic, sandy soil where the Silk Wood
was planted. The differing soils have enabled a large variety of trees and shrubs
to become established. While the Old Arboretum contains many rare and exotic
specimen trees from around the world, Silk Wood provides themed groups such
as the native tree, the oak, ash, cherry and national Japanese maple collections.

Every month provides something specific to look at, with many seasonal events
taking place throughout the year, including the annual Festival of the Tree in
August. The Forestry Commission are keen that the arboretum is not just a place to
look at trees but to encourage people, in particular children, to use woods as places
of activity. Numerous trails lead around the arboretum but every so often you'll
come across 'Naturally Playful' play zones where fallen trees and log pathways make
toys and where children are encouraged to build dens, using their imagination to
make the most of the natural resources around them. Against the norm, children's
entrance to the arboretum is free during the summer holidays.

Food and drink

On site at Westonbirt is the **Maples Restaurant**, serving good, home-cooked and
wholesome food. There's also a small café and a picnic area. Just yards from the
entrance is the **Hare and Hounds Hotel** (*01666 881000; www.cotswold-inns-hotels.
co.uk*) where Jack Hare's Bar serves fresh, seasonal fare from nibbles and sandwiches
to more substantial meals. Children welcome.

9. WILTSHIRE COTSWOLDS

For some, Wiltshire is more associated with Salisbury Plain and the Vale of the White Horse than the Cotswolds, but a reasonable chunk of the Cotswolds does fall into the county. Because the area is less known, its quiet, untouristy nature gives quite a sense of discovery.

Towns such as **Malmesbury**, **Corsham** and **Bradford-on-Avon** all have their own character and just a day spent in each should leave you feeling that you'd like to spend longer. But it's the countryside that is the jewel here, much of it appealingly remote. In the north of this locale, above the M4, the land lends itself to open wolds – Malmesbury sits on top of one of them. But below the M4 corridor the land begins to twist and turn again, providing sharp ridges and secret valleys around the edge of Bath.

One of the best valleys for exploring is **By Brook**. In the north, close to its source, it is relatively well known and tourist orientated, including **Castle Combe**, one of the great showpieces of the Cotswolds. But further south it uncovers equally worthwhile villages such as **Ford** and **Slaughterford**, with plenty of opportunities for walks off the beaten track.

I've sneaked north Somerset and a tiny snippet of Gloucestershire into this locale too, for the ridges of hills know no authoritative boundaries, and secrets such as **St Catherine's**, which lies within ten yards of the Wiltshire boundary, are too good to miss by being overly picky about where the dotted line falls.

When researching this book, I met a man who had been stationed at one of the barracks in the area while performing his National Service in the 1950s. He reminded me of the important role that the military has played here over many years – there are still several military bases and operational units in the area. He told how, on a Friday evening, the roads for miles around, in particular the London road (now the A4 between Bath and Chippenham) out of Bath, were lined with personnel trying to thumb a lift to go home for the weekend.

Getting there and around

Trains
First Great Western (*www.firstgreatwestern.co.uk*) run services to Bath Spa from London, the south, the southwest and the north (the latter too via Bristol Temple Meads). There are local services to Bradford-on-Avon from Bath and Trowbridge on the Bristol to Weymouth line, also run by First Great Western.

Buses
National coach firms stop at Bath. There are local services between Bath and Marshfield and Bradford-on-Avon but local bus journeys around the locale can be tortuous, lengthy affairs with many changes. There is, however, a direct bus from

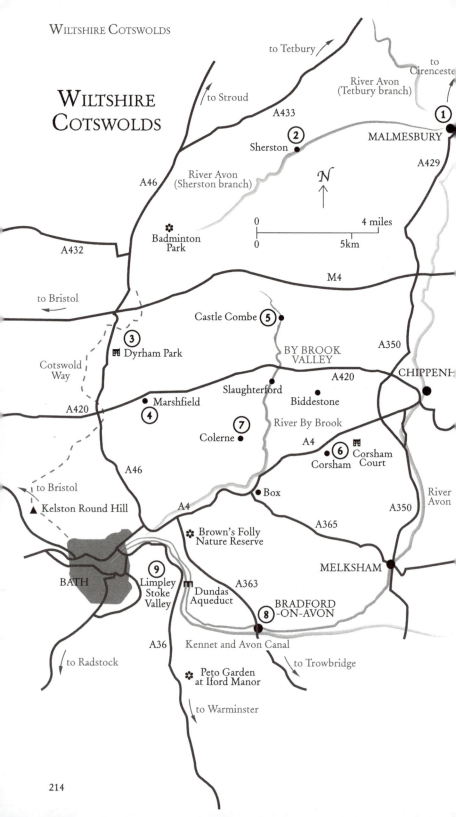

WILTSHIRE COTSWOLDS

to Tetbury

to Cirenceste

River Avon
(Tetbury branch)

to Stroud

A433

① MALMESBURY

② Sherston

A429

River Avon
(Sherston branch)

A46

N

A432

Badminton
Park

0   4 miles

0   5km

to Bristol

M4

Castle Combe ⑤

③
⊞ Dyrham Park

BY BROOK
VALLEY

A350

Cotswold
Way

A420

Slaughterford

A420

CHIPPENH

A420

Marshfield

④

Biddestone

River By Brook

Colerne ⑦

A4

A46

Corsham ⑥ ⊞ Corsham
Court

Corsham

to Bristol

▲ Kelston Round Hill

Box

River
Avon

A4

A350

Brown's Folly
Nature Reserve

A365

BATH

⑨
Limpley
Stoke
Valley

Dundas
Aqueduct

A363

MELKSHAM

A36

⑧ BRADFORD
-ON-AVON

Kennet and Avon Canal

to Radstock

Peto Garden
at Iford Manor

to Trowbridge

to Warminster

214

Bath to **Dyrham Park**. But you will not be able to explore the secret valleys in this locale by bus.

Cycling

A useful dead-straight section of former Roman road is the 12-mile rural byway section of the **Fosse Way**; this begins close to Crudwell, three miles north of Malmesbury, and ends just north of the By Brook Valley, close to Castle Combe. Where the byway ends, the Fosse Way continues as a quiet, country road until it reaches the outskirts of Bath close to Batheaston.

A particularly attractive traffic-free cycle ride runs between Bath and Bradford-on-Avon. It's a part of the **National Cycle Network Route 4** and uses the towpath of the **Kennet and Avon Canal**, which runs alongside the River Avon. Running on the flat through the Limpley Valley, with its wooded slopes either side and a stop-off point midway for a drink at the Dundas Aqueduct, it is a popular route.

Bike hire

Bath & Dundas Canal Co Brassknocker Basin, Monkton Combe BA2 7JD ✆01225 722292 🖰 www.bathcanal.com. On the towpath of the Somerset Coal Canal close to Bath, hire of bikes, trailers and tag-a-longs. Shop selling bikes and accessories. Ideal for exploring the Limpley Stoke Valley.

Towpath Trail and TT Cycles Frome Rd, Bradford-on-Avon BA15 1LE ✆01225 867187 🖰 www.towpathtrail.co.uk. Cycle hire including adults' and children's bikes, trailer bikes, child seats and helmets. All bikes are less than 6 months old. Bike sales and repairs at TT Cycles bike shop. Situated by the Kennet and Avon Canal, the company hires canoes too.

Accommodation

Castle Inn Castle Combe SN14 7HN ✆01249 783030 🖰 www.castle-combe.com. Buildings don't get much prettier than this, and it's in arguably one of the most idyllic locations next to the ancient Market Place with views running down the main street. Full of charm, with little inglenooks and snugs in which to enjoy a drink or afternoon tea and an elegant restaurant for dinner. Eleven beautifully decorated rooms, all with personal character and added touches.

Stowford Manor Farm Wingfield, Trowbridge BA14 9LH ✆01225 752253 🖰 www.stowfordmanorfarm.co.uk. Although on the limits of the locale, and indeed the Cotswolds, it's too good a place to miss and is perfect for visiting the more southerly attractions; you can walk to the Peto Garden at Iford or across the fields to Bradford-on-Avon. Right on the banks of the River Frome, you can choose between B&B in the farmhouse or camping in one of their riverside meadows. Breakfasts for guests staying in the farmhouse usually include produce from the farm. In summer you can sit in the garden and indulge with a cream tea; the scones are made in the farm kitchen and there's Jersey cream from their own cows. You can join the Farleigh and District Swimming Club for a dip in the river or support the local craftsmen and women in the studio workshops on site.

Tourist information centres

Bradford–on–Avon 50 St Margaret's St ☎01225 865797
📶 www.bradfordonavon.co.uk.
Malmesbury Town Hall, Cross Hayes ☎01666 823748.

The young Avon Valley to Malmesbury

The town of **Malmesbury** clusters around the River Avon, which ultimately flows south to Bradford-on-Avon and west to Bath and Bristol. But before it reaches Malmesbury, its young life begins in two halves, the Tetbury branch, obvious enough, and the Sherston branch, which flows from the southwest, rising just over the county border in Didmarton and onto Sherston before meeting up with its twin. A prominent tributary also flows into this river at Sherston, whose source rises within the grounds of the great **Badminton Estate**. It is this Sherston branch of the Avon, together with its tributary, that I'm focusing on here.

① Malmesbury

As a defensive location, Malmesbury has an ideal position upon a hill sandwiched between the two branches of the River Avon. Iron Age settlers were the first to make the most of its natural assets. And while today, the Dyson headquarters is left vulnerable outside the town's defences, at the heart of Malmesbury is its magnificent abbey, visible for miles around and dwarfing all other buildings in the town.

What can be seen today of **Malmesbury Abbey** is only a third of its original size, having, in the 12th century, been built in a cruciform shape. Over the centuries, bits have dropped off and never been replaced. A tower, taller than that on Salisbury Cathedral, was added but fell down, and what remains is essentially the nave, with the transepts – and the monastery – long gone. Since the 16th century, the abbey has been the parish church and inside has an inspiring sense of grandeur, with soaring ceilings. Yet outside, signs of its piece-meal neglect are clearly evident. The south porch once had remarkable stone carving, sadly decaying. From the peaceful Cloister Garden, on the north side, the stone ruins are more obvious, where pigeons roost silently in prayer along the precipice of arched window frames, and pink-tinged valerian clings to life from rocky edges, the stunted posts of once grand archways and giant flying buttresses left suspended.

Of the remaining stained-glass windows, one features the abbey's benefactor, the 'Flying Monk'. In 1010, inspired by the jackdaws who roosted at the abbey, Brother Eilmer strapped wings to his arms and legs and 'flew' from one of the abbey towers. The experiment was not greatly successful and after gliding about 200 yards he fell, breaking both his legs. Banned by his abbot from making another attempt, Eilmer lived on another 50 years or so to become a distinguished scholar. The townsfolk have since taken the budding pilot to their hearts.

Abbey House Gardens

One of the best places from which to view the abbey is next door from the Abbey House Gardens (*01666 822212; www.abbeyhousegardens.co.uk; open daily Mar to Oct*). The former abbot's house (not open to the public) is striking enough but the five-acre gardens in which it sits with views across to the mystical remains of the abbey walls are outstanding. The gardens are in front of the house and are formal but somewhat rambling. A Celtic cross, a delicate knot garden, herbaceous borders, a loggia, fat topiary balls and a medieval herb garden, shaped like a wheel with spokes, interrupt trimmed lawns and grassy paths. But rebellious roses burst out over their neatly trimmed guardian box hedges, weeping perennials sprawl across carefully tended lawns and vines cascade from archways around the herb garden, all defying formal order. It is a delight to wander through.

Behind the house is another world. Steep terraces and criss-crossing paths climb down the rocky hillside to the River Avon and the old monastic fishponds, fed by a cave-like waterfall. Ferns and rhododendrons thrive in damp corners and the vibrant colours of pondside plants reflect in the river. The imagination has been used wisely here and it shows.

Incidentally, Abbey House Gardens are also known as the 'home of the naked gardeners'. It must only be while clipping and snipping at plants that the owners', Ian and Barbara Pollard, are bereft of clothing, for they were happily eating breakfast when I visited, and they were fully clothed.

Food and drink

Malmesbury has numerous independent shops along its High Street, together with a mix of cafés, pubs and restaurants.

Old Bell Hotel Abbey Row 📞01666 822344 🌐 www.oldbellhotel.co.uk. Reputedly the oldest purpose-built hotel in England (built in 1220), traditional Cotswold comfort. The Brasserie Restaurant offers informal dining for lunches and evening meals while afternoon tea can be taken in one of the lounges or outside on the secluded garden terrace. Accommodation and more formal dining in the elegant Edwardian Restaurant available too.

A walk around Malmesbury

Allow 1½ hours minimum.

Begin at the distinctive, octagonal **Market Cross** at the top of the High Street and walk through the Tolsey Gate into the **Abbey precinct**, where you'll come across the grave of Hannah Twynnoy who, according to her gravestone, was mauled to death by an escaped circus tiger in 1703. Coming out of the graveyard by the Old Bell Hotel, walk down Abbey Row, where you'll catch glimpses of the town and the Sherston branch of the River Avon below.

At The Triangle, turn right into the Gloucester road and almost immediately left along St Mary's Street, to the charming **Horsefair**, where an illegal market used to run to dodge the town market's toll.

Leave Horsefair via West Street and, at the end, turn right into Bristol Street. Take the first left into Foxley Road and cross over Turtle Bridge, taking in the views of the town from the Avon. Just past the bridge, turn left onto a footpath that crosses **King's Heath**, the water meadows that were given to the town by King Athelstan. Follow the footpath and the river – these are some of the prettiest views of the town – until you come to a bend in the river with a tiny footbridge. The bulge in the river is called **Daniel's Well** and is great for a summer paddle.

Cross over the footbridge, passing the backs of residential gardens and climb the steep steps back to the Market Cross. Continue past the cross into Oxford Street where, at its end, you'll see **Tower House**. Among the former houseguests were Henry VIII and Charles I but the tower atop was not built until the 19th century, as an observatory. Turn right into Cross Hayes, one of the old marketplaces, and then left into Silver Street. The land falls away sharply at the bottom as you walk down Back Hill Steps towards the Tetbury branch of the **Avon**. Within yards, the two branches of the river join together.

Turn right into St John's Street, past the tiny **almshouses** and then left where you'll see a very pretty 12th-century stone archway that was once the entrance to a medieval hospital. Cross the river using St John's Bridge, where you'll see the old mills that were originally used for wool, but turned to silk production 200 years ago as the wool trade declined. Just over the bridge turn into Cuckingstool Mead and walk through to **St Aldhelm's Mead**. This is a great place for a picnic as the rustle of giant poplar trees overshadows the noise of the nearby road. The park is overlooked by meadows at the western end and, towards town are the backs of the terraced houses above. Their endearing gardens slope down to a spur of the river, where plum trees dangle in the water.

At the playground, turn right and climb up to King's Wall, a delightful narrow street of old stone houses that heads back to the High Street. At the junction with the High Street, look down its lower section where you'll see the terrace of old millworkers' cottages before turning left to return to the Market Cross.

Summer Café 4 High St ☎01666 822639. My pick of places to eat. Small café with a couple of pavement tables. Breakfasts and lunches (homemade quiche, salads, baguettes and the like) and afternoon teas (delicious homemade cakes and biscuits). Open 09.00 on Sun, when breakfast/brunch is popular.

② Sherston, Luckington and Badminton

Winding southwest, back towards its source, the Sherston branch of the Avon skirts around **Sherston**. The focal point of this village is its broad High Street lined with Cotswold stone houses. Every July, Sherston holds an annual carnival, the highlight of which is a French-style boules tournament.

The Romans occupied this area, with the Fosse Way running just to the east, and the remains of a villa were found close to the village, but Sherston's history really comes alive with the Saxons. The Danish king Canute and his men advanced on the village in 1016 but were met by John Rattlebone, so named afterwards because his knockout blows caused the enemy's bones to rattle. The Danes retreated. John Rattlebone has been the village hero ever since and is celebrated at the village pub, the Rattlebone Inn.

You can use a two-mile stretch of the Macmillan Way to walk from Sherston to its southerly neighbour, **Luckington**. In doing so, you'll pass by the church and through the grounds of **Luckington Court**, a bonus for Jane Austen (or Colin Firth) fans. The Queen Anne house was used as 'Longbourn' – the home of the Bennett family – in the 1995 award-winning BBC adaptation of *Pride and Prejudice*. Consequently, Luckington Court is a very popular wedding venue.

The Wiltshire/Gloucestershire border lies just to the west of Luckington, dividing the Badminton Estate and **Badminton Park**. The village of **Badminton** is impressive enough and makes a refreshing change from all the stone villages in the area. Its uncharacteristic colour co-ordinated yellow lime-washed houses seem more in keeping in west Somerset than the Cotswolds. Badminton Park remains essentially private but a public footpath – a metalled track that is perfect for pushchairs and wheelchairs – runs straight through the park linking Badminton with Little Badminton. There's no prospect of a circular walk but the there-and-back stroll provides ample opportunity to watch the deer that roam the park, and to take in the views of the lake and the grand house, home of the Duke of Beaufort. The private gardens are opened just for one day each summer (open days are posted at *www.badmintonestate.co.uk*).

Badminton is, of course, best known for its annual horse trials (*www.badminton-horse.co.uk*), one of the most prestigious events in the cross-country eventing calendar, attracting top riders from across the world, including royalty. It was also the birthplace of badminton when, in 1873, the game was introduced to guests at Badminton House as 'the Badminton game', even though versions had existed for centuries under several guises throughout the world. The nearby Bath Badminton Club cemented the new game by drawing up the first set of written rules in 1877.

Food and drink

Old House at Home Burton SN14 7LT ☎01454 218227 🖰 www.ohhcompany.co.uk.
Ivy-clad pub with abundant internal character. A choice of bar snacks (deluxe bacon
sandwich, smoked salmon and crab salad, etc) or main menu, with masses of choice,
including game. Very popular for Sunday lunch. Usefully placed for nearby Badminton.
Rattlebone Inn Sherston ☎01666 840871 🖰 www.therattlebone.co.uk. Named after
the village hero, a 17th-century village pub with plenty of ambience enjoyed by locals,
including the nearby Beaufort Hunt. Recently refurbished, there's plenty of character
with exposed stone walls and beams, inglenook fireplaces and various nooks and
crannies. The main restaurant is housed in an atmospheric old barn with a classic
British menu. Bar snacks include the Rattlebone steak sandwich and summertime
involves an outdoor barbecue. Regular entertainment includes live music monthly and
the use of three boules pitches, a popular 'sport' in the village. Recently resurrected is
'Mangold hurling', the ancient art of turnip-tossing.

Dyrham and Marshfield

Having run pencil-thin for several miles between Hawkesbury and Old Sodbury,
the Cotswold escarpment begins to broaden again at **Dyrham** creating a great,
knotted lump as it nears Bath. Fighting armies have used the vantage points,
overlooking the Avon and Severn valleys, to their advantage. For example in
AD577 the Battle of Dyrham took place when a West Saxon army, under the
authority of Cuthwine and Caewuln, sprung an attack on the Britons of the West
Country, making use of an Iron Age fort on Hinton Hill, just north of Dyrham.
Three kings of the Britons were killed and, in so doing, Cuthwine and Caewuln
took the cities of Bath, Cirencester and Gloucester.

③ Dyrham Park

Television and film producers clearly love the Cotswolds and none of it more
so than Dyrham Park (*0117 937 2501; www.nationaltrust.org.uk*). My first
encounter of this house, with its imposing deep golden façade, was through the
film, *The Remains of the Day*, when political dignitaries drew up to the entrance
to be waited upon by Anthony Hopkins. More recently, the house has played
host to *Doctor Who*.

The Baroque mansion sits at the foot of the Cotswold escarpment, sheltered
by a bend in the ridge. Its landscaped deer park takes up almost 270 acres of the
escarpment, including Hinton Hill, where the Battle of Dyrham was fought.
Visitors may wander here throughout the year, looking out for the deer, which
have been in the park since it was enclosed in 1620, and enjoying the views over
Bristol and the Severn bridges. The National Trust lays on a minibus to take
you down the long, sweeping drive to the house but, if you're able, winding
your way down the escarpment on foot, stopping at Neptune's Statue to soak up
the view of the house below, is by far the best approach. Then you'll encounter

the changing landscape as you descend: the Frying Pan Pond, a relatively recent addition in 1833, and the Old Lodge buildings where there's a picnic area. You can catch the minibus back to the car park (where a bus from Bath also drops off passengers) if you don't feel like climbing back up the hill on the return.

Inside, the huge rooms have changed little in decoration since William Blathwayt transformed the house and estate in 1691. His taste was for Dutch everything (the landscape park once included a Dutch garden, now disappeared) and the house is filled with Dutch decorative arts, with a large collection of delftware. Consequently, a tulip festival is held each year, usually in April or May.

In contrast to the wildness of the landscape park, the West Garden is a suntrap, perfect in the warmer months for lazing around on the lawns, in the orchard – filled with perry pears, daffodils and wild flowers – or around the pools. Events, such as 'Lazy Jazz on the Lawn' are often put on here to tempt you to linger a while longer and enjoy the rear views – actually the original entrance – to the house. The National Trust can generally be relied upon for tasty food and Dyrham Park is no exception – lunches and afternoon teas are available at the courtyard tea room, close to the main entrance.

④ Marshfield

Southeast of Dyrham is Marshfield, a large village positioned at the top of a south-facing ridge and overlooking a green moonscape of undulations and wooded valleys. Its layout is of one long, long High Street, off which are numerous thin burgage plots, a medieval land rental system consisting of a house and a thin plot of land behind. When I first visited Marshfield I was astounded by its beauty and had visions of its High Street, like so many other locations in the Cotswolds, being used as a film set. As if stepping back in time, the extensive street, which runs virtually the full length of the village, is made up predominantly of elegant and graceful Georgian façades, with numerous architectural features such as balustrades on roofs and scalloped porches. The fascinating street names such as Sheep Fair Lane and Touching End Lane give an indication of

The Marshfield mummers

Every Boxing Day, the village tradition is for 'The Paper Boys', a seven-strong troupe of 'boys' to perform a mummers play. The troupe, costumed in strips of paper, begin in the Market Place and process along the High Street, performing their five-minute play several times along the route. The story is based loosely – oral traditions without anything written down mean that the play has evolved over time – on the legend of St George and the Dragon but remains a fertility rite. According to tradition, therefore, women may not perform.

The troupe is made up from villagers, ideally those whose families have lived in the village for generations.

village history – it was granted market status in 1234 – encouraging you to explore further, away from the High Street. And close to the church is a magnificent tithe barn, now converted to a private house.

Close by are two gastronomic delights that have created fine reputations for the village. The first is the small but expanding **Marshfield Bakery** that began from premises on Marshfield's High Street. Now in purpose-built premises on the A46 just north of Dyrham Park, the 25-year-old business has made its name by making high-quality shortbreads, biscuits and cakes, with recipes originally developed in the Whites' farmhouse kitchen and still handmade using ingredients sourced from Wiltshire and neighbouring counties. One of their products, the Three Shires Biscuit, takes its name from the nearby Three Shires Stone, where Wiltshire, Gloucestershire and Somerset meet.

The whole process of producing **Marshfield Ice Cream** is local indeed. Crops grown on the organic farm are used to feed the cows who supply the milk to make the ice cream. The production of the ice cream takes place on the site too. While the farm allows local community groups to visit, the general public are unable to simply turn up, but the sale of Marshfield Ice Cream is prolific in the area; it is absolutely delicious.

Food and drink

Catherine Wheel High St, Marshfield ☎01225 892220 🖱 www.thecatherinewheel. co.uk. Handsome Georgian building with an inviting restaurant and bar with classic British dishes and a more creative menu (braised pork belly, lamb tagine, venison meatballs). Exposed walls and roaring log fires make winter visits cosy or there's a sunny patio for summer. Open daily. Accommodation too.

Marshfield Bakery Tolldown Barn, Dyrham SN14 8HZ ☎01225 891709 🖱 www.marshfieldbakery.co.uk. The bakery and shop are situated on the A46, half a mile north of the entrance to Dyrham Park. Open 08.00 to 17.15 Mon to Fri and 10.00 to 16.00 Sat. Closed Sun.

Tollgate Tea shop Dyrham SN14 8LF ☎01225 891585. On the A46, half a mile south of the entrance to Dyrham Park. A cosy tea room housed in an old lodge with a conservatory and sweet little garden to the rear that provides panoramic views of the Severn Valley and Welsh hills. Breakfasts, lunches and afternoon teas. Closed Mon.

The By Brook Valley

A 12-mile-long tributary of the River Avon, By Brook provides a backdrop to some of the choicest villages. Its spaghetti-like tangle of meandering loops is unusual for a river so small, and its gracefulness and therapeutically quiet sound make it an ideal companion for walking. Its steep valley sides are reminiscent of other areas of the Cotswolds and indeed its water was important in powering the 20 mills that once worked hereabouts during the years of the wool trade. When wool declined, many of the mills were used to make paper instead; now they have all disappeared.

Beginning close to the village of **Burton**, By Brook sidles through **Castle Combe** then on to **Ford**, **Slaughterford** and **Box** before joining up with the Avon at Batheaston.

The roads between all of these villages and their neighbours are small and narrow, ideal for fairly hilly cycling or pottering about slowly by car. They are not designed for speed; for that, visit Castle Combe Racing Circuit where you can put your own road car through its paces around the track.

⑤ Castle Combe, Ford, Slaughterford and Biddestone

Creating a tour out of these four villages provides the ideal opportunity to explore them all, for while Ford and Slaughterford are free of tourist attractions, they should not be missed and neither should the countryside that surrounds them. Views unveil themselves abruptly, for example as you drop down from Thickwood towards Slaughterford, turning a corner and suddenly coming across the sweetest little stone bridge across By Brook, the roadsides brimming with wild flowers.

The furthest north is **Castle Combe**; I find the most impressive way to arrive is from the south, either along the little lane that runs startlingly close at times to the gorge-like valley below or along the Macmillan Way footpath, which runs close to the stream. The attractiveness of the village is renowned, tucked as it is into the valley, and its unblemished array of Cotswold cottages really pull the crowds. The view from the bridge across By Brook, at the lower end of the main street, is one of the most photographed in the Cotswolds, but sadly that's all many visitors tend to see before moving on. At the top of the main street is the 14th-century market cross, where wool was once sold – Castle Combe also had its own mill and made its wealth from the wool trade – with the Castle Inn behind.

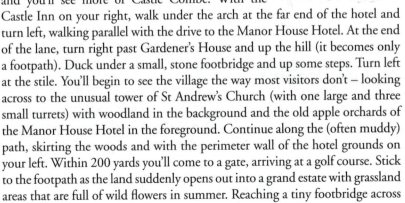

But take a short walk just out of the village and you'll see more of Castle Combe. With the Castle Inn on your right, walk under the arch at the far end of the hotel and turn left, walking parallel with the drive to the Manor House Hotel. At the end of the lane, turn right past Gardener's House and up the hill (it becomes only a footpath). Duck under a small, stone footbridge and up some steps. Turn left at the stile. You'll begin to see the village the way most visitors don't – looking across to the unusual tower of St Andrew's Church (with one large and three small turrets) with woodland in the background and the old apple orchards of the Manor House Hotel in the foreground. Continue along the (often muddy) path, skirting the woods and with the perimeter wall of the hotel grounds on your left. Within 200 yards you'll come to a gate, arriving at a golf course. Stick to the footpath as the land suddenly opens out into a grand estate with grassland areas that are full of wild flowers in summer. Reaching a tiny footbridge across

By Brook, you'll have the stream and the surroundings to yourself with the possible exception of the odd guest from the hotel's golf course. You can either continue along the Macmillan Way or take the ten-minute walk back to the village to enjoy a drink in one of the pubs or tea rooms.

Ford is the next village on the route of By Brook, closely followed by **Slaughterford**, a disjointed village on the valley side with a very handsome church set among meadows. The houses drift down to the stream, which rather than crossing at the end of the village you can follow through the imposing Backpath Woods. This is, I think, the ideal route to reach **Biddestone**. Approximately two miles to the east of both Ford and Slaughterford, Biddestone is one of the most sought-after villages in Wiltshire for property buyers and prices are some of the highest in the area. Reaching it you'll understand why, with its wide main street, lined with some very good-looking stone houses, plus a village green and duck pond in the centre. It's a pleasant spot to sit, open a flask of coffee and enjoy the ducks' company for a moment or two.

Food and drink

The pavement tables of the **Castle Inn** have one of the best views in Castle Combe, overlooking the market place. The **Manor House Hotel**, set well back in its own grounds, provides full afternoon tea – and is a member of the Tea Guild, demonstrating excellence in serving a proper cup of tea. The hotel also has a Michelin-starred restaurant.

White Horse Biddestone ☎01249 713305 🖱 www.thewhitehorsebiddestone. co.uk. Simple village pub serving a basic menu (chips and peas with everything and lots of pastry) but useful for a lunchtime drink. Great location by the village green and duck pond.

⑥ Corsham

Often overlooked in favour of other Cotswold towns simply because they happen to be better known, **Corsham** is every bit worth visiting, not least because it is filled less with tourists and more with locals.

Right on the eastern edge of the Cotswolds, it too made its wealth through the wool trade, but being slightly away from the river and without the means to drive mills, the market town stuck to the less industrial tasks of spinning and weaving. The 17th-century row of **Flemish cottages** in the High Street was built for the weavers who came from the continent.

The town also made a name through quarrying high-quality Bath stone, a pale, creamy-coloured limestone that is significantly different in both colour and texture from the stone of the northern Cotswolds. The industry still continues today in quarries close to the town, with Bath Stone remaining an ever-popular choice for building.

The partly pedestrianised, flagstoned **High Street** is full of attractive façades, with the Georgian town hall, built as a market hall, perhaps the most elegant,

The Burlington Bunker

It's hard to imagine idyllic little towns like Corsham being a seat of power but things are not always what they seem. For beneath the surface, in the abandoned stone quarries under Box Hill, is the Burlington Bunker, also known as Site 3. In the 1950s parts of the old Spring Quarry were developed as a central Government War Headquarters, where the politicians would adjourn in the event of a nuclear strike. The underground bunker was radiation-proof and consisted of a street with Whitehall ministries on each side and included a pub (the Rose and Crown), a bakery, laundry, kitchens and enough facilities for 4,000 government ministers and civil servants. The bunker was decommissioned in the early 1990s but remained a decoy site until 2004.

although the gabled Flemish cottages do perhaps rule with their charm. The street has a good range of independent shops and eating-places. Fifty yards from the southern end of the High Street are the 17th-century **Hungerford Almshouses and Schoolrooms**, Grade I listed and some of the best-preserved structures of their kind. The buildings were built to an extremely high quality, and of a scale or lavishness previously unknown for buildings of this nature. The almshouses are still lived in but you can visit the schoolrooms, which contain many of their original 17th-century fittings. One-hour guided history tours of Corsham are available from the tourist information centre in the High Street.

Corsham Court

Topping both the High Street and the almshouses is Corsham Court (*01249 701610; www.corsham-court.co.uk; open afternoons only, weekends all year plus Tue to Thu Mar to Sep*), where the countryside meets the town. Accessed just 100 yards from the High Street via Church Street, the Corsham Estate was a royal manor during Saxon times and was later owned by royalty in Tudor times too. But the existing house is Elizabethan, built in 1582, with extensions and alterations in the late 18th century. It belonged to the Methuen family for eight generations; you can see the family crest carved into the exterior walls.

The Methuens have been avid collectors of paintings; inside is a distinguished collection of Old Masters from the 16th to 19th century with works by Van Dyck, Filippo Lippi, Reynolds and Romney. The artworks hang in the Picture Gallery, a room commissioned for the purpose and which was designed, along with the other state rooms, by Capability Brown. Brown also landscaped the parkland and gardens, building a Gothic-style bathhouse in the grounds, planting avenues and numerous specimen trees, some of which still survive. Two public footpaths cross the park, where you can catch sight of the 13-acre lake that Brown had planned but was not finished until 40 years after his death.

To walk the park without visiting the gardens means missing out on the herbaceous borders and the folly in the form of a ruined castle – built in

225

order to screen a part of the High Street. You'd also miss the glorious peacocks that roam the gardens and who have become a symbol of Corsham. Quite unphased by people, they hang around the entrance steps to the court, and have even been known to promenade along Corsham's streets.

For an alternative walk on the west side of town, close to **Pickwick** – from which Charles Dickens gained the ideas and names for *The Pickwick Papers* – a friend of mine who lives in the town tells me that strolling up Middlewick Lane and along the footpath to Pickwick Lodge and the woods behind is 'absolutely gorgeous, especially in winter'.

Food and drink

The Deli at Corsham 18 High St ☎01249 716091. Licensed deli and cheesemonger; good for picnic bits. Stocks many locally produced foods and will make up hampers to order. Fresh baked and filled baguettes also available for lunch on the move.

Flemish Weaver High St ☎01249 701929. Classic old tavern located next to the town hall run by locals Mac and Dawn McHugh. Simple food (but includes a gluten-free curry) and friendly atmosphere, where children are welcome. Lots of original features in a 17th-century house; convenient for visiting Corsham Court.

Neston Park Farm Shop Bath Rd, Atworth SN12 8HP ☎01225 700881 ⚑ www.nestonparkfarmshop.com. Selling beef, pork and lamb from the Neston Park Estate along with many other farm-shop goodies, much of it also produced on site. First-class café too with peaceful courtyard garden, where you can watch the livestock roaming in the fields.

Two Pigs Pickwick, Corsham SN13 0HY ⚑ www.the2pigs.info. Eccentric pub that serves drinks, plenty of music but no food at all. A regular CAMRA award-winner, beers are changed frequently to maintain interest, although a regular contender includes 'Swill', the staple bitter of the pub. A 'spit-and-sawdust' pub where comfort is not a priority but atmosphere is, there's some kind of live music – usually blues or rock – every Monday night. Open evenings only (plus Sunday lunchtimes). No children allowed.

⑦ Colerne and St Catherine's

On the opposite side of the valley to Corsham, standing on the ridge, is **Colerne**, a really delightful village that tends to get bypassed by tourists. Yet the views from here out across the By Brook Valley and across to Box are spectacular; you can even make out the lights of Bath at night.

Its prominent hilltop position, with its water tower and distinctive church tower – one of the four pinnacles is significantly larger – also makes it a landmark from which to gather your bearings in the area. And standing beneath the church tower, you'll notice that the clock has only the hour hand, one of only a few churches in Britain to do so, including Westminster Abbey. Frank's Wood, along Eastrip Lane, to the east of the church is a new community woodland. Planted in 2000 in memory of a villager, it's very pleasant to wander through, with the baby oaks and field maples just about at head height, but it's also one of the best spots to view the valley.

East of the village is **Colerne Park and Monk's Wood**, a 132-acre woodland and SSSI owned by the Woodland Trust; you are welcome to wander through. On the western slopes of the valley, its trees provide cover for many rare woodland plants such as meadow saffron, toothwort, green hellebores, lily of the valley and star of Bethlehem. Down by the river is Weavern Farm (*weavern* meaning 'wavering', a description of the meandering river), a derelict property now but once the site of Weavern Mill, where fulling for the wool industry took place, followed in 1793 by paper manufacture.

This area is perfect for a walk where you're unlikely to see another soul. Access from Colerne is via Thickwood. A quarter mile past Thickwood, turn right towards Euridge Manor Farm and park at the end of the lane.

West of Colerne and the Fosse Way, a knotted cluster of valleys covers the landscape. You're only ten minutes from Bath here and yet to be in amongst the valleys feels deliciously remote. I took a gentle drive and walk in the relatively

As I walked out one Sunday morning

It was a simple, ordinary early morning walk, full of far-reaching scenes towards Biddestone and Box. The meadows were mine alone. Near distant bells of Colerne, echoing across this secret valley, inaccessible by car, made way for the chuckling of By Brook a dazzling distance below, through the thick jungle of ash and field maple. Hazels that had not seen the coppicer's tool for many years, made the canopy and ancient ropes of old man's beard twisted their way from tree to tree into a wildlife playground.

Cobnuts, part discarded, were the remains of a fat squirrel's supper, disturbed perhaps from his dessert by the whimsical screeching of a bird. From the 'V' of the valley, the woodland paths become steeper, blackberries ripen although there's no-one to pick them for jam-making – and the berries of lords and ladies grip their pedunculate stems.

As I descend, the trickles amplify and ferns wet with dew turn the wood to rainforest. Abruptly, ferns are swapped for horsetails, the forest floor for open meadow, ash to overhanging willows and banks dip down to a whirlpool of cobalt blue. A dozen Friesian cattle acknowledge my presence with a passing nod but the grass is much too sweet for them to take notice of me for long. Only birds reside in the abandoned farmhouse now, tucked back against the woods, the squatters weaving in and out of the stone mullions. A breeze picks up and carries the brook downstream and I return the way I came, a moment in time captured.

A walk from Euridge Manor Farm through Monks Wood to By Brook and Weavern Farm.

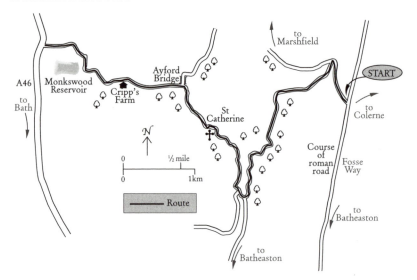

confined area and it's best described by what I saw on my visit, but this is no place for rushing. I spent much of the day exploring and could quite happily have spent longer.

From the Fosse Way 1½ miles north of Batheaston and virtually opposite the turning for Colerne, turn onto the road signposted for Rocks East Woodland, a 100-acre wood with signposted trails that you can walk for a fee. Take the first left on a tight turn. The road descends sharply through very attractive hillside beech woods that remind me more of Scandinavia than the Cotswolds, somehow different from those around the Stroud valleys. Water oozes from springs with the forest floor smothered in ferns, bamboo, common comfrey and horsetails making the most of the damp conditions, the smell sublime, patchy sunlight stroking the leaves. A series of small lakes, occupied by numerous waterfowl, come into view and there are a couple of public footpaths here to delve further into the woods.

Once out of the woods, continue along the narrow, twisting lane for half a mile progressing deeper into the valley, past Oakford Reservoir, where the lie of the land begins to change and further hillsides begin to encroach on the complex landscape. Take the next right, which appears to bend back on itself, and within yards right again. The lane necessarily bends with each curve in this secluded valley. In a mile, on your left is **St Catherine's Court**, a Tudor manor house that looks out across the valley. The house is privately owned and you can do little but admire its beauty as you pass, but next door **St Catherine's Church** stands out among the area's buildings. Its entrance is through ornamental gates of some grandeur hung upon carved stone pillars, and when I visited a tiny courtyard was filled with floaty white cosmos flowers. The view across the valley is magnificent from the churchyard, but inside is the jewel. The church remains a shrine to Captain William Blanchard, a former owner of St Catherine's Court, who died in 1631. Carvings of him and his wife kneel on top of a marble tomb but the decoration that surrounds them is inspirational, with a peacock blue, medieval red-and-gold painted pulpit and mosaic tiles patterned with gold, greens and soft reds on the walls and the altar screen.

Having visited the church, continue on until the road takes a left bend and begins to climb. Look back at the sweeping views along the next remote valley of green pastures and swathes of woodland. Climbing past the end of Monkswood Reservoir don't forget to catch a bird's-eye view of the lake below once the little lane runs along the hillside above. Within yards the land comes to a junction with the busy A46 and your moment of seclusion is over.

Bradford-on-Avon and the Limpley Stoke Valley

In the far southern tip of this locale and right on the border with Somerset is Wiltshire's other Cotswold gem, **Bradford-on-Avon**. This is the Bristol Avon, not the same river as the Avon that flows through Stratford in the north of the Cotswolds. From Bradford the Avon flows west and then curves north, running through the **Limpley Stoke Valley** and taking the **Kennet and Avon Canal** with it to Bath. So very different from other parts of the Cotswolds, there are lots of alternative activities here, like taking a canoe on the canal or watching boats cross the remarkable **Dundas Aqueduct**.

⑧ Bradford-on-Avon

Although on the very fringes of the Cotswolds, few towns could be more Cotswold-like, with weavers' cottages huddled up the hillside and steep paths that once took the workers to the mills lining the river. Bradford, or 'Broad Ford' as it was in Saxon times, has its fair share of agreeable architecture and enticing corners.

The river and its medieval stone bridge in the centre of town combine to make a notable focal point from which emanates so much of interest. As a starting point, climb up **Silver Street** and look back, where you'll see great views of the town, the spires and turrets, cupolas and pinnacles. Silver Street is one of the main shopping streets, along with Market Street, though this is the main thoroughfare through town and can get ridiculously busy with traffic. From Silver Street, climb Coppice Hill. It's a very quiet no-through road, lined with appealing stone cottages and at the top are the most unusual remains of a very grand Wesleyan chapel built in 1818 with only the façade remaining, containing giant window arches and a substantial portico entrance.

Between Coppice Hill and Silver Street is **The Shambles**, one of the shortest streets in town, yet it has a number of tiny shops crammed together – a minute Tardis-like bookshop, a deli, a café and a superb greengrocers whose colourful fruits spill out onto the pavement, each shop decorated with baskets of hanging flowers.

From Market Street cross over to **Church Street** and follow the road to the end, passing by the weavers' cottages and more stately clothiers' homes. Next to the river is **Abbey Mill**, the last cloth mill to be built in Bradford, in 1875. However, its opening almost signalled the closure of a 700-year industry of wool and cloth manufacture and just 27 years later, the mill closed. The Royal Cycling Corps and Australian Forces occupied its vast bulk, a classic chunk of stone and glass, during World War I. The building has more recently been renovated and converted to retirement apartments but remains very stately reflected in the river.

At the end of the street are two churches almost side by side. On the right is the tiny but tall Saxon **church of St Laurence**, the oldest surviving building in town. It is still used as a place of worship, though with a dozen people standing inside it's crowded. Bizarrely the church was once 'lost', having been redeveloped into a school and overshadowed by other buildings. It was not until 1856 that a local clergyman came across some old records and discovered the building to be a 10th-century church.

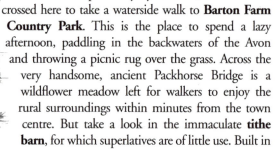

The main parish church sits pleasantly by the river, which can be crossed here to take a waterside walk to **Barton Farm Country Park**. This is the place to spend a lazy afternoon, paddling in the backwaters of the Avon and throwing a picnic rug over the grass. Across the very handsome, ancient Packhorse Bridge is a wildflower meadow left for walkers to enjoy the rural surroundings within minutes from the town centre. But take a look in the immaculate **tithe barn**, for which superlatives are of little use. Built in 1341, this is cathedral-like in stature, 168 feet long and 33 feet wide. Its roof of thick Cotswold stone tiles weighs over 100 tons alone supported by an astounding lattice of timberwork.

Food and drink

Bradford-on-Avon is awash with very good places to eat and drink. My particular favourite though is the Bridge Tea Rooms.

Ale & Porter 25 Silver St ☎01225 868135 🖥 www.aleandporter.co.uk. Café, patisserie and *traiteur* (French for 'caterer'; the owner is French) serving continental café-style food using fresh and seasonal ingredients. Everything sold is made on the premises – and that includes the bread, patisseries and chocolates. Even the organic coffee is roasted in-house.

Bridge Tea Rooms Bridge St ☎01225 865537 🖥 www.thebridgetearooms.co.uk. Not just a place to eat but also one of Bradford-on-Avon's major tourist attractions; visiting these tea rooms is a must. A former blacksmith's cottage dating from 1675; you step back to a bygone age as you walk through the door. Under the low ceilings, costumed waitresses serve light meals and afternoon teas during the day followed by candlelit dinners in the evenings. A regular annual winner of the prestigious Tea Guild's 'UK Top Tea Place'; their awards are celebrated in stained-glass artistry hanging on the walls.

Lock Inn Frome Rd ✆01225 868068 🖥www.thelockinn.co.uk. Vibrant and quirky canal-side café that's something of an institution. Breakfasts, snacks, lunches and dinners served in the multi-coloured café, the tugboat (on the canal) or in the canal-side garden, sheltered under the trees. Plastic tablecloths rule. Beer on draught and local Bath ales. Boat, canoe and cycle hire by the hour or day too.

⑨ Limpley Stoke Valley and the Kennet and Avon Canal

Three miles southwest of Bradford-on-Avon is the **Peto Garden** at **Iford Manor** (*01225 863146; www.ifordmanor.co.uk; open Apr to Oct, see website for variable open days*), an architecturally styled garden created by the celebrated garden designer Harold Ainsworth Peto who bought the manor in 1899. His style of mixing fragments of old buildings and sculptures is shown off to dramatic effect on the steep hillside overlooking the River Frome. Rock gardens mingle with Roman columns, statues gaze over formal terraces and windows in walls peer at silent pools. Specimen trees are used architecturally too. Italian influence is everywhere and one of my favourite areas is the Cloisters, an atmospheric courtyard building at the far end of the garden where fluttering pink clematis flowers are entwined with the graceful marble columns. The roofless structure is used annually for an intimate opera-in-the-round summer festival and is one of the most romantic stage-sets I've seen.

The **Kennet and Avon Canal** lies just a half mile north of the garden and has a stirring backdrop passing through the gorge-like and forested Limpley Stoke Valley. Explorers of the area are spoilt for choice with the entire length of the canal and its towpath between Bradford-on-Avon and Bath accessible to boaters, cyclists and walkers. Within a matter of three miles, the canal boasts two aqueducts – the Avoncliff and Dundas – carrying water sky high over the railway and the Avon. Both notable feats of engineering, their existence stopped the requirement for numerous locks and makes a boat journey much less arduous.

The **Dundas Aqueduct**, with its smooth balustrading above the river, represents beauty in industrial design. It was built from Bath stone in the 18th century, although the chief architect and engineer for the project wanted to use brick, feeling that the stone would not be a sturdy enough material. But stone won the day; as some of the main users of the canal were going to be local quarry owners, it would have been quite a slight on their industry to transport their stone over a brick-built structure.

Those not walking from Bath or Bradford-on-Avon can park in the small car park at the **Brassknocker Basin** to reach the Dundas Aqueduct. This is where the former **Somerset Coal Canal** joins with the Kennet and Avon, a link to carry 'black gold' from the Somerset coalfields to Bath and Bristol. The canal lasted for less than a hundred years in the 19th century and only the few yards, used as the Brassknocker Basin, remain. There's a small, free exhibition about both canals at the basin and a place to hire canoes and electric boats. But the Kennet and Avon Canal Trust (*www.katrust.org*) also plies the water with *Jubilee*, a handsome narrowboat used for public boat trips to Claverton and a 'stop and return' to Avoncliff, giving visitors the chance to explore this weavers' village, where two of the old cloth mills remain.

At the northeast end of the Limpley Stoke Valley, close to the village of Bathford is **Brown's Folly**, a nature reserve with SSSI status and of great importance within the area. It's also a fabulous place to go to before visiting Bath as the views of the city from the cliff-like slopes are some of the best you'll find; it's *the* place to see how the city is laid out. Run by the Avon Wildlife Trust, the nature reserve covers an area where former quarrying of Bath stone has created many giant sunken holes and caves. Much of the area is now covered with mature woodland of mixed, native species, a children's natural playground with lots of space to build dens; we came across a huge rope swing through the trees too.

Following the main path, walk to the far end of the wood until you reach a fence. You can turn left for the actual Brown's Folly, a tall tower sadly misused and looking rather forlorn, or pass through a black kissing-gate and down the steps to walk out onto open scrubland. Be careful of steep drops at the cliff face, where you will find the wonderful views of Bath and the hills beyond, Bathampton Down on the other side of the valley, as well as views west down the Limpley Stoke Valley. A footpath – there are actually numerous tracks – runs for a mile along the top of the ridge providing a regularly changing view among the low-lying shrubs and bushes. My children absolutely love this place and they find the numerous tracks through the undergrowth irresistible.

Brown's Folly is accessed off the Bathford to Monkton Farleigh road but there's a very, very steep hill (1 in 4) out of Bathford to negotiate. An off-road car park for the reserve is just near the brow of the hill.

Food and drink

Angelfish Café Brassknocker Basin BA2 7JD ☎01225 723483. Pleasant, licensed restaurant with terrace next to the Somerset Coal Canal and a great place to watch the boats. Homemade cakes and scones plus snacks (savoury pancakes and chunky sandwiches) and substantial lunches – the portions are large. Boat, bike and canoe hire next door.

Hartley Farm Shop & Café Hartley Farm, Winsley BA15 2JB ☎01225 864948 www.hartley-farm.co.uk. Much of the produce in the farm shop is produced directly at Hartley Farm including meat, eggs, fruit, vegetables and herbs. Dairy products come from a neighbouring farm and the remaining produce sold is sourced solely from producers in the southwest of England. The café serves light meals, freshly prepared sandwiches and homemade cakes.

10. BATH

Could we imagine being without Bath? England, Britain, the World would be significantly poorer if it was suddenly not there, or indeed had never been created, for Bath has culturally enriched our lives over the centuries. That's why the city is classified by UNESCO as a World Heritage Site, a status that it shares with the Taj Mahal, the Pyramids of Giza and the Great Wall of China, for providing 'outstanding universal value to the whole of humanity'.

There are few cities in the world that I would wish to live in, but Bath is one of them. As the birthplace of my mother and the city that launched my grandfather's career in music, I have affection for Bath. But then who doesn't? Its remarkable architecture and town planning, green spaces and attractive location, and associations with the Romans, Jane Austen, civilised living and restoring health maintain its draw as a fashionable city just as much now as it did in historical times.

According to legend as recorded by Geoffrey of Monmouth in the 12th century, the story of Bath begins, not with the Romans but with King **Bladud** in around 863BC. As a young prince he spent time in Greece where he contracted leprosy. Cast out when he returned home to England, he took a job as a swineherd in the marshy Avon Valley and drove his pigs across the Avon in search of acorns. The herd contracted his disease but seemed to be miraculously cured when they rolled around in the mud where hot springs bubbled from the earth's surface. Amazed by what he saw, Bladud bathed in the hot mud too and was cured also.

Free from stigma, Bladud returned home and became King of the Britons (and later father to King Lear, the very one immortalised by Shakespeare). Grateful for his cure, he founded the city of Bath and dedicated the thermal springs to the Celtic goddess, Sul. Nine hundred years later the **Romans**, hearing of the powers of the waters at Bath, came to worship the goddess and named the city Aquae Sulis, or the 'Waters of Sul'. A statue of Bladud and one of his pigs stands in the **Parade Gardens**, next to the river. So if you see pigs, wooden or otherwise, around the city, you'll know why.

I've divided Bath into three areas for the sake of this chapter, taking a line roughly west from Bridge Street through Upper Borough Walls. 'Old Bath', covers the area south of this line, the **Abbey**, the **Roman Baths** and the medieval streets that surround them, such that there are, for the Georgians left little of the old city. North, 'New Bath' focuses on fashionable 18th-century Bath, the **Royal Crescent**, the **Circus**, and the **Assembly Rooms**, whose soirées came to life in the novels of **Jane Austen**.

'East of the River' takes in **Pulteney Bridge**, **Great Pulteney Street**, **Sydney Gardens** and the **Holburne Museum**. And finally, it covers the **Kennet and Avon Canal** and a few attractions that may take additional effort to get to, but shouldn't be missed like **Prior Park** and the **American Museum in Britain**.

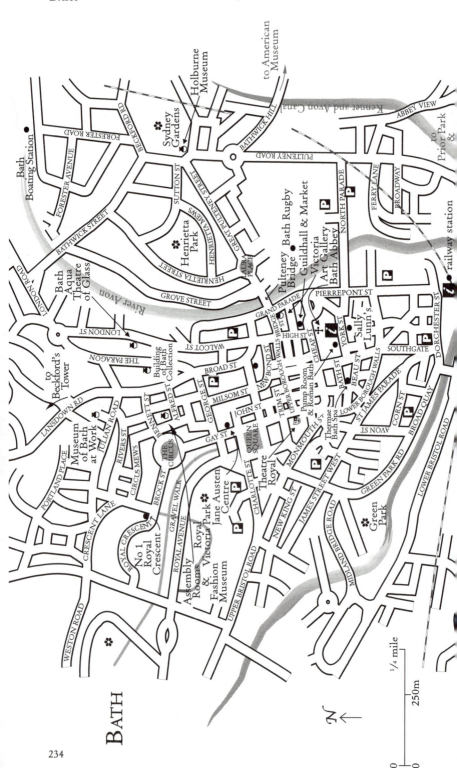

BATH

to American Museum

Kennet and Avon Canal

ABBEY VIEW

to Prior Park &

Holburne Museum

Sydney Gardens

BECKFORD RD

FORESTER ROAD

FORESTER AVENUE

Bath Boating Station

SUTTON ST

Henrietta Mews

HENRIETTA STREET

GREAT PULTENEY STREET

LAURA PLACE

BATHWICK HILL

PULTENEY ROAD

Henrietta Park

BATHWICK STREET

Pulteney Bridge

Bath Rugby

Guildhall & Market

Victoria

Art Gallery

Bath Abbey

NORTH PARADE

FERRY LANE

BROADWAY

railway station

Bath Aqua Theatre of Glass

GROVE STREET

PIERREPONT ST

GRAND PARADE

HIGH ST

CHEAP ST

YORK ST

Sally Lunn's

SOUTHGATE

DORCHESTER ST

River Avon

LONDON ROAD

LONDON ST

THE PARAGON

WALCOT ST

NEW BOND ST

UPPER BOROUGH WALLS

BRIDGE ST

BEAU ST

LOWER BOROUGH WALLS

ST JAMES PARADE

CORN ST

BROAD QUAY

to Beckford's Tower

Building of Bath Collection

BROAD ST

ALFRED ST

GEORGE ST

MILSOM ST

Pump Room & Roman Baths

BATH ST

Thermae Bath Spa

AVON ST

GREEN PARK RD

LANSDOWN RD

JULIAN ROAD

BENNETT ST

RIVERS ST

CIRCUS MEWS

THE CIRCUS

BROCK ST

JOHN ST

QUEEN SQUARE

MONMOUTH ST

ST JAMES STREET WEST

MIDLAND BRIDGE ROAD

LOWER BRISTOL ROAD

Museum of Bath at Work

Royal & Victoria Park

Jane Austen Centre

GAY ST

Theatre Royal

CHARLOTTE ST

NEW KING ST

Green Park

PORTLAND PLACE

CRESCENT LANE

ROYAL CRESCENT

No 1 Royal Crescent

GRAVEL WALK

ROYAL AVENUE

Assembly Rooms

Royal & Fashion Museum

UPPER BRISTOL ROAD

WESTON ROAD

N

¼ mile

250m

234

Getting there and around

Trains

First Great Western (*www.firstgreatwestern.co.uk*) operates services from London Paddington to Bath Spa and from the West Country and south Wales. Services also operate from London Waterloo with **South West Trains** (*www.southwesttrains. co.uk*). From the north, a change is likely at Bristol Temple Meads. Bath Spa station is next to the Southgate shopping centre and a ten-minute walk from the Roman Baths.

Buses

Coaches operate to Bath from most major towns in the UK, with frequent services from London Victoria coach station and direct from major airports. Regular bus services operate around the city, especially from Bath Spa station and these are useful for reaching the outskirts of the city. However, there is no substitute for **walking** in the city centre – indeed it's absolutely necessary with many streets pedestrianised and it would be worth allowing an extra day in Bath to provide time to walk to all the attractions.

Those travelling by **car** are recommended to park at one of the four park and ride sites on the outskirts of the city – on all major routes, just follow the 'P&R' signs – and catch the bus into the centre.

A **hop-on-hop-off** sightseeing tour operates in Bath, with 17 stops or a 45-minute non-stop journey if you use it as an initial introduction to the city in order to gather your bearings. Two routes operate, one around the main city centre, although you will need to walk to most attractions, but useful for reaching the Royal Victoria Park and the Botanic Gardens. The 'Skyline Tour' takes passengers east of the river and is particularly good for getting to the American Museum in Britain and Prior Park. There's no need to book as buses run every few minutes from Bath Abbey (City Centre Tour) and Bath Spa station (Skyline Tour).

Cycling

Perhaps it's because of the hills that you don't see lots of bikes around Bath in quite the same way that you do in Oxford; the hills are indeed hard going. However, the National Cycle Route Network Route 4 does run through the town, connecting Bath with Bristol to the west and Bradford-upon-Avon to the east. Much of the route is traffic-free, either using the very picturesque towpath by the Kennet and Avon Canal, or the disused railway west of the city; pick up the route west at Locksbrook.

Bike hire

Bath Bike Hire Bath Narrowboats, Sydney Wharf, Bathwick Hill BA2 4EL ☎01225 447276 www.bathbikehire.com. Adults' and children's bikes for half- and full-day hire plus trailers and tag-a-longs. Situated by the Kennet and Avon Canal, a 20-minute walk from Pulteney Bridge; you can cycle straight from the hire centre onto the traffic-free cycle route along the towpath.

Walking

Despite its hilly tendencies, Bath is an absolute delight for walking. The city – or the abbey to be precise – is of course the end, or beginning, of the **Cotswold Way** and as such makes it something of a modern-day pilgrimage site. For those who don't wish to trek the full 102 miles, a six-mile 'circular' walk has been devised whereby you can catch a bus from the city centre to the Lansdown park and ride site, walk across Bath Racecourse and then pick up the last few miles of the long-distance trail. On the way you'll get superb views of the city from **Kelston Round Hill** before descending towards the abbey. Full instructions for the 'Journey's End' walk can be downloaded from www.nationaltrail.co.uk/Cotswold.

Bath also has many options for themed walking trails, either guided or self-guided. You can pick up a 'City Trail' leaflet from the Tourist information centre in Abbey Churchyard to take yourself on a 1½-hour self-guided walk of all the sites in Bath that make it a World Heritage Site. Guided tours also begin from here on 'Jane Austen's Bath', taking place every weekend (plus bank holiday Mondays) throughout the year.

You really do get something for nothing in Bath, in the form of **free walking tours**. Operating every day of the year, regardless of the weather, they begin at Abbey Churchyard entrance to the Pump Rooms and are taken by the Mayor of Bath's fully trained honorary guides. Tours last approximately two hours. An alternative is the **Bizarre Bath Comedy Walk** (*01225 335124; www. bizarrebath.co.uk*), which has now been running for 20 years. It's more street theatre than guided walk, and you'll find the evening flies by discovering stories of Bath that stretch the traditional image of the city. Running every evening from April to October, there is no need to pre-book; simply turn up at the Huntsman Inn (on North Parade Passage) at 20.00. Walks take place regardless of weather or dark evenings.

For views over the centre of Bath and some of the idyllic surrounding countryside from the city, take the waymarked **Bath Skyline Walk**. The six-mile circular route gives the chance to explore the area around **Claverton Down** and **Bathampton Down** to the east of the city centre. You'll pass by an Iron Age hillfort, Roman settlements and Sham Castle, an 18th-century folly, as well as taking in wooded valleys and wildlife meadows, owned by the National Trust. Take bus 410 or 418 from the bus station (next to Bath Spa railway station) to the University of Bath where you can pick up the trail, signposted 'Bath Skyline'.

Tourist information centre

Bath Tourist Information Centre Abbey Churchyard ☎0906 7112000 (50p/minute!) 📱 www.visitbath.co.uk.

Accommodation

Beckford's Tower Lansdown Rd ☎01628 825925 🖥 www.landmarktrust.org.uk.
A quirky alternative to B&B, and a unique opportunity to stay in a landmark
structure, Beckford's Tower sits on a hill to the north of Bath. Wealthy collector
William Beckford, who was obsessed by towers and constructed several of them
in his lifetime, built the tower in 1827 – he would retreat to it daily to indulge his
passion for collecting artefacts. This ground-floor, 2-bedroomed (one double, one
twin) apartment gives a flavour of his opulent, but reclusive lifestyle, with rich
furnishings. Guests can climb the spiral staircase to the belvedere for sweeping
views of Bath. A museum, open to the public, on the property is open from Easter
to October. For anyone remotely apprehensive or excited by the prospect, William
Beckford and his architect are buried at the foot of the tower.

The Kennard 11 Henrietta St BA2 6LL ☎01225 310472 🖥 www.kennard.co.uk.
Superb location in the very centre of Bath, close to Pulteney Bridge and 5 minutes'
walk from the abbey and Roman baths. A fine Georgian town house that has
been sympathetically restored with period furnishings and plenty of attention to
detail. Breakfast is served in the old kitchen, now resembling an elegant dining
room with vibrant peacock green walls, swags at the windows, gilt mirrors and
botanical prints plus a glitzy chandelier. Refined bone china and a breakfast menu
serving produce from the Cotswolds. The owners, Mary and Giovanni Baiano,
have also created a formal Georgian town-house garden at the rear, with sources
of inspiration for fashionable plants of the period coming from Jane Austen's
writing. Free car parking permit for duration of stay.

Food and drink

A part of the attraction of Bath is making the most of its remarkable selection of
places to eat and drink. The city is one of the places in Britain that made drinking tea
fashionable and there are plenty of options to experience a civilised afternoon tea.
Beware though, many tea rooms are either closed or stop serving tea by 16.00 in
preparation for dinner service. The city also has numerous very hospitable pubs and
very good restaurants. You will not go hungry in Bath!

Tea rooms and cafés

Hansel und Gretel 9 Margaret's Buildings, Brock St ☎01225 464677
🖥 www.hanselundgretel.com. 'At home in the Alps', a shop on the ground floor
(selling all-things alpine) and strudel bar in the basement. Very cosy *stuberl* with
benches and just 3 tables decorated with red-and-white gingham fabric and lit by
fairy lights. Strudels and cakes from the alpine regions and the Black Forest plus
alpine drinks. My pick of the tea rooms; see also page 247.

The Pump Room Abbey Churchyard ☎01225 444477 🖥 www.romanbaths.co.uk/
the_pump_room. An attraction in its own right and considered one of the most
socially acceptable places to 'be seen' for over 200 years. You will often find a
queue for morning coffee, lunches and afternoon tea; it's best to book for dinner.

Come here to try the spa water and the distinctive 'Bath Bun'. Listen to the Pump Room Trio or the lunchtime pianist perform while you eat.

Riverside Café & Restaurant Below Pulteney Bridge, 17 Argyle St
☎01225 480532. Café under the archways of Pulteney Bridge with small riverside terrace. Very good café with bistro-style food, home-cooked and fresh. Also serving breakfasts, light bites and afternoon teas with homemade cakes. A lovely place for morning coffee. Evening meals served Mar to Sep.

Sally Lunn's The renowned tea room is featured under *Pubs and restaurants*.

Pubs and restaurants

Beaujolais Bistro Bar 5 Chapel Row (by Queen Sq) ☎01225 484200
☝ www.beaujolaisbath.co.uk. A popular haunt with locals. Plenty of atmosphere and great French/continental food, serving classic bistro dishes – plus some British favourites. Lunches and the early dinner (set) menu are good value for money. Wine shop on site too – French influenced but not exclusively so – try before you buy at the bar.

Coeur de Lion Northumberland Pl ☎01225 463568 ☝ www.coeur-de-lion.co.uk. Promoted as 'Bath's smallest pub', the Coeur de Lion is also on one of Bath's narrowest, pedestrianised streets. With a long and celebrated history that includes much petition by locals to prevent the pub from being closed down in recent years, the Coeur de Lion is regularly included in CAMRA's Top 100 British pubs. Oozing character (and people) – it really is small – with stained-glass windows and a long bar, but little else owing to its size. Owned by one of Bath's breweries, Abbey Ales.

Hall & Woodhouse 1 Old King St ☎01225 469259 ☝ www.hall-woodhousebath.co.uk. Owned by the famous Hall & Woodhouse Brewery (Badger Original, Fursty Ferret, Tanglefoot, etc), a very large and magnificent bar-cum-restaurant. Superb food and drink and attentive service but visit for the surroundings alone – choose from several areas, each with its own ambience: by the entrance, a winter garden conservatory-style area with shelves filled like an old grocer's store; to the rear, a large living room with sofas, coffee tables, rugs, a giant fireplace and bookshelf where you can help yourself to a book, copies of the *Beano* or a board game for the evening. Great with families and couples alike. Up the starlit staircase is a silver-panelled restaurant with glass chandeliers; you can watch the chefs at work here. Or head to the Manhattan-style rooftop terrace (open only occasionally) for views of the city. A place to take time and relax.

Pulteney Arms 37 Daniel St ☎01225 463923 ☝ www.thepulteneyarms.co.uk. Five minutes' walk from Pulteney Bridge and Sydney Gardens, in a quiet residential area. Friendly pub with lots of character: exposed stone walls inside, period fireplaces and original gas lighting. Tiny rear terraced garden; guests also spill out onto the pavement where additional tables and seating is provided. Popular with the rugby crowd (Bath Rugby Ground is 5 minutes' walk). Good home-cooked food; Sunday lunches are popular – try the 'Rugby Boy Roast', consisting of beef, lamb and pork if you're famished.

River Cottage Canteen Komedia, 22–23 Westgate St ☎01225 471578 🖥 www.rivercottage.net. A trendy, modern place to eat with deliberately basic (bohemian) décor but good, nutritious food. From breakfast to evening meals, Sunday roasts to afternoon tea, all the organic food is produced either on site (in-house bakery), at River Cottage or from suppliers selected by Hugh Fearnley-Whittingstall.

Salamander 3 John St ☎01225 428889 🖥 www.bathales.com. Unpretentious 'black-and-gold' town-centre pub owned by Bath's other brewery, Bath Ales. On the ground floor is the blackened-wood bar area (wooden bar and shelves, wood floorboards, wood bar stools) and upstairs is the supper room. Bath Ales are obviously the main tack and many of the supper dishes use the tipple too (maybe braised shin of beef or mussels in Bath Ales cider). Breakfast served 10.00 to 12.00.

Sally Lunn's 4 North Parade Passage ☎01225 461634 🖥 www.sallylunns.co.uk. A Bath institution, I've categorised this under restaurants rather than tea rooms because, while Sally Lunn's is celebrated as a place for morning coffee and afternoon tea, it's less known for its quiet candlelit dinners, and yet I've eaten extremely well here. In the quaint old terraced tea shop, full of ambience and friendly staff, you'll find very good, hearty food. Try the 'trencher' meals, served on the famous Sally Lunn Bun (see page 243); meat and gravy on a bun may not sound right but it really works.

Old Bath – around Bath Abbey

Before Bath reinvented itself in the 18th century by creating wide, fashionable avenues, it had a network of small alleyways and streets. There's little truly medieval in Bath such was its sweeping out of the past, but a few streets close to Bath Abbey give an impression of life in the city before its reincarnation. With tiny shopfronts and not-so-high buildings, they provide a fascinating change to the Palladian style of Georgian Bath. Many of the streets around Bath Abbey are pedestrianised so make the most of this walking territory and spend a morning ambling from shop to shop.

Roman Baths

Arguably the beating heart of Bath, the Roman Baths (*01225 477785; www. romanbaths.co.uk; open daily*) is where one of the hot springs that have attracted people for millennia, bubble to the surface. It took up to 10,000 years for the water that once fell on the nearby Mendip Hills to drift down through limestone caves and then push to the surface again; since surfacing it has reached a natural temperature of 46°C with a flow of approximately 250,000 gallons of water per day.

Before you reach the actual baths, you encounter an exhibition on life in the Roman city and the reasons people set up home here. The powerful imagery of the Temple of Sulis Minerva, the goddess they came to worship, is portrayed against a wall, her piercing gaze staring at anyone in the room. Gravestones, tools, money, an attractive mosaic (actually found in a house nearby) bring the history to life, confirming that most 'Romans' in Britain did not necessarily originate from Rome at all but from many other European countries, along with locals who had adopted Roman ways.

I found the explanations of the pre-Roman history the most enlightening, imagining prehistoric times when the inhospitable area was marshy, the valley wooded and how mysterious and potent the landscape with these hot, bubbling springs must have seemed for those coming to worship the Celtic goddess of Sulis (whom the Romano-British very successfully rebranded by being bracketed with the Roman goddess of wisdom, Minerva).

You do have to use every power in your imagination to take you back to Roman times. As one of the most visited attractions in Britain, the baths are consistently busy with people clicking away at the buttons of audio guides. I find the best place to appreciate what these baths are all about – why they are special – is the Roman Spring Overflow where surplus water from the Sacred Spring (seen bubbling in the King's (Bladud's) Bath on your way round) pours into a Roman-built drain before flowing into the river close by. It's hot and steamy there with the pressure and volume – and the noise – of the water intense. The orange deposits of the minerals thickly encrust the stone and brick around as if painted.

Naturally the largest of the baths, the Great Bath, still impresses regardless of how many times you look at it in tourist literature. Don't be fooled by the building or the 'Roman' figures that line the terrace above though: the building is 18th century and the statues are actually late 19th century, put in place when the baths were uncovered and opened to the public for the first time. The terrace is, however, an inspirational place from where to view the abbey next door.

A truly magical experience is to view the Roman baths in the evening, when the rooms and pools are lit up by torchlight as darkness falls. During July and August the baths are open until 21.00 (last entry).

The Pump Room

The 43 minerals within the water, which apparently cured Bladud, were deemed to have healing properties and new medical ideas in the late 17th century made 'taking the water' extremely fashionable. For this purpose, a Pump Room was opened in 1706 and **Beau Nash**, Bath's master of ceremonies, turned the building into a fashion icon. The high-ceilinged vast room that you see today though is the work of massive alterations in 1796 to accommodate all the new residents – Bath's population exploded from 2,000 to 38,000 during the late 18th century.

Taking tea in the Pump Room is 'an attraction' in its own right, but this is still *the* place to take the waters and if you've paid to visit the Roman baths then you are entitled to a free glass of spa water. It's pumped direct from the bubbling King's Spring below to an elegant urn placed sacredly in the bow of a giant window.

'Do I have to drink it all?' I asked the buxom waitress in a meek, schoolgirlish manner. Memories came flooding back of struggling with a glass of the very same sulphurous-cum-ferrous-tasting liquor in a show of macho Britishness to a French exchange student years before. 'Not if you don't want to, but it's good for you!' replied the matronly figure. It may not be the most elegant approach to drinking a glass of water in such an esteemed location, but my best advice is to 'down it' so that the drink barely touches the sides – the water has an undeniably revolting taste.

The alternative is to 'dine' in the Pump Room, when a lemon or strawberry syrup can be added to disguise it. Or do as I did and eat a Bath bun, designed for the very job of hiding the taste of the spring water. (A Bath bun is a little like a toasted teacake with currants and crystallised sugar on the top, served with cinnamon butter.)

Elegance is the word to sum up the Pump Room. Its very nature makes you sit up straight. The giant chandelier – taller than the height of most people's living room – sparkles across the hall and the dashing figure of Beau Nash, holding his set of etiquette rules, peers down from the wall as if to make sure that you hold your teacup correctly and keep your elbows off the table. I cast an ear to the bow-tied Pump Room Trio as they added to the elegance, feeling some sense of connection in the room; this was where my grandfather held one of his first jobs as a conductor in the 1930s, leading the Pump Room Orchestra, allegedly one of the oldest established ensembles in the British Empire, founded by Beau Nash.

Thermae Bath Spa

It's all very well looking at where the Romans enjoyed a bathe, but the spa waters still hold their therapeutic properties and Bath retains its fashionable status as a spa town. From the Roman baths, wander down Bath Street (the only double-colonnaded street in Britain) and at the far end, directly in front of you, you'll come across the Cross Bath and, to your left, the modern-day, glass-caged Thermae Bath Spa (*0844 888 0844; www.thermaebathspa.com*), promoting itself as 'Britain's original and only natural thermal spa'.

'I learnt to swim here as a child, when the "spa" was a municipal swimming pool', said Charlotte Hanna. Charlotte, the sales executive at Thermae Bath Spa, offered to show me around the modern facilities but first, while standing in the middle of Hot Bath Street outside the spa entrance, she suggested that I put my hand to the manhole cover in the middle of the road. It's not a practice I'm occasioned to doing regularly but, mindful of a potential passing car, I did as I was told. The cover felt warm (while the day wasn't) and I could hear the gushing of the hot spring beneath my hands. 'That,' she said, 'is the Hot Spring.'

We looked into the open-air Cross Bath, an intimate thermal pool enclosed by a World Heritage Site Georgian shell, where bathers can book the entire facility for private use. 'It's popular with brides before a wedding,' said Charlotte. Inside the main glass-fronted spa building, numerous pools, steam rooms and treatment rooms all using the healing powers of the naturally heated waters send visitors

A history of bathing in Bath

There are three naturally hot springs in Bath; one is the **King's Spring**, upon which the Roman baths and temple to Sulis Minerva were built. The other two are the **Cross Spring** and **Hetling Spring** close to one another in Hot Bath Street. Though Bath is particularly known as a Roman and Georgian city, many people came in the intervening centuries to visit and make use of the natural waters. The Cross Bath, at the end of Bath Street and situated directly above the Cross Spring, is so called because pilgrims would come to the abbey, leave their cross (or staff) propped up against the wall and bathe there.

While the Georgians made 'taking the water' and bathing particularly fashionable, it was previous generations who paved the way, creating greater interest in Bath and its springs. Charles II, desperate for an heir and unable to produce a legitimate son, came to Bath to take the waters in the hope that their mystical powers would do something. He may have been suffering from syphilis, as was his brother James II, many of whose children conceived with his second wife, Mary of Modena, did not survive. Desperate for a male heir, James and Mary both came to Bath and soon after produced a son, which caused many conspiracy theories about the paternity of the offspring. Regardless, the 'miracle' created something of a boom in tourism for Bath and once Queen Anne had paid a visit in 1702, sealing it as *the* place to be, Georgian Britain came to the city.

Following the Georgian period the spas in Bath continued to wave in and out of fashion for more than 150 years until they closed completely in 1978. The new **Thermae Bath Spa**, which opened in 2006, incorporates modern architecture over the ancient spring, now the **New Royal Bath** and the restored buildings of the Cross Bath and the Hetling Pump Room.

into a trance-like state of relaxation (me included and I hadn't even begun to make use of the facilities). The smell, by the way, is sweet-scented and nothing like that of the spa water I'd drunk previously. But of all the alluring hot pools, massage jets, frankincense-infused steam rooms and body-wraps, the most inviting has to be the open-air rooftop pool. 'Beauty heals,' said Charlotte, and the views of the city, the abbey and the green pastures beyond, which can all be seen while lying back in the steaming pool, are certainly beautiful. It may be all in the mind rather than the water, but bathing here for an afternoon, or an evening as the sun goes down with the lights illuminating the abbey, has to be one of the best ways to enjoy the Cotswolds slowly.

Bath Abbey

The history of Bath Abbey (*www.bathabbey.org; open to general tourists when services are not being held*) is described in an extensive exhibition in the Vaults Museum beneath this illustrious building so I don't feel the need to repeat it here. Instead I'd prefer to focus on a couple of aspects that really caught my eye in a building that's so immense in scale and craftsmanship that the need to focus is a necessity or you become punch-drunk.

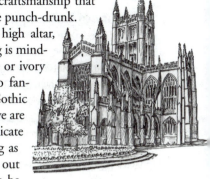

The first is the stone carving behind the high altar, beneath the dazzling east window. The carving is mind-blowing in detail and fragility, like a fine lace or ivory crochet. Knitting-needle columns progress to fan-shaped arches of graceful proportions, Gothic arches frame intimately carved reliefs and above are borders of leaves and flowers so soft and delicate they can't possibly be created from something as hard as stone. It made me look closer to seek out an accidental slip of the chisel that needed to be covered up, and wonder how much the stone carver swore and groaned at the prospect of a job so intricate, where tiny birds hidden among the leaves are carved so that you can see the eye and the tip of the beak.

The other feature that really grabbed my attention is the permanent exhibition – the **Bath Abbey Diptychs**. Created by local artist Sue Symons in 2007, the diptychs depict 'the life of Christ in 35 pairs of panels'. These extraordinary works of art, which took over 3,000 hours to produce, are inspired combinations of calligraphic lettering, painted decoration and needlework.

Each pair are unique, some vibrant and filled with gold, others dark and mysterious, according to which part of the 'story' they tell. They remind one of the illuminated manuscripts created by medieval scholars.

Sally Lunn's House

Something of an institution in Bath, **Sally Lunn's House** (*01225 461634; www.sallylunns.co.uk*) is the only place in the world to buy the famous **Sally Lunn Bun**. A refugee from France, in 1680 Sally Lunn found work with a baker in Bath and introduced him to French brioche. The resulting 'Sally Lunn Bun' as it became known, a plain brioche-like bun, was popular with the new 'Georgian' tourists in Bath for its light texture and its ability to accompany any meal. The recipe for her bun was discovered at the bakery, in a secret cupboard above the fireplace in the 1930s, where the Sally Lunn Bun is still made fresh every day. A small museum on the history of Sally Lunn's House exists in the basement, below the tea rooms and restaurant.

Guildhall Market and Victoria Art Gallery

Just to the north of the abbey, one large Georgian building separates the High Street from Grand Parade and the River Avon. In it is the prestigious Guildhall, used for weddings and events, the covered market and the Victoria Art Gallery. The **Guildhall Market** is already special before you've even entered: just look at the domed building in which it's housed and the ornamental gates at the two entrances; a passageway runs right through the market linking the two streets either side. There's been a market on the site for 800 years – Bath was also a 'wool town' at one

Adopt a picture

The Victoria Art Gallery is running a tremendous sponsorship scheme that almost sounds too good to be true. The gallery has a vast catalogue of paintings that are in need of restoration. New paintings requiring work are put on the gallery's website and you can 'Adopt a Picture', paying for its restoration, which can cost as little as £200. In return, you get to watch some of the restoration process and arrangements can be made to have it hanging in your home or place of work for a year.

stage (Chaucer's 'Wife of Bath' is 'an expert in cloth making') – although much of the internal infrastructure, such as the original weighing room, has disappeared. But look at the market building from the opposite side of the neighbouring river and you can see the windows and doors of the old market vaults, the slaughterhouses and the stables that run beneath Grand Parade, held up by a sturdy stone colonnade.

Still run as a traditional market with many little 'shops' inside, it is full of atmosphere with a good old-fashioned mix of bakery next door to haberdashery, pet supplies next to secondhand paperbacks, a barber's shop close to a cheese stall and a deli where you can buy traditional Bath buns. One of the bye-laws for 1864 caught my eye: 'No person shall throw or fling vegetables, garbage or any missile in the market.'

Next door, but with an entrance in Bridge Street, is the **Victoria Art Gallery** (*01225 477244; www.victoriagal.org.uk; closed Mon*), one of two free-to-enter museums in Bath. There are three centuries of British paintings on display from artists including Gainsborough, Constable and Sickert plus some fascinating local scenes, such as *The Royal Crescent* by Joseph Farringdon. The picture is painted from the river sometime after 1775 and, while we associate this landmark to be in the centre of the city today, in the painting there are no buildings between the river and the Crescent.

The gallery gives excellent background detail about each painting or artist and reminds us that most artists were in Bath to make a living. Gainsborough, for example, as a portrait artist realised that Bath was a good place in which to make a living as many wealthy spa visitors were keen to have their portrait painted during their stay. He did very nicely from the tourist trade, living and working in the city from 1759 until 1774, first at a very grand house close to the Pump Room and later at one of the finest addresses in the city: The Circus.

One local picture really strikes me: *Ladymead House.* The painting was rediscovered in the attic of Ladymead House itself in 1977. The house still stands in Walcot Street today though much altered since the painting was produced in the 1680s. Images of Bath before the Georgian period are rare and this one shows a building that was soon unfashionable, but in this painting the house is not the focal feature. In the foreground, making the house a diminishing dot, is a vast, formal walled garden that runs down to the river, the whole plot surrounded by thick and wild woodland. It gives a glimpse of Bath that is almost impossible to imagine today.

New Bath – 18th-century Bath

No area of Bath was left untouched by the architect's pen when the city was remodelled: even the older streets close to Bath Abbey were tinkered with. But it is as the city moves north, away from the river, that we see the most profound effects. To appreciate the Bath that we see today is to understand something of 18th-century town planning when the city was transformed beyond recognition, and also of the four men who were largely responsible (see below): Ralph Allen (the man with the money) John Wood the Elder, plus his son John Wood the Younger (the architects), and 'Beau' Nash (the dandy).

A man's world – Bath's big four

Ralph Allen

As a teenager he was a post office clerk and postmaster in Bath but over his lifetime he totally reformed the British postal system and earned himself large sums of money. With his wealth he bought quarries at Combe Down and Bathampton Down, providing much of the Bath stone that was used to create Georgian Bath, accumulating an even greater fortune. He worked closely with John Wood the Elder, who built Prior Park on the edge of the city in 1742 for him. You can see Allen's town house and office, with its ornate columns and parapet above, in North Parade Passage, close to Sally Lunn's House. Mayor of Bath as well as a philanthropist, he donated the money and stone to build the Mineral Water Hospital and is still revered in the city.

John Wood the Elder and Younger

An ardent follower of the designs of the 16th-century Italian architect, Andrea Palladio, Georgian architecture in Bath under the hand of John Wood is essentially Palladian in style. He was responsible for requesting that Ralph Allen quarry the stone in smooth, giant blocks rather than rough rubble; hence Wood could achieve the clean lines necessary to create the architectural effects he had in mind. On his death in 1754, his son, **John Wood the Younger**, took on his architectural projects. The Woods' legacy to town planning is huge, as their ideas in Bath became the model for towns and cities worldwide.

Richard 'Beau' Nash

While John Wood the Elder created the buildings, Beau Nash filled them with parties, dances, concerts and gamblers (he was a prolific gambler himself) and turned Bath into the most fashionable place to be seen. A dandy and a fashion icon, Nash's ideas on fashion and how the social classes were expected to behave were followed closely; he even drew up a set of 'Rules to be observ'd at Bath' on etiquette and behaviour. As master of ceremonies he was at the centre of society life and, like Allen, is very much a hallowed name in Bath. He lived in a house where the sumptuous Theatre Royal now stands, at the west end of Upper Borough Walls.

Queen Square, The Circus and the Royal Crescent

These three addresses are some of the most fashionable in Bath today and are linked by their architects, John Wood the Elder and Younger. The first to be built, in 1730, was **Queen Square**, an area of Bath that was badly damaged during World War II in the Baedeker Blitz, when the Luftwaffe targeted places of cultural interest by picking them out from Baedeker guidebooks.

On the west side of Queen Square is the **Bath Royal Literary and Scientific Institution** (*01225 312084; www.brlsi.org*). The cultural centre provides a focal point for talks, discussions and debates, plus exhibitions throughout the year; you do not need to be a member to join events. A list of forthcoming activities, many presented by eminent speakers and lecturers, is shown on the BRLSI website and in the foyer.

Just north of Queen Square, at the top of Gay Street, is **The Circus**. Begun in 1754 by John Wood the Elder, it was the first circular terrace in modern Europe but Wood died soon after the first stone was laid and his son (the Younger) completed the project. The terrace was originally called King's Circus after King Bladud and the acorns that adorn the tops of the buildings are a reference to the king and his swine herd.

Wander along **Gravel Walk**, between Gay Street and Royal Avenue, and you'll see the interesting backs of the properties that introspectively look to The Circus. The backs seem to reveal so much more and are by no means as elegant as the façades. Accessed through a tiny, half-hidden doorway off Gravel Walk is a **Georgian Garden**, recreated following excavations that revealed three garden plans. Formal box hedges, bulbs, roses, herbs and hardy perennials all historically correct fill this secretive, little-frequented space with colour.

To the west of The Circus, connected by Brock Street, is the **Royal Crescent**, designed by both John Wood the Elder and his son, the latter building the

---

Symbolism in Bath's architecture

Shape is crucial to Queen's Square, The Circus and the Royal Crescent, and it's believed that the Woods had connections with the **Freemasons**. Much as he was obsessed with Palladian architecture, John Wood the Elder was also very interested in ancient monuments and Druid activity, believing that there had been Druid temples worshipping the sun and moon on Lansdown Hill in Bath. The Circus is partly derived from Stonehenge (as well as the Colosseum in Rome) and supposedly represents the sun while the Royal Crescent is a symbol of the moon. Queen Square, supposedly representing the earth, is also aligned in such a way that follows the Masonic path of the sun. There are many symbols associated with Freemasonry on the buildings themselves, particularly in The Circus, such as set squares, compasses and shapes. A **Masonic Hall** still operates in Bath, in Old Orchard Street. The original Theatre Royal building (*www.oldtheatreroyal.com*), which you can visit, has a museum and collection of Masonic artefacts.

famous street between 1767 and 1775. Like The Circus, its shape was a first in modern European architecture. The builder effectively sold the façades and owners would then create a house behind so that, while there is elegant uniformity from the front, the rear of the property is a mix of rooflines and styles. It did make me wonder about smog; I tried to count all the chimneys – there are approximately 30 façades, each with two sets of chimneys and each of those with between ten and eleven chimney pots. If they'd all been billowing smoke at once …

Number 1 Royal Crescent
Despite its grandeur, the Royal Crescent by the 1960s was not a pleasant place to live, having fallen into disrepair (some houses were destroyed in the Baedeker Blitz) and disrepute. Number 1, the first property to have been built in the Royal Crescent with, in theory, the best address of the 'street', was one such house, having been converted rather badly into a series of flats and bedsits. Bernard Cayzer, a man passionate about interior design and the Georgian period, bought the place (for £11,000!) having spotted an advertisement in *Country Life*. He gave the property to the Bath Preservation Trust together with the funds to refurbish it.

Number 1 Royal Crescent (*01225 428126; www.bath-preservation-trust.org.uk; closed Mon*) was restored as a museum to show what a grand 18th-century house would have been like to live in. Obviously none of the furniture is original to the house, but each room provides detailed examples of Georgian interior design, with authentic furnishings. Rooms are laid out like stage sets, ready for the men to return to their game of cards, while the drawing room is prepared for visitors calling to take tea. Plastic fruit on the table in the dining room perhaps detracts from the elegance but take the opportunity to look out of the upstairs window and imagine the views, without buildings, all the way down to the river, as in the painting by Joseph Farringdon in the Victoria Art Gallery (see page 244).

Brock Street and Margaret's Buildings
Brock Street, a smart street with several art galleries and stylish restaurants, connects The Circus with the Royal Crescent. Off this, take a wander down the pedestrianised **Margaret's Buildings**. A quietly fashionable street, it too has well-groomed art galleries, antique shops and small clothes boutiques and at the northern end is Hansel und Gretel (see page 237). This shop and strudel-café sells everything alpine and, every Wednesday morning, free German-language sessions take place, irrespective of ability. Every Monday evening (*18.00–20.00*) there's a 'Knitter's Knatter' when knitters, again regardless of ability, get together over balls of wool and knitting needles clicking away, for a chat. Everyone is welcome to simply turn up; the shop sells wool.

Royal Victoria Park and the Botanic Gardens
You'd think, by its very name, that Bath's largest green space is Victorian. To some extent it is, but it was created during the Regency period and named the

Royal Victoria Park by a perhaps rather bumptious Princess Victoria when in 1830, at the age of 11 years, she opened the new park. A park of many parts, extending over 57 acres; the Royal Crescent looks upon the section closest to the city centre. From there it spreads out north and west to incorporate large greens, filled with numerous specimen trees for summer shelter, formal flower borders in town park style, a vast playground, a duck pond, two golf courses and Botanic Gardens.

In the northwest corner, the **Botanic Gardens** are the furthest to reach from the city centre, but is my pick of the green spaces in Bath. Completely restored within the last few years, it provides beauty and interest as well as botanical correctness, with lots of gardens within a garden to give colour throughout the year. Winding pathways draw you from one to another, a rose walk to a magnolia lawn, heather borders to a butterfly garden. Pockets of lawn offer restful places to sit and enjoy the surrounding scents. The main entrance is off Royal Avenue, which curves around the floral part of the garden; to the north, on the opposite side of the road, is the **Great Dell**, an undulating tree garden, where the heady scent of pine rises above you and cyclamen sprout at the roots of trees. It's a restful place, and a world apart from the crowds that gather in front of the Royal Crescent, just ten minutes' walk away.

Gravel paths criss-cross the vast lawns of the park for winter promenading, and for three days in May the lawns play host to the Bath Spring Flower Show. But for the remainder of the year they are the launch site for **hot-air balloons** that drift off early morning and evening to give passengers a stunning view of Bath from above. **Bath Balloons** (*01225 466888; www.bathballoons.co.uk*) take off from the Royal Victoria Park three to four times per week; bookings are essential.

Jane Austen Centre

No author is more closely associated with Bath than Jane Austen. The city had been rejuvenated by the time she was alive, the new architecture in place, with balls and concerts in full swing. Indeed the author was one of the very people who met society in the streets and halls of Bath, observing every mannerism before writing it down.

The Jane Austen Centre (*40 Gay St, 01225 443000; www.janeausten.co.uk; open daily*) resides in a Georgian town house in the same street and just a few doors down from where Jane lived for a while. Similar in style you can get a sense of Georgian living here (although in this respect it doesn't quite match up to Number 1 Royal Crescent), but the exhibition brings Jane's story, and how Bath fits into it, to life. Every visit begins with a live introductory talk, provided at certain times of the day. Occasional temporary displays of reproduction costumes, used for television and film adaptations of Jane Austen's novels, may be on show but be aware that the exhibition is otherwise little more than a collection of information boards giving details of her life in Bath, presented amongst the occasional replica artefact. While there's plenty to read, the centre can therefore be a little disappointing if you're expecting something more. On

Jane Austen in Bath

Jane first came to visit Bath in 1797 and then in 1799. Her experiences of the city were good at that stage, reflected in the happy nature of her heroine in *Northanger Abbey*, Bath being the setting for more than half of the book. Jane then spent five years living in the city, finally leaving in 1806. Following the death of her father in 1804 (he is buried in St Swithin's Church at the junction of The Paragon and London Street) she moved four times within the space of a year to gradually poorer districts of Bath. Perhaps understandably, Jane's later novel, *Persuasion*, reflects a dispirited view of the city.

the second floor are the Regency Tea Rooms, not hugely endowed with character or ambience, but useful enough.

Do not miss the enthusiastically received annual **Jane Austen Festival** when, for nine days every September, Georgian Bath comes alive with Empire line dresses, ribboned bonnets, gloves and lace parasols as perfectly ordinary people dress up to celebrate everything Austen. Numerous festivities take place, with Regency dances, costumed walking tours, talks, Regency meals and workshops. I rather liked the sound of 'Fops and their fancies' from a recent festival, discovering the dandies of Bath in a 'local drinking tavern' decorated in period style, but the event was for gentlemen only. Much more genteel would have been learning to fold napkins ready for afternoon tea with Jane Austen herself!

While in the area of Gay Street and Queen Square, take time to visit **Mr B's Emporium of Reading Delights** (*14–15 John St; 01225 331155; www. mrbsemporium.com*). A bookshop like no other, it has won numerous awards for being different, with many author events that are unlike the usual book signings. Under the title 'Book Lovers Unite', standard author readings are replaced with longer, richer and more interactive literary-themed evenings, with food and drink supplied. Just for a browse the bookshop is a delight too; the 'Bibliotherapy Room' upstairs (passing the Tintin-wallpapered staircase) includes comfy chairs by the fireplace and tables complete with water jugs.

The Assembly Rooms and Fashion Museum

During the 18th century there were two sets of Assembly Rooms. The original rooms, built in 1708 at the request of Beau Nash, were close to the river. When a new set of assembly rooms were built in 1771 close to The Circus, the two were distinguished simply as the lower or upper rooms. The lower rooms burned to the ground in 1820 and all that remains of them, the grand columns from one façade beneath Pierrepont Street, can be seen from the Parade Gardens. So it is the more recent, upper rooms near The Circus that we know now simply as the Assembly Rooms.

Owned today by the National Trust, the Assembly Rooms (*Bennett St; 01225*

477789; www.fashionmuseum.co.uk) were once the hub of Georgian and Regency social life, where dances took place, gamblers lost fortunes, matches were made and new husbands found. The grandeur of the rooms – many visit simply to look at the size and beauty of the nine glass chandeliers that hang from the ceilings – remains today. But don't count on being able to view the rooms, simply because the National Trust guidebook gives opening times and days. Managed by the local council on behalf of the Trust, they are often used for civil functions, weddings, conferences and so on, consequently remaining shut. When I visited recently the rooms were closed for a whole week due to a conference. Many visitors, including a Jane Austen fan from Australia, were understandably disappointed; trying to appease, an official commented that 'the Assembly Rooms are a working building, not a museum'. Access is only guaranteed during August so phone to check if any functions are likely to be taking place.

Beneath the Assembly Rooms is the **Fashion Museum** (note that National Trust members need to pay) where a vast collection of contemporary and historical dress from the past 400 years is showcased. Naturally, there's a large collection of clothes from the Georgian period, all displayed on dressed figures plus lots of hats, gloves and accessories. Visitors, both children and adults, may try on corsets and crinoline petticoats.

Regularly changing temporary exhibitions take place too – past displays have featured the likes of dresses of the late Diana, Princess of Wales.

Museums of Bath

For something a little grittier, the **Museum of Bath at Work** (*01225 318348; www.bath-at-work.org.uk*) off Julian Road illustrates 2,000 years of earning a living in the city. The museum is housed in Bowler's workshops, opened in 1872, an old engineering and brass foundry where nothing that looked vaguely useful was ever thrown away. Consequently the contents are all there. Changing with the times, the company moved into fizzy pop manufacture, hence plenty of machines, bottles and drinks labels from that industry are there too.

It's a fascinating collection of social history, with rooms and tools laid out just as they were when the last shift bell rang, where belts, pulleys, cogs and levers vie for attention. You purchase your ticket in the old stores at a solid wooden counter, in front of a solid wooden set of deep drawers, bulging with brass this and iron that.

Furniture-making workshops have been reconstructed from Keevil and Son, renowned in Bath from the 18th century for cabinet making and later for fitting out department stores and ocean liners. The quarrying of Bath stone is, of course, highlighted, as well as Plasticine, which was invented and made in Bath. There's also the Bath Chair, the Bath Oliver biscuit and numerous other products developed off the back of the high-class 'medical' tourist industry. Providing interest for hours, to my mind it's one of the most absorbing museums in the city.

However, it's closely rivalled by the **Building of Bath Collection** (*The Paragon; 01225 333895; www.bath-preservation-trust.org.uk; open Sat to Mon, mid-Feb to end of Nov*), where visitors can discover how the city was transformed during Georgian times. It amply fleshes out the background to the rebuilding, with information on the principles of Palladian architecture and the ideologies of John Wood the Elder and his son. The construction of a Georgian house and street is illustrated through original materials, with masonry, street signs, ironmongery, railings, street lighting, plasterwork, tiling and architectural decoration featuring throughout the museum. A giant scale model gives an insight into the layout of the city. 'Many visitors don't realise that you can push buttons on the model and a specific area of the city lights up. I love it,' explained one of the volunteer guides.

Walcot Street and London Street

The bohemian side to Bath is shown in Walcot Street together with its continuation, London Street. The long street, running parallel with the River Avon, has a character of its own and is filled with creativity: artisan art-and-craft workshops, furniture, upholstery and interior design showrooms, paintings, architectural salvage yards and the odd eatery. On the west side of the street is **Bath Aqua Glass** (*01225 463436; www.bathaquaglass.com*) – glassware, inspired by the Roman heritage of the city, is handmade on the premises; the products are characteristically coloured by adding copper oxide to the molten glass. You can visit to watch the craftsmen handling the red-hot glass, as they roll and form the molten liquid like sticky toffee; this is the place to visit for warmth in the depths of winter. Whatever piece is being made during the demonstration can be dated and personalised while you're there. Having a go at glass blowing is a possibility and there's always the added bonus of buying factory seconds at reduced prices; there's usually nothing too wrong with these, simply being the practice pieces of apprentices.

On my last visit, one place that really caught my eye in Walcot Street was **The Makery** (*146 Walcot St; 01225 421175; www.themakeryonline.co.uk*). Old sewing patterns and a pile of fabrics in the window and a floor-to-ceiling rack of shelving filled with jars of buttons, scissors, yarns and craft books were enough to draw me in. Sewing machines ready for action stood on standby and in the centre of the room, a giant pine table was the focal piece, like a friendly kitchen table that listens to the daily chatter of people's lives.

Kate Smith, the owner, who set up The Makery in 2009, explained, 'I'm trying to teach people to be resourceful when they come here. Traditional skills of sewing, upholstery and many crafts have been forgotten. People say that they don't have time to make things at home so they come here instead and either learn how to sew through one of our workshops or, if they're already experienced, simply use our space as a place where they can switch off from the world. Visitors have said that with no phone, no television and the chance to focus on a practical project here, they find the experience therapeutic and don't want to go home!'

I could quite see why, with the social interaction around the giant pine table, the wine glasses ready to be filled and music quietly playing in the background. 'The social aspect is very much a part of it,' continued Kate.

'People can drop-in just for a natter and to make something instant; you don't have to be local or a regular, although I do get lots of regular customers now.'

The Makery Café operates every Tuesday evening (*18.00–21.00*) and Friday morning (*10.00–13.00*). You can use the equipment (some people bring their own projects that they're already working on), have some delicious homemade cake and a drink, and get crafty.

Kate organises lots of workshops for both adults and children, from learning to sew clothes, reupholstering tired furniture to garter-making hen parties and messy art workshops for children.

East of the river

Much of the city centre sits in a pocket, tucked into a narrow loop of the Avon. But there's plenty to see east of the river.

The River Avon in Bath

One of Bath's great landmarks, **Pulteney Bridge** was completed in 1773 to the designs of Robert Adam. Like the Ponte Vecchio in Florence which inspired it, it is one of the few European bridges with buildings on it. The bridge, with its row of shops, has a front and back – the front, facing south, being relatively decorative, while the back is somewhat plain.

Beneath the bridge by the Pulteney Weir and sluice gate (the latter is not particularly pretty but it helps to stop Bath from flooding) are starting points for **river cruisers**, which make an idyllic trip, as you sit on board and let the buildings drift past. The more urban views don't last for long; as the boat weaves around the overhanging trees, the snaking river becomes really quite rural and intriguing. The sycamore, ash and chestnuts overhang so much that you cannot see the next stretch of river. The blue flash of a kingfisher is a quite likely appearance as the valley suddenly opens out to river meadows and views of Little Solsbury Hill and Bathampton Down.

The boat turns at Bathampton Weir, manmade 600 years ago and a rural outpost of the city where drivers cross the tiny tollbridge between Batheaston and Bathampton to avoid the city centre; the guide on the boat told us that pence per foot it's allegedly the most expensive toll bridge in Europe.

On the return trip you can stop off at the **Bath Boating Station** (*01225 312900; www.bathboating.co.uk; boats available Easter to Sep*), an attractive black-and-white timber boathouse where you can hire wooden rowing skiffs, punts and canoes, all handmade on the premises by the fourth generation of a boat-building family. Alternatively laze on the very attractive riverside lawns of the **Bathwick Boatman** (*01225 428844; www.bathwickboatman.com*) pub where you can enjoy a meal as the boats come and go. Our boat guide commented that the Avon around Bath is 'as good as it gets', a clean and healthy river with all 36 native coarse fish found in it and even the occasional otter.

Boats cannot access the river west of Pulteney Bridge, so to explore the river here, walk or cycle a section of the **River Avon Trail** (*www.riveravontrail.org.uk*), beginning at Pulteney Bridge and leading 23 miles out of Bath into Somerset.

Bath Rugby

Opposite the 'formal' floral **Parade Gardens** on the west side of the river, where concerts are performed on the bandstand, is **Bath Rugby Ground** (*www.bathrugby.com*) and the Recreation Ground – or The Rec as it's known locally – where fans sing to a different tune in the stands at the ground of one of the nation's top rugby teams. That the pitch is so centrally located is fascinating; you can see the verdant green pastures through the gates along the riverside walk. Better still, you can actually watch a match either from the stands or for free from the pavement at the end of Johnstone Street, a small cul-de-sac off Laura Place.

Bathonians are serious about their rugby so if you want to don the club colours to watch a match, the **Bath Rugby Shop** is in Argyle Street, just east of Pulteney Bridge. You can't miss the shop: it's painted royal blue just like the team strip. Match tickets can be bought from the ticket office behind the 6X Stand by the river.

Great Pulteney Street

North of Bath Rugby, Great Pulteney Street is the grandest, straightest road in Bath at 1,000 feet long and 100 feet wide. Its understated elegance gives competition to the Champs-Elysées in Paris. Not the work of the usual architectural suspects in Bath, the street, built in 1789, was designed by Thomas Baldwin, who was also responsible for the Guildhall west of the river and numerous other streets east of the river. But like so many other streets in Bath, the architect designed only the façades in Great Pulteney Street, with the rear of each property differing from the one next door; Baldwin did, however, live in one of them, marked with a blue plaque.

The Holburne Museum and Sydney Gardens

At the western end of Great Pulteney Street is **Laura Place** while in line at the eastern end is the Holburne Museum, situated in the **Sydney Gardens**. Having undergone a two-year transformation that included a large modern extension to the 18th-century town house, the **Holburne Museum** (*01225 466669; www. holburne.org*) now has double the amount of space to show off its exhibits, put on national exhibitions and educate the public about its artworks.

Inside is the Holburne's collection of 6,500 objects, pictures and books, with an important collection of 18th- and early 19th-century paintings to match the Georgian 'theme' of the city. And the recent acquisition of a collection of theatrical paintings once owned by the playwright Somerset Maugham brings an alternative look at the 18th century; many of the actors and actresses portrayed in the paintings performed in Bath during the heyday of the Theatre Royal. However, a major part of the new space is for education and running alongside the collection and temporary exhibitions are events for people of all ages, from creative workshops for toddlers to adult lectures and study days.

The museum spills out into the Sydney Gardens, where peaceful grassy enclaves among the pines and beech trees provide the perfect place to spend a sunny afternoon with a book. Follies, Palladian columns and decorative bridges are all part of the appeal. A friend who lives in Bath asked me what I thought of the Sydney Gardens. 'I'm not too sure about the railway line running straight through,' I admitted. 'Ah, but that's what's nice about it,' she replied. 'My son loves to visit, stand on the bridges and watch the trains go by.'

I prefer **Henrietta Park** between the river and the Sydney Gardens, accessed either from Henrietta Street or Sutton Street. On many Bath tourist maps, there's mention of a 'Garden for the Blind' but, ironically, I could not find it. Asking a couple of gardeners in the park they responded that the garden we were standing in was it. 'It did have Braille labels 20 years ago!' they responded. But it was completely redesigned and is now a sensory garden. True to their word, it is a little haven, where scented roses brush up against rosemary and lavender, vibrant canna lilies fight with sword-like spiky agave and pergolas surround a symmetrical pool.

Kennet and Avon Canal

Large villas and town houses line the broad avenue that is **Bathwick Hill**, climbing out of Bath towards **Claverton Down**. Turn to face the city and the whole centre is laid out in front of you. Bathwick Hill, and indeed the Sydney Gardens, cross over the Kennet and Avon Canal, which begins in Bath, connected to the River Avon in **Widcombe**, a small, delightful Georgian suburb rarely explored by tourists.

Like its disused counterpart, the Thames and Severn Canal further north in the Cotswolds, the Kennet and Avon links the Severn with the Thames. But the section through Bath is truly historic: a mile-long stretch north from the canal's junction with the Avon, known as the Widcombe Lock Flight, includes 19 listed structures along its length, such as giant chimney stacks (used for steam pumps to help boats through the series of locks), and old lock-keeper's cottages. Many have been recently restored to mark 200 years of the canal. A walk along the towpath here is magical, with the sharply rising escarpment to Claverton Down terraced with smart Bath stone town houses to one side, and views over the centre of Bath to the other, together with the odd splash of colour from a passing narrowboat. At the Bathwick Hill entrance to the canal, you can hire dayboats from **Bath Narrowboats** (*01225 447276; www.bath-narrowboats.co.uk*) to take a gentle cruise out of Bath towards the Limpley Stoke Valley and the Dundas Aqueduct. Making the most of the canal is a must, either walking the towpath or working the locks with a boat.

Prior Park Landscape Garden

Prior Park (*01225 833977; www.nationaltrust.org.uk/Wessex; open daily except Tue Feb to Oct; weekends only Nov to Jan*) is relatively old and relatively new. Completed in 1764 by John Wood the Elder, it was commissioned by Ralph Allen, the postmaster and owner of the Bath stone quarries, as a home for himself from which he could 'see all of Bath and for all of Bath to see'. The vast house and buildings have been used as a private school for the last 150 years but couldn't manage the upkeep of the 28-acre garden so gave it to the National Trust in 1993. Since then the trust has spent every year reclaiming the garden, based upon old drawings.

Far removed from formal parterres and topiary statues, Prior Park is entirely naturalistic in style making the most of the sharp descent from the house down towards Widcombe. While the view of Bath is the key component, one of the most attractive parts of the garden is at the bottom, the Wilderness Area where you can sit by the Serpentine Lake and gaze into the waters from the Palladian Bridge. It is a wonderful place to stretch the legs and stretched they will be, as the climb back to the exit is punishing unless you take it slowly. To break the return climb I spent half an hour watching a not-very-nocturnal badger snuffling amongst and rooting out carefully planted bulbs and rhizomes from a woodland bank.

Prior Park is considered a green tourism site by the National Trust. There is no parking on site and it is preferred that visitors catch a bus (Bath to Combe Down) from Dorchester Street in the city centre; the bus stops outside the entrance to Prior Park. Alternatively Prior Park is one of the Skyline Tour stops on the City Sightseeing bus.

American Museum in Britain

It takes a little bit of effort to reach (see page 235), but the American Museum in Britain (*01225 460503; www.americanmuseum.org; open Mar to Oct and Dec, afternoons only, closed Mon except bank holidays and in Aug*) on Claverton Down is a delight. Tranquilly set away from the city centre in the handsome Claverton Manor it has magnificent gardens and views over the Limpley Stoke Valley.

It's essentially dedicated to exhibiting and educating about colonial America. The museum, the only one of its kind outside the United States, gives a fascinating insight into the 'quiet' America, even if the history it's portraying isn't quiet. Period rooms such as Conkey's Tavern, bring the history to life, with most of the furnishings coming from colonial homes in the States. The museum particularly focuses on finding America and colonising it, and encountering Native Americans; it has a strong emphasis on the crafts of both natives and colonials.

The museum holds one of the finest textile collections in the world, and I particularly liked the Textile Room, where antique quilts, hooked rugs, tapestries and samples hang. It's an inspiring room where every Tuesday afternoon anyone interested in quilting can join in the making of a quilt. The idea is to recreate the companionship of a traditional quilting bee, where quilters work together and interact socially. On a panel in the room is the 'Quilters' Community' board, filled with advertisements for patchwork classes, quilting groups and societies – I noticed one for men making quilts.

The Orangery serves delicious homemade American fare (Brunswick chicken, chilli and tortillas, shortnin' bread) and you can watch the cookies being made. Numerous courses, events and family activities take place, including important temporary exhibitions staged in the purpose-built exhibition gallery.

Index

Numbers in bold indicate major entries; numbers in italic indicate maps.

Abbey House Gardens 217
Ablington 123
accommodation 146
    Bath 237
    Four Shires 48
    High Cotswolds 78–9
    North Cotswolds 22–3
    Southern Cotswold Scarp and
        Five Valleys 182
    Stratford-upon-Avon 3–4
    Thames Tributaries 110
    Thames Valley 163
    Wiltshire Cotswolds 215
Adderbury 53
Adlestrop 133
Akeman Street 116, 119, 130, 140
Alice in Wonderland 89, 156, 159
Alscot Park 24
American Museum in Britain
    235, **255**
Ampney St Mary 169
Anne Hathaway's Cottage 9
Arden, Mary 9
Arlington Row 123–4
Arnold, Matthew 143, 159
art and craft activities 41, 44, 87,
    125, 132, 194, 247, 251–2, 255
Arts and Crafts Movement vii, 27,
    33, 35, 40, 101, 177–8, 197,
    209
Arts and Crafts Movement,
    contemporary 34, 192, 194
Ashbee, C R 33
Ashmolean Museum 150
asparagus 27, 30
Assembly Rooms, Bath 233,
    249–50
Asthall Manor 115
Aston-sub-Edge 30
Atherstone-on-Stour 23
Austen, Jane 233, 236, **248–9**
Avening 209
Avon Valley Footpath 15, 18
Avon, River (Bristol) 216, 217,
    222, 229, 230, 233, 243, 252
Avon, River (Warwickshire) 11,
    14–15, 18
Avoncliff 231, 232

Badminton 201, 219
Badminton Estate/Park 216, 219
Badminton Horse Trials 219
Baldwin, Thomas 253
Banbury Cakes 54–5
Banburyshire 47
Bancroft Gardens 12, 16
Barcheston 66–7
Barnsley 124–5
Barnsley Herb Garden 125
Barnsley House (Hotel) 110,
    124–5, **126–7**
Barnsley, Ernest 209

Barrie, J M 44
Barringtons, the 113
Barrow Wake 187, 188
Barton Farm Country Park 230
Bath 227, 229, 231, 232, **233–5**,
    234
Bath Abbey 233, **242–3**
Bath Abbey Diptychs 243
Bath Aqua Glass 251
Bath Boating Station 252
Bath bun 238, 241, 244
Bath Royal Literary and Scientific
    Institution 246
Bath Rugby 253
Bath Skyline Walk 236
Bath stone 224, 231, 245
Bathurst Estate 131, 185
bats 204
Batsford 115
Batsford Arboretum 80
Battle of Blenheim 139
Battle of Dyrham 220
Battle of Edgehill 50
Beau Nash 240, 241, 245, 249
beavers 166
Beckbury Camp 94
Beckford, William 237
Beckford's Tower 237
beech woods 187, 189, 202, 228
Belas Knap 98
Belloc, Hilaire 133
Betjeman, Sir John 81
Bibury 123–4, 167
Bibury Trout Farm 124
Biddestone 224
bike hire 2, 22, 77, 109, 145, 162,
    181, 215, 235
birdwatching 165, 175
Bishop's Palace, Witney 117
Bisley 186
Bisley Boy 186
Bizarre Bath Comedy Walk 236
Blackwells 153
Bladud, King 233, 246
Bledington 134
Blenheim Estate/Palace 138,
    139–41
Bliss Tweed Mill 62
Blockley **37–9**
Blossom Trail 40
Bloxham 53
bluebells 70, 136, 189, 198
Boars Hill 143, 159
boat hire 14, 252, 254
boat trips 14, 151, 157, 159, 173,
    232, 252
Bodleian Library 67, **152**
bookshops 35, 63, 153, 249
Botanic Garden, Oxford 157
Botanic Gardens, Bath 248
boules 219, 220
Bourton House Garden 79

Bourton-on-the-Hill 79
Bourton-on-the-Water **105–6**,
    111
Bouthrop *see* Eastleach Martin
Bradford-on-Avon 229–1
Brailes 67–9
Brailes Hill 58, 68, 69, 82
brass rubbing 17, 208
Brassknocker Basin 231
Bredon Hill 19, 22, 40, **45**
Bretforton 30
breweries 51, 84, 106, 174, 197,
    238, 239
Bridge Tea Rooms 230
Bridget Jones' Diary 42
Bristol Aero Collection 163
Bristol and Gloucester Gliding
    Club 196
British Asparagus Festival 30
Broad Campden 36
Broad Ride 131, 185
broadcloth 194, 199
Broadway **39–1**
Broadway Tower 21, 40
Broadway Tower Country Park 41
Broadwell 134
Brockhampton 103
Brook Cottage Garden 51
Brother Eilmer 217
Broughton Castle 52
Brown, Ford Madox 177
Brown's Folly 232
Buckholt Wood 187, 189, 191
Bugatti Owners' Club 98
Building of Bath Collection 250
Burford 113–14
Burlington Bunker 225
Burne-Jones, Edward 149, 156,
    176, 177, 195
bus travel *see* getting there and
    around
bus, hop on–hop off sightseeing
    Bath 235
    Stratford-upon-Avon 2
Buscot 176
Buscot Park 175–7
Buscot Weir 176
butterflies 99, 100, 195, 206
By Brook 213, **222–8**

cafés *see* places by name
Cam Long Down 196
camping 49, 57, 96, 110, 137,
    185, 186, 215
canoe hire 175, 215, 231, 252
canoeing 173, 229
Capability Brown 40, 139, 225
Carfax Tower 148
Carroll, Lewis 89, 148, **156**, 159
Castle Combe 223
Cathedral of the Feldon 68
Centenary Way 26, 50, 64

Cerney House garden 129
Chalford 186–7
Charlbury 137
Charlecote Park 8, **18**
Charles Dodgson *see* Lewis Carroll
Charles I, King 97, 192
Chastleton 72
Chastleton House 72–3
Chavenage 211
Chedworth 122
Chedworth Roman Villa 122
Chedworth Woods 122
cheese-rolling 188
Cheltenham 75, 95, **100–2**
Cheltenham Gold Cup 99, 102
Cheltenham Literature Festival 102
Cheltenham Museum & Art Gallery 99, 101
Cheltenham Racecourse 93, 95, 102
Cherington, Gloucestershire 209
Cherington, Warwickshire 69
Cherwell Valley 53, **54–7**
Cherwell, River 53, 54, 154, 155
children's activities 5, 89, 102, 117, 122, 138, 166, 198, 207, 212, 232, 252
chilli festival 95
Chipping Campden 32–5
Chipping Norton 62–3
Chipping Norton Theatre 63
Chipping Sodbury 201
Christ Church College 144, 148, **155**, 156
Christ Church Meadow 155
Churchill 135
Churchill, Sir Winston 139
Churn Valley **128–32**, 161
Churn, River **128–32**, 161
Cider with Rosie 188, 191, 193
Circus, The, Bath 233, **246**
Cirencester **129–2**, 185
Cirencester Park 131
Cirencester Park Polo Club 131
Claude Duval Bridle Route 48
Claverton Down 236, 254, 255
Cleeve Common 75, 98, **99**
Clopton Bridge 14
coach travel *see* getting there and around
Coaley Peak Viewpoint 196
Cogges Manor Farm Museum 117
Colerne **226–7**, 228
Colerne Park and Monk's Wood 227
Colesbourne Park 129
Coln St Aldwyns 125
Coln Valley 104, **121–8**
Coln, River 104, **121–8**
Combe 138
Combe Mill Museum 138
Conran, Sophie 91
cookery schools 91, 121, 129, 134
Cooper's Hill 187, **188**
Corinium Museum 130

Cornbury Festival 56
Cornbury Park 136
Corsham **224–6**
Corsham Court 225–6
Cotswold and Feldon Cycle Route 68
Cotswold brie 88
Cotswold canals 172
Cotswold Canals Trust 172, 173
Cotswold Commons and Beechwoods National Nature Reserve 189, 191
Cotswold Farm Park 92
Cotswold Ice Cream Company 112
Cotswold Line Railbus 48, 107
Cotswold Lion *see* Cotswold sheep
Cotswold Olimpicks 31
Cotswold pennycress 92
Cotswold Sheep Society viii–ix, 74
Cotswold sheep vii, **viii–ix**, 92, 132
Cotswold Show 131
Cotswold stone 113
Cotswold Water Park 161, **164–7**, 175
Cotswold Way Circular Walks x
Cotswold Way x, **21**, 31, 32, 40, 42, 44, 94, 95, 99, 103, 181, 188, 198, 236
Cotswold Woodland Crafts 190
Cotswold Woollen Weavers 120
Cotswolds and Malvern Line 19, 47, 107
Cotswolds AONB viii–x, 19, 23, 119
Cotswolds Conservation Board ix, 90, 119
Cotswolds Grazing Animals Project 190
Court Barn Museum 33
Cranham 189
Cranham Common 189, 190
Cricklade 161, **167–9**
Crickley Hill 179, 187, **188–9**, 190
croquet 73
cycling 48, 68, 77, 93, 109, 137, 144–5, 162, 181, 215, 235

damselflies 165, 196
Daneway 172, 182, **184–5**
Davies, W H vi, 202
Daylesford Organic Farmshop 133, 134
Deddington 53
Devil's Chimney 100
Dexter, Colin 148
Diamond Way 32, 36, 91, 93, 105
Dikler, River 84, 85, 86, 111
Dirty Duck, Stratford-upon-Avon 4
dodo 154
Domestic Fowl Trust 30
Donnington 84

Donnington Brewery 84
Donnington Way 84
Dover, Robert 31
Dover's Hill 21, 31, 32
Dowdeswell Wood 102
Down Ampney 169–70
Downham Hill 196
drystone walls ix, **90–1**
Duchy Home Farm 132, 212
Duke of Marlborough 139
Dundas Aqueduct 229, **231**, 254
Dunkirk Mill 204
Dursley 197–9
Duval, Claude 55
Dyrham Park 220–1

Eastleach Martin 120, 153
Eaton Hastings 177
Ebrington 35
Edgehill **50–1**, 64
Edward Sheldon wine merchant 65
English Civil War 50, 52, 72, 85, 155, 192
Ernest Wilson Memorial Garden 34
Escape to the Cotswolds! x, 119
Evenlode Valley 82, **132–41**
Evenlode, River 82, **132–41**
Ewelme Valley 197

Fairford 126
Fairford Park 125
fairtrade town 97
Faringdon Collection *see* Buscot Park
farm shops *see* places by name
Farmcote 94
Farmcote Herbs and Chilli Peppers 94
Farmers' market 85, 149, 173, 194, 198, 199
Farmington 112
Farncombe Estate 41
Fashion Museum 250
Feldon 63–9
Festival of the Tree 212
Fiennes family 52
Filkins 120
fishing 110, 124, 126, 128, 167, 175, 176
Five Valleys **179–212**, *180*
Fleece Inn, Bretforton 30
Flemish Cottages, Corsham 224
Flying Monk, The 217
Foodworks Cookery School 129
football in the river 106
Fosse Way vii, 73, 79, 118, 130, 163, 215, 219
Fossebridge 123
Four Shires Stone 47, 69
Foxholes Nature Reserve 136
Freemasons 246
Frome Valley 179, 182, **183–7**
Frome, River 183
fruit farm 95

Gainsborough, Thomas 244
gardens to visit 10, 16–18, 27, 38, 51, 54, 79, 80, 81, 97, 125, 127, 129, 157, 176, 183, 192, 197, 200, 211, 217, 231, 246, 248
gargoyles 97
Garrick Inn 15
Gatcombe Horse Trials 207
Gatcombe Park 207
Gateway Centre 164
Georgian Garden, Bath 246
getting there and around
  Bath 235–6
  Four Shires 47–8
  High Cotswolds 75–8
  North Cotswolds 19–22
  Oxford 143–5
  Southern Cotswold Scarp and Five Valleys 181–2
  Stratford-upon-Avon 1–3
  Thames Tributaries 107–10
  Thames Valley 104
  Wiltshire Cotswolds 213–15
Gifford's Circus 207
gliding 196
Gloucestershire Guild of Craftsmen 192
Gloucestershire Morris Men 36
Gloucestershire Warwickshire Railway 75, 95
Gloucestershire Way 104
Golden Valley 179
golf courses 58, 99, 198, 247
Gordon Russell Museum, Broadway 40
Gower Memorial 12, 16
Great Barrington 113
Great Pulteney Street, Bath 253
Great Rissington 111
Great Tew 56
Great Witcombe Roman Villa 188
Greenway, The 2, **18**, 22
Greystones Farm Nature Reserve 105
Guild Gallery, Painswick 192
Guildhall Market, Bath **243–4**, 253
Guiting Festival 91
Guiting Power 91

Hailes Abbey 95
Hall, Dr John 10, 11
Hall's Croft 10
Haresfield Hill 190, 191
Harry Potter 155
Harvard House 15
Hathaway, Anne 9
Heart of England Way 21, 26, 28, 32, 36, 82
Henrietta Park, Bath 254
Henson, Adam 92
Hetty Pegler's Tump 196, 197
Hidcote Manor Garden 27
Highgrove 211
Highgrove Shop 211

Holburne Museum 253
Holst Birthplace Museum 101
Holst, Gustav 101
Holy Trinity Church, Stratford-upon-Avon 7, 8, **11**
Honeybourne 29
Honington 64
Hook Norton 59
Hook Norton Brewery 51, 59, **60–1**
Hook Norton Pottery 59, 147
horseracing 93, 102
horseriding x, 18, 48, 99, 131, 187
hot-air balloon trips 248
HRH Prince of Wales 210, 211, 212
Hugh the Drover 171
Hunts Court Garden 200

ice cream 88, 112, 147, 222
ice hockey 158
ice rink 158
Idlicote 64
Iford Manor *see* Peto Garden 231
Ilmington 26
Ilmington Downs 26, 27, 41, 82
Ilmington Morris Men 26, 36
Inglesham 170–2
Inglesham Lock 172, 173
Inspector Morse 143, 147, 148, 149
ironstone 26, 51
Isis (Thames), River 155, 159

Jane Austen Centre 248
Jane Austen Festival 249
Jericho 150, 159

Keble College 120, 153
Keble, John 120, 153
Keith Harding's World of Mechanical Music 119
Kelmscott 177–8
Kelmscott Manor 161, **177–8**
Kemble 163
Kennet and Avon Canal 215, 229, **231–2**, 233,
  in Bath **254**
Kiftsgate Court Gardens 27
Kiftsgate rose 27
Kiftsgate Stone 31
King Edward VI Grammar School 8, 15
Kingham 135

Ladymead House, Bath 244
Leach Valley *see* Leach, River
Leach, River 118–21
Lechlade-on-Thames 161, 167, **173–5**
Leckhampton Hill 98, **100**
Lee, Laurie 179, 188, 191, 193
Levellers, The 114, 149
Liddell, Alice 156, 159
lidos 63, 101

limestone grassland 189, 190, 195, 206
limestone vi, 90, 99, 100, 137, 154, 224
Limpley Stoke Valley 229, **231–2**, 254
Lineover Wood 103
Little Rissington 111
Lodge Park 119
Long Compton 25, 71, 72
Longborough 82
Longborough Festival Opera 82–3
Lords of the Manor Hotel 87
Lower Oddington 134
Lower Quinton 25
Lower Slaughter 87–8
Lower Swell 86
Luckington Court 219
Lygon Arms, Broadway 40

Macmillan Way 50, 70, 122, 184, 223, 224
Made in Stroud 194
Magdalen College 154
Makery, The 251
Malmesbury 216–19
Malmesbury Abbey 216
mangold hurling 220
maps, Ordnance Survey xi
Margaret's Buildings, Bath 247
Marshfield 221–2
Marshfield Bakery 222
Marshfield Ice Cream 222
Marshfield mummers 221
Mary Arden's Farm 9
Masonic Hall, Bath 246
May Morris 178
Meon Hill 25, 26, 28, 50
Mickleton 28
microbreweries *see* breweries
Mill Dene Garden 38
Minchinhampton 206–8
Minchinhampton Common 179, 182, 190, **206**
Mini plant, Cowley 155, 158
Minster Lovell 115–16
Minster Lovell Hall 115
Misarden Park Gardens 183
Miserden 183–4
Mitford family 58, 80–1, 110, 115, 116
Modern Art Oxford 157
Monarch's Way 15, 21, 26, 32, 36, 82, 118, 122
Montpellier Quarter, Cheltenham 100
Moreton Show 74
Moreton-in-Marsh 73–4
morris dancing 26, **36**, 171
Morris, William 22, 40, 123, 149, 161, 170, 177, **177–8**, 195
Morris, William vii
Museum in the Park 194
Museum of Bath at Work 250
Museum of Oxford 154–5

Museum of the History of Science, Oxford 153
music festivals and concerts 53, 56, 82, 91, 136, 137, 231

Nailsworth 204–6
Nailsworth Valley 179, **202–5**
Nash, Richard 'Beau' *see* Beau Nash
Nash, Thomas 10, 11
Nash's House **10**
National Hunt Festival *see* Cheltenham Gold Cup
nature reserves 17, 99, 100, 102, 105, 122, 136, 165, 168, 175, 189, 191, 232
Naunton 88–9
Naunton dovecote 89
Neigh Bridge Country Park 165
New Place, Stratford-upon-Avon 10
Newark Park 201
North Cerney 129
North Leigh Roman Villa 137
North Meadow 168
North Nibley 200
Northanger Abbey 249
Northleach 118–19
Northwick Park Estate 36
Nottingham Hill 98
Number 1, Royal Crescent 247
Nympsfield Long Barrow 196

O'Neil, Jonjo 93
Oakridge 186–7
Offa, King 96
Old Father Thames 161, 174
Old Silk Mill, Chipping Campden 34
Old Town, Stratford-upon-Avon 10, 16
On Form sculpture exhibition 115
Operation Market Garden 170
Owlpen Manor 197
Oxfam 153
Oxford 89, **142–59**, *142*
Oxford Canal 54, 144, 150
Oxford Castle 158
Oxford Covered Market 152
Oxford marmalade 152, 158
Oxford Martyrs 153
Oxford Open Doors 149
Oxford Union 149
Oxford University **144**, 146
Oxford University Press 150
Oxfordshire Cotswolds 107
Oxfordshire Museum 138
Ozleworth 201
Ozleworth Bottom **201**

Painswick 187, **192–3**
Painswick Beacon 187, 191
Painswick Rococo Garden 192–3
Painswick Valley 179, **187–93**
Palladian architecture 239, 245, 246, 251

Parade Gardens 253
Parr, Catherine 97
peacocks, Corsham 226
Persuasion 249
Peto Garden at Iford Manor 231
Peto, Harold 176, 231
Pickwick 226
Pickwick Papers, The 226
Pitt Rivers Museum 153–4
Pittville Park, Cheltenham 101
Port Meadow 159
pottery 59, 71
Pre-Raphaelites vii, 40, 149, 156, 176, 177, 178, 195
Prescott Hill Climb 98
Prestbury Hill Reserve 99
Prestbury Park *see* Cheltenham Racecourse
Preston-on-Stour 23
Prinknash Abbey 189–90
Prinknash Abbey Watercolour Gallery 190
Prinknash Pottery 191
Prior Park 235, 245, **254**
pubs *see* places by name
Pudding Club 23, **28–9**
Pulteney Bridge 252
Pump Room Trio 238, 241
Pump Room, Bath 237, **240–1**
punting 156–7

quarries 89, 100, 113
Queen Square, Bath 246

Radcliffe Camera 148, 152
Radcliffe Square, Oxford 152
Radcliffe, John 153
rail travel *see* getting there and around
Ralph Allen 245, 254
Randolph Hotel 149
Rare Breed Survival Trust 92
Red Arrows Display Team 111, 163
restaurants *see* places by name
Richardson and Amey Nature Reserve 175
River Avon Trail 253
Riverside Festival 137
Robert Welch, silversmith 34, 35
Rocks East Woodland 228
Rodborough Common 179, 182, 190, **206**
Rodmarton Manor 209
Rollright Stones 71–2
Roman Baths, Bath 233, **239**, 240
Roman snails 100, 122
Roman villas 97, 122, 137, 188
Rossetti, Dante Gabriel 149, 176, 178, 195
round houses 172, 186
Rousham House and Gardens 54
Royal Agricultural College 131–2
Royal Crescent, Bath 233, 244, **246–7**
Royal International Air Tattoo 127

Royal Shakespeare Company **5–7**, 11, 12, 13
Royal Shakespeare Theatre 5
Royal Victoria Park 247–8
RSC Garden 17
RSC *see* Royal Shakespeare Company
RSC theatre tours 5
rufous grasshopper 189
rural skills courses ix, 91, 191
Rye Hill Golf Course 58

Sabrina Way 99
Sally Lunn Bun 239, 243
Sally Lunn's House 238, 239, **243**
Salperton 104
Salt Way 95, 104, 125, 173
Sapperton 172, 182, **184–5**, 209
Sapperton Canal Tunnel 184, 186
Sealed Knot 50
Selsley 195
Selsley Common 182, **195**
Sevenhampton 103
Sezincote 81
Shakespeare Centre 7, 8, **10–11**
Shakespeare Centre Library and Archive **12–13**
Shakespeare Club 11
Shakespeare Express steam train 1
Shakespeare in Love 52
Shakespeare Institute 10
Shakespeare, William 1, 3, **4–13**, 17, 18, 148
Shakespeare's Birthplace **8**
Shakespeare's Birthplace Trust 7
Shakespeare's Church *see* Holy Trinity Church
Shakespeare's grave 11
Shakespeare's Way **3**, 21, 25, 48, 64, 67, 145, 148
Sheepscombe 187, 190, **191**
Sheldon family, Weston Park 66–7, 70
Sheldon Tapestries 67, 70
Sheldonian Theatre 153
Shelley, Percy Bysshe 174
Sherborne 112
Sherborne Estate 112
Sherston 219
Shipston Wool Fair 65
Shipston-on-Stour **64–6**, 68
shopping *see* places by name
Shotover Country Park 158
Shottery 9
Sibford Ferris and Gower 58
Skyline Tour 235, 254
Slad 188, 193
Slad Valley 179, **187–93**
Slaughterford 223, **224**
Slaughters, The *see* Lower Slaughter *and* Upper Slaughter
snakeshead fritillary 154, 168
snowdrops 129
Snowshill 42–3
Snowshill Lavender 43
Snowshill Manor 42

Society for the Protection of Ancient Buildings 171
Somerset Coal Canal 231
Somerset Monument 201
Southrop 120
Spencer-Churchill family 37, 39, 139
Spoonley Villa 97
St Aldates 154
St Catherine's 213, 228
St Giles Fair 150
St John's Lock 174
St Michael at the North Gate 151
stained glass 111, 128, 156, 170, 176, 217
Stanton 44
Stanway 44
Stanway House and Fountain 44
steam trains 1, 75, 95
Stinchcombe Hill 198
Stonesfield 137
Stonesfield slate 137
Stour Valley 63–9
Stour, River 19, 23, 58, 59, 63, 64, 70
Stow Art Group 87
Stow-on-the-Wold 84, **85–6**
Stratford Brass Rubbing Centre 17
Stratford Town Walk 3
Stratford-upon-Avon Canal 15
Stratford-upon-Avon xii–18, *xii*
Stroud 194–5
Stroud Scarlet 194
Stroudwater Canal 172
Stroudwater Textile Trust 194
Sudeley Castle 97
Suffolks, Cheltenham 100
Sul, Celtic goddess 233
Summertown 158
Swalcliffe 58
Swan Theatre 5, 7
Swinbrook 115
Sydney Gardens, Bath 253–4

Temple Guiting 91
Tetbury 206, **210–12**
textile mills 193, 194, 198, 204, 218, 232
Thames and Severn Canal 172, 184, 186
Thames Head 161, 163
Thames Path 145, 159, 162, 165, 171, 174, 177
Thames Valley 107, 128, 150, 155, 160, **160–78**
Thames, River 107, 128, 150, 155, 160, **160–78**
thankful villages 88
Theatre Royal, Bath 245, 253
TheGallery@TheGuild, Chipping Campden 34
Thermae Bath Spa 241–2
Thomas, Edward 133
Three Ways House Hotel 23, **28**
Thyme at Southrop 121
tithe barn, Bradford-on-Avon 230

tithe barn, Swalcliffe 58
Toadsmoor Valley 179, **186–7**
Todenham 72
Tolkien, J R R 147
tourist information centres 3, 22, 48, 78, 110, 146, 183, 216, 236
Traitor's Ford 59
transport *see* getting there and around
Treasure Trails 89
Twinberrow Wood 198
Tyack, Irene, artist 135
Tyndale Monument 200
Tyndale, William 200

Uley 197
Uley Blue 194, 197
Uley Bury 196
UNESCO World Heritage Site 233
University Church, Oxford 153
University Museum of Natural History 153–4
Upper Quinton 26
Upper Slaughter 87–8
Upper Swell 86
Upton House 50–51
USAF Upper Heyford 57

Vale of Evesham 19, 22, 27, 29, 30, 31, 40, 45
Vaughan-Williams, Ralph 169–70, 171
Verey, Rosemary 110, 124, **126–7**
Victoria Art Gallery, Bath **243–4**, 247
volunteer work 103, 137, 167, 172

Wade, Charles 42
Walcot Street, Bath 251
walks (specific)
  Atherstone-on-Stour 23, 24
  Blenheim Great Park 140–1, *141*
  Cirencester History Walk 130
  farm walk 80
  Malmesbury 218
  Sapperton 185, *185*
  Sherborne Estate 112
  Walks on Wheels x
  Windrush Valley 115–16, *116*
Walkers are Welcome 78
walking *see* getting there and around
walking tours
  Bath 236
  Oxford 145
  Stratford 3
Warden's Way 78, 87, 89, 90, 93, 97
water vole 164, 166–7
Watledge 202
Welcombe Hills Country Park 17
Wellington Aviation Museum 74
West of England cloth 204
Weston Park 66, 70
Weston-sub-Edge 30

Westonbirt Arboretum 206, **212**
Whichford 70
Whichford Pottery 71, 82
Whichford Wood 59, 70
Whispering Knights see Rollright Stones
Whittington 103
Whittington Court 103
Widford 114
Wigginton 58
wild flowers 99, 105, 168, 195, 206
Willersey 39–40
Willow Walk 177
Winchcombe 75, 78, 94, **96–8**
Winchcombe Walking Festival 78
Windrush Valley Cycle Route 109
Windrush Valley *see* Windrush, River
Windrush Way 78, 89, 97
Windrush, River 88, 91, 105, 106, **111–18**
wine cellar tours 65
witchcraft 25, 71
Withington 122
Witney 111, **116–18**
Witney Wool and Blanket Trail 117
Wood, John the Elder 245, 246, 251, 254
Wood, John the Younger 245, 247
Woodchester Mansion 203–4
Woodchester Mosaic 203
Woodchester Park 202
Woodstock 138–41
wool town
  Bradford-on-Avon 229–31
  Burford 113–14
  Castle Combe 223
  Chipping Campden 32–5
  Chipping Norton 62–3
  Cirencester 129–32
  Corsham 224–6
  Dursley 197–9
  Fairford 128
  Painswick 192–3
  Shipston-on-Stour 64–6
  Stroud 194–5
  Tetbury 210–12
  Witney 116–18
  Wotton-under-Edge 199–200
Woolsack Races 210
Wotton-under-Edge 199–200
Wroxton 51
Wroxton Abbey 51
Wychwood Forest 109, 132, 136
Wychwood Forest Fair 137
Wychwood Project 137
Wychwoods, the 136
Wyck Rissington 111

Yellow Hat Tribe Gallery 135
yew trees, Painswick 192
yurts 49, 110, 182